Russian Foreign Policy

Russian Foreign Policy

The Return of Great Power Politics

Jeffrey Mankoff

A Council on Foreign Relations Book

ROWMAN & LITTLEFIELD PUBLISHERS, INC.
Lanham • Boulder • New York • Toronto • Plymouth, UK

The Council on Foreign Relations (CFR) is an independent, nonpartisan membership organization, think tank, and publisher dedicated to being a resource for its members, government officials, business executives, journalists, educators and students, civic and religious leaders, and other interested citizens in order to help them better understand the world and the foreign policy choices facing the United States and other countries. Founded in 1921, CFR carries out its mission by maintaining a diverse membership, with special programs to promote interest and develop expertise in the next generation of foreign policy leaders; convening meetings at its headquarters in New York and in Washington, DC, and other cities where senior government officials, members of Congress, global leaders, and prominent thinkers come together with CFR members to discuss and debate major international issues; supporting a Studies Program that fosters independent research, enabling CFR scholars to produce articles, reports, and books and hold roundtables that analyze foreign policy issues and make concrete policy recommendations; publishing *Foreign Affairs*, the preeminent journal on international affairs and U.S. foreign policy; sponsoring Independent Task Forces that produce reports with both findings and policy prescriptions on the most important foreign policy topics; and providing up-to-date information and analysis about world events and American foreign policy on its website, www.cfr.org.

THE COUNCIL ON FOREIGN RELATIONS TAKES NO INSTITUTIONAL POSITION ON POLICY ISSUES AND HAS NO AFFILIATION WITH THE U.S. GOVERNMENT. ALL STATEMENTS OF FACT AND EXPRESSIONS OF OPINION CONTAINED IN ITS PUBLICATIONS ARE THE SOLE RESPONSIBILITY OF THE AUTHOR OR AUTHORS.

ROWMAN & LITTLEFIELD PUBLISHERS, INC.

Published in the United States of America
by Rowman & Littlefield Publishers, Inc.
A wholly owned subsidiary of The Rowman & Littlefield Publishing Group, Inc.
4501 Forbes Boulevard, Suite 200, Lanham, Maryland 20706
www.rowmanlittlefield.com

Estover Road, Plymouth PL6 7PY, United Kingdom

British Library Cataloguing in Publication Information Available

Library of Congress Cataloging-in-Publication Data

Mankoff, Jeffrey, 1977–
Russian foreign policy : the return of great power politics / Jeffrey Mankoff.
    p.   cm.
Includes bibliographical references and index.
ISBN-13: 978-0-7425-5794-9 (cloth : alk. paper)
ISBN-10: 0-7425-5794-4 (cloth : alk. paper)
ISBN-13: 978-0-7425-5795-6 (pbk. : alk. paper)
ISBN-10: 0-7425-5795-2 (pbk. : alk. paper)
[etc.]
    1. Russia (Federation)—Foreign relations—21st century.   I. Title.
JZ1616.M36   2009
327.47—dc22

                                        2008053725

Printed in the United States of America

♾ ™ The paper used in this publication meets the minimum requirements of American National Standard for Information Sciences—Permanence of Paper for Printed Library Materials, ANSI/NISO Z39.48-1992.

Dedicated to Caitlin Barrett,
and to the memory of Bill Odom

Contents

Acknowledgments

I would like to take this opportunity to thank the many people and organizations who made the writing of this book possible—and to absolve them of responsibilities for its shortcomings. The book began as a smaller research project conducted under the auspices of Yale University's Studies in Grand Strategy, on the basis of research conducted during the summer of 2005 at the Carnegie Moscow Center. I want to express my gratitude to Yale and to the Smith-Richardson Foundation for their intellectual and financial support. I am also grateful to Natalia Bubnova at Carnegie Moscow for placing Carnegie's resources at my disposal and for giving me a home base during my initial forays into the complexities of Russian foreign policy, and to the scholars at Carnegie who took the time to speak with me about my work.

After taking a break from this project to focus on completing my dissertation, I returned to it in the fall of 2006 as a John M. Olin National Security Fellow at Harvard University. With its wealth of resources and numerous Russia specialists, Harvard was in many ways an ideal place to write the bulk of the manuscript. Particular thanks are due to Stephen Peter Rosen, head of the Olin Institute, to the other Olin Fellows (especially Terence Lee and Dima Adamsky), to Carol Saivetz, who read and commented on an early draft of two chapters, to Mark Kramer, who gave unstintingly of his time and encouragement, and to Lt. Gen. Kevin Ryan, Charles Cogan, Paige Duhamel, and the unflappable Ann Townes.

Perhaps fittingly, the book was finished exactly where it was started, at Yale's International Security Studies (ISS), to where I returned in 2007 as a Henry Chauncey Fellow. I am particularly grateful to John Gaddis, who encouraged me to turn what had started as a mere seminar paper into a book, who read a complete draft, and whose faith in the project never wavered. Thanks are also owed to Paul Kennedy, Charles Hill, Keith Darden, Ann Carter-Drier, Susan Hennigan, Ted Bromund, Minh Luong, and Monica Ward. It is thanks to all of them that Yale has been such a welcoming and intellectually vibrant place to work and one of those rare outposts in academia where tackling big, complex questions is actively encouraged. A special word of thanks is also owed to the late Lt. Gen. William Odom, a man whose knowledge of Russia was unsurpassed and whose gruff manner could not hide the fact that he was the best teacher I knew at Yale.

For guiding the project from manuscript to book, I would also like to extend my gratitude to Jessica Gribble and Susan McEachern at Rowman & Littlefield, along with the anonymous reviewer whose comments helped me polish the arguments. Besides my work at Yale, I have also for the past year been an adjunct fellow at the Council on Foreign Relations (CFR), and additional thanks are due to my CFR colleagues who helped bring the manuscript out in the CFR Books series. In particular I want to thank Council President Richard N. Haass, Vice President and Director of Studies Gary Samore, George F. Kennan Senior Fellow for Russia and Eurasia Studies Ambassador Stephen Sestanovich, Assistant Director of Studies Melanie Gervacio, Director of Publishing Patricia Dorff, and research associate John Elliott.

Last but certainly not least I want to thank Caitlin Barrett, whose support and companionship have always been more crucial, and more appreciated, than I can adequately communicate.

Abbreviations

ABM	antiballistic missile
APEC	Asia-Pacific Economic Cooperation organization
ASEAN	Association of Southeast Asian Nations
BRICs	Brazil, Russia, India, China
BTC	Baku-Tbilisi-Ceyhan oil pipeline
BTE	Baku-Tbilisi-Erzurum gas pipeline
CACO	Central Asian Cooperation Association
CDC	Community of Democratic Choice
CDU	Christian Democratic Union (Germany)
CFE	Conventional Forces in Europe (Treaty)
CFP	Common Foreign Policy (EU)
CIS	Commonwealth of Independent States
CNPC	Chinese National Petroleum Company
CPC	Caspian Pipeline Consortium oil pipeline
CSTO	Collective Security Treaty Organization
DPNI	Movement Against Illegal Immigration
EEC	European Economic Community
ENP	European Neighborhood Policy (EU)
ESDP	European Security and Defense Policy (EU)
ESM	Eurasian Union of Youth
EU	European Union
EurAsEc	Eurasian Economic Association
FSB	Federal Security Service (*Federal'naya Sluzhba Bezopasnosti*)
G8	Group of Eight
GDP	gross domestic product
GU(U)AM	Georgia-Ukraine-(Uzbekistan)-Azerbaijan-Moldova group
IAEA	International Atomic Energy Agency

IMEMO	Institute of International Economics and International Relations
IMF	International Monetary Fund
IMU	Islamic Movement of Uzbekistan
IRI	International Republican Institute (U.S.)
KGB	Committee on State Security (*Komitet Gosudarstvennoi Bezopasnosti*)
KPRF	Communist Party of the Russian Federation
LDPR	Liberal Democratic Party of Russia
LNG	liquefied natural gas
MAP	membership action plan (NATO)
MED	International Eurasian Movement
MGIMO	Moscow State Institute of International Relations
NATO	North Atlantic Treaty Organization
NDI	National Democratic Institute (U.S.)
NGO	nongovernmental organization
NPT	Non-proliferation Treaty
NRC	NATO-Russia Council
NSC	National Security Council (U.S.)
OSCE	Organization for Security and Cooperation in Europe
PCA	Partnership and Cooperation Agreement
PfP	Partnership for Peace (NATO)
PJC	Permanent Joint Council (NATO)
PSA	Production Sharing Agreement
RATS	Regional Anti-Terrorist Structure (SCO)
SCO	Shanghai Cooperation Association
SORT	Strategic Offensive Reductions Treaty
SPS	Union of Right Forces (*Soyuz Pravykh Sil*)
START	Strategic Arms Reduction Treaties
SVOP	Council on Foreign and Defense Policy (*Sovet vneshnei i oboronoi politiki*)
UK	United Kingdom (of Great Britain and Northern Ireland)
UN	United Nations
U.S.	United States of America
USSR	Union of Soviet Socialist Republics
WEU	Western European Union
WTO	World Trade Organization

Introduction

The Guns of August

While the world's attention was focused on the opening of the Beijing Olympics in early August 2008, Russian tanks poured across the border into the breakaway Georgian province of South Ossetia. In a matter of days, the Russians had smashed the Georgian military, seized control of South Ossetia, and threatened the Georgian capital of Tbilisi. Days later, Russia announced its recognition of South Ossetia and another separatist province of Georgia, Abkhazia, all while dismissing the protests and threats of the West. To a world that had grown used to seeing Russia as a dysfunctional shell, the invasion of Georgia was a stunning announcement that Russia had again become a force to be reckoned with.

Even as Russian troops continued to linger in Georgia throughout the autumn, systematically dismantling the country's military infrastructure and demonstrating the impotence of outside powers to stop them, the Russian economy began spiraling rapidly downward. Fearing increased political and economic risk, foreign investors began withdrawing capital from Russia only days into the conflict with Georgia, causing severe declines on the stock market. Russia's economic difficulties were only beginning, however, as the implosion of a massive housing bubble in the United States set off a worldwide freeze in credit markets. With a global recession in the offing, oil prices fell from a high of $147 per barrel in July to less than $50 a barrel in late November. Russia—its economy heavily dependent on oil and gas—was hit extremely hard, forcing the Kremlin to intervene by orchestrating a bailout of several leading banks, propping up the ruble, and repeatedly halting trading on the stock market to prevent further slides. The war and the economic crisis highlighted one of the central dilemmas confronting modern Russia, namely, the tension between an imperative to harness the forces of globalization to make the country a fully integrated member of the modern economy, and a deep-seated desire to fall back on a tradition of claiming global influence on the basis of the ability to project hard power. This tension, based on competing narratives on the nature and identity of the Russian state, is clearly reflected in the man nominally in charge of the country throughout both the war in Georgia and the financial crisis, President Dmitry Anatolievich Medvedev. A lawyer (and fan of Western rock music), Medvedev was long seen in the West as the most liberal and reform-minded of the potential successors to former president Vladimir Putin. While Medvedev has repeatedly stated his belief in the need for Russia to become a fully modern country, he, as well as those who still wield power behind the scenes, continues to support the notion that Russia remains very much a traditional Great Power, operating in a world where the traditional measures of power continue to define relationships among states.

Russia still confronts the burdens of history in a way few large states do. Russia and the Soviet Union attained their greatest power and glory in periods when the state was at its strongest. Consolidation at home and expansion abroad were always the keys to securing Russia against its marauding neighbors, whether Tatars, Turks, Poles, or more recently, Germans. Without defensible frontiers, Russia historically fell back on the establishment of buffer zones between itself and its rivals. Ukraine played this role against the Turks and Tatars for centuries; Poland played it against Germany in the nineteenth century and again after the 1939 Nazi-Soviet Pact. During the Cold War, it was the USSR's Eastern European satellites (again with Poland at the forefront) that served to insulate the Russian heartland against foreign aggression. This interest in using its neighbors as cannon fodder long made Russia feared. Fear bred respect until the final days of the Soviet Union, when even the periphery of the USSR itself stopped fearing Moscow. When the Soviet Union collapsed in December 1991, the rump Russian Federation was a shadow of its Soviet self. The country's frontiers were pushed backed farther than they had been since the seventeenth century, while the once-mighty Red Army simply collapsed. And when Russia was no longer feared, it was no longer accorded the respect given to major powers. Its objections were ignored as NATO moved to take in its closest neighbors. Even pieces of the former Soviet Union began freeing themselves from the Russian yoke. A distinct Weimar syndrome began making itself felt in 1990s Russia, while little was done to overcome the historic association between power and respect.

Russia's recovery, which has been shocking mostly for its rapidity, has provided the foundation for a reassertion of old patterns. Once again, many Russians see a hostile world, now comprising not just the old bogeyman of

NATO, but newer threats such as jihadism, lapping at their borders. For the political elite at least, the response has been to fall back on the tried and true—a strong state backed by a strong military, and a foreign policy that emphasizes strategic depth. Only the world of the twenty-first century is not the world of the nineteenth century, and the old certainties of Russian foreign policy are not entirely suited to the new threats and challenges. Consequently, a major underlying tension in contemporary Russia's foreign policy discourse exists between past and future, autarky and integration. As Dmitry Medvedev took office in mid-2008, Russia was still struggling to graft its historically determined identity as a Great Power onto the new realities it faces.

The war between Russia and Georgia provides the backdrop for this book's fundamental theme: the resurgence of Russia's power and autonomy as an actor in the international system. In the course of the decade from 1998 to 2008, Russia went from weak and fractious to possessing the strength and confidence to launch a massive military assault on a neighboring state in the face of worldwide condemnation; even the battering of the country's economy has not dampened Russian leaders' aspirations to play a greater role on the world stage. Russia's internal transformation, based on booming revenue from the sale of its energy resources and the political stability provided by the rule of President Putin (2000–2008), is by now common knowledge. Yet much less attention has been paid to the impact of this transformation on Russian foreign policy.

Certainly, Russia's greater coherence, stability, and confidence all contributed to Moscow's willingness to use force in the dispute with Georgia. Relative power, however, is only one factor that statesmen must consider in the making of foreign policy. A state's identity in the international system—whether it sees itself as a satiated or a revisionist power, a nation-state or an empire—provides the intellectual framework that shapes decisions about how power is employed. The same is true for how a country and its leadership articulate their national interest, which is less an objective goal than a subjective understanding of what will benefit different actors in the state. In short, recognizing that Russia at the start of Medvedev's presidency is a stronger, more stable state than it was when Putin became acting president on the last day of 1999 is necessary, but it is not sufficient to understanding the evolution of Russian foreign policy during the intervening period.

Understanding the nature of Russia's interactions with the rest of the world in the second decade of the twenty-first century (and after) is impossible without at least appreciating the continuities between Medvedev's Russia and the rapidly changing, often unpredictable country that emerged from the breakup of the Soviet Union in 1991. The central contention of this work is that the assertive, narrowly self-interested foreign policy that has characterized Russia during the Putin-Medvedev years is merely the cul-mination of a process that began over a decade earlier, during the presi-dency of Boris Yeltsin, at a time when the bulk of the Russian elite came to recognize that integration with the West and its institutions was neither possible nor desirable, at least in the short run. With Russia's own instabil-ity and the West's inability to make a Russia after its own image, Kremlin leaders began laying the foundation for Russia to return to its accustomed international position as one pole in a system of shifting, competitive states. Arguments in the 1990s over NATO expansion or the West's response to ethnic cleansing in Kosovo merely foreshadowed the more serious dis-putes a decade later over the war in Georgia.

The years of Vladimir Putin's presidency featured Russia's re-emergence as a global power with interests—and the capacity to pursue them—across the world. Such a position as one of a handful of Great Powers is something many Russian elites have long wanted for their country, but only with the economic and political recovery of the Putin years did that ambition start to seem attainable. As Putin's semisuccessor (Putin remains in power as prime minister, with a greatly expanded portfolio of responsibilities and power relative to his predecessors), Medvedev will have to confront a dan-gerously unstable world, where Russia's interests are not always clearly defined and where it will be necessary—as it was under Putin and Yelt-sin—to balance Russia's engagement with the West with the need to con-tain the arc of instability around Russia's borders, while simultaneously managing relations with an increasingly vibrant East Asia.

Medvedev will also have to deal with the not-inconsiderable foreign pol-icy legacy of his immediate predecessor. Under Putin, Moscow's approach to dealing with challenges as diverse as instability on its borders, the rise of China, and the expansion of NATO became notably more prickly and assertive.[1] The actual process of making Russian foreign policy also changed. The chaotic pluralism of the 1990s gave way to a system domi-nated on the surface by the president and his staff, though characterized by an ongoing, if submerged, struggle for influence among actors within the security services, the military-industrial complex, large state-owned compa-nies, and possibly between the president and prime minister. Indeed, such a struggle may hold part of the answer to Russia's decision to invade Geor-gia in the face of Medvedev's proclaimed interest in improved relations with the West. Under Putin, this power struggle was less about ideology than about control of and access to resources. With the exertion of Russian power against Georgia, there is evidence that ideological disputes within the elite are beginning to make a comeback.[2]

Despite Russia's larger presence on the international stage, the overall set of ideas and preferences driving Russian foreign policy has remained broadly similar since at least the mid-1990s. The more assertive, confrontational approach to dealing with the rest of the world that characterized Putin's term in office is thus only in part a direct result of Putin himself. It is also the consequence of a broad elite consensus about the role Russia should play in the world as well as an increase in Russia's relative international power.

This upsurge in Russian power has many sources: most important have been the persistently high prices for oil and gas, of which Russia is a major exporter. Russia's energy-fueled economic growth allowed Moscow to begin the process of reversing the precipitous decline of its military forces, freeing itself from dependence on foreign creditors, and exerting pressure on customers of its oil and gas. Less quantifiably, Russia's energy boom contributed to a new sense of confidence among the country's elite, which has become less reticent about standing up for what they believe to be Russia's national interests. Finally, the wars in Iraq and Afghanistan have fed into a perception that the United States is tied down elsewhere and that the era of U.S. hegemony in the world is past. Thanks to these developments, the Russian Ministry of Foreign Affairs boasts that "the main accomplishment of recent years is Russia's newly attained foreign policy autonomy."[3]

Overall, the Russian elite's conception of itself and its place in the world looks much the same as in the mid-1990s. After the collapse of the westernizing strategy initially pursued by Yeltsin and young reformers such as acting prime minister Yegor Gaidar, head of the State Property Committee and privatization guru Anatoly Chubais, and foreign minister Andrei Kozyrev, the Russian governing class turned its back on the idea of seeking integration with the West and its institutions. In foreign affairs, the transition from Kozyrev to Yevgeny Primakov as foreign minister symbolized (but did not cause) the shift to a new approach emphasizing Russia's role as a sovereign Great Power in an anarchic, self-help international system where power, rather than international norms or institutions, remained the *ultima ratio* in international relations.

This new approach found broad support within the Russian elite of the mid-1990s and has continued to inform Russian foreign policy ever since. Putin largely succeeded in mastering the Byzantine world of Russian bureaucratic politics by embodying and adhering to a wide-ranging elite consensus that emphasizes Russia's historic Great Power role, a balance between Russia's western, southern, and eastern flanks, and an active diplomacy in pursuit of what most of the elite perceived as Russia's interests as a state. Some of these factors (including the record oil and gas prices that underpinned Russia's economic recovery until mid-2008) may be transient, but others are likely to endure. With a managed transition to a new president handpicked by his still-powerful predecessor there is little reason to suppose the underlying assumptions of Russian foreign policy behavior will change significantly under Medvedev.

Following years of post–Cold War irrelevance and decline, Russia has more recently gone to great lengths to prove to the rest of the world that it matters internationally—at times in ways other powers perceive as aggressive, nationalistic, and threatening. Whether supporting separatist groups in neighboring states, cutting off gas to Belarus and Ukraine, or standing up for Iran at the UN Security Council, Russia's "new" foreign policy often appears dangerously anachronistic in the West—even apart from the decision to invade neighboring Georgia in alleged defense of an unrecognized separatist regime in South Ossetia. Actions that Moscow sees as justified by its greater strength and confidence seem in the West aggressive and malevolent. The editor-in-chief of *Russia in Global Affairs*, Fyodor Lukyanov, aptly likens the foreign policy behavior of Putin's Russia to that of the infamous "new Russians" of the early 1990s, a nouveau riche whom others perceive as arrogant and lacking refinement and who will continue his escapades "until he runs into someone even richer or smarter, or else manages to offend just about everyone."[4]

Over the past few years, this pushy parvenu seems to have been increasingly out to challenge the post–Cold War order, which has been predicated above all on the dominant international position of the United States. For this reason, it has become more common to hear about Russia as a rival to the U.S. and Europe, intent on using what levers of influence it possesses to subvert its neighbors and prevent the expansion of free-market democracy around its borders. The two sides' increasingly frosty relationship in Central Asia and the Caucasus, Eastern Europe, the Middle East, and elsewhere reflects this perception of Russia as a rival to the West. As a report released by the Council on Foreign Relations in March 2006 lamented, the mounting rivalry between Russia and the West means that "cooperation [between Russia and the West] is becoming the exception, not the norm."[5]

Of course, a more assertive Russia affects not just the West. Russia's neighbors, including both the former Soviet republics and nearby countries such as China, Iran, and Turkey also have a direct stake in how Russia chooses to interact with the rest of the world. China, another rapidly rising state uncomfortable with a world order in which Western norms dominate, has been at times a useful partner but also a worrisome rival for the Kremlin. Chinese traders have kept the economy of the vast Siberian and Far Eastern border regions afloat as their Russian population has shriveled. Beijing's purchases of Russian military equipment propped up the Russian military-industrial complex at a time when orders from Russia's own military were negligible. In geopolitical terms, China's discomfort at the constraints imposed by U.S. power has encouraged Beijing and Moscow to seek common cause on a range of issues, from the war in Iraq to the presence of U.S. forces in Central Asia. Such cooperation, however, has not eliminated the deep-seated fear many Russians feel about their giant neighbor with its huge population, booming economy, and history of Sino-Soviet and Sino-Russian border disputes. China's clear preference for economic integration and a peaceful rise have also at times put it at odds with a Russia less invested in the persistence of the status quo, notably during the Georgian conflict, when Beijing refused to endorse Moscow's recognition of the breakaway republics.

The states most directly impacted by Russia's assertive foreign policy are those immediate neighbors who were once also members of the Soviet Union. Since the collapse of the USSR in 1991, the successor states have sought to establish (or re-establish) a new identity for themselves out of the shadow of Russia. Some, like Belarus, have renounced little of their Soviet past, while others, particularly Georgia, have sought to maximize the cultural, political, and historical distance between themselves and Moscow. For the Kremlin, keeping the former Soviet republics from becoming jumping-off points for hostile forces has been the dominant theme. As with the war in Georgia, Russian policy inside the borders of the former Soviet Union has sometimes looked like naked imperialism, but here more than anywhere, context is critical. The fall of the USSR turned the areas around Russia's borders into a contested zone for the first time since the Russian Civil War of the early 1920s, and Russia's leaders gave the incursion of foreign forces (including both NATO and foreign NGOs) the worst possible interpretation. Russia's sometimes manic approach to the former Soviet Union is thus part of the larger dynamic of Great Power competition that has characterized Russian foreign policy for the past decade-plus. It is also a response to what Moscow perceives as the West's hypocritical policy over, for instance, Kosovo. Why, Moscow wonders, will the United States and European Union use their political and military power to secure Kosovo's independence from Serbia, a Russian ally, but react neuralgically when Russia attempts to do the same for South Ossetia?

During the late 1990s, Russia appeared to have been so weakened by political, economic, and military collapse as to be finished as a shaper of world affairs. Even as analysts and diplomats in the West dismissed Yeltsin's Russia as a prickly but ultimately irrelevant nuisance, Russia's elites chafed at what they saw as their country's temporary eclipse. No matter Yeltsin's affinity for the West and no matter Russia's continued dependence on foreign assistance, most of Russia's ruling class continued to think of their country as destined by history and geography to be one of the principal guardians of world order. It took Yeltsin's departure, along with the consolidation of state power and skyrocketing energy prices, to give substance to such ideas. Putin and Medvedev's Russia has not embarked on a new, more threatening path in the world but has merely recovered enough to act in a way that even most Yeltsinites desired. The changed tone of Russian diplomacy under Putin at times masked the continuity of these aims. That new tone, however, resulted more from changed circumstances than changed goals. These circumstances—state consolidation, high energy prices, the passing of U.S. supremacy—will not end anytime soon.[6] Even if the recession into which Russia was thrust during the second half of 2008 proves deep and prolonged, it, too, is unlikely to result in a fundamental shift, any more than the economic disasters of 1992 and 1998 did.

Medvedev may well turn out to be more of a liberal than the ex-KGB man Putin. Whether or not that is the case, and whether or not Putin continues to shape events from behind the scenes in his capacity as prime minister (or even if he returns as president in 2012), Russia's international behavior will continue to operate on the basis of the same considerations that have driven it since the implosion of Kozyrev's integration strategy around 1994–1995. Even though Putin did not come to power until 2000 (he became prime minister in 1999), Russia's foreign policy has been essentially Putinist for well over a decade. Given the enduring nature of the Russian elites' preferences as well as the external environment confronting it, Russian diplomacy will most likely continue to bear the hallmarks of this grand strategic vision in the Medvedev years as well.

NOTES

1. Among the slew of recent articles debating the strength and durability of Russia's foreign policy revival, see Paul Dibb, "The Bear Is Back," *The American Interest,* Nov–Dec 2006, 2(2); Yury E. Fedorov, "'Boffins' and 'Buffoons': Different Strains of Thought in Russia's Strategic Thinking," Chatham House Briefing Paper, Mar 2006; Andrei P. Tsygankov, "Projecting Confidence, Not Fear: Russia's Post-Imperial Assertiveness," *Orbis,* Aut 2006: 677–90; Dmitri Trenin, "Russia Leaves the West," *Foreign Affairs,* Jul–Aug 2006, 85(4): 87–96; Thomas Ambrosio, *Challenging America's Global Pre-eminence: Russia's Quest for Multipolarity* (Aldershot: Ashgate, 2005). For a more skeptical take, see S. Neil MacFarlane, "The 'R' in BRICs: Is Russia an Emerging Power?" *International Affairs,* 2006, 82(1): 41–57; "Russia's Dangerous, but Mostly for Russians," *The Economist,* 2 Dec 2006. Not surprisingly, Russian assessments have tended to be more confident that Russia's re-emergence is both real and positive for Russia as well as for the world generally. See Igor Ivanov, "A New Foreign-Policy Year for Russia and the World," *International Affairs: A Russian Journal of World Politics, Diplomacy and International Relations,* 2003, 49(6): 33–38; Yevgeny Primakov, "Russia's Foreign Policy in 2005 Was Successful in Every Area," *International Affairs: A Russian Journal of World Politics, Diplomacy and International Relations,* 2006, 52(2): 13–22; Vladimir Degoev, "Fenomen Putina kak faktor mirovoi politiki," *Svobodnaya mysl',* 2006 (6): 17–26; Yuri Baluyevsky, "Strategic Stability in a Globalized World," *Russia in Global Affairs,* Oct–Dec 2003 (4).

2. Daniel Kimmage, "Russian 'Hard Power' Changes Balance in Caucasus," *RFE/ RL Analysis,* 12 Aug 2008.

3. Russian Ministry of Foreign Affairs, "Obzor vneshnei politiki Rossiiskoi Federatsii," 27 Mar 2007, http://www.mid.ru/brp_4nsf/sps.

4. Fyodor Lukyanov, "Time for a New Foreign Policy Look," *Moscow Times*, 28 Dec 2006.

5. "Russia's Wrong Direction: What the United States Can and Should Do," Independent Task Force Report No. 57 (New York: Council on Foreign Relations, 2006), 4.

6. On the passing of U.S. hegemony, see Richard Haass, "The Age of Nonpolarity: What Will Follow U.S. Dominance?" and Kishore Mahbubani, "The Case against the West," *Foreign Affairs*, May–Jun 2008, 87(3).

1

Contours of Russian Foreign Policy

Since the collapse of Communism, Russia has endured a confusing, often torturous process of self-definition. Stripped of the geopolitical and ideological certainties at the heart of Soviet politics, contemporary Russia has been forced to answer a series of fundamental questions about its relationship to the post–Cold War world system and its own identity as a state. No longer controlling an imperial hinterland in Europe and freed from a zero-sum relationship with the United States based primarily on the logic of mutually assured destruction, Russia in the early twenty-first century is in many ways a state in search of itself.

A major component of this process of self-definition has been the attempt to elaborate a new foreign policy vision befitting a weakened but still formidable power confronting a world of emerging and uncertain threats. The formulation of a new approach to foreign policy in Russia has continued unevenly since the last days of the Soviet Union, when Mikhail Gorbachev first evoked the vision of a "common European home" stretching from the Atlantic coast to the Urals. In the early 1990s, Yeltsin presided over a country that appeared to be moving rapidly to join its onetime Cold War enemies in a new, democratic West. This rush to the West quickly foundered on the rocks of domestic opposition and foreign skepticism. By the middle of the decade, this vision of Russia's mission had been replaced by a determination to restore Russia as an independent international actor whose interests remained distinct from those of the liberal capitalist West. The new approach to foreign policy rested on a deep-seated consensus among the Russian elite about the nature of international relations and about the identity of Russia as a state.

Upon his emergence from obscurity in the late 1990s, Vladimir Putin pursued a strategic design that both reflected basic elements of this consensus and used it to fashion a long-term vision of Russia's role in the world.

11

Strengthened by high oil prices and a booming economy, today's Russia has succeeded in achieving many of the goals to which the Russia of the 1990s merely aspired. Under the Putin-Medvedev duopoly that emerged in 2008, the question of Russia's long-term identity and interests has taken on a new urgency, as the war in Georgia forced outside powers to reassess a number of assumptions about Russia's international role.

Putin's ability to shape Russian foreign policy to a large extent depended on his adherence to a general strategic consensus that has prevailed since the mid-1990s. The transition to Medvedev's presidency in mid-2008 exposed the lack of institutionalization long bedeviling Russian governance, while raising significant doubts about the ability of any leader to depart from the shared understanding about the nature of Russia's interests. The foundation of this consensus is the notion that Russia is a Great Power, albeit a weakened one, with interests in many corners of the globe and a responsibility to look out for itself in a dangerous, indifferent world.[1] Russia's elite is therefore inclined to envision its country playing a role in the world analogous to that of the United States, rather than integrating with the less realpolitik-inclined European Union, even though many of its closest diplomatic partners are in Europe.[2]

Consequently, Russian foreign policy continues to focus on upholding (or creating) a system of international relations in which large states are the primary guardians of global order, free to pursue their national interests as they deem fit, respecting one another's primacy within a circumscribed sphere of influence, and maintaining a general balance of power among themselves. Despite the chaos of the 1990s, Russia's leaders never ceased regarding their own country as one of these major powers. Beginning with former foreign minister Yevgeny Primakov, Russian diplomats and policy makers have repeatedly emphasized that Russia must therefore have an independent foreign policy, rather than function merely as an appendage of the West or a supplier of natural resources to the world market.[3]

Official strategy documents, particularly the Foreign Policy Concept and the National Security Concept, reflect this understanding of the world. Although the importance of these documents should not be overemphasized—they are the work of bureaucratic horse trading and are often left deliberately vague in order to satisfy competing constituencies—the language they use does provide some insight into how the men responsible for Russian national security view the world. More a guide to the broad principles behind policy than a catalogue of responses to specific challenges, the Concepts define the mental universe within which policy decisions are supposed to be made. Particularly instructive in this regard are the differences between the Foreign Policy Concept adopted in December 2000, almost a year into Putin's presidency, and its replacement, which was approved by Medvedev barely a month into his term in office in 2008.

The Putin-era document lists as the first priority of Russian foreign policy:

Promoting the interests of the Russian Federation as a great power and one of the most influential centers in the modern world [by] ensuring the country's security, preserving and strengthening its sovereignty and territorial integrity and its strong and authoritative position in the world community [in order to promote] the growth of its political, economic, intellectual, and spiritual potential.[4]

This statement, along with the Concept's subsequent priorities ("shaping a stable, just, and democratic world order . . . [based] on equitable relations of partnership among states") is notable for the attention it gives to notions such as sovereignty, Great Power, and partnership among states.[5] The language of the Foreign Policy Concept is that of geopolitics—a world of states seeking power and pursuing their national interests, while subject to a balance of power. Such language, and such a worldview, would be unthinkable in official statements from the United States, much less the European Union.

Shortly after taking office in May 2008, Medvedev signed an updated Foreign Policy Concept.[6] The 2008 version copies about 80 percent of the text of its predecessor verbatim. The differences, however, are significant. The term *Great Power* (*velikaya derzhava*) is gone, replaced by a reference to Russia as "one of the leading centers of the contemporary world" and repeated mention of a "new Russia." Russian analysts argue that the changes reflect a greater emphasis on Russia's position as a rising power, a work in progress with lingering socioeconomic weaknesses that belie the blustery tone of the Putin-era document, although the notion of striving for Great Power status remains an important subtext.[7] In addition to repeating the above paragraph, the top priorities of Russian foreign policy under Medvedev include:

Creating favorable external conditions for the modernization of Russia, transformation of its economy through innovation, enhancement of living standards, consolidation of society, strengthening of the foundations of the constitutional system, rule of law and democratic institutions, realization of human rights and freedoms and, as a consequence, ensuring national competitiveness in a globalizing world.[8]

One final important difference is that the new document also specifies that the cabinet, which is headed by the prime minister, carries responsibility for implementing Russia's foreign policy. This addition allows Putin, who became prime minister immediately on stepping down from the presidency, to maintain a hand in foreign affairs, though previous prime ministers were denied this role.

Given the war with Georgia that broke out barely a month after

Medvedev signed the 2008 Concept, it is difficult to square the new document's emphasis on development, the rule of law, and other liberal reforms with the hard-line response to mounting tensions with Tbilisi. To be sure, the 2008 Concept dropped its predecessor's almost ritualistic reference to the need for a belt of good neighbors around the Russian Federation's borders. Still, the contrast speaks to a certain confusion in Russian foreign policy thinking, or, more likely, a still unresolved debate. Medvedev, after all, was an outsider when elevated to the presidency, and his views (with their emphasis on competitiveness and soft power) have long been at odds with those of the *siloviki* (members of the security and intelligence services) with whom Putin surrounded himself and who continue to some extent to surround Medvedev nearly a year into his presidency. It almost appeared as if the war in Georgia was cooked up in order to knock the new president off balance and demonstrate that, for all his liberalizing rhetoric, true power rests elsewhere.

The National Security Concept, confirmed by Putin just weeks after his ascension to the presidency in January 2000, further elaborates the ideological assumptions underlying Russian foreign policy. It identifies two mutually contradictory trends defining the future development of the international order. On the one hand, international relations in the post–Cold War world seem dominated by "the strengthening economic and political positions of a substantial number of states and their integration in a complicated mechanism of multilaterally directed international processes." At the same time, however, this tendency toward greater integration and multipolarity is offset by "attempts to create structures of international relations founded on the world community's domination by the developed countries of the West led by the U.S. and predicated on the unilateral—especially in the power-military sense—resolution of the key problems in world politics."[9] The focus on states and power generally, coupled with the belief that Russia's position in the world is threatened by the formation of a world order from which it is excluded, are the basic tenets of what could be termed a geopolitical understanding of world politics.[10]

The understanding of how the world works contained in the Foreign Policy and National Security Concepts has important implications for the way Russian foreign policy is actually conducted. Russian diplomacy is focused on bilateral relations with other states, especially large states such as the U.S., China, and India, rather than multilateral pacts based on commitments to shared values. Moscow largely even prefers to deal with transnational problems such as terrorism within the framework of bilateral relations. Unlike multilateral forums, bilateral state-to-state relations have the advantage, from the Russian perspective, of avoiding the creation of intrusive behavioral norms while preserving (at least for the major powers) states' sovereign equality. The Russian government prefers to work through those multilateral organizations that, like the UN Security Council or the G8, are essentially Great Power clubs that do not limit Russia's sovereignty over its domestic affairs and that impose limits on the United States' ability to act without the support of other major powers.[11]

Worry about the overarching role of the U.S. in international affairs has led Russia's foreign policy makers to increasingly focus on the concept of multipolarity (*mnogopolyarnost'*) as the key to international stability. In its most basic form, this term simply refers to a kind of concert arrangement among the Great Powers, akin to the nineteenth-century Concert of Europe or an idealized version of Franklin Roosevelt's "Four Policemen." It is at once an attempt to negate the continued dominance of the United States and a broader framework for thinking about the nature of modern international relations, where knowledge, technology, and power are more widely distributed than at any previous moment in history.[12]

Multipolarity implies a world of states more or less equal, if not in their inherent power capabilities (few Russian officials are rash enough to claim that Russian "hard power" will match that of the United States anytime soon), then at least in their entitlement to shape the international order. For Primakov in the 1990s, a multipolar order was largely something Russia should aspire to create.[13] For officials of the twenty-first century, it is increasingly seen as an existing phenomenon. Factors seen contributing to the emergence of a multipolar world order include the divergence of priorities between the United States and the European Union in the war on terror and the rise of states such as Brazil, India, and China (which make up, along with Russia itself, the so-called BRIC group of rising powers). Furthermore, as the Russian Ministry of Foreign Affairs argued in its annual 2007 review of foreign policy, "The myth of a unipolar world crumbled completely in Iraq."[14] Similar gloating emanated from the Kremlin during the late 2008 economic crisis, set off by the end of a massive housing bubble in the U.S.—even though the consequences of the downturn were quite severe for Russia itself.

If the world in the twenty-first century is destined to be multipolar, the Russian elite is largely unanimous in believing Russia must be one of the poles. For all the talk of integration with the West in the aftermath of the September 11, 2001, terrorist attacks, there was never any real belief in Russia's giving up its identity as an autonomous actor in world affairs. The ongoing discussion about the concept of "sovereign democracy" as a description of the Russian political system focuses to a great degree on this issue. A truly sovereign democracy, as defined by the originator of the term, Kremlin ideologist Vladislav Surkov, is one whose goals and methods—both at home and abroad—are made solely on the basis of calculations of national interest, rather than because of external pressure to conform to behavioral norms. This emphasis on sovereignty is invoked both in domestic politics (e.g., to reject Western criticism of Moscow's clampdown on civil society) and in foreign affairs, where the Kremlin seems less and less interested in coordinating its policies with those of the West. The focus on sovereignty as a value, coupled with the revival of Russia's economic fortunes over the past several years, has greatly enhanced Moscow's ability to conduct an independent foreign policy. Foreign Minister Sergei Lavrov underlined the importance of this autonomy in a September 2006 address in Los Angeles:

> And for us, this autonomy [*samostoyatel'nost'*] is a key issue, and we will continue to act on this basis both within the country and in the international arena. . . . I think that the rapid revival of Russia's foreign policy autonomy is one of the issues which is complicating relations between us, since far from everyone in the U.S. has gotten used to this. But they must get used to it.[15]

The existence of a multipolar world order requires, in the Russian analysis, the strengthening of those international institutions and laws promoting the sovereignty and equality of the world's major states.[16] Consequently, the Kremlin continues to favor a system of international relations in which large states are the primary upholders of global order, their intramural relations dictated by calculations of national interest.[17] Consequently, Russian diplomats are wont to argue that the cause of stability is best served by upholding those norms and institutions (above all, the UN Security Council) that formalize the existence of a Great Power concert. According to Putin, "We must clearly recognize that the critical responsibility . . . for securing global stability will be borne by the leading world powers [*vedushchie mirovye derzhavy*]—powers possessing nuclear weapons [and] powerful levers of military-political influence."[18] In a world dominated by Great Powers, smaller states are left to fend for themselves as the large states jockey for influence over them.

THE WEST IN RUSSIAN FOREIGN POLICY

Relations with the West constitute the primary frame of reference for Russian foreign policy. Moscow's interactions with other parts of the world, including the former Soviet states around its borders, are conditioned upon the state of relations with the Western community and especially the leading member of that community, the United States. The Cold War legacy of bipolarity is the main reason for the ingrained Western-centrism of Russian foreign policy; Russia's ruling elite grew up during an era when Moscow and Washington largely directed the fate of the world. Besides, given the United States' recent predominance, it is hardly surprising that Russia's leaders should think of their relationship with Washington as central to their country's international position since "there is almost no regional or global policy issue that Russia could presently decide without taking into consideration the 'American factor.'"[19]

The West's importance as a frame of reference for Russia has not generally been reciprocated by Western leaders since the end of the Cold War. In part, the West's lack of attention has to do with the realization that today's Russia is in many ways a weaker, less threatening power than was the Soviet Union; in a world containing al Qaeda terrorists, rogue states seeking nuclear weapons, and a China rapidly becoming both an economic and military rival, Russia does not normally figure in the top rank of problems competing for the attention of Western statesmen. Part of the West's lack of attention also has to do with uncertainty about what today's Russia is and what tomorrow's Russia will be—and hence how to frame policy toward it.

To a large degree, outside assessments of Russian foreign policy seem to center on the question of whether or not Russia is moving toward or away from the West in cultural and institutional, as well as diplomatic, terms. The United States, as the remaining superpower and the mirror to which many Russians hold up their own country, occupies a special place in the elites' thinking about Russia's place in the world.[20] At the same time, the European Union, which is closer geographically and more closely intertwined in social and economic terms, offers Russian elites an alternative more critical of Russia's internal failings, but also rather uncomfortable with America's global hegemony. For this reason, some Russian thinkers have (especially in the run-up to the Iraq war and in the aftermath of the war with Georgia) reanimated the old Cold War idea of trying to play Europe off against the United States. Nonetheless, the West as a collective abstraction remains the key reference point for the conduct of foreign policy. Such is particularly the case in discussions about the domestic transformations Russia has endured over the past two decades.

The debate about Russia's relationship with the West centers in particular on the degree of institutional and ideological convergence between Russia and its former Cold War enemies, that is, about Russia's interest in and ability to "join the West." Although Russia's convergence with the West seemed somewhat inevitable in the last days of Soviet power, the deep-seated differences between Russia and even its immediate neighbors in East-Central Europe have repeatedly intervened.[21] And while there has been much debate over the past two decades about Russia's ability and interest in "joining the West," there has never been a comparable level of interest in the idea of Russia "joining the East." Consequently, a Russia that is not firmly anchored in Western institutions is one that is largely on its own internationally, maneuvering between East and West or pursuing what Russian diplomats since Primakov have referred to as a "multivector" foreign policy.

For much of the 1990s, even as then-President Yeltsin was shelling his recalcitrant parliament and presiding over a corruption-ridden privatization scheme, most observers in the U.S. and Europe operated on the assumption that Russia had made some kind of fundamental choice about joining "Western civilization"—even though major disagreements on issues such as the war in Chechnya and the Kosovo crisis perpetually complicated relations.[22] Somewhat ironically given later developments, the ascension to power of Vladimir Putin in 1999 (first as prime minister, then as president) was welcomed in Western capitals for reversing the slide toward kleptocratic decay taking place under Yeltsin and for confirming Russia's generally westward course.[23] Putin, a former KGB operative in East Germany who had been a key adviser to the reformist mayor of St. Petersburg, Anatoly Sobchak, was praised for putting Russia back on a westward vector. In contrast to the ill and erratic Yeltsin, Putin was the calm professional who would bring competence and stability back to the Kremlin after the drift of Yeltsin's last years in power. This assumption provided the context in which, after meeting the new Russian leader for the first time, U.S. president George W. Bush famously claimed to have looked into Putin's soul and seen a man who was "straightforward and trustworthy," and "deeply committed to his country."[24]

The September 11, 2001, attacks in the United States reinforced this newfound faith in Russia's westward course. Putin was widely praised for the alacrity with which he declared his country's readiness to assist the United States and to put aside old suspicions about U.S. intentions. This decision to cooperate in the U.S.-led war on terror was perceived as a confirmation of Putin's fundamentally Western orientation and of Russia's unshakable determination to recast its identity as a Western rather than a global or a Eurasian power.[25]

Yet even during the post–September 11 rapprochement between Russia and the U.S., there were warnings that the era of good feeling should not mask the fact that Putin's vision of foreign policy was an expansive one that could cause problems for Russia's Western partners. Despite Putin's acceptance of U.S. initiatives during this period, there were signs of more difficult times to come; as early as 2002, Russia's quest for greater influence in the former Soviet states—in particular an apparent attempt to wrest control of the strategically and economically valuable Kerch Strait from Ukraine—was causing unease in Western capitals.[26] Moscow saw the attacks of September 11 as the culmination of trends that had been under way for many years (Russia's experience in Chechnya and Central Asia had awakened Moscow to the dangers of Islamic terrorism well before 2001). The events of that day, and even more, the muscular U.S. response to them—invading not only Afghanistan, but Iraq as well—reinforced Russia's interest in a world of many powerful states, rather than a single hegemon, as did Washington's willingness to ignore strenuous Russian objections to policies such as NATO expansion or withdrawal from the Anti-Ballistic Missile (ABM) Treaty.[27] Objections to the fruits of U.S. unilateralism only fed skepticism within Russia about whether Russia could, or indeed should, aspire to join the Western community of nations.

The end of the post–September 11 honeymoon in relations between Russia and the West was for many a profound disappointment, but hardly the first time that hopes for post-Communist Russia's integration into Western institutions and adoption of Western norms were not fulfilled. Indeed, Western perceptions of Russian foreign policy since 1991 have been characterized above all by a dialectical process of expectation and disappointment about Moscow's integration with the institutions that make up the West.[28] Establishing the actual moment of Russia's turn away from the West is important, because it tells us something about the reasons for that turn and the likelihood that it will endure. It is a question that has lingered in the background of much commentary on Russian politics and foreign policy.

Dmitri Trenin observed in 2006 that, "Until recently, Russia saw itself as Pluto in the Western solar system, very far from the center but still fundamentally a part of it. Now it has left that orbit entirely: Russia's leaders have given up on becoming part of the West and have started creating their own Moscow-centered system."[29] Since the start of Putin's second term in 2004, few would quarrel with that observation; still fewer would object since the fallout of the Russo-Georgian conflict of 2008 has become clear. Yet if scholars and diplomats are in agreement that Russia is now charting its own international course, there is much less agreement about precisely when Russia decided to abandon its putatively Western identity. Trenin dates Russia's divorce from the West to 2005, in the aftermath of the "colored revolutions" in Georgia, Ukraine, and Kyrgyzstan. The authors of a 2006 report to the Trilateral Commission (all high-ranking diplomats) also noted a growing divergence between Russian and Western priorities but date the change to late 2003, when reactionaries in the Putin government seized control from a group of Western-leaning liberals, halting economic reform and pursuing a more confrontational policy toward the West in the run-up to the 2003 parliamentary and 2004 presidential elections.[30]

These observers may cite different dates, but they at least locate Russia's estrangement from the West during Vladimir Putin's presidency and connect it to policy choices made by Putin's Kremlin. But what if the roots of this estrangement stretch further back, into the Yeltsin years (or beyond)? It is worth remembering that after a brief flirtation with Western integration in the early 1990s, Yeltsin's Russia was also subjected to harsh criticism both for its turn away from democracy and for its resistance to Western foreign policy initiatives (especially in the Balkans). It was Yeltsin, after all, who used tanks to defeat his parliamentary opposition in 1993, and it was under Yeltsin's watch that Russian troops seized the airport in Priština, Kosovo, in 1999, nearly causing a firefight with NATO soldiers. As early as 1994, some observers noted that for the foreseeable future Russia's foreign policy would be driven by "the championship, above all, of Russia's own national interests" and self-perception as one of the world's Great Powers rather than by partnership with the West.[31] Or, as the Duma deputy and scholar Alexei Arbatov also pointed out in 1994, "There is an overwhelming consensus on the main goal of strategic and national security: that Russia should remain one of the world's great powers."[32]

Even the 2001 terrorist attacks in the United States did not fundamentally alter the Kremlin's approach to the world and Russia's role in it. Though Putin took the lead in seeking to bring Russia and the Western powers (particularly the U.S.) together in the struggle against terrorism, he did not in the process abandon Russia's long-standing claim to an autonomous role. Failure to appreciate this fact no doubt contributed to the disappointment many Western leaders expressed regarding Russia's more recent retreat from cooperation. The point is that the desire to remain outside of the West as a political (and moral) grouping is a deep-seated one among the Russian political class that has less to do with a particular configuration of power in the Kremlin than with the Russian political and cultural elites' understanding of their country's own history and role in the international system.

While Russia's foreign policy priorities did not undergo a fundamental transformation during the Putin years, the functioning of the political system in Russia did, with consequences at least for the way Russia was perceived beyond its borders.[33] Today's Russia is no doubt a much less free place than the Russia of the 1990s, and the security services are much more pervasive. Elections, where held at all, are tightly controlled by the Kremlin, as opposition figures such as former Prime Minister Mikhail Kasyanov and onetime chess champion Garry Kasparov discovered when they sought to challenge the Kremlin's tightly managed succession process. Much of the independent media have been swallowed up by the state or its proxies (such as natural gas monopoly Gazprom), and a not inconsiderable number of independent journalists, most notably Anna Politkovskaya of *Novaya Gazeta*, have turned up dead. Even big business has been forced to adhere to the government's line, and the Kremlin has shown no hesitation in going after obstreperous oligarchs such as Vladimir Gusinsky, Boris Berezovsky, and Mikhail Khodorkovsky with the entire coercive apparatus of the state.

Given the importance of democratic values and practices in the West's self-perception, the evident failure of Russia's democratization cannot but have consequences for Russia's prospects of integration with the Western world. Nonetheless, Western powers have managed to have cooperative, even close, relations with a variety of nondemocratic states such as Saudi

Arabia, Egypt, and China. Russian observers, especially those sympathetic to the West, thus sometimes complain that Russia is being held to a double standard on the issue of democracy.[34] The state of democracy in Russia has important consequences for foreign policy but does not, in and of itself, determine the extent to which Moscow can find common cause with the United States and Europe.

Among Russians, perceptions about the institutions of governance have foreign policy consequences because of a persistent link between attitudes toward Russia's domestic political development and toward interactions with the West. On the one hand, polls continually show that most Russians would prefer the government to be more socially oriented, even at the expense of Russia's leading global role. Meanwhile, the work of William Zimmerman in the 1990s showed repeatedly that Russians who favored a market economy and democratic politics also supported close cooperation with the West, while supporters of a Soviet-style political and economic system were equally consistent in advocating a more confrontational approach to dealing with the West.[35]

The existence of such splits between elite and mass opinion about Russia's identity in the world and the role of the state more than a decade and a half after the fall of the Soviet Union is in part the result of the fact that Russia's fundamental identity, including its degree of belonging to the Western/European community, remains ill defined.[36] The challenge for Russia's post-Soviet elites has thus been "to reconcile traditional national interests with the newly emerging social and political entity."[37] The process of scripting a new national identity out of the collective memory of the populace has been one of the most challenging tasks for all post-Communist states in Eastern Europe and Eurasia. In a rather short span of time, these states have had to free themselves from the shackles of Communist orthodoxy, reintegrate their pre-Communist pasts into collective memory, and work out a new relationship with a European Union that was itself busy undermining the traditional foundations of national distinctiveness. Some formerly Communist states have been more successful than others in establishing an identity that allows them to pursue a successful, stable foreign policy in the context of a vastly changed European landscape.[38] Russia has been notably less successful than states such as Poland in doing so, and the lure of the West continues to compete for attention with Russia's autarkic, imperial past as a model for future development.[39]

A Russia that is firmly anchored to Western institutions is one that, like Germany and Japan after 1945, has decided to trade its foreign policy autonomy for prosperity and security within an increasingly integrated community of nations whose priorities are economic rather than political. Yet the analogy with postwar Germany and Japan has never been widely accepted in Russia. While many average Russians would be willing to see their country relegated to the role of a medium-sized regional power if such a diminution resulted in greater prosperity, Russia's elites largely are wedded to the idea of their country as a major power.[40] Given the top-heavy configuration of the Russian political system, it is largely the elites' priorities that matter, especially on questions of foreign policy.

Whatever their other political and ideological differences, Russia's elites are generally in agreement that Russia is, and should remain, a power with global interests and global reach. To be sure, Putin and Medvedev have often spoken of Russia as being part of Europe.[41] On the other hand, officials and diplomats have made no secret of their interest in Russia playing a truly global role, analogous to that of the United States or, indeed, of the Soviet Union during the Cold War. As then-Foreign Minister Igor Ivanov cautioned (before the September 11 attacks), neither Russia's jettisoning of Communist ideology, its democratization, nor hope for better relations with the West would cause the country to "narrow the scope of its foreign policy interests."[42] Russia's relatively modest international role early in Putin's presidency thus had more to do with the overall weakness of the Russian state and economy at the time than with any broad conceptual shift.

The fact that Russia's ambitions are increasingly global does not by itself determine the nature of Moscow's relations with other countries. A Russia that operates outside the institutional and normative bounds of the West can set itself up as a rival and a spoiler if it so chooses. However, it is worth remembering that despite its impressive growth in the years leading up to 2008, Russia remains significantly behind major Western powers in economic and military terms, and in the Kremlin's more active foreign policy lies a recognition of this underlying power reality as well as a profound resentment at having its interests ignored when it was weaker. As the authors of the 2006 Trilateral Commission report judiciously caution:

> Russia is essentially defensive and independent rather than aggressive and expansionist. Russia will use pressure of many kinds on less powerful neighboring states and use leverage with the major powers where it has it . . . but it does not seek confrontation with them. . . . The ambition of the present leadership, supported by the majority of the electorate, is to re-establish Russia as a strong, independent, and unfettered actor on the global stage.[43]

Of course, the inhabitants of Georgia might have a different perspective on Russia's putative defensiveness. Georgia and other pieces of the former Soviet Union have always posed something of an exception for the Russian Federation. The lingering distinction in Russian public discourse between the so-called Near Abroad of the ex-USSR and the Far Abroad everywhere else reflects this duality. As onetime hinterlands of not just the USSR, but in some cases also the Russian Empire and even the Kingdom of Muscovy, the states of the CIS (from which Georgia withdrew following its disastrous conflict with Russia) have often been portrayed as less than full members of the global community by Russian politicians and diplomats. Shortly before stepping down as president, Putin approved the formation of a separate Federal Agency for CIS Affairs separate from the Foreign Ministry, a step at least implying that the former Soviet republics are not really "foreign" at all.[44] Even during the war in Georgia, Lavrov and others sought to draw a line between Russian behavior in the Near Abroad and desire for continued good relations with the major powers of the Far Abroad, which Moscow has repeatedly said it hopes to de-ideologize.[45]

PUTIN'S LEGACY

Russia's return as a major international player, as well as its increasingly frosty relationship with the Western world, largely coincided with Vladimir Putin's term in the Kremlin (i.e., 2000–2008). This worsening of relations with the West, not to mention Putin's background in the KGB and the consolidation of authoritarianism on his watch, made Russia's second president a rather reviled figure in Western capitals and (especially) in the Western press. Though initially hailed in much of the West as a capable, energetic modernizer, by the time he left office, Putin carried with him a decidedly sinister reputation only exacerbated by the appearance of him upstaging Medvedev in prosecuting the Georgian war.[46] Given the highly centralized nature of the Russian political system, Putin's direct impact on foreign policy has been considerable and remains so since his move from the Kremlin to the White House (seat of the Russian prime minister and his cabinet). Yet despite significant Western criticism of Russian foreign policy during Putin's second term, his actual legacy as a statesman is quite complex. Putin's emphasis on rebuilding Russian power led him to approach the West in different ways at different times, depending on the needs of Russia's international position. Underlying his entire grand strategic approach has been a commitment to the restoration of Russia as a major power.

Putin, of course, did not originate the Great Power aspirations at the heart of Russia's interactions with much of the rest of the world. On the other hand, and to a much greater degree than his predecessor, Putin succeeded in translating that aspiration into a concrete reality. His ability to position Russia as one of the indispensable pillars of the international system owes much to fortuitous circumstances (above all the sustained rise in global prices for Russia's major export, energy). At the same time, Putin's success was in part the result of his ability to pursue a clearly articulated vision of the world and Russia's place in it and to mobilize the resources necessary to achieve his ends.

Putin was also careful to operate within the broad elite consensus about Russia's role as one of the world's leading powers. In this way, he managed to neutralize opposition and give himself substantial freedom to maneuver at the tactical level. By positioning himself as a defender of Russia's international prerogatives, Putin largely managed to defuse opposition to particular initiatives, above all when he sought to avoid fruitless quarrels with other major powers.

For the first half of Putin's presidency, the most notable fact about Russian foreign policy was its generally passive, reactive nature—a development that led some analysts to argue that a historic turning point had been reached, bringing an end to the era of confrontation between Russia and the West once and for all. In Putin's second term, and in particular since 2006, such optimism gave way to a new round of philippics about the resurrection of Russia's imperial instincts that reached unprecedented levels during the war in Georgia. The changing nature of Russia's international behavior during the course of Putin's presidency makes sense as part of a broader strategy based on restoring Russia's ability to play the global role preferred by its elites. In bandwagoning with the United States after September 11, 2001, and seeking to minimize quarrels with the West thereafter, Putin made a strategic calculation that international cooperation—along with restoring the domestic bases of Russian strength—was the most effective means of recapturing Russia's lost global influence. When the external and internal environments changed as a result of rising energy prices, the war in Iraq, and the colored revolutions in the CIS, so, too, did the Kremlin's strategy for attaining its geopolitical aims.

During Putin's second term, this pattern of deferring to Western initiatives, notably in connection with the war in Afghanistan, gave way to a much more determined assertion of Russian power, at times in direct contravention of U.S. and EU aims. Russia's newfound oil and gas wealth underpinned a sense of power and independence that continues to shock observers used to a Russia whose menace lay in its weakness rather than its strength. The changed tone of Russian diplomacy became particularly clear during the course of 2006. The year began with Moscow's decision to shut off gas supplies to Ukraine, ostensibly to force Kyiv[47] to pay market price for deliveries of Russian energy. The subtext to this dispute over energy prices, however, centered on the 2004 Orange Revolution, which brought to power a strongly pro-Western Ukrainian president, Viktor Yushchenko, who had campaigned on a platform of reducing Ukraine's dependence on Russia and seeking membership in Western institutions (including NATO). It seemed that Moscow was using its dominant position in Ukraine's energy market as a way of forcing Kyiv to hew to a more pro-Russian foreign policy. Ukraine, like other former Soviet republics still dependent on Russian gas, was in essence given a choice: "Either loyalty . . . or independence, at the highest [possible] price."[48]

While 2006 began with a crisis over gas, the end of the year was marred by the assassinations of Anna Politkovskaya, the investigative journalist gunned down in the lift of her Moscow apartment building, and of the ex-KGB agent and political dissident Aleksandr Litvinenko, who was poisoned in London with the rare radioactive element polonium. Whatever the motivation for the killings, they had a chilling impact on relations with the Western world. Critics of Putin—including a dying Litvinenko—blamed the Kremlin for complicity in the assassinations. Officials in the U.S. and Europe claimed that the assassinations were part of "the steady accumulation of problems and irritants [that] threatens to harm Russia's relations with the West."[49] Moscow pointed out that there was no evidence of Kremlin involvement in either case and warned its Western counterparts against jumping to conclusions (though also refusing in line with the Russian constitution to extradite the prime suspect in Litvinenko's killing, ex-KGB agent and current Liberal Democratic Party Duma deputy Andrei Lugovoi, to Britain to face charges). Regardless of who was responsible, the damage to Russia's image was done.

Nor were Russia's relations with the U.S. and Europe helped by the fact that the Kremlin was busy launching assaults on some of the biggest and most influential Western energy companies. Moscow sought to take control of massive extraction operations on Sakhalin Island and in the Far North (Shtokman) that had been ceded to firms like Royal Dutch Shell and British Petroleum in the 1990s. Realizing they had few options, the oil majors meekly assented to, in effect, the nationalization of their largest assets in Russia.[50] Their travails added one more charge to the bill of indictment being presented against Putin's Russia.

The 2006 assassinations, the Kremlin's response to the colored revolutions, its decision to nationalize the Yukos oil company (which was negotiating the sale of a major stake in its operations to ExxonMobil or Chevron Texaco), the gas cutoffs, reluctance to end Russian participation in Iran's nuclear program, suspension of the Conventional Forces in Europe (CFE) Treaty, attempts to block the independence of Kosovo, hostile response to the planned deployment of NATO antimissile systems in the Czech Republic and Poland, and finally the invasion of Georgia contributed to the perception that Putin's Russia was bent on aggressively promoting its exclusive interests at the expense of partnership and cooperation with the West.

For many Russians, though, that partnership as originally constructed had been a failure, and Russia's international resurgence was merely a sign that Moscow had had enough of being alternately hectored and ignored by its alleged partners. Western support for anti-Russian regimes like that in

Georgia, the relentless expansion of NATO, U.S. scorn for arms control agreements, the deployment of weapons systems close to Russia's borders, the dismemberment of Russian ally Serbia—all seemed incongruous with the rhetoric of partnership, too.

RUSSIA AND THE NON-WEST

How Russia defines itself with relation to the West is in many ways the country's key foreign policy question. That relationship will continue to play the central role in determining the nature of Russia's interactions with other countries and with international institutions. Even if Russia's leaders do not see their country as belonging to the West in some fundamental way, their foreign policy has nonetheless inevitably been Western-centric. Moscow's relations with the other former Soviet republics, with Asia (especially China), and elsewhere are all a function of its position with respect to Europe and, more fundamentally, the United States.

Moscow might seem increasingly interested in the idea of a partnership with China or India, for instance, but largely as a way of balancing what it perceives as Western hegemony and unilateralism. For much of the past decade, Russia's complicated relationship with the Western powers drove it to seek both a greater, at times exclusive, role inside the CIS as well as closer relations with powerful non-Western states such as Iran, India, and China.[51] Like Russia, these states remain committed to the notion of absolute sovereignty, at least for themselves, and opposed to what they perceive as Western attempts to impose a single system of values and practices onto the world.

Yet the overall direction of Russian foreign policy also affects countries outside the West in important ways. Moscow's relations with its former dependencies in the CIS provide something of a test case for how Russia's evolving post-Soviet identity has shaped its external relations, with Moscow's atavistic imperial instincts vying with a newer and narrower conception of the Russian Federation's national interests. After a decade of neglect and selective engagement, Putin's Russia sought to play a much more active role in the Near Abroad, in part as a way of forcing the West to take its claims to Great Power status seriously.

In part, this increased activity was connected to Russia's more active diplomacy generally, with the former Soviet republics seen as the natural sphere of influence for a Great Power Russia. Moreover, given the strategic location and extensive oil and gas reserves of many CIS states, Russia's growing involvement around its borders is in a sense a symptom of the more global foreign policy Russia began pursuing during the Putin years. If Russia's more active international stance is the main factor "pushing" Moscow into the CIS, then instability within several of the former Soviet republics (including the rise of Islamic radicalism and terrorism in the Caucasus and Central Asia) served to "pull" Russia into the region.[52] Russia's growing interest in Central Asia as well as its open intervention in the politics of Belarus, Georgia, Azerbaijan, Moldova, and Ukraine have been a source of continuing discord with the West and one that, given the conjunction of ideas and capabilities driving Russian foreign policy, is likely to persist. Medvedev's declaration, shortly after Moscow recognized the independence of Abkhazia and South Ossetia, that Russia would regard the area around its borders as "a region where it has privileged interests," is a clear indication that the CIS will remain the primary object of Russia's more active foreign policy.[53]

China is a power in many ways analogous to Russia, and Moscow's relations with Beijing have, like its role in the CIS, often served as a reflection of the state of relations with the West. Russian statesmen have often seen China as a kind of alternative to the West, whether as a model for economic development without political liberalization or as a geopolitical pole toward which Russia can align in opposition to the West. China is moreover one of the major customers for Russian energy as well as military technology. At the same time, Russia and China have maintained a wary partnership (formalized in the Shanghai Cooperation Organization, or SCO) based on economic cooperation, an uneasy détente in Central Asia, and a shared commitment to checking the expansion of U.S. influence in the region.

A large, rapidly growing country uneasy with Western hegemony in the world, China is in a sense a natural partner for a Russia keen on the establishment of a multipolar world. On the other hand, Russo-Chinese relations suffer from a long history of mistrust and rancor. Territorial disputes, immigration (especially in sparsely populated Siberia and the Far East), and competing ambitions in Central Asia mean that while Beijing and Moscow have often found it expedient to cooperate in checking the exercise of U.S. power, they remain wary partners, as indeed they were for much of the past half century. Russian leaders in particular have expressed real worry about China's future plans and ability to dominate the Russian Far East.

PAST, PRESENT, AND FUTURE

The identification of Russia as something other than Western is arguably one of the most important developments in relations between Russia and the rest of the world since the fall of the Soviet Union in 1991 and has broad implications for the future. It is particularly important to understand whether Putin's course of aggressively promoting Russia as an independent

Great Power with global ambitions was an aberration that will be repudi-
ated once Putin and his circle are no longer in power, or whether it is the
result of deep-seated structural and institutional factors that will endure
under Medvedev (and likely, after), regardless of what role Putin continues
to play.

To place the Putin era into its proper context, it is necessary to understand how Russian foreign policy evolved and changed before Putin came
to power in 2000. Putin, of course, did not take over a tabula rasa, and
while his term in office saw the displacement of Yeltsin's ruling circle (the
so-called Family, led by Yeltsin's daughter Tatyana Dyachenko and the now-
exiled oligarch Boris Berezovsky), Putin did not completely displace Russia's ruling elite or the basic assumptions underlying Russian foreign policy.
Indeed, in the realm of foreign policy, the change was less pronounced than
elsewhere.

In this regard it is worth reconsidering in particular the career of Yevgeny
Primakov, foreign minister from 1996 to 1998, later prime minister and
then rival of Putin for the presidency. Despite the vitriol Primakov encountered from Putin's circle when the two men were rivals for the 2000 presidential nomination, Putin followed several of the foreign policy
prescriptions laid out by Primakov during (and before) his tenure as foreign
minister. Primakov continues to matter because if anything, the real turning
point came not in 2000, when Putin became president, but much earlier,
around 1992 or 1993, when it became clear that then-Foreign Minister
Andrei Kozyrev's call for Russia to join the Western community of nations
was not sustainable, either domestically or internationally. Primakov, who
would replace Kozyrev as foreign minister in 1996, embodied the newly
assertive tenor of Russian foreign policy that has, more recently, coexisted
uneasily with a desire for a productive, equal partnership with the West.[54]
Primakov and his backers represented a particular conception of Russian
national identity, one that has proven to have substantial resonance among
the Russian political class.[55]

Russia's foreign policy "revolution" was the result of the mounting frustrations evinced by the Russian population (elites as well as masses) over
the course of the country's reforms in the early 1990s, the failure of the
West to step in to rescue the Russian economy or integrate Russia into Western security structures, and the perception that Kozyrev was kowtowing to
the West without achieving anything appreciable in return. For a Russian
elite (especially the new elite that had come to prominence in the early Yeltsin administration from positions in the middle ranks of the bureaucracy
or the provincial leadership) that never ceased to think of the country as a
major world power, Kozyrev's approach was both humiliating and counterproductive. A number of influential economic players in the military-
industrial complex and other large state-owned industries likewise felt their

own interests threatened by Kozyrev's desire to open up the Russian economy to outside competition.[56]

Resistance to Kozyrev's ideas also stemmed from the fact that the external world confronting Russia continued to look much as it had during the Cold War. Institutions such as NATO had not themselves undergone sufficient transformation since the end of the Cold War and were in the mid-1990s torn between attracting Russia and containing it in the event that democracy failed. With no formal institutional mechanisms for managing Russia's integration with the West, Moscow often felt itself faced with a series of faits accomplis that it had no ability to influence, above all in connection with the expansion of NATO. Resentment over the West's perceived double standards and attachment to zero-sum thinking has been a constant complaint among Russian politicians and academics, who charge that the end of the Cold War merely gave Western powers an opportunity to roll back Russian influence, seize Russian markets (especially in the arms trade), and establish a semicolonial economic relationship in which Russia exports raw materials and imports advanced technology.[57]

Even worse, Russia had difficulty articulating a convincing justification for deferring to Western leadership since it had not yet developed a coherent vision of its own interests. To many observers inside Russia, the pursuit of integration with the West in the early 1990s was less a strategic decision than an indication that Russia lacked a strategy entirely.[58] In one now infamous and symptomatic exchange, then-foreign minister Kozyrev asked former U.S. president Richard Nixon, "if you . . . can advise us on how to define our national interests, I will be very grateful to you."[59]

The pursuit of integration under Kozyrev and acting Prime Minister Yegor Gaidar in the early 1990s did not bring improvement to the lives of most ordinary people, who suffered abysmally from the economic and political chaos of the 1990s. In the mind of the Russian electorate, democracy increasingly came to be associated with poverty and instability. The almost inevitable result was a backlash against the idea of the West as well as against Russia's own "artificial Westernization."[60] The fault was not entirely that of Gaidar or Kozyrev, or of Yeltsin himself, but nonetheless they and the ideas they represented took much of the blame. As a result, notions of convergence and integration with the West lost their appeal, and Russia's leaders began shifting their nation back onto a more Westphalian, Great Power course.

It was not long before the mounting opposition to Kozyrev began having an effect on the actual conduct of Russian foreign policy. As early as August 1992, opposition from hard-liners in the Supreme Soviet and the military forced Yeltsin to cancel a visit to Japan because of the territorial dispute over the Kuril Islands. With Kozyrev still in office, Moscow adopted a document called "Russia's Strategic Course toward Members of the Commonwealth of

Independent States" (*Strategicheskii kurs Rossii s gosudarstvami-uchastnikami Sodruzhestva Nezavisimykh Gosudarstv*) in September 1995. This document laid out a series of threats toward the CIS states, in particular with regard to establishing sovereignty and sharing resources from the Caspian Sea, serving notice that Moscow would not lightly accept the rollback of its influence over its neighbors.[61]

In the meantime, Yeltsin had bombarded the Supreme Soviet in October 1993 to oust the coalition of nationalists and Communists intent on deposing him, but the elections that followed left the protofascist Liberal Democrats of Vladimir Zhirinovsky as the largest party in the new State Duma. Then, in 1994, Russian troops entered Chechnya to put down, brutally, an uprising by the restless population of that region. Both the rise of Zhirinovsky and the war in Chechnya reflected the depth of hostility to the post-Soviet status quo that had emerged between 1991 and 1994. They also helped create a more defensive tone in Russia's interactions with an outside world that looked on with incredulity at what was transpiring.[62]

Primakov, who took over at Smolenskaya Ploshchad (headquarters of the Ministry of Foreign Affairs) when Kozyrev was finally ousted in 1996, inherited the reins of Russian foreign policy at a time when developments were already pushing Russia in a more assertive direction. He pursued a foreign policy course that was at once more consensual domestically and more confrontational internationally. It sought to establish Russia as one of the leading states in the international system (commensurate with its position as a permanent member of the UN Security Council) and to limit the influence of the United States in the area of the former Soviet Union. Primakov at times also toyed with the idea of building a counterhegemonic bloc among countries hostile to or distrustful of the United States, including Iran, Libya, North Korea, Cuba, and China, albeit without result.

Primakov declared that under his watch Russia would reject both the strident anti-Westernism of the Soviet Union and the naïve romanticism of the early 1990s in favor of an approach that would emphasize Russia's "status as a great power" and an "equal, mutually beneficial partnership" with the United States and Europe.[63] What these concepts meant in practice was not always clear. Primakov and his backers rejected a subservient relationship to the West but were less clear as to what other principle would serve as the foundation for their strategy, leading one Western analyst to lament that Russian foreign policy under Primakov "is difficult to define. It is difficult even to detect."[64] Primakov sought to overcome the domestic political rifts opened by Kozyrev's strategy of integration as a prelude to Russia's re-emergence as an active, autonomous international player, but lacked a grand strategic vision about this role this new Russia would play. Some alarming incidents soon occurred, most notably the near-firefight between Russian and NATO troops over control of the airport in Priština in 1999.

Serious clashes between post-Soviet Russia and its partners in the U.S. and Europe are thus nothing new, even if the consequences of such clashes have become more serious in recent years; nor for that matter is the elite's general set of priorities a recent development. What has changed since the mid-1990s is Russian power (economic, military, and soft) relative to the West, along with the Kremlin's growing ability to dominate the foreign policy-making process. Russia's transformation into an energy superpower, whether or not it is ultimately sustainable or beneficial to the country as a whole, left Moscow in a much stronger international position as long as energy prices remained high. The Kremlin used this energy revenue to tighten its hold on the state and rebuild the foundations of national power.

In relative terms, Russian power has also been aided by the United States' preoccupation since 9/11 with the wars in Afghanistan and Iraq, and what Bush termed the global war on terror, which many Russians believe will force the U.S. to scale back its geopolitical ambitions for the foreseeable future.[65] Russian observers and politicians continue to cite rising demand for energy and the diminution of U.S. power to assert that a multipolar world order, which for Primakov was an aspiration for the future, already exists.[66]

The continuity between past and present becomes clear when looking at how Medvedev articulated the priorities of Russian foreign policy. In an interview given shortly after the end of active hostilities in Georgia, Medvedev summarized the five overriding positions guiding Russia's foreign relations, namely: (1) "Russia recognizes the supremacy of the basic principles of international law"; (2) "the world must be multipolar," since a world dominated by one power "is unstable and threatened by conflict"; (3) "Russia does not desire confrontation with any country"; (4) "protecting the lives and dignity of our citizens wherever they are located"; and (5) "Russia, like other countries of the world, has regions in which it maintains privileged interests."[67] These principles, which some termed the "Medvedev Doctrine," were sharply criticized in the West, especially the fourth and fifth points.[68] After all, it was in defense of Russian "citizens"—residents of South Ossetia who had received Russian passports—that the Kremlin justified its invasion of Georgia. And the notion that Moscow would explicitly claim a region of privileged interests seemed a needless throwback to the days of balance-of-power politics, spheres of influence, and other seemingly anachronistic concepts.

Despite being poorly received in the West, the "Medvedev Doctrine" was on the whole less revolutionary than it might seem. Indeed, the creation of a multipolar world governed by international law, with the major powers working among themselves to solve problems, has been the basic aim of Russian foreign policy for close to two decades and has been widely expressed elsewhere. Russia's privileged interest in the former Soviet Union

has also been central to Russian foreign policy ever since the USSR collapsed, even if Medvedev's declaration was somewhat more explicit than
what Moscow had stated openly in the past. The claim to protect Russian
citizens "wherever they are located" was more of a departure, though tensions over the status of ethnic Russians in the Baltic states have long been
an irritant in Russia's relationship with Europe. In any case, Medvedev's
fourth point aside, the tenets of the "Medvedev Doctrine" could just as easily have been made by a Primakov or a Putin (even if Primakov would not
have systematized them). Only the fact that the doctrine was elaborated in
the wake of a war that took the West badly by surprise made it seem like
some sort of basic reversal.

ECONOMICS AND FOREIGN POLICY

Part of the reason Russia under Putin and Medvedev has been more effective at pursuing an independent foreign policy has been its remarkable economic transformation since 2000, a transformation that in late 2008 was
imperiled by the unexpected (to the Kremlin) flight of foreign investment
from the country following the war in Georgia and the freezing up of credit
markets worldwide. At least until the implosion of the Russian stock market, Russia's leaders no longer felt themselves economically dependent on
the West, thanks in particular to persistently high prices for oil and gas,
which allowed the Kremlin to pay off its debt to the International Monetary
Fund and other Western creditors ahead of schedule—while forcing much
of Europe to recognize its own dependence on Russian energy. Moscow
consequently felt it had a greater degree of autonomy in foreign affairs and
the freedom to engage in balancing against the West where it served Russian
interests to do so.

One element of the Russian approach to foreign policy that did change
during the Putin years was precisely the increased attention given to economic factors as a component of national power.[69] In a major departure
from Soviet days, Russia's leadership has been very explicit about the connection between economic success, prosperity, and the ability to project
power in the world. In its last years, the Soviet Union was an economic
basket case—"Upper Volta with rockets," as *The Economist* famously
described it in 1988. The Russia of the 1990s was not much better off, particularly after the financial crisis of 1998 derailed Russia's tentative recovery
and fed an atmosphere of political instability.[70]

Putin was initially appointed prime minister in August 1999 in part to
provide new leadership in resolving the financial emergency. As both prime
minister and president, Putin has been very cognizant of the importance of
the economy for Russia's political and diplomatic activity. While Russia's

leaders worked during Putin's first years in office to close the gap between their country and the rapidly developing economies of the Far East, an assertive, expensive foreign policy was a luxury Moscow simply could not, in Putin's estimation, afford. This realization set Putin apart not only from many others in the leadership during his first term, but also from members of the Yeltsin-era foreign policy establishment like Primakov, who were much less attuned to the economic and financial elements of their foreign policy.

Putin told the Security Council in mid-2006 that "the level of military security depends directly on the pace of economic growth and technological development."[71] Putin's annual addresses to the Federal Assembly (Duma and Federation Council) repeatedly emphasized the importance of social and economic recovery as a prerequisite for the more active foreign policy he and much of Russia's elite favored. In his first such address, in July 2000, Putin warned that "the growing gap between ourselves and the leading states is turning Russia into a Third World country."[72] In his final address to parliament, in April 2007, Putin listed his economic accomplishments and told the assembled representatives, "Contemporary Russia, in restoring her economic potential and recognizing her possibilities, is striving for a relationship of equality with all nations."[73] The focus on economic and social consolidation was reflected as well in the Kremlin's creation and initial funding of the so-called National Projects aimed at improving public health, education, agriculture, and housing. The stated importance and visibility of the National Projects is also partially responsible for the fact that they were initially assigned to Dmitry Medvedev as the Kremlin built him up to be Putin's anointed successor—though once Medvedev was safely ensconced in the Kremlin and the Russian economy was tanking, the government sought to revisit its commitment to fully funding these initiatives.[74]

Putin's government also made conscious policy choices designed to stimulate and harness economic growth for the purpose of enhancing state power, though results were mixed. Despite impressive economic growth for most of Putin's presidency, the Russian economy remains dominated by the extraction and refining of hydrocarbons, and the state continues to be a major economic player in a way that limits opportunities for private investors. And though Russia benefited from high oil prices during most of Putin's presidency, significant structural problems remain, including too many unprofitable factories kept open and an underreformed banking sector. Oil and gas production have also begun leveling off (significant expansion would require massive investment to increase extraction from remote, inaccessible fields in places such as the Barents Sea and the Far North's Yamal Peninsula), while capital flight remains substantial.[75] These problems will likely pose a limit to Russia's future power potential.[76] Still, GDP growth in 2007 was estimated by the government at 7.6 percent, and according to the World Bank, even with the financial upheaval of 2008, Russian growth will remain around 3 percent, even as much of the world faces negative growth.[77]

The economic expansion of the decade after the 1998 crisis further underpinned Putin's policy of strengthening the state by keeping government coffers full. The funds were heavily spent on strategic initiatives such as reducing Russia's foreign debt and modernizing the military. Putin used the boon of higher oil revenues (transferred to the government by way of a windfall tax on high oil prices) to pay off Russia's international debt burden early, reducing foreign leverage over Russian policy. Moscow's debt payments to both the IMF and the Paris Club of sovereign creditors proceeded ahead of schedule; by 2003 Moscow had discharged all of its sovereign debt to the IMF.[78] By the end of Putin's presidency, the country had accumulated foreign reserves totaling over $476 billion, behind only Japan and China internationally (though it was forced to spend several tens of billions of dollars to prop up the economy in the latter part of 2008 and early 2009). The windfall profits from the energy sector also allowed Moscow to establish a massive stabilization fund, designed to cushion the domestic economy against future price shocks as well as to guard against so-called Dutch disease.[79]

In keeping with its view of the world as an arena for Great Power rivalry, Russia also moved to take advantage of its newfound wealth to upgrade the military. The early months of Putin's presidency were marred by the sinking of the *Kursk* submarine, an event that showcased both the decay of the Russian military machine and the president's seemingly poor grasp of military matters. Starting around 2003, Russian military spending began increasing rapidly. In 2006, Russia's defense budget was 668.3 billion rubles, an increase of 22 percent over the previous year.[80] By 2007, the Kremlin was spending 822 billion rubles on the military.[81] Much of this additional spending initially went toward upgrading existing facilities, higher salaries for servicemen, and introducing contract service in place of conscription in a slowly increasing number of units, rather than on enhancing Russia's offensive capacity.

More recently, Moscow embarked on an ambitious program of upgrading its military hardware. A new class of gigantic nuclear submarines was introduced in February 2008 with the launching of the *Yuri Dolgoruky*. The Kremlin also went on a buying spree for strategic bombers, ballistic missiles, submarines, and next-generation tanks.[82] Important at least in symbolic terms is also the renewal of Russian Tu-95 and Tu-160 bomber patrols over the Mediterranean, Atlantic, and Pacific, including off the coast of the United States, as well as the resumption of large-scale naval exercises in international waters. The effectiveness of the Russian military's drive into

Georgia in August 2008 showcased how the armed forces had revived their operational capability since the dark days of the Chechen conflict, including the ability to conduct complex combined arms operations.[83]

Then again, the recognition that power in the modern world is as much a function of wealth and stability as of sheer military might has had profound implications for how Moscow has pursued its interests. As Putin cautioned in 2006, "We must not repeat the mistakes of the Soviet Union, the mistakes of the Cold War era. . . . We must not solve the problem of military construction at the expense of the development of the economic and social spheres. This is a dead end that will only lead the country to waste its resources."[84]

Although Russia has largely eschewed integration with Western political institutions, one of its most urgent priorities has been to integrate into the global economy. And while natural resources currently account for the bulk of Russia's exports, Putin has been clear about the need for the country to diversify its economy and become a leader in the information economy if it hopes to achieve the status of a first-rank global power. The negotiation of an agreement that seemed to clear the way for Russia's entry into the WTO in late 2006 was hailed in Moscow as one of the signal triumphs of Putin's diplomacy and was notable for being negotiated by a coterie of liberal economic advisers who otherwise saw their influence diminish during Putin's second term in office.[85] Russia's gradual movement toward WTO ascension seemed to stall in the aftermath of the conflict in Georgia, however, as several Western countries began rethinking their support for any kind of agreements with the Kremlin while Moscow suspended its implementation of a number of agreements that had already been reached.

Despite Putin's intermittent support for integration, economic nationalism remains strong inside Russia. Consolidation of state control over the oil and gas sectors has been one of the key ways the Kremlin has sought to amass power. Russia's natural resource monopolies Gazprom and, to a lesser degree, Rosneft have been in part tools with which the Kremlin has pursued its diplomatic ends through economic means. Putin himself described Gazprom as "a powerful political and economic lever of influence over the rest of the world," and Russian attempts to gain control of downstream assets in Europe and the former Soviet states attest to the reach of this and similar levers.[86]

The assertion of state control over the economy is usually depicted inside Russia as reversing the corruption-riddled privatization of the early to mid-1990s. The opening bell in the government's struggle for control of the energy sector was sounded with the campaign to seize control of the assets belonging to the Yukos oil company and its founder, Mikhail Khodorkovsky. It is unlikely any single factor was responsible for the decision to nationalize Yukos and imprison its founder. Certainly the official line that

Khodorkovsky had dodged billions of dollars' worth of taxes had a grain of plausibility, though given the scale of corruption and tax evasion in the oil sector in the early 1990s, Khodorkovsky was likely no guiltier than any number of other oligarchs. His outspoken opposition to Putin and funding of opposition political parties, which the Western press generally claimed to have been Khodorkovsky's principal sin, most likely played a role as well.

The seizure of Yukos was also part of a larger pattern of state-driven consolidation in the energy sector and other pieces of the economy's "commanding heights."[87] The surge in oil and gas prices since the start of the U.S. invasion of Iraq drastically increased the value and importance of energy worldwide. As Mikhail Delyagin of the Russian Institute for the Study of Globalization argues, with prices likely to continue rising in the long run, despite the downturn of late 2008 (due to chronic instability in the Middle East and the inexorable rise in demand from India and China), the world is entering a new period of segmented markets and energy mercantilism. With the passing of the age of a global energy market, Delyagin argues countries will rush to lock up what energy supplies they can in order to reduce their vulnerability to outside pressure.[88] At the same time, revenues from the energy sector have been a key component of the government's burgeoning budget surplus and a tool for buying the loyalty of the elite. Even the dramatic fall in energy prices in late 2008 has not altered the fundamental belief that a combination of rising demand from the developing world and supply constraints as existing oil and gas fields decline will contribute to a future of sustained higher prices and energy mercantilism.

The record prices for oil and gas lasting from the start of the war in Iraq until the second half of 2008 had a profound impact on the way the Kremlin uses energy reserves as a tool of its foreign policy. According to former deputy energy minister Vladimir Milov, during the early part of Putin's first term, when oil and gas prices remained low, privatization of the energy sector was a key objective for the Russian government, then dominated by free-market liberals like prime minister Mikhail Kasyanov and economic adviser Andrei Illarionov.[89] The subsequent rise in oil prices produced a windfall for the state, which continued to dominate the energy sector while a privatization program was under development, allowing the Kremlin to pay off its entire $17 billion foreign debt by 2003 and transfer billions of dollars to the stabilization fund. With analysts forecasting a more or less permanent rise in oil and gas prices, control of energy suddenly appeared to offer the government a secure route to huge amounts of money for the budget. The result was an end to talk of privatizing the energy sector, the departure of Kasyanov, Illarionov, and other economic liberals, and increasing state control of oil and gas production.[90] Scarcity and the existence of fixed pipeline routes also meant that energy, in addition to providing an infusion of cash, could serve as a lever with which to exert influence over Russia's neighbors.

Seen in this light, the Russian government's campaign against Yukos seems connected to a series of other attempts to establish control over energy resources for geopolitical purposes. The price wars that broke out between Moscow and a number of former Soviet states (most damagingly with Ukraine) make sense in the context of realizing that control of oil and gas supplies confers greater leverage than possession of unreliable satellite states. Demanding market prices from Kyiv and other post-Soviet capitals allowed Gazprom to realize higher revenues and to sow political chaos in countries seen as turning their backs on Russia.

Control of energy supplies and transit routes is not merely a regional concern either. Before its nationalization, Yukos had been heavily involved in lobbying the Kremlin over the route of a pipeline to supply gas to East Asia and was also engaged in discussions with ExxonMobil and Chevron Texaco that would have opened the way for significant Western investment in the Russian energy sector. By seizing control of Yukos, the Kremlin ensured that it will have the final say over the pipeline route and that foreign investors will be prevented from grabbing hold of an industry Russia considers strategically vital.[91] For similar reasons, the Kremlin blocked attempts by a Chinese oil company to buy a stake in Yukos after its seizure.[92] Moscow's relations with China and Japan meanwhile continue to be complicated by a dispute about the routing of a major pipeline to the Pacific coast. The Kremlin has also made little secret of its interest in acquiring downstream assets inside Europe as part of its quest for energy security. As a supplier, Russia's definition of energy security is quite different from that of its European customers, a circumstance that has contributed to the two sides' inability to agree on a framework for regulating the energy trade.[93]

Even while aggressively keeping foreign investors out of controlling positions in the oil and gas sector, the Kremlin sought to attract foreign investment and expertise elsewhere. The result was a certain economic schizophrenia, as the Kremlin has had to reassure foreign investors enough to encourage them to continue betting on Russia, even as its actions have continually raised questions about its commitment to economic openness and the rule of law, which the 2008 Law on Investment in Strategic Sectors was designed to remedy.[94] The common denominator uniting the closed nationalistic and liberal integrationist strands of Russian economic policy has been the preoccupation with geopolitical power. Controlling its neighbors' access to strategic oil and gas supplies is a blunt form of power, while the wealth generated from foreign investment and through increasing exports (as a result of eventual membership in the WTO) is a subtler but no less important aspect of enhancing the state's strength and opportunities to play a larger geopolitical role.

CONCLUSION

It remains to be seen whether Russia's newly assertive foreign policy remains viable in the longer term, especially if Medvedev and Putin do not accelerate Russia's economic diversification. To be sure, the preferences of Russia's elites are unlikely to change in any substantial way in the near future. It also seems unlikely that the Russian political system will undergo the kind of fundamental democratization that would allow the general public's preference for a more socially oriented (and hence less internationally active) approach to be realized. On the other hand, the objective factors underlying Russia's re-emergence as a major international player may not prove to be as durable as Putin and others hope. A foreign policy based on the revenues from high energy prices is necessarily hostage to fluctuations in the global energy market, as indeed it was during the Soviet Union's economic boom of the 1970s and the subsequent bust of the 1980s.[95] Overall, the economy is still inflexible and uncompetitive. Meanwhile, despite increased spending and attempts to reform the outdated system of conscription, the military remains deeply corrupt and inefficient.[96] Xenophobia is rampant and growing.[97]

Most critically, Russia's unfavorable demographic situation could severely limit the country's capabilities over the long term. Already, the Russian population has declined from 148.7 million people at the start of 1992 to 144.5 million when the last census was conducted a decade later. The decline would have been even more severe if not for the large-scale and unrepeatable in-migration from the other post-Soviet republics.[98] In percentage terms, the decline of the Russian population is among the most severe in history for a country not in the throes of war or famine.

While some of the decline is attributable to couples' reluctance to have children amidst the disastrous economic conditions of the 1990s, other contributing factors appear more intractable. Rates of premature death, especially for Russian men, remain among the highest in the world—largely as a result of lifestyle choices (drunkenness, smoking, poor diet, homicide/suicide). Rates of HIV infection are high and growing, particularly among the country's large number of intravenous drug users. Nor is the demographic decline spread evenly among regions of the country or ethnic groups. On the whole, the birthrate among traditionally Muslim peoples was notably higher during the 1990s—with a range of potential consequences for the social cohesion of a country increasingly in the throes of Slavic-Russian nationalism.[99]

These weaknesses are real and most likely will act as constraints on any Russian attempt to assert itself globally. At the same time, though, their impact, at least in the immediate term, is likely to be modest. Even in its still-troubled state, the military can be used to intimidate and bully neighboring states—as Georgia discovered to its cost—while the possession of a large nuclear arsenal will continue to assure Russia some degree of world power and respect on the part of Washington and Beijing. The demographic crisis is a more serious impediment, but apart from its impact on the armed forces (which are in any case increasingly moving away from conscription to fill their ranks), its impact will primarily be regional. Russia's population decline is being felt most in Siberia and the Far East, that is, along the border with China. Managing relations with Beijing will be among the most critical tasks of Russian foreign policy in the next century, and the demographic disparity is only one component of that relationship between a relatively diminished Russia and a rapidly growing China.

To the extent that Russia under both Yeltsin and Putin pursued a consistent, grand strategic approach to the country's role in the world, that approach has been predicated on the re-emergence of Russia as a major power capable of pursuing what it perceives as its national interests in a still-anarchic world order—though Putin paid greater attention in particular to the domestic foundations of international power. The overall focus on power and anarchy accounts for much of the divergence between Russian and Western perspectives on international affairs, as Moscow has not embraced the notions of integration, collective security, and pooled sovereignty that have predominated in the West since at least the end of World War II.[100] Within Russia, assessments of Putin's success or failure as a statesman hinge largely on the degree to which he is seen as having restored Russia to Great Power status and stood up for the country's interests, both within the former Soviet space and globally.[101] Medvedev will be similarly judged.

While Russian foreign policy is global in scope, it also remains constrained—significantly—by domestic political considerations and the unfolding struggle to define a post-Soviet, postimperial identity for Russia. Strengthening the state, the economy, and the military are all prerequisites for Russia's eventually living up to the expansive vision of its role in the world that has emerged over the past decade. Russia's foreign policy has emphasized tactical flexibility and caution as it seeks a breathing space to recover the country's strength; the war in Georgia may be a signal that the period of recovery and consolidation has ended, even though the Kremlin sought to limit the long-term strategic consequences of the conflict. This strategy of pursuing global stability and internal regeneration has many precedents in Russian history. It was adopted by Tsar Alexander II and Aleksandr Gorchakov after the Crimean War, and again by Sergei Witte and

Pyotr Stolypin following the Russo-Japanese War and the 1905 Revolution. These men and their ideas have been consciously adopted as models by a number of current Russian statesmen who see their own task in equally stark terms.[102]

Gorchakov termed his approach *sosredotochenie*, "reconcentration," while Stolypin used the term *peredyshka*, or "breath catching." In both cases, the underlying principle was that the country should focus on resolving its domestic problems—serfdom, labor unrest, and so on—before embarking on an expansive foreign policy. In post-Soviet Russia, too, the scope of the country's domestic problems was such that the kind of global, Great Power foreign policy advocated by Primakov (and much of the Russian elite) was largely unattainable. Still, Yeltsin's Russia tried, even confronting the U.S. directly on a handful of occasions, over Kosovo, Chechnya, and elsewhere. The first years of Putin's presidency, by contrast, were marked by a much greater degree of deference to Western initiatives, even ones that the Russian establishment strenuously opposed (such as the inclusion of the Baltic states in NATO). In contrast to the Gorbachev and Yeltsin-Kozyrev years, however, this deference appears to have resulted less from any basic convergence between Russian and Western policy goals or any attempt to appease the Western powers than from a recognition of Russia's weakened position in the international system and of the need for domestic consolidation. For that reason, the changes in Russia's approach to foreign policy since the start of Putin's second term seem to have less to do with political change, turnover among elites, or the emergence of new ideas than they do with Russia's stronger relative position in the international balance resulting from high energy prices, economic recovery, and the fallout from the U.S. misadventure in Iraq—a change in tactics rather than strategy.

In political science terms, both neorealist and constructivist approaches to international relations have some relevance in explaining the twists and turns of Russia's post-Soviet foreign policy.[103] Neorealists emphasize the existence of international anarchy, where states' behavior is conditioned by the distribution of power among them.[104] A state like Russia that experiences a precipitous decline in relative power (at the end of the Cold War) would be expected to retract its geopolitical ambitions commensurate with its reduced standing in the world, while a state whose relative power is increasing should seek a more expansive international role as it seeks to assert influence and defend its security. This pattern seems to hold reasonably well for Putin's Russia—seeking security through retrenchment when weak and through assertion when strong—but is less helpful in explaining why Yeltsin's Russia refused to scale back its ambitions in the late 1990s, even as the war in Chechnya and the 1998 financial collapse revealed the depth of Russia's decline. Or, as one Russian journalist noted:

In 2001 when George Bush gazed trustingly into Vladimir Putin's eyes, the price of oil on the world market was $20 a barrel. Today it is almost three times as much. . . . But the problem, of course, is not just about oil. When, for example, Moscow sees the main problem in the Middle East as the West's refusal to recognize Hamas, rather than Hamas' refusal to recognize Israel, there will never be an agreement. No matter the price of oil.[105]

Here, constructivist theories provide some insight, which is also applicable, albeit in a different way, to the Putin era and beyond. Constructivists emphasize that states' international behavior is above all a function of their self-perception and the identity constructed by their elites.[106] Russia's insistence on acting and being treated like a Great Power, which has endured through both the Yeltsin and Putin eras and which is widely shared among policy makers and thinkers in Russia, is in many ways a constructivist tale. Politics continues to matter, and Russian foreign policy continues to be determined as much by its leaders' choices and domestic constraints as by objective international factors.[107] While post-Communist Russia has struggled to define itself culturally and politically, there has been much greater agreement about Russia's international role. Russian elites have long viewed their country in Great Power terms, with interests that stretch around the world and with a right to be consulted on a wide variety of international issues that do not necessarily affect Russia's interests in any direct way. Liberals like Kozyrev have been no less forthright than their political enemies in propounding the thesis that Russia remains a Great Power whose interests must be taken into account by others, including more powerful states like the U.S.[108]

While this conception of Russia as a Great Power has been critical in setting the course for Russian foreign policy, it does not explain the vacillations and inconsistencies that have characterized that policy since 1991. It is possible to argue, as Andrei Tsygankov does, that these vacillations are the result of different identity coalitions having power at different times over the past decade and a half.[109] To be sure, Kozyrev embodied a radically different set of values than did Primakov or Putin. Yet one of the key discontinuities in Russia's recent diplomatic history is between the interest in cooperation with the West evinced by Putin in 2001–2002 and the more confrontational attitude adopted by the same Putin a few years later. Moreover, under Kozyrev, Primakov, and Putin, despite a host of other disagreements, officials have not questioned Russia's fundamental identity as an autonomous Great Power and key actor in the international system. Identity and identity coalitions thus do not explain the full range of variation over time, and it is necessary for this reason to turn back to neorealist thinking about power and the search for security.

Given the important continuities (especially in the realm of preferences and identity) that have existed across the post-Soviet period in terms of Russia's approach to foreign policy, it seems safe to say that the primary constraints on Russian foreign policy in the near future will be more economic than political. The consensus surrounding Russia's role as a fully sovereign Great Power is so secure that Medvedev will have little choice but to pursue the creation of a multipolar world dominated by Great Powers pursuing their respective national interests. The debate about what constitutes Russia's national interest remains vigorous, though, despite the greater political centralization of the Putin years. Indeed, at times it seems that Russia is more interested in gaining recognition of its special responsibility than in using that responsibility to present constructive solutions to a given problem (the Mideast peace process being one example).[110] Still, this approach has been the dominant thread in foreign policy thinking since the mid-1990s and faces no serious challenge within Russia today. The success of the Medvedev-Putin tandem in carving out a space for Russia to act as one of these Great Powers will be determined above all by Russia's ability to resolve its domestic difficulties and retain the economic capacity to force others to take its concerns seriously.

NOTES

1. Russian analysts, even liberals, are generally keen to emphasize Russia's importance as an independent pole in world affairs. See Vladimir Lukin, "Rossiiskii most cherez Atlantiku," *Rossiya v global'noi politike*, Nov–Dec 2002 (1): 103. Lukin, a former ambassador to the United States, is a leading figure in the liberal Yabloko party. See also A. Pushkov, "Quo Vadis? Posle vstrechi Putin-Bush," *Mezhdunarodnaya zhizn'*, Jun 2002, 8–9. For a critique of this tendency to see the world in geopolitical, balance-of-power terms, see Paul Goble's essay, "In Moscow, Geopolitics Is the Scientific Communism of Today," *Radio Free Europe/Radio Liberty (RFE/RL) Newsline*, 11 Aug 2005.

2. Dmitri Trenin, "Pirouettes and Priorities," *The National Interest*, Win 2003–04 (74): 80.

3. See "Primakov on Russian Relations with the West," *OMRI Daily Digest*, 30 May 1996.

4. Russian Ministry of Foreign Affairs, "Kontseptsiya vneshnei politiki Rossiiskoi Federatsii," 2000, http://www.ln.mid.ru/ns-osndoc.nsf/0e9272befa3420974 3256c630042d1aa/fd86620b371b0cf7432569fb004872a7?OpenDocument.

5. Ibid.

6. Russian Ministry of Foreign Affairs, "Kontseptsiya vneshnei politiki Rossiiskoi Federatsii," 2008, http://www.mid.ru/ns-osndoc.nsf/0e9272befa342097432 56c630042d1aa/d48737161a0bc944c32574870048d8f7?OpenDocument.

7. Fyodor Rumyantsev and Aleksandr Artemev, "Konets velikosti," *Gazeta.ru*, 15 Jul 2008.

8. Russian Ministry of Foreign Affairs, "Kontsepsiya vneshnei politiki Rossiiskoi Federatsii," 2008.

9. Security Council of the Russian Federation, "Kontseptsiya natsional'noi bezopasnosti Rossiiskoi Federatsii," http://www.scrf.gov.ru/documents/decree/2000_24_1.shtml.

10. As Putin's presidency ended in 2008, a new Military Doctrine was being prepared by the Ministry of Defense and the General Staff. Drafts of the new Military Doctrine, as well as the commentary of top officers, including the former chairman of the General Staff Gen. Yury Baluevsky, confirm that the new document will continue to emphasize the primacy of state-based threats to Russia's military security. See Makhmud Gareev, "General Gareev: Rossiya menyaet svoyu voennuyu doktrinu," RIA-Novosti, 16 Jan 2007, http://www.rian.ru/analytics/20070116/5912 4252.html. With Medvedev's inauguration, the Security Council is preparing to replace the National Security Concept as well (though as of autumn 2008, a full draft had not been made public).

11. Celeste A. Wallander, "The Challenge of Russia for U.S. Policy," testimony to U.S. Senate Committee on Foreign Relations, 21 Jun 2005.

12. Mikhail Margelov, "Bor'ba za mnogopolyarnost'," *Nezavisimaya Gazeta*, 20 Sep 2005.

13. Dmitri Trenin, *The End of Eurasia: Russia on the Border between Geopolitics and Globalization* (Washington, DC: Carnegie, 2002), 306–8.

14. Russian Ministry of Foreign Affairs, "Obzor vneshnei politiki Rossiiskoi Federatsii," 27 Mar 2007, http://www.mid.ru/brp_4nsf/sps.

15. Sergei Lavrov, "Rossiya i SShA: Mezhdu proshlim i budushchim," *Mezhdunarodnik.ru*, 26 Sep 2006, http://www.mezhdunarodnik.ru/magazin/5308.html.

16. Igor Ivanov, "A New Foreign-Policy Year for Russia and the World," *International Affairs: A Russian Journal of World Politics, Diplomacy and International Relations*, 2003, 49(6): 34; Ye. Primakov, "Is the Russia-U.S. Rapprochement Here to Stay?" *International Affairs: A Russian Journal of World Politics, Diplomacy and International Relations*, 2002, 48(6): 88.

17. Primakov does deserve much of the credit for adopting the notion that Russia must remain an independent pillar of the global order. See "Primakov on Russian Relations with the West," *OMRI Daily Digest*, 30 May 1996.

18. V. Putin, "Poslanie Federal'nomu Sobraniyu Rossiiskoi Federatsii," 10 May 2006, http://www.kremlin.ru/text/appears/2006/05/105546.shtml. A more radical version of this idea, termed "collective neo-imperialism," was recently put forward by two influential Russian analysts. See Vladislav Inozemtsev and Sergei Karaganov, "Imperialism of the Fittest," *The National Interest*, Sum 2005 (80): 74–80.

19. Irina Isakova, *Russian Governance in the Twenty-First Century: Geo-strategy, Geopolitics and Governance* (London: Frank Cass, 2005), 87–89.

20. Andrew Monaghan, "'Calmly Critical': Evolving Russian Views of US Hegemony," *Journal of Strategic Studies*, Dec 2006, 29(6): 987–1013.

21. See "The New Post-Transitional Russian Identity: How Western Is Russian Westernization?" World Policy Institute/Harriman Institute Project Report, Jan 2006.

22. Fukuyama's notion of history's end was first stated in his "The End of His-

tory?" *The National Interest*, Sum 1989 (16). A more detailed and philosophically grounded expression of this argument can be found in Fukuyama, *The End of History and the Last Man* (New York: Free Press, 1992). Other scholars looking specifically at Russia argued that the end of Communism had finally removed any realistic basis for Russia to seek a role in the world outside the West. See especially Trenin, *The End of Eurasia*.

23. For instance, Jack Matlock, former ambassador to the Soviet Union, praised Putin for his "unequivocal" commitment to democracy and preference for good relations with the West. See Jack Matlock Jr., "Russia Votes: Will Democracy Win?" *New York Times*, 26 Mar 2000.

24. Caroline Wyatt, "Bush and Putin: Best of Friends," BBC News, 16 Jun 2001, http://news.bbc.co.uk/2/hi/europe/1392791.stm.

25. Lilia Shevtsova, *Putin's Russia*, trans. Antonina W. Bouis (Washington, DC: Carnegie, 2003), 4; Thomas M. Nicholas, "Russia's Turn West," *World Policy Journal*, Win 2002-2003, 19(4): 13-14. On a more philosophical level, Dmitri Trenin argued that the implosion of the Soviet Union shattered the political unity of Eurasia, leaving Russia too weak to resist the rising powers of India and, especially, China. Only by fully anchoring itself to the culture and institutions of Europe could Russia avoid the dolorous possibilities of seeking futilely to re-create the USSR or complete disintegration. According to Trenin, only the "full demilitarization of its relations with the West" and a long-term strategy of seeking to join Western institutions (including the EU and NATO) can save Russia from geopolitical marginalization. Dmitri Trenin, *The End of Eurasia*, 259, 311-12.

26. See Vladimir Kuchkanov, "Demokraticheski orientirovannye perevoroty v SNG i geopoliticheskie perspektivy Rossii v regione," *Mezhdunarodnik.ru*, 28 Sep 2005, http://www.mezhdunarodnik.ru/magazin/1439.html; Janusz Bugajski, "Russia's New Europe," *The National Interest*, Win 2002-03 (74): 84-91.

27. A. Ye. Safonov, "Terrorizm apokalipsisa," *Mezhdunarodnaya zhizn'*, 2006 (5).

28. See James M. Goldgeier, "The United States and Russia: Keeping Expectations Realistic," *Policy Review*, Oct-Nov 2001: 47-56.

29. Dmitri Trenin, "Russia Leaves the West," *Foreign Affairs*, Jul-Aug 2006, 85(4).

30. Roderic Lyne, Strobe Talbott, and Koji Watanabe, "Engaging with Russia: The Next Phase," Report to the Trilateral Commission, Triangle Paper 59, 2006: 40-44. A similar date was chosen by Janusz Bugajski, who sees the arrest of Mikhail Khodorkovsky and Moscow's diplomatic tussle with Kyiv over the strategically vital Kerch Strait in 2004 as heralding the new era of Russian assertion. See Bugajski, "Russia's New Europe."

31. Nodari A. Simonia, "Priorities of Russian Foreign Policy and the Way It Works," in *The Making of Foreign Policy in Russia and the New States of Eurasia*, ed. Adeed and Karen Dawisha (Armonk, NY: M. E. Sharpe, 1995), 38-39. See also R. Craig Nation, "Beyond the Cold War: Change and Continuity in U.S.-Russian Relations," in R. Craig Nation and Michael McFaul, *The United States and Russia into the 21st Century* (Carlisle Barracks, PA: Strategic Studies Institute, U.S. Army War College, 1997), 9-13.

32. Alexei G. Arbatov, "Russian National Interests," in *Damage Limitation or Crisis? Russia and the Outside World*, ed. Robert D. Blackwill and Sergei A. Karaganov

(Washington, DC: Brassey's, 1994), 55. Arbatov was not alone in seeing the germ of Russia's re-emergence as a Great Power in the appointment of Primakov. See, among others, Sergei A. Karaganov, "Russia's Elites," in Blackwill and Karaganov, eds., *Damage Limitation*, 54, and Uri Ra'anan and Kate Martin, eds., *Russia: A Return to Imperialism?* (New York: St. Martin's, 1995), especially the chapters by Ra'anan and Sergei Grigoriev.

33. On the role of the security services (*siloviki*), see Ian Bremmer, "Who's in Charge in the Kremlin?" *World Policy Journal*, Win 2005–2006: 1–3; Ian Bremmer and Samuel Charap, "The *Siloviki* in Putin's Russia: Who They Are and What They Want," *Washington Quarterly*, Win 2006–2007, 30(1): 83–92; Olga Kryshtanovskaya and Stephen White, "Putin's Militocracy," *Post-Soviet Affairs*, 2003, 19(4): 289–306; Pavel K. Baev, "The Evolution of Putin's Regime: Inner Circles and Outer Walls," *Problems of Post-Communism*, Nov–Dec 2004, 51(6): 3–13. Of course, the term *siloviki* elides a range of distinctions among the members of this class, many of whom were already in positions of power under Yeltsin. See Brian D. Taylor, "Power Surge? Russia's Power Ministries from Yeltsin to Putin and Beyond," PONARS Policy Memo #414, Dec 2006. As Taylor points out, it is not *siloviki* as such who have attained newfound prominence under Putin, but specifically members of the FSB (rather than the Interior Ministry, Foreign Intelligence Service, military, or other armed organizations).

34. Mariya Gamaleeva, "Formirovanie obraza Rossii kak aspekt publichnoi vneshnei politiki," *Mezhdunarodnik.ru*, 2 Aug 2006, http://www.mezhdunarodnik .ru/magazin/4812.html.

35. William Zimmerman, *The Russian People and Foreign Policy: Russian Elite and Mass Perspectives, 1993–2000* (Princeton, NJ: Princeton University Press, 2002), 14–17.

36. Ilya Prizel, *National Identity and Foreign Policy: Nationalism and Leadership in Poland, Russia, and Ukraine* (Cambridge: Cambridge University Press, 1998), 1–11; Vladimir Shlapentokh, "Two Simplified Pictures of Putin's Russia, Both Wrong," *World Policy Journal*, Spr 2005: 61–72.

37. Gabriel Gorodetsky, "Introduction," in *Russia between East and West: Russian Foreign Policy on the Threshold of the Twenty-First Century*, ed. Gabriel Gorodetsky (London: Frank Cass, 2003), xi.

38. Timothy Snyder shows, for example, how Poland's post-Communist elites renounced their country's traditional civilizing mission to the East, in the process opening the way to membership in the Western community of nations symbolized by NATO and the European Union. Timothy Snyder, *The Reconstruction of Nations: Poland, Ukraine, Lithuania, Belarus, 1569–1999* (New Haven, CT: Yale University Press, 2003), 277–93.

39. Ted Hopf, *Social Construction of International Politics: Identities & Foreign Policies, Moscow 1955 and 1999* (Ithaca, NY: Cornell University Press, 2002), 156.

40. Anastasiya Kornya, "Imperskie ambitsii ne aktual'ny," *Vedomosti*, 23 Jan 2007.

41. V. Putin, "Poslanie Federal'nomu Sobraniyu Rossiiskoi Federatsii," 16 May 2003, http://www.kremlin.ru/appears/2003/05/16/1259_type63372type63374type 82634_44623.shtml.

42. Igor Ivanov, "The New Russian Identity: Innovation and Continuity in Russian Foreign Policy," *Washington Quarterly*, Sum 2001, 24(3): 11–12.

43. Lyne, Talbott, and Watanabe, "Engaging with Russia," 162.

44. Paul Goble, "Window on Eurasia: Putin Restricts Russian Foreign Ministry's Role in CIS Countries," 14 May 2008, http://windowoneurasia.blogspot.com/2008/05/window-on-eurasia-putin-restricts.html.

45. Rustem Falyakhov, "More of Pragmatism," *RBK Daily, Johnson's Russia List* [hereafter *JRL*] #2008-133, 17 Jul 2008.

46. Dmitri Simes calls Putin Russia's "elected emperor." See Adi Ignatius, "Person of the Year 2007: A Tsar Is Born," *Time*, http://www.time.com/time/specials/2007/personoftheyear/article/0,28804,1690753_1690757_1690766,00.html. Other Western commentators are even more scathing. Several authors have in recent years accused Putin of leading a fascist revival in Russia on the basis of enforced youth mobilization through groups such as Nashi as well as openly aggressive rhetoric toward neighboring countries. See, for example, Gavin Knight, "The Alarming Spread of Fascism in Putin's Russia," *New Statesman*, 24 Jul 2007. See also Cathy Young, "Putin's 'Young Brownshirts,'" *Boston Globe*, 10 Aug 2007. On the Putin-Medvedev tandem's operations during the Georgian war, see Steven Lee Myers and Thom Shanker, "West Baffled by 2 Heads for Russian Government," *New York Times*, 21 Aug 2008.

47. Since Ukraine is now an independent state using Ukrainian as its official language, I have chosen to use the spelling *Kyiv*. *Kiev* has a strongly imperial overtone, which I prefer to avoid, especially when talking about relations between Ukraine and Russia.

48. Fyodor Lukyanov, "Dve Rossii," *Vedomosti*, 28 Dec 2006.

49. John D. Negroponte, "Annual Threat Assessment," testimony to U.S. Senate Select Committee on Intelligence, 11 Jan 2007; *JRL* #8, 12 Jan 2007.

50. Steven Lee Meyers, "Putin's Assertive Diplomacy Is Seldom Challenged," *New York Times*, 27 Dec 2006.

51. See Tarique Niazi, "Pushback to Unilateralism: The China-India-Russia Alliance," *Foreign Policy in Focus, JRL* #3, 3 Jan 2008.

52. "Demokraticheski orientirovannye perevoroty v SNG i geopoliticheskie perspektivy Rossii v regione," *Mezhdunarodnik.ru*, 28 Sep 2005, http://www.mezhdunarodnik.ru/magazin/1439.html.

53. Andrew E. Kramer, "Russia Claims Its Sphere of Influence in the World," *New York Times*, 31 Aug 2008.

54. It is notable, too, that in his current position as head of the Russian Federation Chamber of Commerce, Primakov has been a vocal and enthusiastic supporter of Putin's foreign policy course. Yevgeny Primakov, "Russia's Foreign Policy in 2005 Was Successful in Every Area"; *International Affairs: A Russian Journal of World Politics, Diplomacy, and International Relations*, 2006, 52(2): 13–22; Fyodor Lukyanov, "Perspektiva: 2008—ne problema," *Vedomosti*, 6 Feb 2007.

55. Andrei Tsygankov, *Russia's Foreign Policy: Change and Continuity in National Identity* (Lanham, MD: Rowman & Littlefield, 2006), xxiv. Tsygankov argues that Primakov and Putin represent different, albeit related strands in thinking about Russian national identity and foreign policy. He calls Primakov's policy "Great

Power Balancing," emphasizing the element of rivalry in U.S.-Russian relations during the Primakov interlude as well as how Russia sought to check the expansion of U.S. power. Conversely, Tsygankov terms Putin's approach "Great Power Pragmatism," which, he argues, has been less confrontational toward the West while still emphasizing Russia's role as a major power and pillar of the international system.

56. Yury Fedorov, "Vneshnyaya politika Rossii: 1991–2000. Chast' I," *Pro et Contra*, 2001, 6(1–2).

57. A. Pravda, "Putin's Foreign Policy after 11 September," in *Russia between East and West: Russian Foreign Policy on the Threshold of the Twenty-First Century*, ed. Gabriel Gorodetsky (London: Frank Cass, 2003), 50; Andrey Kolesnikov, "Ivanov, Medvedev Seen Projecting Contrasting Facets of Russian Foreign Policy," *Gazeta.ru*, *JRL* #27, 4 Feb 2007.

58. "Report of the Russian Working Group," *U.S.-Russian Relations at the Turn of the Century* (Washington, DC: Carnegie Endowment for International Peace; Moscow: Council on Foreign and Defense Policy, 2000), 59.

59. Quoted in Dmitri Simes, "The Results of 1997: No Dramatic Upheavals," *International Affairs*, 1998, 44(1): 28. A stunned Nixon replied that he would not presume to tell the Russian foreign minister what his own country's national interest was.

60. Dmitry Shlapentokh, "Looking for Other Options: Russia's National Identity Cannot Be Based on Western Models," *Russia Profile*, 30 Oct 2006. See also Samuel Huntington, "The West and the World," *Foreign Affairs*, Nov–Dec 1997, 75(6): 37; Lawrence Freedman, "The New Great Power Politics," in *Russia and the West: The 21st Century Security Environment*, ed. Alexei Arbatov et al. (Armonk, NY: M. E. Sharpe, 1999), 22.

61. Ibid.

62. Andrei Kozyrev, "Partnership or Cold Peace?" *Foreign Policy*, Sum 1995 (99): 3–5.

63. Leon Aron, "The Foreign Policy Doctrine of Postcommunist Russia and Its Domestic Context," in *The New Russian Foreign Policy*, ed. Michael Mandelbaum (New York: Council on Foreign Relations, 1998), 29–30.

64. Michael Mandelbaum, "Introduction: Russian Foreign Policy in Historical Perspective," in *The New Russian Foreign Policy*, ed. Michael Mandelbaum (New York: Council on Foreign Relations, 1998), 1.

65. Aleksei Bogaturov, "Lovushki detsentralizatsii: V SShA vozvrashchaetsya mysl' o privlekatel'nosti shirokikh koalitsii," *Nezavisimaya Gazeta*, 5 Feb 2007.

66. "Obzor vneshnei politiki." Even Kozyrev warned, back in 1994, that "the international order of the [twenty-first] century will not be a Pax Americana or any other version of unipolar or bipolar dominance. The United States does not have the capability to rule alone." Jeffrey Mankoff, "Russia and the West: Taking the Longer View," *Washington Quarterly*, Spr 2007, 30(2): 128; Andrei Kozyrev, "The Lagging Partnership," *Foreign Affairs*, May–Jun 1994, 73(3): 59–71.

67. Dmitry Medvedev, "Interv'yu Dmitriya Medvedeva telekanalam 'Rossiya', Pervomu, NTV," 31 Aug 2008, http://www.kremlin.ru/appears/2008/08/31/1917_type63374type63379_205991.shtml.

68. George Friedman, "The Medvedev Doctrine and American Strategy," *Stratfor*

Geopolitical Intelligence Report, 2 Sep 2008, http://www.stratfor.com/weekly/medve dev_doctrine_and_american_strategy.

69. Bobo Lo, *Vladimir Putin and the Evolution of Russian Foreign Policy* (London: Royal Institute of International Affairs, 2003), 51–53. Primakov was, in fact, the first to make economics a central component of Russia's power projection capabilities, emphasizing Russia's capability to manipulate energy supplies to the former Soviet republics to ensure their loyalty to Moscow. Yeltsin's long-time premier, Viktor Chernomyrdin, who was also a former head of Gazprom, envisioned forcing the former Soviet republics to invest in Gazprom and other natural resource monopolies as a way of more closely tying them to Russia economically. See Tsygankov, *Russia's Foreign Policy,* 114–15.

70. On the reasons for the 1998 financial crisis, see Brian Pinto, Evsey Gurevich, and Sergei Ulatov, "Lessons from the Russian Crisis of 1998 and Recovery," *Managing Volatility and Crises: A Practitioner's Guide,* available at http://www1.worldbank .org/economicpolicy/documents/mv/pgchapter10.pdf.

71. V. Putin, "Vstupitel'noe slovo na zasedanii Soveta Bezopasnosti, posvyash- chennom meram po realizatsii Poslaniya Federal'nomu Sobraniyu," 20 Jun 2006, http://www.kremlin.ru/text/appears/2006/06/107450.shtml.

72. V. Putin, "Poslanie Federal'nomu Sobraniyu Rossiiskoi Federatsii," 8 Jul 2000, http://www.kremlin.ru/appears/2000/07/08/0000_type63372type63374type 82634_28782.shtml.

73. V. Putin, "Poslanie Federal'nomu Sobraniyu Rossiiskoi Federatsii," 26 Apr 2007, http://www.kremlin.ru/appears/2007/04/26/1156_type63372type63374type 82634_125339.shtml.

74. The National Projects were first announced in 2005 and have been aggres- sively promoted in the media as an example of the state taking a proactive approach to Russia's deep-seated social problems. His identification with the National Proj- ects has also no doubt helped Medvedev's political ascent. For 2007, the Kremlin eventually budgeted $10.2 billion for the four National Projects. "Russia to Raise National Project Spending 12% to $10bln in 2007," RIA-Novosti, 23 Oct 2007, http://en.rian.ru/russia/20070823/73753727.html.

75. Clifford Gaddy and Fiona Hill, "Putin's Agenda, America's Choice: Russia's Search for Strategic Stability," Brookings Institution Policy Brief #89, May 2002. See also Opening Statement of Senator Joseph R. Biden Jr. to Senate Committee on For- eign Relations hearing on "U.S. Policy toward Russia," 21 Jun 2005. According to Biden, capital flight in 2005 may have reached the equivalent of $7 billion.

76. See "Annual Forecast 2008: Beyond the Jihadist War—Former Soviet Union," Stratfor Analytical Report, Jan 2008, http://www.stratfor.com/analysis/annual_ forecast_2008_beyond_jihadist_war_former_soviet_union. Moscow is aware of the political and diplomatic limitations imposed by the current economic model and is in the process of outlining a new economic development strategy for the coming decade that will advocate lessened reliance on commodity exports. See "The Econ- omy Needs Restructuring, but How?" RIA Novosti, *JRL* #6, 8 Jan 2008.

77. "PM Outlines Goals for Next Three Years," RosBusinessConsulting, *JRL* #7, 8 Jan 2008; Charles Clover and Catherine Belton, "Retreat from Moscow: Investors Take Flight as Global Fears Stoke Russian Crisis," *Financial Times,* 17 Sep 2008;

Michael Stott, "Russia Acknowledges Financial Crisis Hit Hard," Reuters, 21 Nov 2008, http://www.reuters.com/article/reutersEdge/idUSTRE4AK4L620081121. Some financiers are less optimistic than the World Bank and believe that overall Russian growth will be negative over the course of 2008.

78. "Russia 'to Pay Paris Club Early,'" BBC News, 3 Feb 2005, http://news.bbc.co.uk/2/hi/business/4233547.stm.

79. Carlos Pascual, "The Geopolitics of Energy: From Security to Survival," Brookings Institution, Jan 2008, http://www.brookings.edu/papers/2008/01_energy_pascual.aspx. At the start of 2008, the Stabilization Fund held $156.81 billion. "Stabfond RF za 2007 god vyros na 1,5 trln rublei," RIA-Novosti, 9 Jan 2008, http://www.rian.ru/economy/finance/20080109/95837964.html.

80. Valeria Korchagina, "Cabinet Set to Back Higher Spending," *Moscow Times*, 18 Aug 2005, 1.

81. Christian Neef, "Russian Bear Roars: Why Is Moscow Risking a New Cold War?" *Der Spiegel* online, 25 Jun 2008, http://www.spiegel.de/international/world/0,1518,562073,00.html.

82. Ibid.

83. On the effectiveness of Russia's military during the Georgian conflict, see Felix K. Chang, "Russia Resurgent: An Initial Look at Russian Military Performance in Georgia," Foreign Policy Research Institute (FPRI) analysis paper, 13 Aug 2008.

84. V. Putin, "Poslanie federal'nomu sobraniyu," 10 May 2006, http://www.kremlin.ru/appears/2006/05/10/1357_type63372type63374type82634_105546.shtml.

85. See Anders Åslund, "Russia's WTO Ascension," testimony at the Hearing on EU Economic and Trade Relations with Russia, European Parliament Committee on International Trade, 21 Nov 2006, http://www.iie.com/publications/papers/paper.cfm?ResearchID=686.

86. See Lyne, Talbott, and Watanabe, "Engaging with Russia," 65.

87. Anders Åslund, *Russia's Capitalist Revolution: Why Market Reform Succeeded and Democracy Failed* (Washington, DC: Peterson Institute, 2007), 247–59.

88. Many Russian analysts have recently been stepping up their calls for the state to consolidate its control over energy resources and pipeline routes in order to have a means of exerting control over the policies of their neighbors and limiting Russia's vulnerability to external pressure. See Mikhail Delyagin, "Energeticheskaya politika Rossii," *Svobodnaya mysl'*, 2006 (9–10): 5–14.

89. V. Milov, "The Future of Russian Energy Policy," address to the Brookings Institution, 30 Nov 2006: 15, http://www.brookings.edu/comm/events/20061130.htm. See also Åslund, *Russia's Capitalist Revolution*, 214–21.

90. Milov, "The Future of Russian Energy Policy," 17–19. The downside, as Milov makes clear, has been the extreme lack of investment in the energy sector, rent seeking, inefficiency, and shortages on the (still subsidized) Russian domestic market. The growing state role in the economy has also, of course, limited growth and investment, especially given that oil and gas account for such a large section of Russia's GDP.

91. Wallander, "Challenge," testimony to U.S. Senate Foreign Relations Committee.

92. Alexander Koliandre, "Russia Keeps China Energy Options Open," BBC News, 21 March 2006, http://news.bbc.co.uk/2/hi/business/4830768.stm.

93. Brookings Institution, "The Russian Federation," 28–29.

94. Åslund, *Russia's Capitalist Revolution*, 272–76.

95. Yegor Gaidar, "The Soviet Collapse," AEI Online, On the Issues, 19 Apr 2007, http://www.aei.org/publications/pubID.25991,filter.all/pub_detail.asp.

96. Rajan Menon and Alexander J. Motyl, "Why Russia Is Really Weak," *Newsweek*, Sep 2006.

97. For figures on xenophobic attitudes and incidents, see Yelena Novoselova, "Mnogonatsional'naya nenavist'," *Rossiiskaya Gazeta*, 11 Jan 2008.

98. Nicolas Eberstadt, "The Russian Federation at the Dawn of the Twenty-first Century: Trapped in a Demographic Straightjacket," *National Bureau of Asian Research (NBR) Analysis*, Sep 2004, 15(2): 7.

99. Judyth Twigg, "Differential Demographics: Russia's Muslim and Slavic Populations," Center for Strategic and International Studies PONARS Policy Memo No. 338, Dec 2005: 136–37. Twigg notes that births among Russia's Slavic population began increasing around 1999 while Muslim births started declining shortly thereafter. The percentage of Muslim conscripts will thus peak around 2016–2017—assuming conscription has not been abolished by then.

100. Mankoff, "Russia and the West," 127–29.

101. "Russia Recognition as One of World Leaders Main Result of Year," Itar-Tass, *JRL* #285, 20 Dec 2006. See also Primakov, "Russia's Foreign Policy in 2005 Was Successful in Every Area."

102. Gorchakov's diplomacy, which aimed at rebuilding and reintegrating Russia into the European Concert following the Crimean War, has in particular been evoked as a model for what Russia today requires. Former foreign minister Igor Ivanov consciously identified his approach with that of Gorchakov, and a number of scholars and pundits have invoked Gorchakov or Stolypin as appropriate historical models. See Igor Ivanov, *The New Russian Diplomacy* (Washington, DC: Nixon Center/Brookings Institution, 2002) 26–28. See also Flemming Splidsboel-Hansen, "Past and Future Meet: Aleksandr Gorchakov and Russian Foreign Policy," *Europe-Asia Studies*, 2002, 54(3): 377–96.

103. As Pursianinen points out, current debates about the relative importance of power and ideology in framing the outlines of Russian foreign policy are in many ways reminiscent of similar debates that long simmered over the Soviet Union. See Christer Pursianinen, *Russian Foreign Policy and International Relations Theory* (Aldershot: Ashgate, 2000), 48.

104. Kenneth N. Waltz, *Theory of International Politics* (Reading, MA: Addison Wesley, 1979), 102–28.

105. Sergei Strokan, "Tsena voprosa," *Kommersant*, 5 Feb 2007.

106. Alexander Wendt, *Social Theory of International Politics* (New York: Cambridge University Press, 1999), 1–7, 103–19.

107. On this point see Richard Rosencrance and Arthur A. Stein, "Beyond Realism: The Study of Grand Strategy," and Michael W. Doyle, "Politics and Grand Strategy," in *The Domestic Bases of Grand Strategy*, ed. Richard Rosencrance and Arthur A. Stein (Ithaca, NY: Cornell University Press, 1993), 3–21, 22–47; David A. Lake and

Robert Powell, "International Relations: A Strategic Choice Approach," in *Strategic Choice and International Relations*, ed. David A. Lake and Robert Powell (Princeton, NJ: Princeton University Press, 1999), 3–38.

108. Lo, *Vladimir Putin and the Evolution of Russian Foreign Policy*, 13–14. See also Andrei Kozyrev, *Preobrazhenie* (Moscow: Mezhdunarodnye otnosheniya, 1995), 221.

109. Tsygankov, *Russia's Foreign Policy*, 26.

110. See Steven Pifer, "What Does Russia Want? How Do We Respond?" (lecture at Texas A&M University, 11 Sep 2008), http://www.brookings.edu/speeches/2008/0911_russia_pifer.aspx.

2

Bulldogs Fighting under the Rug

The Making of Russian Foreign Policy

In any country, establishing precisely who makes foreign policy, and how, is difficult. In a country like Russia with weak formal institutions and a political system that has been in more or less constant flux for the past two decades, the challenge is even greater. The collapse of the Soviet Union and the Communist bloc left the Russian Federation awkwardly balanced between its imperial-authoritarian past and what was hoped by many to be a democratic future. Even as the Russian political system evolved under presidents Yeltsin and Putin, it failed to develop the sturdy institutions that would lend a degree of continuity and predictability to its behavior. Russia's failure to institutionalize eventually resulted in a very centralized form of government, with enormous power concentrated at the top and few of the constraints that exist in the pluralistic countries of the West: parliaments, a free press, or a loyal opposition. Still, Dmitri Trenin's observation that, despite the centralization and authoritarian tendencies of Russia under Putin, "the Russian political system rests on the acquiescence of the governed" remains germane.[1] An increasingly narrow elite may make foreign policy, but the wider public constrains the range of choices available to that elite.

The consolidation of decision making means both that foreign policy in Russia is a preserve of an elite and that the elite itself is smaller and more directly connected to the regime than in the 1990s. To some extent, this observation is rather banal, since in most countries, foreign policy is viewed as the province of a fairly select intellectual and economic elite. Moreover, even in a country as politically regimented as Russia, the elite is far from homogeneous, and various strands of opinion on the nature of Russia's national interest are clearly visible, even within the Kremlin itself. Putin's centralization certainly did not re-create the political structure of the Soviet Union, which, with its ideological underpinnings and rigid *nomenklatura* system of appointments, had a much narrower group of individuals capable of influencing foreign policy.[2]

In institutional terms, foreign policy decision making in early-twenty-first-century Russia is concentrated inside the presidential administration and, since Putin's move from the Kremlin to the Russian White House, in the office of the prime minister—not, it should be noted, in the Ministry of Foreign Affairs (*Ministerstvo Inostrannykh Del*, MID), the Security Council, or the cabinet. Constitutionally, the presidency completely overshadows the prime minister in the realm of foreign policy. Under the Medvedev-Putin "tandemocracy," however, much of the de facto responsibility for foreign policy followed Putin to the prime ministership, a development highlighted above all by the summer 2008 conflict with Georgia. Putin's ability to carry authority with him is further testimony to the weakness of formal institutions.

Likewise, the Russian parliament has never played a major role in the making of foreign policy. The Federation Council (the upper house) was made purely appointive in 2003, and its role has been increasingly subordinated to the presidential administration that is indirectly responsible for choosing its members.[3] Although the lower house, the State Duma, remains elective and some of its members are true experts in foreign affairs, the Kremlin's manipulation of the electoral system and political parties has drastically reduced the Duma's ability to act autonomously. With the pro-government United Russia (*Edinaya Rossiya*) Party controlling over two-thirds of the seats in the Duma, the legislature quickly became a reliable ally of the Kremlin rather than an independent force.[4]

While theoretically responsible for playing the lead role in defining and implementing foreign policy, the Foreign Ministry also became rather peripheral during Putin's presidency. This eclipse stems from a number of sources. On the one hand, the Foreign Ministry did not adjust well to the collapse of the Soviet Union. Upon becoming foreign minister in 1991, Andrei Kozyrev dismissed many high-ranking officials (including all the deputy ministers) left over from his Soviet predecessor. Among those who remained, most still possessed a fundamentally Soviet worldview and remained extremely skeptical of Kozyrev's attempts to build a positive-sum relationship with the United States.[5] At the same time, the Foreign Ministry was not ready for the more pluralistic policy-making environment of the early 1990s. Accustomed to a more hierarchical system of decision making, the Foreign Ministry's post-Soviet leadership was caught off guard by the emergence of alternative power centers and ceded much of the initiative to groups such as the military-industrial complex, the Ministry of Defense, and the armed services, as well as large businesses and regional leaders with their own set of foreign policy priorities.[6]

With the strong-willed Yevgeny Primakov as foreign minister and President Yeltsin weakened both personally and politically, the Foreign Ministry became more visible and influential in the late 1990s. Primakov came to embody a consensual approach to foreign affairs that encompassed most of the players in the unfolding foreign policy debate. With the rise to power of Vladimir Putin, the post of foreign minister has been held by men—Igor Ivanov followed by Sergei Lavrov—from the ranks of career diplomats lacking strong political connections or strongly articulated views about the direction of Russian foreign policy. Thus while it makes sense to speak of a Kozyrev foreign policy or a Primakov foreign policy, the same does not hold for a Lavrov foreign policy, since Sergei Vladimirovich's role has been principally to implement the concepts developed by his political superiors in the Kremlin. Under Putin, a few close associates, including Sergei Ivanov (former chairman of the Security Council, defense minister, and first deputy prime minister) and presidential aide Sergei Prikhodko, were the president's key foreign policy advisers.

The Security Council (*Sovet Bezopasnosti*), whose importance has ebbed and flowed over time, is mainly a forum for drawing up broad conceptual documents and an advisory group for the president, designed, like the NSC in the United States, to resolve competing bureaucratic priorities. Under Sergei Ivanov's leadership the Security Council played a key coordinating role within the administration, thanks to the close personal ties between Ivanov and President Putin. A similar dynamic operated under Yeltsin, when the Security Council's importance varied directly with the level of trust its chairman enjoyed with the president.[7] From 2004 to mid-2007, when Igor Ivanov, the technocratic former foreign minister, served as the council's chairman, its role in foreign policy diminished again.[8] Medvedev's appointment of the *silovik* Nikolai Patrushev as head of the Security Council (and of retired general staff chairman Gen. Yury Baluevsky as deputy chairman) was interpreted by Russian analysts as an attempt to give the council renewed authority—or to banish potential rivals to prestigious but irrelevant posts.[9]

The centralization of foreign policy making in the Kremlin, part of a process Putin termed "strengthening the power vertical," allowed Putin to impose a fairly coherent vision of the national interest in a way that was not consistently possible during the Yeltsin-Primakov years, when regional and sectoral interests often took predominance. The transition to Medvedev reopened some of the broader ideological debate about Russia's foreign policy priorities. The transformation of the Federation Council into a purely appointive institution and the creation of seven super-regions overseen by presidential appointees deprived the regional governors of much of their power, including the power to freelance in foreign policy. The state's growing role in the economy has had more mixed results. On the one hand, the nationalization of Yukos (and the example it set) means that the top officials of major companies have become state employees subject to discipline from above.[10] On the other hand, given its size and concentration in strategic industries like energy, the state sector of the economy has become a powerful actor in its own right, potentially acting as a veto player on foreign policy decisions affecting its interests directly; the gas industry in particular retains the ability to frustrate the center's initiatives if its interests are at stake.

Despite this success in centralizing the foreign policy decision-making process within the Kremlin, Putin's Russia was not a monolith, and Medvedev's duopolistic Russia appears even less so. Whatever his aspirations, Putin was not able to make foreign policy into a completely top-down affair. While the role of the legislature and regional leaders may have been greatly circumscribed, other groups remain important players in the policy process. Two groups in particular deserve mention in this regard: large energy companies and the security services (including the military).[11] High energy prices, the fact that Russia is heavily dependent on oil and gas exports for foreign exchange earnings, and the symbiotic relationship between big business and the state all limited the government's ability to rein in major corporations such as the natural gas monopoly Gazprom, so much that one respected analyst termed big business, rather than the insipid state-controlled press, Russia's true "fourth estate."[12]

Big business can at times and in certain areas impede the implementation of the government's foreign policy agenda. The directors of inefficient, state-owned companies, especially natural resource monopolies, worked hard to block Russia's ascension to the World Trade Organization (WTO), which Putin identified as a priority.[13] As Gazprom is the country's principal cash cow, it will no doubt continue to exert substantial pressure on foreign policy, though the Kremlin has tried at times to limit its power by replacing its leadership (Aleksei Miller for Rem Vyakhirev) and stocking its board with Kremlin insiders, including Dmitry Medvedev himself, who served as Gazprom's chairman before his elevation to the presidency.

The security services are another institution with strong views on foreign policy that Putin did not entirely manage to bring under Kremlin control. Much of the military command advocates prioritizing the former Soviet Union in Russia's foreign policy and adopting a confrontational approach toward the United States; the war with Georgia thus found strong backing among the brass. Likewise, the debate over Russia's new Military Doctrine, which will be released in late 2008 or 2009, is indicative of how the high command understands the world and the threats facing Russia. One notable aspect of the new Doctrine is the fact that it continues to focus on state-based threats, especially from established states (i.e., the West and NATO members). Baluevsky, former chief of the Russian General Staff, argued that "the struggle for spheres of influence among the developed countries claiming for themselves world and regional leadership" is one of the principal destabilizing factors in the post–Cold War world.

For this reason, the Military Doctrine will reportedly emphasize conventional military threats on the part of the West alongside the newer dangers of terrorism and failed states as the main security threats facing Russia— even though Putin, Medvedev, and their associates have made clear that they consider the military's focus on conventional, state-based threats to be outmoded. Criticizing Baluevsky, then-defense minister Sergei Ivanov claimed that "Russia has no military or political enemies."[14] Such tension between the Defense Ministry's political leadership and the uniformed services is one of the main reasons the military continues to challenge the Kremlin's supremacy in the making of foreign policy, a problem that could get worse as Medvedev attempts to pursue a more comprehensive reform (and downsizing) of the military.[15]

Meanwhile the notorious *siloviki*, members of the various internal security forces descended from the Soviet-era KGB, have increasingly spread their influence throughout the state and the economy. While much of their activity has been connected to sewing up lucrative economic fiefdoms, their growing power cannot but have an impact on the making of foreign policy. The Soviet-era KGB was considered something of an intellectual elite (and unusually cosmopolitan in its outlook). To the extent that the foreign policy preferences of leading *siloviki* can be known, however, they appear to have a strong Eurasianist, anti-Western undertone. Certainly Igor Sechin, Putin's deputy chief of staff and security expert, was long reputed to be one of the Kremlin's leading hard-liners (though Sechin was careful to stay out of the public eye and to keep his opinions to himself).[16]

Some elements of the security services are less ideological—much of the defense industry, for example, favors improved relations with the West in large part as a way to open new markets for Russian military technology.[17] Moreover, given the scale of Russia's military collapse in the years since the end of the Cold War and the sheer cost of full-scale rearmament, the newer generation of military leadership has softened to some degree on the nature of the threat from the West. By downplaying the likelihood of confrontation with the U.S. or NATO even as the armed forces continue to see the West as the principal threat to the country, the Kremlin has been able to focus on economic development and integration as well as on expanding Russian influence in the CIS. Putin's halting success in downsizing the military (especially the ground forces) and moving toward contract service in place of the draft are good indications of the struggle among different bureaucratic and ideological factions that continues behind the façade of Kremlin unity.[18]

Nor is the military itself homogeneous. With the winding down of the war in Chechnya and the appointment of Putin loyalists to important positions in the Ministry of Defense, the Kremlin has been trying to rein in the uniformed services' political autonomy. Early in his first term, Putin moved to sideline some particularly outspoken generals who had been calling for Russia to adopt a harder line in dealings with the West, including former defense minister Marshal Igor Sergeev and then-head of the Defense Ministry's International Department Colonel-General Leonid Ivashov.[19] Indeed, the cause of military reform has been held back in large part because of the continuing distrust between Putin's inner circle, drawn heavily from the nonmilitary components of the national security bureaucracy (mainly the intelligence services) and the military leadership in the Defense Ministry and General Staff. Even the appointment of Sergei Ivanov, with his close ties to the president, was unable to fully contain the military's discontent.[20]

In early 2007, Ivanov was promoted to first deputy prime minister and replaced as defense minister by Anatoly Serdyukov, a former furniture salesman and tax inspector with no background in defense issues. It is notable that both Ivanov, a career intelligence officer and close associate of the president, and Serdyukov are not from the career military ranks, as Yeltsin's defense ministers had been. The appointment of a complete outsider like Serdyukov signaled how little trust the Kremlin had in the upper ranks of the military.[21] Baluevsky's departure as chief of the General Staff in mid-2008 was likewise connected to attempts by the Ministry of Defense to rein in the military's autonomy and subject it to modernization in line with a perception on the part of the country's civilian leadership that the military has failed to adapt in order to confront the range of nontraditional security threats facing Russia.[22]

On balance, the Russian state under Putin and Medvedev has much greater autonomy in foreign affairs than it did during the 1990s, when not only business and the military, but also local governors and the legislature often pursued their own foreign policy agendas. Yeltsin's Kremlin was often completely unable to coordinate the activities of the Security Council, Foreign Ministry, Defense Ministry, and a plethora of short-lived bureaucratic actors (the Foreign Policy Council and Defense Council, created and later abolished by Yeltsin) nominally under the president's control.[23] Yet much of that autonomy remains dependent on the president's ability to balance competing interests and factions within his administration, a task Putin managed in large part by never identifying too closely with any particular group or clan.

THE CONSTRAINTS OF MASS OPINION

The Kremlin's domination of the foreign policy-making landscape extends to public opinion as well. While it may be true that, even more so than in most Western democracies, foreign policy in Russia is the preserve of a narrow elite, the role of public opinion in setting Russia's external course cannot be entirely discounted. True, with elections to the Duma and for the presidency largely ritualistic, the traditional avenues for the public to influence foreign policy have largely been blocked. Even in the Yeltsin years, though, the Russian public had a low sense of what political scientists term "external efficacy"—or the belief that their preferences can have an impact on public policy.[24] At the same time, Russia is far from a closed society, and the intensity of debates played out in the media (especially print media and the Internet) reflect the degree to which public opinion is engaged in discussions of foreign policy. Opinion polls show that the public at large continues to have strong preferences on issues of international politics and national security policy.

Moreover, even if Russian elections are not entirely free or fair, neither are they completely meaningless as they were under Communism. So far, at least, the votes in national elections appear to have been fairly tallied (albeit after the authorities have sharply limited which names may appear on the ballot or have access to the media). The outcomes of Russian elections at the federal level therefore offer at least an approximation of public sentiment; in contrast to the Soviet era, ballots are generally cast in secret and overt compulsion to vote a particular way is limited (voting in some republics, notably Chechnya, has stronger Soviet overtones). Putin claimed, plausibly enough given his persistently high approval ratings, to base his rule on the consent of the governed; the fact that Medvedev received close to 70 percent of the vote in the March 2008 election to replace Putin allowed the new president to effectively claim the mantle of public legitimacy from Putin.

Even without real elections, maintaining consent requires adhering to at least a minimum level of accord with the sentiments of the public. The public in Russia thus acts as a constraint, limiting the range of policy options the government can adopt—at least in a range of high-visibility policy areas such as relations with the former Soviet republics. The Kremlin makes foreign policy, but it depends on the acquiescence of the public in doing so, and its range of choices is constrained to a certain degree by what the public will accept.

That pubic opinion does not actually drive foreign policy in Russia can be seen in the divergence between public and elite sentiment and between public opinion and the government's actual policy choices. Repeated polls have shown that, on the whole, Russian public opinion is more isolationist and less confrontational than elite opinion.[25] Typical is a poll taken in November 2008 showing 47 percent of Russians believing that the military should only defend Russian territory, while only 30.4 percent believed it should intervene abroad.[26] Thus the elite consensus based on Russia's role as a Great Power does not necessarily hold at the level of public opinion, suggesting that a more democratic Russia with better institutions might embark on a rather different course in the world than the one pursued by the current semi-authoritarian regime.[27] Still, Russian citizens are aware of their government's efforts to enhance Russia's global role and are largely appreciative of the successes the Kremlin has achieved in the past few years.[28] A majority of Russians believe that their country should be either a superpower or at least one of the ten to fifteen leading world powers—though when asked what being a superpower actually entails, most respondents list high living standards, rather than any measure of political or military power, as the main criterion of that status.[29]

It should be noted, however, that such comparative isolationism does not correlate with more positive attitudes toward other countries, especially the U.S. In almost every year examined by William Zimmerman, elites were less inclined to view the U.S. per se or the growth of U.S. power as a threat to Russian security than was the public at large.[30] The U.S.-led invasion of Iraq led to an upsurge in hostility to the U.S., in large part because of a drumbeat of hostile coverage in the state-controlled media. According to polling done by the Levada Center, in March 2002, 29 percent of Russians viewed relations with the U.S. as "normal, calm [*normal'nye, spokoinye*]," 30 percent saw them as "cool [*prokhladnye*]," and 18 percent saw them as "tense [*napryazhennye*]." By February 2005, with the U.S. occupation of Iraq an established fact, the numbers were 45 percent, 22 percent, and 7 percent, respectively.[31] Sharply negative press coverage of the U.S. also coincided with the war in Georgia in 2008, and once again, public attitudes toward the United States took a turn for the worse. Shortly after the outbreak of hostilities between Moscow and Tbilisi in August 2008, the respective figures in the Levada Center polls were 16 percent, 29 percent, and 38 percent.[32]

On the whole, the Russian public tends to be less interested in the Great Power ambitions of its leaders and more interested in the quotidian details of everyday life. The public does seem to appreciate the fact that, over the past several years, the country has become more prominent and respected around the world. Yet appreciating what has been accomplished at relatively little cost is not the same as actually demanding a more assertive international posture. Given the gap in attitudes between members of the security services and the public at large, as well as autocracies' need to foment an atmosphere of perpetual crisis in their foreign relations as a justification for blocking reform, the consolidation of "managed democracy," or later, "sovereign democracy" in Russia does have important implications for how the state pursues its foreign policy goals.[33]

Putin, for one, seemed to have a good understanding that while the public does not oppose an assertive foreign policy, its priorities are elsewhere. His heavy emphasis on domestic concerns during his annual messages to the Federal Assembly as well as in his scripted interactions with the public (e.g., his periodic appearances on televised call-in shows) reflected a belief the public cares more about butter than guns. In this regard it hardly seems accidental that Medvedev initially sought to acquaint the public with his talents by taking on a number of highly visible domestic initiatives as Putin's first deputy prime minister in charge of National Projects, or that his own initial remarks about Russia's priorities for the future focused on improving national competitiveness.

IDEAS AND IDEOLOGIES OF THE ELITE

If public opinion at most sets the bounds of what is acceptable, elite opinions matter more in shaping the state's foreign policy agenda. The overall direction of elite opinion about the scope and content of Russia's national interest has changed substantially since the early 1990s. Calls for full-scale integration with the West, which were a staple of public discourse in the late 1980s and early 1990s, are now confined to a small liberal fringe. Cooperation with the West (especially on security issues) remains important to many Russian leaders, but few elites still believe in using integration with Western institutions as a means of anchoring Russia's domestic political transformation, or in Russia pooling its sovereignty with the democracies of the West. In other words, many Russian leaders—including, it should be noted, both Putin and Medvedev—largely advocate cooperation with the United States and Europe against common threats (such as Islamic terrorism) but do not support moving beyond such a realpolitik-infused relationship to a partnership based on shared values and institutions or to actually "joining the West."[34]

In part, this development is the result of the disappointments Russia experienced in the 1990s as a consequence of its overtures to the West not being reciprocated. At the same time, the pervasiveness of Great Power ideology—*derzhavnost'*—in the thinking of Russia's political elites has to do with long-standing traditions of conceptualizing the world and Russia's place in it dating back to the tsarist era. The Russia of 1991, of course, was not a tabula rasa, and the influence of ideologies left over from the Soviet period remains strong today, even if only an extreme fringe would actively seek to restore the Soviet Empire as such.

While the notion of Russia as an independent Great Power in an anarchic world has long existed within the elite, the ascension of Primakov to the post of foreign minister in 1996 marked a real post-Soviet turning point. In constructivist terms, the transition from Kozyrev to Primakov reflected the emergence of a new consensus about Russia's identity as a state and its role in the global system. This identity is characterized by etatism (or *gosudarst-vennost'*)—namely the idea that the state should play a leading role in the economic and political life of the country, and that the national interest in foreign policy should be defined in reference to the well-being of the state itself (rather than the protection of its citizens or the upholding of international law, for example). This identity also entails an emphasis on power as the principal criterion by which to judge the state's health. *Gosudarstven-nost'* and *derzhavnost'* are the two major components of the geopolitical worldview that has predominated among the Russian elite since the 1990s, and in many ways grow out of a much older, even pre-Soviet intellectual tradition. Within that worldview, however, are many shades of emphasis, and it is the interplay among these shades that forms the substance of the Russian foreign policy debate.

The contours of that debate have changed to some extent since the mid-1990s. Nonetheless, a spectrum of views continues to exist, despite the Kremlin's success in consolidating the process of decision making.[35] Scholars often identify a number of camps or schools of foreign policy thinking among the Russian elite.[36] While it is no doubt true that a few well-defined ideologies exist (particularly on the extremes), what is striking about the Russian elite is the size of the political spectrum's center and the range of opinions within the general consensus about Russia as a Great Power. During the Putin years, this *derzhavnost'-gosudarstvennost'* consensus was all but ubiquitous, which is one reason Putin's foreign policy generated so little controversy. A range of opinions continues to exist within this geopolitical framework, but the differences are, for the most part, about emphasis or particular policy choices rather than about overall strategy. For this reason, while the notion of distinct camps or schools remains a useful heuristic device, and given the size and breadth of the mainstream, thinking about the center as a continuum rather than as a series of discontinuous units offers greater insight into the interplay of forces. Many of the most influential foreign policy thinkers and practitioners in Russia do not fit neatly in any of these boxes anyway. Certainly Putin, who at the same time tried to re-establish Russian dominance within the area of the CIS and sought a cooperative, at times even close relationship with the United States, defies easy categorization.

Some of the more salient and visible approaches include extreme Russian ethnonationalism, imperialistic Eurasianism, a kind of centrist *derzhavnost'*, and liberal Atlanticism. Actual policy, especially since the fall of Kozyrev, has been a sometimes uncomfortable balance among these trends.[37] Given the general stability of this consensus, there is reason to think that the foreign policy of early-twenty-first century Russia will look fairly similar under Medvedev and beyond.

Particularly influential is the centrist tendency, which is characterized by an eclectic borrowing of ideas and initiatives from the other, more ideologically coherent camps. Less an ideological movement than an attempt to synthesize the competing priorities of the other three camps and an attempt to promote the private interests of certain well-connected officials, Russian centrism has remained the dominant approach since around 1993–1994, precisely because of its success in appealing to a broad constituency among the elite.[38] Within this broad middle, different individuals and groups have different shades of emphasis (Primakov tilted more toward the Eurasianists, for instance) but are united by a shared belief that Russia should play a pivotal role in world affairs, that it should maintain a sphere of influence around its borders, and that a relationship of equals with the other large powers (especially the United States) provides the basic foundation for the country's international behavior. Individuals such as Primakov, and indeed Putin and Medvedev themselves, have in practice largely appealed to a centrist constituency, if only by default.[39]

Russian Nationalism

On one extreme is a loose collection of activists and groups espousing racially tinged Russian nationalism, the most prominent of which is the Movement Against Illegal Immigration (*Dvizhenie protiv nelegal'noi immigratsii*, DPNI), which, despite its name, has also played an important role in Russia's policy toward its southern neighbors in the CIS.[40] The DPNI and others in the nationalist camp are essentially in favor of a smaller, more homogeneous Russia—in contrast to the "Red-Brown" alliance of the 1990s, when the far right (then embodied by Vladimir Zhirinovsky's Liberal Democrats) advocated an expansionist foreign policy. Rather than promoting integration within the post-Soviet space, the DPNI and its acolytes support a kind of "fortress Russia" mentality, particularly against the Muslim republics in the Caucasus and Central Asia, but also against China, which is rapidly becoming a major source of new immigrants to the Russian Far East and the source of much xenophobic angst along the Russo-Chinese border.

Since their enmity is directed primarily at the former Soviet republics to the south, the nationalists are, in comparison with the Eurasianists, relatively sanguine about the West. After participating in a march together with the Kremlin-supported Eurasian Union of Youth (*Evraziskii Soyuz Molodezhi*, ESM) in St. Petersburg in November 2005, DPNI leader Aleksandr Belov (a nom de guerre from the Russian *belyi*, meaning "white") told journalists that his group had essentially hijacked the march from the Eurasianist group. "We marched against migrants, not against the expansion of Western influence, as ESM had planned," he said.[41]

The DPNI rapidly became one of Russia's largest mass political organizations, in large part by tapping into a well of discontent and anxiety about the future among the Russian Federation's ethnically Russian population. The group's emphasis has been on combating what it portrays as ethnic gangs (mostly comprising Caucasians and Central Asians) who had allegedly taken over the commercial trade in Russian markets in the late 1990s and early 2000s. It was also prominent in Moscow's confrontation with Georgia in the autumn of 2006, which resulted from one of Tbilisi's attempts to bring Abkhazia and South Ossetia back under the control of the Georgian government. As the confrontation between Moscow and Tbilisi took on overtly xenophobic overtones (with Georgian-run businesses in Russia being targeted by the police and ethnic Georgians, even those with Russian citizenship, rounded up for deportation), the DPNI became one of the loudest proponents of the Kremlin's aggressive tactics targeting not only the Georgian state but members of Russia's Georgian diaspora as well. The symbiosis between the DPNI's calls to target ethnic Georgians in Russia and the Kremlin's increasingly heavy-handed campaign of intimidation led to much speculation that the DPNI was in fact a Kremlin creation designed to channel discontent away from the regime and toward a vulnerable ethnic minority.[42] Similar allegations were made regarding the Motherland (*Rodina*) Party, which took a surprising 9 percent of the vote in the 2003 parliamentary elections while campaigning on a platform of promoting Russian national values and removing ethnic minorities (especially Caucasians) from positions of power and influence inside Russia.

While the nationalist camp is not primarily interested in foreign policy, its preferences do have an impact, particularly with regard to countries with substantial numbers of immigrants in Russia (like Georgia) or with significant populations of ethnic Russians. Rampant racism and xenophobia discourage many would-be migrants from moving to Russia, despite the country's demographic problems and labor shortages. Russia's fraught relationship with the Baltic states is also in part the result of attempts to appease nationalist opinion outraged by Latvia and Estonia's treatment of their Russian minorities. Since the Baltic states are now also members of the EU and NATO, Moscow's vigorous campaign on behalf of Russian speakers has broader implications for its relationship with Europe.

Eurasianism

The worldview generally termed Eurasianism (*Evraziistvo*) has a long pedigree in Russian academic and political circles, dating back in its original incarnation to the years immediately after the Russian Revolution. The meaning and significance of Eurasianism is much debated by scholars of Russian politics and international relations. At the most literal and basic level, Eurasianism simply means the belief that Russia's fundamental identity, and hence foreign policy priorities, are linked to its geographical position at the crossroads between Europe and Asia. Eurasianism ranges from the imperial and aggressive to various attempts at synthesizing the traditional antipodes of Westernizers and Slavophiles into a kind of Third Way.[43]

Eurasianist thinkers of all stripes are fond of employing the language of traditional geopolitics, particularly the theories of Sir Halford Mackinder, who spoke of Eurasia as the world's "Heartland" and the "pivot of history," the control of which would give a country the resources and transportation routes to exercise global dominance.[44] The anti-American strain in much Eurasianist writing also receives a boost from the attention given to traditional geopolitical principles in much American foreign policy writing. Russian strategists of a Eurasianist bent frequently cite former U.S. national security adviser Zbigniew Brzezinski, who has referred to the post–Cold War world as a "grand chessboard," in order to justify their own aggressive impulses.[45]

Extreme Eurasianism (sometimes termed Neo-Eurasianism), often associated with the ideologist Aleksandr Dugin, is a bizarre, occasionally paranoid philosophy that bears more than a whiff of Nazism.[46] This outlook also has roots in a variety of Western European antiliberal movements, especially the Franco-Belgian *Nouvelle Droite* (or New Right, a group that encompasses the French National Front of Jean-Marie Le Pen and the Flemish nationalist *Vlaams Belang*) and postwar West German conservatism, as well as a variety of rightist philosophies that emerged among the White Russian émigrés of the 1920s and 1930s.[47] Eurasianism in contemporary Russia is in many ways a recipe for the reconstruction of a state looking very much like the USSR, both in terms of frontiers and in terms of its authoritarian political system, which is allegedly the only appropriate one for Eurasia's unique civilization.

At the same time, by virtue of its expansive geographic vision, Eurasianism for the most part rejects the narrow racial focus of groups like the DPNI. Its proponents advocate a statist version of Russian patriotism in which adherence to their ideas of a great Russian Empire transcend ethnic boundaries. In this essentially Hegelian worldview, the state is the embodiment of the people's characteristics and the focal point of the people's loyalties. Because the Russian state encompasses a wide array of racial, ethnic, and religious groups, most Eurasianists hold that all groups sharing a common Eurasian history and identity are part of the larger Eurasian "superethnos," which is more expansive than the DPNI's Russian nation (*russkii narod*). Consequently, Eurasianists see the ethnically based Russian nationalism of the DPNI as a danger to Russia's coherence as a civilization and to its role as a force for integrating the Eurasian landmass. Dugin and others have been sharply critical of the nationalists' role in precipitating violence against other Eurasian peoples, especially the Caucasians, who have become the focal point for the DPNI's campaign against illegal immigrants.[48]

This focus on the Russian state as a force for integrating various ethnicities into a common civilization front does not mean that the Eurasianists are committed to the idea of ethnic or racial tolerance per se. While accepting that the indigenous peoples of Eurasia (Slavs as well as the various Turkic and Finnic inhabitants of central Russia, Siberia, and Central Asia) are constituent parts of a Eurasian "super-ethnos," Dugin and his ilk see a large gap between native Eurasians and the peoples of the West, particularly the Jews, who supposedly are compelled by biological and cultural factors to oppose the Eurasians' communalistic values. Extreme Eurasianism thus combines aspects of Nazi-style biological racism and anti-Semitism with a kind of geographic and cultural determinism.

In terms of foreign policy, the more extreme version of Eurasianism essentially sees the West as a direct geopolitical competitor to Russia, much as it was during the days of the Cold War. Adherents of Eurasianism urge Russia to act as the nucleus for a new bloc of states able to stand up to what Col.-Gen. Leonid Ivashov, one of its most outspoken publicists, termed the global "military dictatorship of the United States."[49] The competition between Russia and the West is at times cast in crude racist terms, as in the writings of the philosopher and historian Lev Gumilev, who, along with Pyotr Savitsky and others, was responsible for adapting Eurasianist ideals that originated with the 1920s White émigrés to the circumstances of the disintegrating USSR of the 1980s. Gumilev (son of the famous Acmeist poets Anna Akhmatova and Nikolai Gumilev, who was executed by the Cheka in 1921) charged that the Soviet Union failed because it was a bastardized version of Russian statehood that incorporated the foreign ideology of Marxism and fell under the sway of Jewish leaders who were alien to the Russian national psyche.[50]

The most important Eurasianist thinker is Aleksandr Dugin, author of *Foundations of Geopolitics* (*Osnovy geopolitiki*), which may be the most widely read theoretical work on strategy and foreign policy in post-Communist Russia. Dugin is also a frequent commentator in the Russian media on politics and foreign policy.[51] His underlying message is the need for Russia to re-emerge as a great empire, dominating the Eurasian space and challenging the United States and the West more generally for world supremacy. Dugin rejects the historic and cultural legitimacy of all the post-Soviet states except Russia itself and Armenia (a Christian state with a history stretching back thousands of years).

As the pivot between East and West, a restored Russian Empire must, according to Dugin, act as the central component of a broad alliance stretching from Western Europe to Japan. In Dugin's view, constructing a Eurasian empire of this sort requires the reabsorption of states like Ukraine and Kazakhstan into a new Russia that has recommitted itself to the supremacy of the collective over the individual and to the leading role of the Orthodox Church. The emphasis on winning over Europe for an anti-U.S. coalition (a policy Moscow briefly attempted during the period leading to the U.S. invasion of Iraq in 2003) rather than seeing the West as a cohesive bloc is another distinguishing feature of the Eurasianist approach. Such an alliance of European and Asian states is necessary in order to isolate the U.S. Stripped of its connections to Europe and to its major ally in the Far East, the United States' geopolitical position would thus be fatally undermined. As the nerve center for an all-out assault on U.S. global dominance, Dugin even mentions pulling Latin America from under U.S. influence and fomenting unrest within the United States on the basis of racial and economic discontent.[52]

These geopolitical reveries would be little more than armchair philosophizing if not for the close connections Dugin, and the Eurasian movement more generally, has developed with key figures in the Russian national security bureaucracy. As John B. Dunlop has shown, leading military figures, including Lt.-General Nikolai Klokotov of the General Staff Academy as well as Ivashov, formerly of the Defense Ministry's International Department, participated in the drafting of *Foundations of Geopolitics*, which thus reflects at least in part the thinking of the Russian high command about the nature of the post–Cold War world. Dugin himself served as a consultant to former federation council speaker Gennady Seleznev and, more importantly, managed to forge links between his Eurasianist movement and the FSB. Through contacts with the official ideologist Gleb Pavlovsky and former defense minister Col.-Gen. Igor Rodionov, Dugin also gained access to the inner circle of Putin's Kremlin. As a result of these connections, Dugin played a central role in drafting the 2000 National Security Concept. Dugin's International Eurasian Movement (*Mezhdunarodnoe evraziiskoe dvizhenie*, or MED), meanwhile, is funded in part by the Russian Presidential Administration as well as the Moscow Patriarchate and the Central Spiritual Administration for Russian Muslims.[53] Adherents of the Eurasianist philosophy continue to hold influential positions in the bureaucracy as well as inside the Kremlin itself (examples include Pavlovsky and Putin's security adviser Igor Sechin, who became first deputy prime minister under Medvedev).[54]

Among the onetime members of the MED's supreme council are former culture minister Aleksandr Sokolov, Federation Council First Deputy Speaker Aleksandr Torshin, and the chairman of the Federation Council's International Affairs Committee Mikhail Margelov.[55] Eurasianist commentators are also well represented in the press and on television, a fact that has given their ideas a certain level of respectability.[56] Dugin was also a source of influence with former foreign minister Primakov, whose approach to foreign policy rhetoric at times seemed to borrow from the Eurasianists.

Centrism: Between Eurasia and the West

A combination of the Eurasianists' emphasis on Russia's leading role in the former Soviet space with a desire for productive, nonconfrontational relations with the West is the foundation for the centrist tendency in Russian geopolitical thought and practice. While paying significant attention to the territory of the former USSR, the centrists reject some of the mistier notions of Russia's special identity and civilization affinities with the peoples of Eurasia.[57] Instead, the centrists have a more traditional conception of Russia's national interests, reject confrontation with the West for its own sake, and merely suggest that Russia pursue a balanced foreign policy that pays as much attention to its interests and obligations in the East as it does to those in the West. In the words of a leading sinologist at the Foreign Ministry's Moscow State Institute for International Relations:

> Russians are Europeans who were carried to and left in Asia by history and fate. So conclusions should be made[,] but not the conclusions after exotic Eurasian theories about Asian essence of Russians. It is necessary to understand that Russia's future depends a lot on the relations with Asian neighbors and on Russia's approach to them.[58]

Other thinkers with good connections to the Putin-Medvedev leadership are also supporters of this approach—with Russia as the central pillar of a bloc of states encompassing more or less the frontiers of the Soviet Union, but not necessarily in direct opposition to the United States and Europe. Such thinkers tend to hold that, while productive relations with the West are essential for Russia's future (particularly her economic future), Moscow cannot neglect the fact that its hinterland is in Asia. Consequently, Russian foreign policy must be active in Asia as well as in Europe, Moscow has a special responsibility for the territory of the CIS, and Russia should never put itself in a position where it must choose between the West and its neighbors to the south and east. Moscow's work on the Iranian nuclear program and decision to sell high-tech weapons to China over Western objections are manifestations of this multivectoral approach to foreign policy. Other centrists—especially those associated at one time with the Yabloko Party—tilt more toward the West, arguing that while Russia cannot escape its responsibility for upholding order in Eurasia, its long-term interest is in a strategic rapprochement with the liberal Western powers.

In an analysis of Russia's foreign policy options following the September 11 attacks and the U.S. decision to invade Iraq, the centrist Council on Foreign and Defense Policy (*Sovet vneshnei i oboronoi politiki*, SVOP) warned against full-scale security integration with the Western powers, a course that would be rejected by a wide range of Russian politicians and would result in Russia's playing a subordinate role to the economically more powerful states of the United States and the European Union. A more realistic alternative, the council argued, was for Russia to press for the formation of a "security alliance of the leading powers" that would continue to respect the distinct interests of each partner.[59] Such a course, which would allow Russia to play an independent role apart from the West, would be more in keeping with the country's unique Eurasian identity. As SVOP head Sergei Karaganov wrote in 1997:

> Russia is returning [to] its historic, Janus-like position—looking east and west simultaneously. Neither Asian, nor European, this middle ground is not mere compromise, it is the authentic Russia.[60]

Despite his belief in Russia's Janus-like identity, Karaganov has also supported improved relations between Russia and the West. In the aftermath of September 11, he called for full-scale cooperation with the West against the common threat of Islamic terrorism.[61] Today, the SVOP continues to favor close relations between Russia and the U.S., even more so than with the EU.[62] This relationship, however, must be a partnership of equals, where the U.S. will have to respect the rights of the other Great Powers, which, in the Russian case, means allowing Moscow to seek further political and economic integration with the other states of the CIS and pursuing its own path of political development.[63]

Among the centrists are other thinkers who emphasize the overall importance of the United States and the West generally, even while accepting that Russia must continue to play the leading role in the former Soviet space. A good example of this phenomenon is Vladimir Lukin, one of the founders of the Yabloko Party (whose name, meaning "apple," was derived from its three founders' surnames—Grigory Yavlinsky, Yury Boldyrev, and Lukin— hence YABL-oko), former ambassador to Washington, deputy speaker of the Duma, and Russia's human rights ombudsman. Lukin, a committed democrat for whom good relations with the United States are one of the core principles of Russian security, is nonetheless wary about the notion that Russia is essentially a Western country. Shortly after the fall of the Soviet Union, during the high point of Kozyrev's strategy of pursuing Russia's integration with the West, Lukin warned that it was a mistake to ignore Russia's unique identity as a civilization, as he argued many well-meaning Western politicians and academics had done.[64]

Any attempts to force Russia solely into either Asia or Europe are ultimately futile and dangerous. Not only would they cause a serious geopolitical imbalance, but they would also undermine the historically established social and political equilibrium within Russia itself.[65]

Following the calamity of September 11, Lukin came to increasingly emphasize the importance of close ties between Russia and the major Western powers. Yet he also insisted that rapprochement take place in such a way as to ensure the preservation of Russia's unique attributes as a society. Russia should adopt, Lukin argued, those fundamental European values, such as respect for human rights, that are not inimical to its own unique identity and should in time seek to join European structures on a fully equal basis while also seeking close cooperation with the United States. The key to the success of such a strategy, according to Lukin, was for Russia's Western partners to recognize that Russia is in many ways unique. "I am pro-Europe and think Russia should be part of Europe," Lukin wrote, "but not in the sense that Russia should cease being Russia."[66]

This approach also has advocates among the "patriotic" opposition, including now the Communist Party of the Russian Federation (KPRF) and Vladimir Zhirinovsky's Liberal Democratic Party of Russia (LDPR). To be sure, the KPRF and the LDPR both advocated a much more aggressive, confrontational approach to the West in the early 1990s. However, for opposite reasons—in the Communist case to appeal to a broader range of voters, and for the LDPR, to take advantage of the Kremlin's patronage—these groups moved toward a less confrontational position during the Putin administration. Adopting a more forward policy in the CIS is portrayed as a defensive maneuver, a way to protect Russia and its allies against foreign encroachment, rather than as a step toward sparking a confrontation with the West. KPRF chairman Gennady Zyuganov wrote in 2006:

> Russia is the heir to the Russian Empire and the Soviet Union. The Belovezha Accords [dissolving the USSR in December 1991] were illegal and criminal. Russia must strive intently but peaceably to overturn them, in full accordance with international law and in full agreement with those former republics and territories of the USSR ready for the restoration of a fraternal union with Russia in the framework of a unified statehood.[67]

Understanding the depth and breadth of such sentiment is one key to grasping why Russia has been unable and unwilling to bring itself fully into the Western camp as men like Kozyrev advocated, and why Russia after Putin will likely continue to think of itself as a separate piece of the international order.

It is Primakov who, among the Yeltsin-era elite, is most connected with the transition to a more centrist foreign policy. His appointment was widely hailed inside Russia as ending the quixotic experiment with joining the West that Kozyrev had undertaken. He promised that on his watch Russia would pay more attention to its neighbors, which he charged Kozyrev with neglecting in favor of his vain pursuit of integration with the West. For his conviction that Russia "has been and remains a Great Power" and his renewed focus on the CIS states, Primakov was lauded at home for restoring Russian dignity and building consensus around his foreign policy goals.[68]

In the West, Primakov was seen initially as an inveterate Eurasianist whose background in the intelligence services and good relations with leaders like Saddam Hussein and Fidel Castro portended a new era of confrontation with the United States. In practice, however, Primakov's interest in building consensus at home meant that his policy initiatives were largely in favor of preserving the status quo and preventing any further slippage in Russia's weight in international affairs—which at times required standing up to the United States—especially over Kosovo. Despite the hostility with which his appointment was greeted in the West, Primakov was always careful to point out that while he (and Russia) would not accept a subservient role, he did not share the strident anti-Westernism associated with the Soviet-era security establishment or the extreme Eurasianists.[69] Primakov's enthusiastic support for Putin's own foreign policy course was also indicative of the distance between the former foreign minister and the ideologues of extreme Eurasianism.[70]

Atlanticism

Even after the fall of Kozyrev and the installation of a new, more state-centric and more Eurasianist foreign policy under Primakov, the influence of pro-Western sentiment remained substantial. This sentiment, associated largely with the now defunct Union of Right Forces (*Soyuz Pravykh Sil*, or SPS) Party, some economic officials in Putin's government, and a variety of academic specialists, emphasizes above all Russia's need to cooperate with the highly developed countries of the U.S. and Europe as part of an overall strategy of transforming Russia itself into a liberal democratic state and member of the "democratic world community."[71] For the most part, support for integration with the Western world and its institutions is accompanied by support for liberal—that is, democratic and market-oriented—domestic priorities. The connection, of course, lies in the fact that supporters of an Atlanticist foreign policy believe that only adherence to international norms will allow Russia to achieve integration with Western institutions. In this way, the Atlanticists emphasize the similarities rather than the differences between the United States and Europe and believe Russia should cooperate with both more or less equally.

A number of officials with liberal leanings remained in prominent positions under Putin—especially in positions related to economic policy.[72] Such Yeltsin-era heavyweights as Anatoly Chubais (who oversaw the crash privatization of state industry in the early 1990s before heading the Unified Energy Systems electricity monopoly) remained important during the Putin era. Medvedev himself made his name as a prominent economic liberal. His frequent calls during his transition to the presidency for Russia to become a rule-of-law state and to overcome its culture of "legal nihilism" grew out of an understanding that the country would be unable to achieve its full economic, and hence geopolitical, potential as long as investors remained distrustful of Russian institutions.[73]

To be sure, the position of economic liberals has never been secure. Putin's former economic adviser Andrei Illarionov, one of the most consistent advocates of economic openness and integration, resigned in protest in late 2005 against what he saw as the curtailing of economic freedoms and the emergence of what he termed a "corporate state" in Putin's Russia.[74] Former economics minister German Gref, who played the lead role in Russia's negotiations to join the WTO, saw his years of handiwork at least put on hold when Moscow withdrew from the negotiations during the war in Georgia.

Nonetheless, liberal and Atlanticist ideas remain well represented among the intellectual elite in Russia. Intellectual liberalism in its Russian context is above all defined by its focus on the economic component of foreign policy, its emphasis on good relations with the West (including in some cases support for Russia truly becoming a Western country with all that implies), and support for democratization at home. These priorities are fairly consistent throughout the liberal camp, despite the quite deep divisions that exist among different liberal thinkers and movements.[75] Chubais, for example, advocated an assertive foreign policy on liberal lines, with a democratic Russia leading a campaign to unite the world's democracies into a bloc that would be responsible for upholding order and promoting liberal values worldwide.[76] Dmitri Trenin of the Carnegie Moscow Center, meanwhile, favors a Russia that is closely associated with Europe, ultimately joining European institutions on a fully equal basis. What unites them is a belief that the era of geo-economics has replaced the era of geopolitics, that Russia is historically and culturally a European power, and that political democratization at home is necessary both for its own sake and as a means of tying Russia's fate to the most advanced states of the West.

In contrast with even the softer Eurasianists who would prefer to move closer to Europe while keeping a respectful distance from the U.S., Atlanticist thinkers tend to focus on both the United States and the European Union (or at least Western Europe) as an essentially unified West that Russia must, eventually, join. In the Atlanticist narrative, Russia has little choice but to pursue integration with the network of institutions that collectively make up "Europe" (even if never formally joining the EU or NATO), on the basis of historical affinities as well as the growing economic linkages between Russia and the EU. Meanwhile, Atlanticists look toward the United States, a country that still exists very much within history, as a strategic partner and a model for the role that a restored Russia can play in the world.

Russia's Atlanticist foreign policy thinkers are principally associated with a handful of Moscow-based research institutes and think tanks, including the Carnegie Moscow Center, the Gorbachev Fund, the Institute of World Economics and International Relations (*Institut Mirovoi Ekonomiki i Mezhdunarodnykh Otnoshenii*, IMEMO), and the Institute of the United States of America and Canada (*Institut SShA i Kanady*), both at the Russian Academy of Sciences. Political figures, many once associated with SPS (Boris Nemtsov, Irina Khakamada), and Yeltsin-era officials such as former acting prime minister Gaidar and former prime minister Sergei Kirienko are also prominent members of the Atlanticist camp. Gaidar in particular has emphasized the need for Russia to moderate its international ambitions on economic grounds, arguing presciently that the record oil prices that fueled Putin's assertive foreign policy would not last.[77] A handful of newspapers, particularly those focusing on business and finance such as *Kommersant*, *Tochka.ru*, and to a lesser degree *Nezavisimaya Gazeta*, have also promoted Russia's deepening involvement in the Euro-Atlantic world.

In terms of foreign policy, probably the most visible and trenchant advocate of the liberal tendency has been Dmitri Trenin. In particular, Trenin—a former career military intelligence officer—has set out to debunk the notion of Russia's Eurasian destiny. He argues that Russia is not only historically and culturally part of Europe but that, as a medium-sized power with a weak economy and deep social problems, Russia's future survival depends on its ability to make the transition to a posthistorical world where Mackinder's precepts about controlling the Heartland have been replaced by a commitment to economic opportunity, growth, and development.

In the twenty-first century, Trenin, Gaidar, and other liberal thinkers continue to base their argument for Russia's integration with the West on the historical and cultural linkage between Russia and Europe—a formulation Putin has often repeated with his references to Russia's "European choice." Trenin has made the case that Russia's survival as a pillar of the international system depends on its willingness to abandon its superpower fantasies and link its fate with that of the liberal democratic West. Directly challenging Primakov, Trenin argues that the post-1945 examples of Germany and Japan are the best analogy for the strategy that Russia of the twenty-first century must pursue, trading foreign policy autonomy for integration in a Western-led system of collective security.

Trenin was also a sharp critic of the Putin government's approach to foreign policy. He saw Moscow's intervention in the Ukrainian and Georgian colored revolutions as signaling an end to Russia's second, post–September 11 honeymoon with the West. By alienating its potential partners, Moscow found itself even more isolated from both an increasingly integrated West and the more dynamic economies and societies of Asia. Trenin charged that, with its attempts to bring the recalcitrant regimes in Kyiv and Tbilisi to heel, Russia had abandoned its course toward a West in which it was condemned to playing a secondary role (being "Pluto in the Western solar system") in favor of constructing an entirely new geopolitical solar system within the space of the former Soviet Union—in other words, of following a policy of rank Eurasianism that it was demonstrably too weak to effect. Of course, Putin's Kremlin in many ways proved a disappointment to Eurasianists as well, and Trenin more recently decried what he sees as the elite's myopic pursuit of its own self-interest, which puts the pursuit of profits above all else, including considerations of ideology or any real thought about the nature of the international system.[78]

KREMLIN, INC.

While the transition period between the Putin and Medvedev presidencies opened more space for public debate of Russia's foreign policy priorities, the ability of any faction to impose its will in the end may be sharply limited by what may prove to be Putin's most lasting legacy—the state's growing hold on the economy, especially in the energy sector.[79] The cross-fertilization between the Kremlin's inner circle and the boards of major companies such as Gazprom, Rosneft, and Transneft has already given a new class of officials and managers an extraordinary degree of influence. The success of these bureaucratic clans would ultimately mean further entrenching a foreign policy that seeks to maximize profits for particular individuals and state-owned companies at the expense of broader political and ideological goals, a process already visible in Moscow's energy diplomacy and in the so-called war of the *siloviki* that broke out among competing factions in the security services during the last year of Putin's presidency.[80]

Wealth and power were linked under Yeltsin as well, as men like Boris Berezovsky and Vladimir Gusinsky used their riches to buy political access. Under Putin, members of the bureaucratic elite like Sechin, presidential administration economic adviser Arkady Dvorkovich, Minister of Industry Viktor Khristenko, and Medvedev himself were installed by the Kremlin on the boards of major state-owned enterprises such as Gazprom (Medvedev and German Gref), Rosneft (Sechin), and Transneft (Khristenko, Dvorkovich).[81] Moreover, many of the individuals placed by Putin's Kremlin in key positions in the economy were *siloviki*, and hence also have extensive ties to the security services, which became something of a state within a state under Putin. The Kremlin portrays the presence of state officials on the boards of corporations such as Gazprom as ensuring that Russia's largest corporations behave in the public interest, yet their presence also exacerbates the problem of corruption.[82] Meanwhile, Russia's private sector saw its power and access to leading officials diminish during the Putin years, with the Yukos case being only the most dramatic example of business's reduced influence.[83]

The resulting nexus between wealth and power—a situation some analysts have termed "Kremlin, Inc."—means that many well-connected individuals have their own very lucrative fiefdoms to protect. If, to paraphrase Calvin Coolidge, the business of Russia is business, then the philosophical and ideological argument about the relative importance of the West and Eurasia in Russian foreign policy matters much less than does ensuring that Russia's oil and gas reserves continue to bring the state and its servitors as much revenue as possible.[84]

Yet the existence of Kremlin, Inc., does have foreign policy implications, especially insofar as the Kremlin's model for economic development centers on the creation of a handful of national champions in industries such as shipbuilding, nanotechnology, and other sectors—not to mention energy—at the expense of private business. This emphasis on national champions downplays the importance of global economic trends in favor of an essentially autarkic development plan. If Russia chooses this path, its ability to pursue economic integration, for example, through the WTO, will be compromised, with consequences for the aspiration to make Russia a responsible stakeholder in an increasingly globalized world.

The essentially mercantilist approach to foreign policy favored by Kremlin, Inc. was evident in the parallel crises over Russian gas supplies to Ukraine and Belarus that broke out in 2006 and 2007, respectively. In both cases, seeking higher prices for Russian energy came into direct conflict with important Russian foreign policy objectives. In 2006, the dispute with Ukraine ultimately disrupted Russian gas deliveries to the EU (since Ukraine began siphoning gas earmarked for the EU to make up for the shortfall), cast serious doubt on Moscow's reliability as a supplier, and drew stinging rebukes from the West for appearing designed to undermine Ukraine's sovereignty.[85] While the Kremlin was happy to turn the screws on the recalcitrant Ukrainian regime, pressure from Gazprom contributed to the decision to cut deliveries even as it became clear that doing so would drag the EU into the dispute. Gazprom and its highly placed directors certainly profited from the higher prices squeezed out of Ukraine and Belarus as well as the example they set of vigorous action to collect on unpaid debts, but the benefits to Russia as a whole seem more questionable since the crisis sped up European attempts to diversify and reduce its dependence on Russia.

The same is true with regard to Russia's participation in building the Iranian nuclear reactor at Bushehr. The military-industrial complex, which is closely tied to the Ministry of Atomic Energy, stands to reap hundreds of millions of dollars in profits from the Bushehr deal alone (not to mention the free publicity that comes with it). Yet the diplomatic cost to Russia is potentially high if Iran obtains a nuclear weapons capacity that even the Kremlin sees as dangerous.[86] On the whole, the Russian model of state capitalism creates perverse incentives for managers and has the potential to undermine the country's long-term growth by crowding out private investment and thwarting attempts to create a more transparent legal order, despite Putin's and particularly Medvedev's call for greater legality.[87] By throwing up barriers to economic integration, this model also undermines the interdependent relationships central to a globalized world economy. The more Russia remains outside the increasingly global world order, the smaller its stake in the preservation of the status quo.

THE KREMLIN UNDER PUTIN AND MEDVEDEV

As for Russia's second and third presidents themselves, gauging the influence of different ideologies is difficult. Putin was a bureaucrat and (to a limited extent) a politician, while Medvedev was a lawyer by training; neither is an ideologue as such. The Kremlin has also been, especially since 2004 or so, exceptionally closed and difficult to penetrate. In practical terms, the Putin government gave something to members of each ideological camp—the Russian nationalists got an assault on illegal migrants, especially Georgians, and increased rhetorical concern for ethnic Russians in the Baltics and Central Asia; the Eurasianists got increased military spending and a concerted campaign to bring Ukraine and Georgia back into the Russian orbit following their colored revolutions; and the liberals got an apparent agreement on Russian membership in the World Trade Organization and a strategic partnership with the United States following September 11, 2001. Overall, the Putin government's approach to foreign policy focused on enhancing Russia's power and influence (both within Eurasia and globally) while preserving productive working relations with the United States and Europe.

To get a sense of the Putin-Medvedev team's "official" ideology, it is also helpful to look briefly at the pronouncements of the man often referred to as the Kremlin's ideologist, Vladislav Surkov. Surkov was the godfather of the late Putin-era discussion about Russia's program of becoming a "sovereign democracy [*suverennaya demokratiya*]," and while his relationship with

Medvedev is complicated, Surkov nonetheless held onto his post under Putin's successor.[88] What "sovereign democracy" means in practice is not always clear, but the basic outlines include the re-establishment of the state's role in the economy with the ultimate aim of freeing Russia from its economic dependence on the West. In other words, despite the centripetal force of globalization, Russia has to maintain its unique identity and place its national interest above all other concerns.

According to Surkov, in order for Russia to be a truly sovereign state, capable of standing up for its own interest in the world, it cannot be under the influence of foreign companies, foreign investors, or foreign NGOs—and its native elite has to come to regard itself as intrinsically Russian. As part of this process, Russia must regain control over its most valuable strategic resources, namely its oil and gas reserves, from foreign companies that acquired stakes in them for a song when Russia was desperate for foreign cash in the mid-1990s. Yukos, whose exiled co-chairman Leonid Nevzlin was once Surkov's boss at Bank Menatep, played a major role in bringing Western capital, and hence Western control, into the Russian energy sector through its partnership agreements with foreign oil majors. This cosmopolitan attitude toward Russia's oil and gas, as much as Yukos's spotty tax records, appears to have been an important consideration in the Kremlin's decision to break up the company.[89]

The problem with the West, from Surkov's point of view, is not that it is incorrigibly hostile to Russian interests, but that its interests are not Russia's (in this view, Surkov has much in common with some of the more moderate Eurasianists). True, some thinkers and leaders in the West will never accept a powerful, sovereign Russia out of sheer hatred, but the more fundamental problem is that for the time being, Russia depends on its exports of oil and gas to undergird its national power. As a supplier of energy, Russia's interests differ fundamentally from those of the West, which is a consumer of Russian oil and gas.

For all his skepticism of Western intentions, Surkov is not a Eurasianist or an inveterate opponent of cooperation with the West. Like Putin himself, Surkov emphasizes Russia's membership in European civilization, a reality that serves to constrain the geopolitical possibilities available to any Russian leader. Russia may have fallen behind the rest of Europe over the course of several centuries, but on the most fundamental level, Russia is following the European path of development, and will—eventually—arrive at the same historical moment as the rest of the continent. To do so, it must consciously take advantage of Europe's own intellectual resources and traditions.

As Surkov told the Business Russia forum:

> It would be good to flee to Europe, but they will not receive us there, [sic] Russia is a European civilization. It is a badly illuminated remote area of

Europe but not Europe yet. In this regard, we are inseparably tied with Europe and must be friends with it. They are not enemies. They are simply competitors. So, it is more insulting that we are not enemies. An enemy situation is where one can be killed in a war as a hero if there is conflict. There is something heroic and beautiful in it. And to lose in a competitive struggle means to be a loser. And this is doubly insulting, I think.[90]

Surkov directly criticized the Eurasianists' assumption that the Russian Federation as it exists in the early twenty-first century is capable of demanding complete equality with the most powerful states of the world, especially the United States.[91] In this regard, Surkov's notion of sovereignty is not the same as that of the Eurasianists. Eurasianist thinkers like Dugin, who have supported the idea of a foreign policy that emphasizes Russia as a sovereign power, focus on sovereignty as the factor necessary for balancing against the U.S. For Surkov and his supporters in the Kremlin, however, sovereignty is more about allowing the Kremlin to have freedom of action—supporting or opposing Washington as Russian national interest dictates without allowing international institutions or norms to act as constraints.

For Surkov, Western notions of multilateralism and political integration are modish ideas whose worth has not yet been proven. For Russia to sacrifice its sovereign statehood to such fads would be little better than the Kremlin's previous mistake of "chasing Karl Marx's specters [*sledit za karlmarksovymi prizrakami*]."[92] Surkov's fundamental argument is that, given Russia's present state of economic, educational, and political development, it is not realistic to think of it in the same terms as the members of the European Union, much less the United States.

Ideology aside, the naked pursuit of profit certainly cannot be dismissed as a factor motivating Russian foreign policy either. Nonetheless, ideas about the nature of the world continue to matter in a fundamental way. Given the influence of Eurasianist thinking in many parts of the Russian national security bureaucracy (including among *siloviki* such as Sechin) and the general consensus of *derzhavnost'* and *gosudarstvennost'*, actual policy often seems to follow Eurasianist prescriptions, especially within the borders of the CIS.

The war in Georgia in particular exposed the limits of the corporatist de-ideologizing of foreign policy. The economic impact of the war was severe, with the Russian stock market getting pummeled by investors suddenly worried that Russia had become a force for regional instability. Between May and September 2008, Russia's benchmark RTS index lost over 46 percent of its value, a decline of $700 billion on paper, and following the war trading had to be shut down for several days in mid-September to prevent a complete collapse.[93] The rest of 2008 was no better.

To be sure, Russia could stand to benefit economically in the long run if the instability in the South Caucasus ends up shelving Western plans for an energy corridor bypassing Russia. By dramatically heightening the perception of political and economic risk, the war and its aftermath greatly complicated this strategy. Still, if Russian foreign policy were only about making money, the war would never have happened or would have been completely wound down as soon as the financial consequences for the country and its elite became clear (given the concentration of wealth in Russia and lack of widespread investment in securities, the brunt of the initial economic plunge fell on members of the elite, including a number of oligarchs with close Kremlin connections, most notably metals magnate Oleg Deripaska, recipient of a massive government bailout). The war seemed much more about Russia's long-standing interest in controlling a sphere of influence around its borders and sending a message to the Western powers about its renewed capabilities. Indeed, it was Eurasianists in the military and security services, not Kremlin-connected magnates, who appeared to be the driving force behind the war.

At the same time, the relatively nonconfrontational approach Putin typically tried to adopt with regard to the United States is indicative of the fact that the broader influence of Eurasianists is limited. The decision to cooperate with the United States in Afghanistan in the aftermath of September 11 was made by Putin personally, over the opposition of almost all his advisers.[94] Medvedev has never given any indication of a strong affinity for the Eurasianists, despite his seemingly contradictory behavior during the Georgian war. Rhetorically at least, Medvedev took up Putin's definition of Russia as a fundamentally Western country, telling an audience in Berlin in June 2008 that "the end of the Cold War created conditions for building truly equal cooperation among Russia, the European Union, and North America as three branches of European civilization."[95] Even Medvedev's controversial proposal for a pan-European collective security organization was at least predicated on the notion of Russia belonging fundamentally inside Europe.

Putin gave contradictory utterances about Russia's location in the West/ Europe or Eurasia (of course, the former Russian president's ability to tailor the message to the audience was hardly limited to this issue).[96] In 2000 at the Asia Pacific Economic Cooperation group (APEC) summit in Brunei, Putin declared, "Russia always felt itself a Eurasian country."[97] In his 2005 address to the Federal Assembly, he simultaneously spoke of Russia's "civilizing mission on the Eurasian continent" and his conviction that Russia "was, is, and always will be a leading European nation."[98]

On other and more frequent occasions, Putin made reference to Russia's European identity. In his 2003 annual address, Putin said that integration with Europe "is our historical choice."[99] In his first meeting with U.S. secretary of state Madeleine Albright (two years before September 11, 2001), Putin "categorically insisted" that Russia was part of the West.[100] Putin repeated this conviction that, in the long run at least, Russia's destiny will converge with Europe's in an article he penned for the European press marking the fiftieth anniversary of the Treaty of Rome in March 2007. Speaking this time to a European audience, Putin wrote that "the full unity of our continent can never be achieved until Russia, as the largest European state, becomes an integral part of the European process."[101] Sergei Ivanov, Putin's closest national security adviser for most of his term, likewise believed, "We are Europeans and not Asians. . . . We are eastern Europeans, that's the right way to describe it." On the other hand, Ivanov does adopt some of the Eurasianists' rhetoric about the U.S. posing a threat to Russia's interests in Eurasia.[102]

Russia's government apparatus appears fairly conscious of its connection to both the Eurasian and liberal camps in its foreign policy. The Foreign Ministry's 2007 foreign policy review thus adopts the Eurasianists' focus on Russia as a bridge between East and West while emphasizing the overall centrality of Europe and the United States in Russia's global strategy. As one of its central recommendations, the report calls for a new initiative to promote an "inter-civilizational dialogue," with Russia playing a central role by virtue of its pivotal position between Europe, the Islamic world, and Asia. It declares that "an objective multivectoral civilizational approach is becoming a key asset for our diplomacy."[103] At the same time, the report portrays such an intercivilizational dialogue as one way to counter the West's quest to add new members to its camp (e.g., through colored revolutions). The theme of Eurasia as a playing field where Russia and the West are vying to establish their influence is a strong undercurrent throughout the report, and indeed, the 2008 war in Georgia gave concrete form to that conception of the CIS.[104]

Putin also pursued a more active policy in Asia than his predecessors, and in doing so sought to emphasize the commonalities and shared interests between Russia and major Asian states like China, India, and Iran. Where Putin truly departed from the true Eurasianists is in his continued search for cooperation with the United States, even within the territory of Eurasia.[105] Moscow may have a range of common interests it wants to pursue in tandem with Beijing, Delhi, and Tehran, but Putin attempted (for the most part) not to allow these interests to come at the expense of good working relations with the U.S. Despite the heated rhetoric that the war in Georgia generated, Moscow remained officially committed to partnership with the Western powers—as long as they accepted Russia's claim to a sphere of influence that included Georgia.

Equally important, Putin largely followed the liberals' economic prescriptions (internationally—the Yukos affair is a different story), and his stated interest in raising Russians' standard of living through economic growth is somewhat at odds with the Eurasianists' emphasis on traditional "hard" measures of security and autarky. Indeed, Putin's emphasis on economic integration (e.g., joining the WTO, signing trade agreements with Europe) runs directly counter to the Eurasianists' call for regional consolidation within the CIS and rejection of the global capitalist order.[106] Putin's Kremlin largely pursued an Atlanticist, integrationist economic policy, even while trying to uphold the Eurasianists' preference for creating a zone of Russian geopolitical influence across the territory of the former USSR—and presiding over the expansion of state control over the commanding heights of Russia's own economy.[107]

Economic integration remains controversial, however. The establishment of national champions outside the energy sector and vacillation over meeting the conditions for WTO entry show the extent to which economic openness remains a subject of debate in Russian political circles.[108] Meanwhile, whatever their underlying intent, in practice the dismantling of Yukos and the establishment of a "state corporatist" model of industrial relations (with the state itself designating which representatives of business it will engage) have thrown up impediments to Russia's economic integration.[109]

Despite the Eurasianists' ability to tap into a deep-seated well of resentment over Russia's post–Cold War decline and the ubiquity of their ideas in official pronouncements like the National Security Concept, they have been less successful in translating their policy prescriptions into action. Putin's strategy for Eurasia was in any case only sporadically confrontational, and then primarily as a way of standing up for Russian interests against perceived U.S. challenges to the status quo (above all with the colored revolutions or NATO expansion).[110] Part of the problem is that much of what the Eurasianists recommend is either impossible or dangerous for Russia to adopt. Constructing an anti-American, counterhegemonic bloc akin to what used to be known as the Second World is almost certainly beyond the Kremlin's ability. Without an organizing ideology like Marxism-Leninism around which other malcontents can rally, a weakened Russia has little capacity to induce others to follow its lead.

Even if countries like China, India, and Iran were consistently lined up with Russia against the United States, the distribution of power within that grouping (both current and potential) would presumably give China, and perhaps India, a greater say in the bloc's direction than Russia.[111] Already, Russia's leaders have recognized that cooperation with China can be a Faustian bargain, especially in the vast Central Asian region that both Moscow and Beijing see as a natural sphere of influence. Moreover, as many elites came to realize during the Primakov interlude, baiting the West can be dangerous, given the existence of constituencies in both Russia and Western countries who would like to see a reversion to the bipolar confrontation of the Cold War.[112] Standing up to the West rhetorically is one thing, but actually seeking confrontation with it is another, altogether too dangerous contingency.

CONCLUSION

Foreign policy under Putin achieved a kind of balance between the prescriptions of the Eurasianists and the liberal Atlanticists. In spite of the difficulties in relations between Russia and the United States during Putin's second term in office, Russia never sought to follow the Eurasianists' prescriptions for constructing a counterhegemonic bloc. True, the Kremlin has attempted, at times quite forcefully, to limit the foreign policy autonomy of states like Ukraine and Georgia, but even within the CIS it has pursued a rather narrowly defined national interest rather than any expansive vision of imperial restoration, as evidenced by its refusal to continue providing gas subsidies to close ally Belarus or to seek the annexation of South Ossetia and Abkhazia. Empire is expensive, and the Soviet Union's need to subsidize its allies and dependents around the world proved to be a major strain on the state's budget. Putin's Russia moved aggressively in the opposite direction, reducing unproductive investment overseas and cutting Russia's foreign military presence in countries like Cuba and Vietnam. Eurasianism is a philosophy of integration—Russia as the centerpiece of a coalition of like-minded states that can, collectively, arrest the world's slide toward unipolarity. Putin's Russia, though, has largely eschewed political integration, not only with Western institutions but also with regional or ideological blocs within Eurasia, in favor of what the Polish statesman Roman Dmowski once termed "a healthy national egoism."[113] Eurasianism is an important undercurrent in Russian political life, but it is far from the major organizing principle of Russian foreign policy.

The August 2008 Georgian war was no doubt a Eurasianist venture, despite Moscow's unwillingness to annex South Ossetia or Abkhazia as the first step in a plan of imperial restoration. Its timing was also significant, coming less than three months after Medvedev took office and while the functioning of the Putin-Medvedev "tandemocracy" was still being worked out. Medvedev came into office in favor of improving the frigid relationship between Moscow and Tbilisi (albeit without outside interference).[114] When the war started following Georgian president Mikheil Saakashvili's ill-advised attempt to seize the breakaway regions by force, Medvedev initially spoke of the conflict's limited nature and Russia's willingness to abide by a cease-fire negotiated by French president Nicolas Sarkozy (Putin, in contrast, flew to the combat zone and made a show of directing the troops in the field). Over time, Medvedev's statements became more menacing, laced with the kind of rough language for which Putin was famous, referring, for instance, to Saakashvili as a "political corpse" the West should jettison.[115]

The strange evolution of Dmitry Medvedev's role during the crisis hints at the jockeying for influence taking place below the surface of Russian politics. It is doubtful the war was Medvedev's brainchild. Putin's own role in the crisis is no clearer, although his personal antipathy for Saakashvili was long known. Without a doubt, an aggressive streak of Eurasianism and nostalgia for the Soviet Union exists among many members of the Russian military and security services. It appears that these groups took advantage of Medvedev's uncertain grip on power (plus Saakashvili's poor judgment) to precipitate a crisis and leave the new Russian president little choice but to be the instrument of their aims.

Even if they succeeded in precipitating a war with Tbilisi, the Eurasianists' emphasis on the CIS as Russia's natural sphere of influence at the expense of relations with the West is somewhat unrealistic. Even after its chastening experience in Iraq, the United States remains the most powerful state in the world, while Europe is crucial for the Russian economy. Russia's ability to achieve its goals of economic modernization and geopolitical influence cannot be attained without the development of close relations with both.

Putin, with his focus on economic integration and geopolitical aloofness, seemed to be charting a course between a moderate version of Eurasianism and the more liberal Westernism of the early 1990s. Medvedev's focus on domestic policy and lack of a tie to the security services argue against his seeking a fundamental revision of Russia's strategic course. Of course, Putin himself was Boris Yeltsin's anointed successor, which did not stop him from turning against many of his erstwhile patrons in Yeltsin's inner circle. Still, apart from a few groups on the Eurasianist (or liberal) fringe, there are few voices in today's Russia calling for a fundamental revision of Putin's foreign policy course. Strengthening Russia as a major international player, pursuing a dominant position inside the CIS, and seeking pragmatic cooperation with the West is a course whose very expansiveness ensures its acceptance by the majority of influential political actors.

To be sure, controversies will arise. In the aftermath of the Georgian conflict, relations with the other CIS states, especially those still burdened by "frozen conflicts" left over from the collapse of the Soviet Union, will be a prime source of discord. Russia's leaders will need time to digest the lessons of Georgia—some will no doubt argue that the conflict showed the West's impotence in an area Russia considers its own backyard; others will argue that the economic consequences of the war have been too severe to risk a repetition.

Another likely bone of contention has to do with Russia's potential entry into the WTO. Putin's pursuit of economic integration as a means of enhancing Russia's geopolitical position and his support for economic reformers like Kasyanov, Illarionov, Dvorkovich, and Gref did not sit well with influential constituencies among the security services or the large state-owned natural resource monopolies. Of course, the fates of Kasyanov and Illarionov, who both broke very publicly with Putin over the Kremlin's inconsistent commitment to economic liberalism, show that balancing between the incompatible demands of the liberals and those committed to economic *gosudarstvennost'* is not always possible, even for as talented a juggler as Putin. Russia's entry into the WTO, which Gref nearly succeeded in negotiating in late 2006 and from which Moscow retreated in 2008 when it became clear other states would use the conflict in Georgia to block Russian entry anyway, may prove to be a bridge too far for the *siloviki* and their backers in the state-owned sectors of the economy. Openness and the adherence to internationally recognized trading rules have the potential to devastate the uncompetitive, inefficient state sector of Russia's economy. WTO rules might also threaten the Kremlin's ability to dominate strategic sectors and companies such as Gazprom.

Finally, relations with the United States will, as always, remain a prime subject for debate. For all his talk of Russia becoming a Great Power and looking out for its own interests internationally, Putin on the whole pursued cooperation with the U.S. to a significant degree. Whether offering a strategic partnership and the right to base troops in the CIS following September 11 or calmly swallowing American withdrawal from the ABM treaty, the Putin administration was about as pro-American as a Russian government could have afforded to be, given the political configuration prevailing in Moscow. As with the question of WTO ascension, the threat to this policy lies with the military and security services that Putin empowered. As in the conflict with Georgia, the non-*silovik* Medvedev will continue facing pressure to adopt a more confrontational approach. Putin was no Kozyrev, but his place in history may prove similar if important constituencies in the Russian elite come to feel that such cooperation with the U.S. was done at the expense of Russia's own national interests and without regard for Russia's Great Power role.

NOTES

1. Dmitri Trenin, "Russia: Back to the Future?" testimony to U.S. Senate Committee on Foreign Relations, 29 Jun 2006.

2. William Zimmerman, *The Russian People and Foreign Policy: Russian Elite and Mass Perspectives, 1993–2000* (Princeton, NJ: Princeton University Press, 2002), 1–3, 11–13. Zimmerman identifies elites as "those who controlled the instruments of coercion or persuasion, dominated key parts of the economy, had specialized knowledge, or occupied key formal political positions." Sergei A. Karaganov, "Rus-

sia's Elites," in *Damage Limitation or Crisis? Russia and the Outside World*, ed. Robert D. Blackwill and Sergei A. Karaganov (Washington, DC: Brassey's, 1994), 41–42. See also Harold Lasswell et al., *The Comparative Study of Elites* (Stanford, CA: Stanford University Press, 1952).

3. Under the reform scheme introduced by President Putin in 2004, members of the Federation Council are chosen by the heads of administration from each of Russia's eighty-seven juridical regions (*oblast, krai*, autonomous *okrug*, and autonomous *oblast* governors; republic presidents; and the mayors of Moscow and St. Petersburg). Most of these officials, in turn, are now appointed by the Kremlin.

4. In the December 2007 parliamentary elections, United Russia officially received 64.30 percent of votes cast, while among the opposition, only the Communists (11.57 percent), the Liberal Democrats (8.14 percent), and the Just Russia coalition (7.74 percent) surpassed the 7 percent threshold to receive seats in parliament. Foreign observers strongly criticized the conduct of the vote for depriving opposition parties of access to the media and opportunities to campaign. Official results are available at the website of the Central Election Commission of the Russian Federation, Svedenie o provodyashchikhsya vyborakh i referendumakh, http://www.vybory.izbirkom.ru/region/region/izbirkom?action = show&root = 1&tvd = 100100021960186&vrn = 100100021960181&region = 0&global = 1&sub_region = 0&prver = 0&pronetvd = null&vibid = 100100021960186&type = 242.

5. Karaganov, "Russia's Elites," 43; Bobo Lo, *Vladimir Putin and the Evolution of Russian Foreign Policy* (London: Royal Institute of International Affairs, 2003), 33–34. As Lo points out, MID's role is much more central at the working level, where it continues to maintain a high level of technical expertise, in contrast to the political level, where weak leadership has increasingly shunted MID aside as an incubator of new foreign policy ideas. The same is true of the Duma, which has largely lost its role as an initiator of policy but continues, in its Foreign Affairs Committee, to analyze international problems and Russia's response to them. The Putin-era Duma is not the rubber stamp that the old USSR Supreme Soviet was, but neither is it a real parliament with fully developed legislative powers. See B. Makarenko, "Rossiiskii politicheskii stroi: Opyt neoinstitutsional'nogo analiza," *Mirovaya ekonomika i mezhdunarodnye otnosheniya*, Feb 2007 (2): 32–42.

6. Andrei P. Tsygankov, *Russia's Foreign Policy: Change and Continuity in National Identity* (Lanham, MD: Rowman & Littlefield, 2006), 83.

7. Robert H. Donaldson and Joseph L. Nogee, *The Foreign Policy of Russia: Changing Systems, Enduring Interests*, 2nd ed. (Armonk, NY: M. E. Sharpe, 2002), 141–49. The Security Council's importance in coordinating foreign policy was at its apex during the First Chechen War, when it was headed by Yeltsin's close associate Oleg Lobov. As Donaldson and Nogee note, the formation of the Security Council in 1992 was widely perceived at the time as an attempt to rein in the overly Atlanticist tendencies of Kozyrev's Foreign Ministry.

8. Amina Azfal, "Russian Security Policy," *Strategic Studies*, Spr 2005, 25(1): 68. Under Yeltsin, the Security Council was subject to repeated turnover and was often ignored on key issues by Yeltsin and his administration. See "Report of the Russian Working Group," *U.S.-Russian Relations at the Turn of the Century* (Washington, DC: Carnegie Endowment for International Peace/Moscow: Council on Foreign and

Defense Policy, 2000), 59; Aleksandra Samarina et al., "Sovbezu khotyat vernut' deesposobnost'," *Nezavisimaya Gazeta*, 20 Oct 2004. The two Ivanovs are not related. The appointment of another technocrat, Vladimir Sobolev, to replace Igor Ivanov in July 2007 did nothing to upgrade the Security Council's role.

9. "Ot redaktsii: Gorizontal'nyi razmen," *Nezavisimaya Gazeta*, 6 Jun 2008.

10. Such is one official justification for the state's growing role in the strategic energy sector. See "News Conference of Presidential Aide Vladislav Surkov, Deputy Head of the Presidential Administration," press conference at the July 2006 G8 summit in St. Petersburg, http://en.g8russia.ru/news/20060704/1168817.html. Also see the discussion of Vladislav Surkov's worldview below.

11. See Lo, *Vladimir Putin*, 39–40.

12. Archie Brown, "Vladimir Putin's Leadership in Comparative Perspective," in *Russian Politics under Putin*, ed. Cameron Ross (Manchester: Manchester University Press, 2004), 11–12. Note that Brown is discussing the period of Putin's leadership after the crackdown on tycoons Vladimir Gusinsky, Boris Berezovsky, and Mikhail Khodorkovsky had already taken place. Under Putin, the faces of the oligarchs may have changed, but the oligarchy remains. It should be mentioned in this regard that the defunct political party Our Home Is Russia (*Nash Dom—Rossiya*), which was established by former premier Viktor Chernomyrdin in the mid-1990s as a party of power akin to today's United Russia, was derisively known in the press as Our Home Is Gazprom (*Nash Dom—Gazprom*) for the close links between its officials and leaders of the gas monopoly.

13. Vladimir Kvint, "The Internationalization of Russian Business," lecture at Kennan Institute, 16 Oct 2006, *JRL* #237. With the 2008 war in Georgia, Moscow announced it was ending (at least for a time) its attempts to join the WTO.

14. Yury Baluevsky, "Struktura i osnovnye soderzhanie novoi Voennoi doktriny Rossii," 20 Jan 2007, http://www.mil.ru/847/852/1153/1342/20922/index.shtml; "Sergei Ivanov: 'U Rossii net voenno-politicheskikh vragov,'" *Izvestiya*, 11 Feb 2007.

15. Dmitry Babich, "The Army's Pain: Servicemen Do Not Understand the Aims of Military Reform, but Are Terrified by Its Scope," *Russia Profile*, 12 Nov 2008.

16. "Igor Sechin vyshel v informatsionnoe pole," *Kommersant*, 13 Dec 2007. Sechin is also reputed to have been a leading figure in the campaign againt Khodorkovsky and Yukos and to have blocked attempts to make Gazprom more open and transparent. See "Sechin, Igor," *Lentapedia* (*Lenta.ru*), http://lenta.ru/lib/14160890/full.htm.

17. Irina Isakova, *Russian Governance in the Twenty-First Century: Geo-strategy, Geopolitics and Governance* (London: Frank Cass, 2005), 38–39; Karaganov, "Russia's Elites," 48–50.

18. Dmitri Trenin, "Russia's Security Integration with America and Europe," in *Russia's Engagement with the West: Transformation and Integration in the Twenty-First Century*, ed. Alexander J. Motyl, Blair A. Ruble, and Lilia Shevtsova (Armonk, NY: M. E. Sharpe, 2005), 283–92; Nikolai Poroskov, "Pushka chesti ne otdast: V Rossii gotovitsya novaya voennaya doktrina," *Vremya Novostei*, 1 Feb 2007; "Oboronnaya politika Rossii," SVOP report, 14 Oct 2003, http://www.svop.ru/live/materials.asp?m_id=7271&r_id=7272.

19. Aleksandr Chuikov, "'Yastreb' uletel?" *Izvestiya*, 12 Jul 2001. The ouster of

Sergeev as defense minister in late 2000 came about after a very public quarrel between the defense minister and Chief of the General Staff Gen. Anatoly Kvashnin. Sergeev, with a background in the Strategic Rocket Forces, had argued for upgrading this branch of the military (which implied prioritizing a potential conflict with the West over the more local threats posed by terrorism and the war in Chechnya, for which strategic rockets served little purpose). See Pavel K. Baev, "The Trajectory of the Russian Military: Downsizing, Degeneration, and Defeat," in *The Russian Military*, ed. Steven E. Miller and Dmitri V. Trenin (Cambridge, MA: American Academy of Arts and Sciences, 2004), 57–59. The outspoken and frequently insubordinate Kvashnin was himself pushed aside as part of a purge of the security services' upper echelons following Putin's re-election in mid-2004, with Baluevsky taking over as chief of the General Staff. See Viktor Myasnikov et al., "Mozgu armii sdelali peresadku," *Nezavisimaya Gazeta*, 20 Jul 2004.

20. Baev, "Trajectory," 60–67; Pavel K. Baev, "Putin's Court: How the Military Fits In," PONARS Policy Memo #153, Nov 2000; Vladimir Mukhin, "Deputaty opasayutsya ofitserskogo bunta," *Nezavisimaya Gazeta*, 16 Feb 2005. The military brass has continually tried to sabotage efforts to move to an all-volunteer military force, which would require a greater degree of attention to the actual conditions of service. Dale R. Herspring, "Putin and Military Reform," in *Putin's Russia: Past Imperfect, Future Uncertain*, ed. Dale R. Herspring (Lanham, MD: Rowman & Littlefield, 2005), 193.

21. See Vladimir Shlapentokh, "Serdiukov as a Unique Defense Minister in Russian History: A Sign of Putin's Absolute Power," comment on *JRL* #76, 1 Apr 2007; Stephen Blank, "Russia's Serdyukov and His Generals," *RFE/RL Endnote*, 11 Dec 2007.

22. "Glava Genshtaba Baluevsky otpravlen v otstavku," *Polit.ru*, 3 Jun 2008, http://www.polit.ru/news/2008/06/03/otstav.html.

23. Dale R. Herspring and Peter Rutland, "Russian Foreign Policy," in *Putin's Russia: Past Imperfect, Future Uncertain*, ed. Dale R. Herspring (Lanham, MD: Rowman & Littlefield, 2005), 261. Jeffrey Checkel, "Structure, Institutions, and Process: Russia's Changing Foreign Policy," in *The Making of Foreign Policy in Russia and the New States of Eurasia*, ed. Adeed Dawisha and Karen Dawisha (Armonk, NY: M. E. Sharpe, 1995), 45–47. As a result of the institutional chaos of the Yeltsin years, foreign policy was increasingly politicized, in contrast to the more centralized and consensual approach of the Putin team.

24. Stephen White and Olga Kryshtanovskaya, "Russia: Elite Continuity and Change," in *Elites, Crises, and the Origins of Regimes*, ed. M. Dogan and J. Higley (Lanham, MD: Rowman & Littlefield, 1998), 127. See also Richard Rose, *New Russia Barometer III: The Results* (Glasgow: Strathclyde University Press, 1994), 28.

25. Zimmerman, *Russian People and Foreign Policy*, 16. Jack Snyder, "Democratization, War, and Nationalism in the Post-Communist States," in *The Sources of Russian Foreign Policy After the Cold War*, ed. Celeste A. Wallander (Boulder, CO: Westview, 1996), 36. Snyder argues that, as an unstable society with weak political institutions, Russia (in the mid-1990s) was liable to fall victim to the pressures of nationalism, popular upheaval, and an aggressive foreign policy in the pattern described by Gerschenkron, Polanyi, and Barrington Moore in the mid-twentieth century.

26. Angus Reid Global Monitor Poll, "Russians Reject Army's Intervention Abroad," *JRL* #220, 1 Dec 2008.

27. The role of domestic political institutions in shaping foreign policy outcomes is a topic somewhat neglected in the international relations literature, which largely focuses on system-level variables or looks at questions of state identity apart from the question of institutions. For a clear statement of the thesis that domestic institutions affect foreign policy in meaningful ways, see Ronald Rogowski, "Institutions as Constraints on Strategic Choice," in *Strategic Choice and International Relations*, ed. David A. Lake and Robert Powell (Princeton, NJ: Princeton University Press, 1999), 115–36. More generally, see Richard Rosencrance and Arthur A. Stein, eds., *The Domestic Bases of Grand Strategy* (Ithaca, NY: Cornell University Press, 1993).

28. "Russians Appreciate Putin's Foreign Policy Efforts—Opinion Poll," *Interfax*, 27 Mar 2007, *JRL* #73.

29. Anastasiya Kornya, "Imperskie ambitsii ne aktual'nye: Grazhdane ne khotyat chtoby Rossiya stala energeticheskoi sverkhderzhavoi," *Vedomosti*, 23 Jan 2007; "Russians Want to See Their Country as a Superpower—Poll," *Interfax*, 25 Jan 2007, *JRL* #18.

30. Zimmerman, *Russian People and Foreign Policy*, 91–92. For 1999–2000 (the last years for which Zimmerman presents data), 62 percent of elites saw the United States as a threat, compared with 68 percent of the public at large. On the question of the growth of U.S. power, 60 percent of elites perceived it as a threat versus 73 percent of the public.

31. Levada Center poll, "Rossiya i SShA," http://www.levada.ru/russia.html. A different Levada Center poll found that over 80 percent of respondents regarded the war in Iraq negatively a year after it began. Levada Center poll, "Voennaya operatsiya SShA v Irake," http://www.levada.ru/irak.html.

32. Levada Center poll, "Vliyanie konflikta v Gruzii na otnoshenie rossiyan k Gruzii, SShA, i Ukraine," 21 Aug 2008, http://www.levada.ru/press/2008082103.html.

33. See especially Anders Åslund, "Putin's Lurch toward Tsarism and Neoimperialism: Why the United States Should Care," *Demokratizatsiya*, Win 2008: 17–25.

34. Angela E. Stent, "America and Russia: Paradoxes of Partnership," in *Russia's Engagement with the West: Transformation and Integration in the Twenty-First Century*, ed. Alexander J. Motyl, Blair A. Ruble, and Lilia Shevtsova (Armonk, NY: M. E. Sharpe, 2005), 272; Dmitri Trenin, "Russia Leaves the West," *Foreign Affairs*, Jul–Aug 2006, 85(4): 87–96.

35. Of course, even within the most tightly controlled regimes, such as the pre-perestroika Soviet Union, elites are by their nature somewhat heterogeneous, based in differences in background, occupation, and a variety of personal factors. See Mattei Dogan and John Higley, "Elites, Crises, and Regimes in Comparative Analysis," in *Elites, Crises, and the Origins of Regimes*, ed. Mattei Dogan and John Higley (Lanham, MD: Rowman & Littlefield, 1998), 14–19; Douglas A. Borer and Jason J. Morrissette, "Russian Authoritarian Pluralism: A Local and Global Trend?" *Cambridge Review of International Affairs*, Dec 2006, 19(4): 571–88.

36. For example, Margot Light and others talk about "liberal Westernizers," "pragmatic nationalists," and "fundamentalist nationalists." See Margot Light, John

Löwenhardt, and Stephen White, "Russia and the Dual Expansion of Europe," in *Russia between East and West: Russian Foreign Policy on the Threshold of the Twenty-First Century*, ed. Gabriel Gorodetsky (London: Frank Cass, 2003), 63–64. This three-way division (often with slightly different names for the different tendencies) is employed by many analysts. See, for example, A. G. Arbatov, *Rossiiskaya natsional'-naya ideya i vneshnyaya politika (mify i realnosti)* (Moscow: Moskovskii obshchestvennyi nauchni fond, 1998), 48–50; Ilya Prizel, *National Identity and Foreign Policy: Nationalism and Leadership in Poland, Russia, and Ukraine* (Cambridge: Cambridge University Press, 1998), 240; James Richter, "Russian Foreign Policy and the Politics of National Identity," in *The Sources of Russian Foreign Policy After the Cold War*, ed. Celeste A. Wallander (Boulder, CO: Westview, 1996), 70. Trenin employs a similar scheme implicitly. See Dmitri Trenin, *The End of Eurasia: Russia on the Border between Geopolitics and Globalization* (Washington, DC: Carnegie Endowment, 2002), 206–8. Andrei Tsygankov, who has written the most comprehensive account of the intra-elite foreign policy debate, offers a slight variation, in that he identifies four camps, termed "New Thinking" (mostly associated with Gorbachev-era reformists), "Integration with the West," "Great Power Balancing," and "Great Power Pragmatism." See Andrei Tsygankov, *Russia's Foreign Policy*, 26. Irina Isakova also identifies four schools, which she terms "Westernism," "Eurasianism" (geographic determinism of the kind advocated by Communist leader Gennady Zyuganov or Liberal Democratic leader Vladimir Zhirinovsky), "Neo-Eurasianism" (extremist anti-Americanism, as advocated by Dugin in the 1990s), and "Pragmatism." See Isakova, *Russian Governance*, 16–17. Bobo Lo, meanwhile, suggests quite rightly that "the ultimate goal [of the liberal Westernizers] differed little from that of the *derzhavniki* and quasi-imperialists." See Lo, *Vladimir Putin*, 13–14. A slightly different approach is adopted by the social constructivist Ted Hopf, who portrays the different foreign policy orientations in terms of competing "discursive formations" that he labels "New Western Russia," "New Soviet Russia," "Liberal Essentialist," and "Liberal Relativist." See Ted Hopf, *Social Construction of International Politics: Identites & Foreign Policies, Moscow 1955 and 1999* (Ithaca, NY: Cornell University Press, 2002). Because he is interested in broader social discourses, Hopf understands these categories as all-encompassing worldviews that structure perceptions of self-identity and relations with an internal or external "Other." The most nuanced outline of the competing approaches to foreign policy in Putin's Russia is provided by Yury Fedorov of the Moscow State Institute of International Relations (MGIMO), who refers to "hard traditionalists" (or "buffoons"), "neo-imperialists," and "pragmatists." See Yury Fedorov, "'Boffins' and 'Buffoons': Different Strains of Thought in Russia's Strategic Thinking," Chatham House Russia and Eurasia Program Briefing Paper, Mar 2006.

37. This scheme most closely approximates the one employed by Irina Isakova. The designation of "Pragmatism," which Fedorov, Isakova, and Tsygankov all employ in some form as a separate ideological tendency, appears overly deterministic. The pragmatists, by and large, have been those in power who do not have the luxury of ideological purity but are forced to employ a range of sometimes incompatible policies. Saying that Putin is a pragmatist is a rather banal observation. Determining which areas of his foreign policy are influenced by pro-Western liberals and which by extreme Eurasianists provides a more nuanced picture of actual pol-

icy. It should be kept in mind, of course, that Kozyrev himself called for a "geopolitical" foreign policy in 1992, in contrast to what he termed the "ideological" approach of the Soviet Union. Jonathan Valdez, "The Near Abroad, the West, and National Identity in Russian Foreign Policy," in *The Making of Foreign Policy in Russia and the New States of Eurasia*, ed. Adeed Dawisha and Karen Dawisha (Armonk, NY: M. E. Sharpe, 1995), 89.

38. The breakdown of elite ideologies and their relative strength looked quite similar in late 1993. See Alexei G. Arbatov, "Russia's Foreign Policy Alternatives," *International Security*, Aut 1993, 18(2): 5–43. Arbatov predicted at the time that "Russian foreign policy most probably will shift . . . to a centrist or moderate-conservative position" that would place greater emphasis on protecting Russian prestige and national interests, especially within the CIS.

39. Dmitri Trenin, "Russia's Security Integration with America and Europe," in *Russia's Engagement with the West: Transformation and Integration in the Twenty-First Century*, ed. Alexander J. Motyl, Blair A. Ruble, and Lilia Shevtsova (Armonk, NY: M. E. Sharpe, 2005), 289. Some scholars, particularly Tsygankov, see a significant discontinuity between the foreign policy views of Primakov and Putin. Tsygankov labels Primakov's approach "Great Power Balancing" in contrast to Putin's "Great Power Pragmatism." The distinction between the two appears more subtle, however, especially since Primakov has been a firm supporter of Putin's foreign policy.

40. See Steven Lee Myers, "Anti-Immigrant Views Catching on in Russia," *New York Times*, 22 Oct 2006.

41. Nabi Abdullaev, "Nationalists Step Forward to Make Political Claims," *St. Petersburg Times*, 22 Nov 2005. The ESM leader later complained about the DPNI's use of xenophobic rhetoric during the march, charging St. Petersburg police with complicity.

42. Fred Weir, "Putin Taps into a Growing Anti-Minority Fervor," *Christian Science Monitor*, 10 Oct 2006.

43. Victor Yasmann, "Red Religion: An Ideology of Neo-Messianic Russian Fundamentalism," *Demokratizatsiya*, Spr 1993, 1(2): 22–24; Donaldson and Nogee, *The Foreign Policy of Russia*, 125–26.

44. H. J. Mackinder, *Democratic Ideals and Reality* (London: Constable, 1919). See also Mackinder, "The Geographical Pivot of History," *Geographical Journal*, Apr 1904, 23(4): 421–37.

45. Zbigniew Brzezinski, *The Grand Chessboard: American Primacy and Its Geostrategic Imperatives* (New York: Basic Books, 1997); Brzezinski, *Game Plan: A Geostrategic Framework for the Conduct of the U.S.-Soviet Contest* (Boston: Atlantic Monthly Press, 1986). See also Francis P. Sempa, *Geopolitics: From the Cold War to the 21st Century* (New Brunswick: Transaction, 2002), 100–114.

46. Yasmann, "Red Religion," 25–28. See also Vladimir Malashenko, "The Russian-Eurasian Idea (Pax Rossica)," *Russian Analytica*, Sep 2005 (6): 5–14.

47. Andreas Umland, "The Rise of Integral Anti-Americanism in the Russian Mass Media and Intellectual Life," History News Network, 26 Jun 2006, http://hnn.us/articles/26108.html.

48. See A. Dugin, "Kondopoga: A Warning Bell," *Russia in Global Affairs*, 2006, 4(4): 8–13.

49. Leonid Ivashov, "Vpolzanie v 'myatezhevoinu,'" *Nezavisimaya Gazeta*, 13 Nov 2002.

50. Yasmann, "Red Religion," 25–31.

51. John B. Dunlop, "Aleksandr Dugin's *Foundations of Geopolitics*," *Demokratizatsiya*, Win 2004, 12(4): 41–42; A. G. Dugin, *Osnovy geopolitiki: Geopoliticheskoe budushchee Rossii* (Moscow: Arktogeya, 1997).

52. Dunlop, "Foundations," 49–52; Dugin, *Osnovy*, 248–60, 367, 377.

53. Dunlop, "Foundations," 43–46.

54. Andrei P. Tsygankov, "Misreading Putin," comment on *JRL* #45, 23 Feb 2007.

55. Umland, "The Rise of Integral Anti-Americanism."

56. Umland, "Neoevraziistvo, vopros o russkom fashizme i rossiiskii politicheskii diskurs," *Zerkalo nedeli*, 16–22 Dec 2006, 48(627), http://www.zn.ua/1000/1600/55389.

57. See L. N. Klepatskii, "The New Russia and the New World Order," in *Russia between East and West: Russian Foreign Policy on the Threshold of the Twenty-First Century*, ed. Gabriel Gorodetsky (London: Frank Cass, 2003), 9; Dmitry Polikanov and Graham Timmins, "Russian foreign policy under Putin," in *Russian Politics under Putin*, ed. Cameron Ross (Manchester: Manchester University Press, 2004), 223–28; Prizel, *National Identity and Foreign Policy*, 269–71; Arbatov, *Rossiiskaya natsional'naya ideya*, 7–8. See also S. N. Baburin, *Territoriya gosudarstva: Pravovye i geopoliticheskie problemy* (Moscow: Izd-vo MGU, 1997), 407–8. A 2001 report by the U.S. National Intelligence Council argues that this trend is essentially power maximizing and nonideological, though arguments about Russia's civilizational identity are by their nature ideological. See "Russia in the International System," Conference Report of the National Intelligence Council, 1 Jun 2001, http://www.dni.gov/nicconfreports_russiainter.html.

58. Aleksandr Lukin, "Litsom k Kitayu: Rossiyane nikak ne otvyknut' smotret' na soseda svysoka," *Kommersant*, 9 Nov 2006.

59. SVOP, "Novye vyzovy bezopasnosti i Rossiya," 11 Jul 2002, http://www.svop.ru/live/materials.asp?m_id=6729&r_id=6758.

60. Sergei Karaganov, "Russia Pulled East and West," trans. Project Syndicate, Feb 1997, http://www.project-syndicate.org/commentary/kar5.

61. Sergei Karaganov, "The NATO Summit," *RFE/RL Newsline*, 19 Nov 2002. See also Mette Skak, "The Logic of Foreign and Security Policy Change in Russia," in *Russia as a Great Power: Dimensions of Security under Putin*, ed. Jakob Hedenskog et al. (London: Routledge, 2005), 91–95.

62. Sergei Karaganov, "Russia and the West After Iraq," trans. Project Syndicate, Jun 2003, http://www.project-syndicate.org/commentary/karaganov8.

63. Sergei Karaganov, "Russia and the International Order," *Military Technology*, Jan 2006: 221–26; Vladislav Inozemtsev and Sergei Karaganov; "Imperialism of the Fittest," *The National Interest*, Sum 2005 (80): 74–80; Sergei Karaganov, "Farsovaya 'Kholodnaya voina,'" *Rossiiskaya Gazeta*, 26 Dec 2006.

64. V. P. Lukin and A. I. Utkin, *Rossiya i Zapad: obshchnost' ili otchuzhdenie?* (Moscow: Yabloko, 1995), 7–9.

65. Vladimir Lukin, "Our Security Predicament," *Foreign Policy*, Aut 1992 (88): 57–58.

66. Vladimir Lukin, "New Century, Greater Concerns," *International Affairs: A Russian Journal of World Politics, Diplomacy and International Relations*, 2002, 48(2): 49.

67. G. A. Zyuganov, "Kak vernut'sya Rossii doverie i uvazhenie mezhdunarodnogo soobshchestva," *Pravda*, 6 Sep 2006. In the mid-1990s, a major struggle broke out within the KPRF over the party's foreign policy orientation. Zyuganov then stood for an aggressive Eurasianist position, emphasizing the Russian people's role in reconstituting a powerful Eurasian state capable of challenging the West's supremacy. His opponents in the party adhered to a traditional Marxist internationalist approach that was no less anti-West but that emphasized the Communist Party's commitment to the international proletariat, without Russia per se occupying any special position in the global division of labor. See Vladimir Bilenkin, "The Ideology of Russia's Rulers in 1995: Westernizers and Eurasians," *Monthly Review*, Oct 1995.

68. Donaldson and Nogee, *Foreign Policy of Russia*, 130.

69. Leon Aron, "The Foreign Policy Doctrine of Postcommunist Russia and Its Domestic Context," in *The New Russian Foreign Policy*, ed. Michael Mandelbaum (New York: Council on Foreign Relations, 1998), 29–30. Aron argues that Primakov was essentially a Russian Gaullist.

70. Yevgeny Primakov, *Russian Crossroads: Toward the New Millennium*, trans. Felix Rosenthal (New Haven, CT: Yale University Press, 2004), 3, 126. See also Primakov, "Russia's Foreign Policy in 2005 Was Successful in Every Area," *International Affairs: A Russian Journal of World Politics, Diplomacy, and International Relations*, 2006, 52(2): 13–22. Of course, even under Putin, and in spite of the post–September 11 rapprochement with the United States, several diplomatic initiatives continue to bear traces of the Eurasianist approach. Most notable of these has been the construction and expansion of the Shanghai Cooperation Organization (SCO), uniting Russia, China, and the Central Asian states apart from Turkmenistan into a regional bloc. See K. V. Vnukov, "Russkii s kitaitsem brat'ya navek?" *Mezhdunarodnaya zhizn'*, 2006 (1–2); Chen Yun, "Kitai i Rossiya v sovremennom mire," *Svobodnaya Mysl'*, 2006 (3): 6–7.

71. E. G. Solov'ev, *Natsional'nye interesy i osnovnye politicheskie sily sovremennoi Rossii* (Moscow: Nauka, 2004), 15.

72. Of course, even Sergei Ivanov, the former intelligence operative identified as Putin's most likely successor, describes himself as "liberal enough" on economic policy. At the same time, Ivanov has expressed a fair degree of skepticism regarding Western-style democracy and expressed little interest in Russia's political and security integration with the West. See Neil Buckley and Catherine Belton, interview with Sergei Ivanov, *Financial Times*, 18 Apr 2007.

73. "Medvedev Calls for Strengthened Fight against Corruption in Russia," *International Herald Tribune*, 22 Jan 2008.

74. "Top Presidential Adviser Quits . . ." *RFE/RL Newsline*, 29 Dec 2005.

75. Eduard Solov'ev, "The Foreign Policy Priorities of Liberal Russia," *Russian Politics and Law*, May–Jun 2006, 44(3): 52–53.

76. A. B. Chubais, "Missiya Rossii v XXI veke," *Nezavisimaya Gazeta*, 1 Oct 2003. Yu. Arkhangel'sky and P. Yermolaev, "Politicheskaya elita i strategicheskie prioritety

RF: Mezhdu 'metologicheskim idealizmom' i 'naivnym realizmom,'" *Mirovaya eko-nomika i mezhdunarodnye otnosheniya*, Nov 2006 (11): 100. Chubais's idea is similar to the superimperialism advocated by Karaganov and Vladislav Inozemtsev. See Inozemtsev and Karaganov, "Imperialism of the Fittest."

77. Yegor Gaidar, "The Collapse of the Soviet Union: Lessons for Contemporary Russia," address to the American Enterprise Institute, 13 Nov 2006, http://www.aei .org/events/filter.all,eventID.1420/transcript.asp. Also see Gaidar, *Gibel' imperii: Uroki dlya sovremennoi Rossii* (Moscow: ROSSPEN, 2006).

78. Trenin, "Russia Leaves the West"; Trenin, "Russia Redefines Itself and Its Rela-tions with the West," *Washington Quarterly*, Spr 2007, 30(2).

79. Petr Ovrekhin and Evlaliya Samedova, "Korporatsiya 'Kreml' uspeshno pora-botala," *Nezavisimaya Gazeta*, 26 Jul 2005.

80. Brian Whitmore, "Russia: Uncertainty over Putin Succession Fuels 'Siloviki War,'" *RFE/RL Feature*, 9 Nov 2007. The "war" pitted factions in the security services associated with Putin's deputy chief of staff Igor Sechin and Federal Counternarcot-ics Service head Viktor Cherkesov. More a struggle for resources than an ideological battle, the clash involved *kompromat*, arrests, bribery, and more than a few murders.

81. According to reporting by the *Financial Times*, eleven members of Putin's presidential administration chaired between them six state companies and held twelve additional directorships. Neil Buckley and Arkady Ostrovsky, "Back in Busi-ness—How Putin's Allies Are Turning Russia into a Corporate State," *Financial Times*, 19 Jun 2006.

82. News conference of presidential aide Vladislav Surkov, Deputy Head of the Presidential Administration.

83. Philip Hanson and Elizabeth Teague, "Big Business and the State in Russia," *Europe-Asia Studies*, Jul 2005, 57(5): 657–80.

84. Trenin, "Russia Redefines Itself."

85. For a sharp criticism of Russia's use of energy to exert influence on its neigh-bors, see "Russia's Wrong Direction: What the U.S. Can and Should Do," Council on Foreign Relations Independent Task Force Report No. 57, Mar 2006.

86. Robert O. Freedman, "Putin, Iran, and the Nuclear Weapons Issue," *Problems of Post-Communism*, Mar–Apr 2006, 53(2): 39–48.

87. Buckley and Ostrovsky, "Back in Business."

88. "Kadrovyi zapas Dmitriya Medvedeva," *Kommersant*, 11 Dec 2007; "The Future Medvedev Team," *RFE/RL Analysis*, 23 Mar 2008, http://www.rferl.org/con-tent/Article/1079678.html.

89. Catherine Belton, "Russia Revising Great Game Rule Book," *Moscow Times*, 15 Apr 2004.

90. "Vladislav Surkov's Secret Speech."

91. "Stenogramma: Suverenitet—eto politicheskii sinonim konkurentosposob-nosti (chast' 1)," http://surkov.info/publ/4-1-0-13.

92. V. Surkov, "Natsional'naya budushchego (polnaya versiya)," http://surkov .info/publ/4-1-0-37.

93. Andrew E. Kramer, "Russian Stock Market Fall Is Said to Imperil Oil Boom," *New York Times*, 12 Sep 2008.

94. See Lo, *Vladimir Putin*, 18–20. Putin's decision to join in the U.S.-led war on

terror has been described in detail by Grigory Yavlinsky, who was one of the members of Russia's political elite summoned to the Kremlin by Putin immediately after the terrorist attacks in the United States to discuss Russia's response. According to Yavlinsky, of the twenty-one members of the Duma and State Council present at this secret Kremlin conclave, only two (including Yavlisnky himself) advocated supporting the U.S. (one unnamed deputy argued for backing the Taliban, while the other eighteen argued for some form of neutrality or balancing). At the end of the meeting Putin declared that Russia would support the U.S. response unconditionally. Putin also explicitly rejected seeking any kind of quid pro quo, such as loans or investment in the Russian economy. Grigory Yavlinsky, "Domestic and Foreign Policy Challenges in Russia," speech to Carnegie Endowment for International Peace, 31 Jan 2002, *JRL* #6059, 6 Feb 2002. As a political opponent of Putin, Yavlinsky has little reason to inflate the president's role in this decision. In order to defuse opposition from within the bureaucracy, Putin agreed that Russia itself would play a very limited role in the U.S.-led campaign in Afghanistan. See Lena Jonson, *Vladimir Putin and Central Asia* (London: I. B. Tauris, 2004), 60.

95. Dmitry Medvedev, "Vystuplenie na vstreche s predstavitelyami politicheskikh, parlamentskikh i obshchestvennykh krugov Germanii," 5 Jun 2008, http://www.kremlin.ru/appears/2008/06/05/1923_type63374type63376type63377—202 133.shtml.

96. Bobo Lo, "The Securitization of Russian Foreign Policy under Putin," in *Russia between East and West: Russian Foreign Policy on the Threshold of the Twenty-First Century,* ed. Gabriel Gorodetsky (London: Frank Cass, 2003), 12–15.

97. Matthew Schmidt, "Is Putin Pursuing a Policy of Eurasianism?" *Demokratizatsiya,* Win 2005, 13(1): 92.

98. Putin, "Poslanie Federal'nomu Sobraniyu Rossiiskoi Federatsii," 25 Apr 2005, http://www.kremlin.ru/appears/2005/04/25/1223_type63372type63374type 82634 ... 87049.shtml.

99. Putin, "Poslanie Federal'nomu Sobraniyu Rossiiskoi Federatsii," 16 May 2003, http://www.kremlin.ru/appears/2003/05/16/1259_type63372type63374_ 44623.shtml.

100. James Collins, foreword to *Putin's Russia: Past Imperfect, Future Uncertain,* ed. Dale R. Herspring (Lanham, MD: Rowman & Littlefield, 2005), xiv–xv.

101. V. Putin, "50 Years of the European Integration and Russia," translated in *JRL* #72, 25 Mar 2007. See also "Ot redaktsii: Truba Dostoevskogo," *Vedomosti,* 26 Mar 2007.

102. Buckley and Belton, interview with Sergei Ivanov.

103. Russian Ministry of Foreign Affairs, "Obzor vneshnei politiki Rossiiskoi Federatsii," 27 Mar 2007, http://www.mid.ru/brp_4.nsf/sps.

104. Russian Ministry of Foreign Affairs, "Obzor."

105. Mark N. Katz, "Primakov Redux? Putin's Pursuit of 'Multipolarism' in Asia," *Demokratizatsiya,* Win 2006, 14(1): 148–49.

106. Isakova's argument that Putin is seeking both economic and security integration with Western institutions is somewhat overstated. See Isakova, *Russian Governance,* 40. As Lo points out, security engagement and integration are sharply limited and remain subordinate to the larger goal of Russia reasserting itself as a central global player. See Lo, *Vladimir Putin,* 111–13.

107. Schmidt, "Pursuing," 93.

108. Arbatov, *Rosiiskaya natsional'naya ideya*, 45–48; Lo, *Vladimir Putin*, 4. Adeed Dawisha, introduction to *The Making of Foreign Policy in Russia and the New States of Eurasia*, ed. Adeed Dawisha and Karen Dawisha (Armonk, NY: M. E. Sharpe, 1995), 4.

109. Philip Hanson and Elizabeth Teague, "Big Business and the State in Russia," *Europe-Asia Studies*, Jul 2005, 57(5): 657–58.

110. See Dmitri Simes, "Losing Russia," *Foreign Affairs*, Nov–Dec 2007, 86(6).

111. S. Neil MacFarlane, "The 'R' in BRICs: Is Russia an Emerging Power?" *International Affairs*, 2006, 82(1): 41–57.

112. Yury Fedorov, "Vneshnyaya politika Rossii: 1991–2000. Chast' I," *Pro et Contra*, 2001, 6(1–2).

113. Quoted in Adam Zamoyski, *The Polish Way: A Thousand Year History of the Poles and Their Culture* (London: John Murray, 1987), 329.

114. "Nachalo vstrechi s prezidentom Gruzii Mikhailom Saakashvili," 6 Jun 2008, http://www.kremlin.ru/appears/2008/06/06/1618_type63377_202182.shtml.

115. Ellen Barry, "Russian President Dismisses Georgia's Leader as a 'Political Corpse,'" *New York Times*, 2 Sep 2008.

3

Partnership Imperiled

Russia and the United States

Immediately after the terrorist attacks of September 11, 2001, Putin was the first foreign leader to call U.S. president George W. Bush and pledge his country's cooperation in the unfolding war on terror. Following Putin's declaration of solidarity with the United States, Bush solemnly proclaimed the dawn of a new era in U.S.-Russian relations, characterized by the revival of the "strategic partnership" between the two former Cold War rivals that had existed in the first glow of the post–Cold War world. Putin immediately welcomed this new characterization of the relationship and declared his hope for a continued rapprochement between Moscow and Washington.[1]

Seven years later, as Russian tanks rolled into Georgia, Bush denounced a move that he claimed would isolate Russia and damage its relationship with the free world. Putin, still at the center of Russian decision making despite his move into the prime minister's office, downplayed Bush's words and with them the importance of the strategic partnership with the United States he had been instrumental in forging during his time as president. In the course of seven years, Moscow had gone from seeking a privileged partnership with Washington to actively scorning the importance of its relationship with the world's most powerful country.

Needless to say, the partnership that Bush and Putin hailed in the aftermath of the 9/11 attacks never successfully took root. This stunning reversal was perhaps the most visible and important result of Russia's changed approach to foreign policy that has come with the revival of Russia's geopolitical might. While it remained weak, Russia saw a special partnership with the United States as the most effective route to power and influence in the world. With Russia's pre-2009 energy-fueled revival, Moscow once again found itself in a position to act autonomously on the international stage and less in need of a United States that never seemed to take Russia's interests seriously anyway.

Even earlier, the promise of the U.S.-Russian strategic partnership proclaimed at the outset of Putin's term as president came to seem increasingly hollow on both sides. In the U.S., disappointment has been connected to the growing authoritarianism of the Russian government under Putin and Medvedev, Russia's willingness to engage with regimes Washington wishes to isolate (including the Iranians, North Koreans, and the Palestinians' Hamas government in the Gaza Strip), and Russia's increasingly aggressive policy toward its neighbors in the CIS. Russia's leaders in turn have expressed disappointment and a feeling of betrayal over what they perceive as Washington's continued pursuit of a containment policy even amidst loud declarations that the Cold War is a relic of the past. U.S. support for expanding NATO (particularly to the states of the former Soviet Union), for stationing antimissile batteries in Eastern Europe, and for building a system of energy pipelines bypassing Russian territory are all cited in Moscow as proof that the United States continues to see Russia as a potentially dangerous rival rather than an erstwhile partner.

The frustrations on both sides mounted steadily even before the crisis in Georgia brought grim talk of a new Cold War. The rhetorical confrontation was especially fierce. In mid-2006, Putin lashed out at American critics of his increasingly forceful dealings with the outside world. Essentially telling Washington to mind its own business, Putin invoked an old Russian proverb, growling, "Comrade Wolf knows whom to eat. He eats without listening to anyone else. And he is not going to listen."[2] This outburst came shortly after U.S. vice president Richard Cheney sounded the tocsin in a speech in the symbolically resonant city of Vilnius in April 2006, warning that Russia was using access to its energy resources to undermine the independence of neighboring states.[3] Perhaps the starkest prewar warning of the downward trend in relations between the two countries came in Munich in early 2007, when Putin dropped the metaphors and openly accused the U.S. of being a threat to world peace. The Russian president declared:

> More and more we are witness to the flouting of the basic principles of international law. Above all the rights of one state are overtaking separate norms, indeed the entire system of [international] law. The United States is overstepping its national borders in every field: in economics, in politics, even in the humanitarian sphere. . . .
>
> In international affairs we are witnessing with increasing frequency attempts to resolve this or that problem on the basis of so-called political expediency, based on the present conjuncture of forces [i.e., U.S. primacy].
>
> And this, of course, is very dangerous.[4]

Not for the first time, observers glumly warned that Putin's speech heralded a return to the kind of U.S.-Russian standoff not seen since the days of the Cold War.[5]

For Russia, as for most countries, relations with the world's richest and most powerful state are the central element in its overall foreign policy strategy. In the Russian case, this is particularly so because of the legacy of the Cold War, when U.S.-Soviet relations dominated the global security agenda. With the more active foreign policy course Russia embarked on during the Putin years—underpinned by political consolidation, economic growth, high energy prices, and higher military spending—relations with the United States have become increasingly tense and difficult. The optimism prevailing in both Moscow and Washington following Putin's decision to aid the U.S. in its war on terror has given way to recriminations over the war in Iraq, the colored revolutions in Georgia and Ukraine, and Russia's own retreat into authoritarianism. Yet the substance of disputes between Moscow and Washington today looks much like that of the 1990s: Russian leaders resent being ignored, while the U.S. fears Russian attempts to overturn the post–Cold War status quo. However, because Russian actions have been more assertive and consequential with the potential to do greater harm to U.S. interests around the world, today's U.S.-Russian disputes have been more serious.

Given the general continuity that has prevailed in Russia's foreign policy strategy for the past decade or so, the current difficulties in the relationship stem primarily from long-term structural changes affecting Russia's position in the international order, rather than from any new approach to Russian foreign policy on the part of the Kremlin. A stronger, and hence more assertive Russia is going to cause difficulties for the United States, regardless of who sits in the White House or the Kremlin. Indeed, there has been no shortage of such difficulties. To pick just one six-month period, in the first half of 2007 alone, serious disputes broke out between Moscow and Washington over U.S. plans for missile defense systems in Eastern Europe, Russia's decision to suspend its participation in the Conventional Forces in Europe Treaty in response, agreements by the U.S. to provide military training to Bulgaria and Romania, negotiations over Kosovo's status, and Russian support for separatist regimes in Transdniestria (Moldova), South Ossetia, and Abkhazia (Georgia), not to mention the ongoing crackdown on pro-democracy protesters in Russia itself.[6] In all these instances, the real underlying problem remains Russia's newfound confidence and willingness to pursue objectives it has long supported but lacked the political, diplomatic, economic, and military wherewithal to attain.

Of course, the nature of U.S.-Russian relations has changed fundamentally since the end of the Cold War, and much as some Russians continue to believe in the relevance of a bipolar model of international relations, today's Russian Federation is hardly suited to play the Soviet Union's role of superpower rival to the United States. While the U.S. remains the central reference point for Russian foreign policy, for the United States, Russia no longer occupies a central position in the minds of policy makers. The collapse of the Soviet Union, along with the emergence of new threats like international terrorism and an increasingly powerful China, have all contributed to Russia's retreat from the position held by the Soviet Union as the number one security threat to the United States.[7] This demotion continues to rankle many Russian leaders, for whom acceptance of a subordinate international role seems out of keeping with Russia's superpower legacy and Great Power aspirations.

The increased power disparity between Russia and the United States along with very different ideas about the nature of the post–Cold War world and its threats have contributed to the disappointment and occasional crises that have permeated U.S.-Russian relations ever since 1991; so, too, has the failure to formulate a new framework to define the relationship in place of bipolar confrontation. Even though the Cold War is over, U.S.-Russian relations remain dominated by "hard" security issues such as strategic arms control and the geopolitics of energy pipelines. When Russia has been an American ally, as in Afghanistan, it has done so as part of a "coalition of the willing," rather than on any more formal institutional basis.[8]

The few attempts at institutionalizing cooperation have faltered. Kozyrev's strategy of partnership and integration with the West foundered in large part because, in the minds of most Russians, it was never seen to be reciprocated by Western powers, above all the United States.[9] Instead of a new Marshall Plan, which many Russians expected as their reward for terminating the Cold War, post-Soviet Russia got large quantities of advice about the virtues of a free market and comparatively meager Western assistance. When that free market ended up leaving millions of Russians cold, hungry, and unemployed, the fault was laid at the door of the United States—whose representatives at times appeared more interested in making their own names and fortunes than in aiding the Russian transition—and those Russians who had advocated closer ties with Washington.[10]

Meanwhile, the United States' often unilateral foreign policy (under both presidents Bill Clinton and George W. Bush) also contributed to the feeling among Russian elites that their concerns no longer mattered to Washington. The result was a deep-seated sense of grievance on the part of Russian leaders reluctant to accept their country's diminished global stature. The strength of *derzhavnost'* within the Russian elite stems at least in part from nostalgia for the days when Washington could not act anywhere in the world without carefully considering the Russian response.

U.S. actions, including the decision to attack Serbia without United Nations approval in 1999, support for the expansion of NATO into Eastern

Europe and the Baltic states, talk of bringing Ukraine and Georgia into the Atlantic Alliance, withdrawal from the Anti-Ballistic Missile (ABM) Treaty, support for Kosovo's independence, and reluctance to sign off on Russia's membership in the World Trade Organization are signals to many Russians that Washington has not accepted the idea of Russia as a genuine partner. Even on issues not directly affecting Russian security, such as the decision to invade Iraq, Washington's willingness to downplay and ignore Russian opposition fed into a perception in Moscow that the strategic partnership was something of a sham.

The result of this belief has been deep-seated resentment among the Russian political class toward the United States.[11] Rather than working together to build a new world order, a substantial number of Russians blame Washington for taking advantage of the country's weakness and vulnerability in the 1990s to further isolate Russia.[12] Consequently, as Russian economic, political, and military strength has increased since the nadir of the 1998 financial crisis, Russian leaders (Yeltsin as well as Putin and Medvedev) have not hesitated to stand up to the U.S. to defend what they see as Russia's vital national interests.

At the same time, of course, regardless of specific actions on the part of the United States, Russian leaders (like leaders in most countries) have an incentive to resist U.S. pressure as a means of appealing to their own nationalists and showing that Russia still matters. In this regard, it is notable how broad the criticism of U.S. policy toward Russia is, with even pro-Western politicians (such as the leadership of the liberal Yabloko Party) criticizing America's perceived tendency to act without regard for Russian interests. What was therefore notable about Putin's approach was the degree to which he emphasized the maintenance of a basically positive relationship with the U.S., even at the cost of unpopular short-term sacrifices.

If Russians too often see the United States as an arrogant power that ignores their interests, the U.S. tends to see the Russian Federation as a country that has not completely broken with its imperial past and refuses to play the role of a responsible stakeholder in the international system.[13] As a result, Washington continues to pursue a dual policy toward Russia, working to limit the expansion of Russian influence (especially around Russia's borders) even while proclaiming its interest in a more cooperative relationship, for instance, in the fight against international terrorism. Russia's own actions have often made things worse, but on the most basic level, the United States' leadership has not figured out how to define the nature of its relationship with post-Communist Russia.

This confusion is manifested in the vastly different narratives prevailing in the two countries. For instance, where Russians tend to see their country's defense of Serbia in 1999 as a refusal to bow to Western diktat, the U.S. and its allies see Russian support for a mercurial war criminal like then-Yugoslav president Slobodan Milošević as proof of Russia's dangerous unpredictability. More recently, the U.S. saw Moscow's decision to cut off gas supplies to Ukraine as a decision to punish Kyiv for its independent foreign policy line, Moscow's refusal to end its involvement in Iran's nuclear program as an attempt to check U.S. influence in the Middle East, and the Russian invasion of Georgia as an effort to restore Russia's domination of its neighbors. Meanwhile, most Russians saw the gas crisis as the result of Ukraine's chronic payment arrears, the Iranian nuclear program as an opportunity for the Russian atomic energy industry, and the invasion of Georgia as a justified response to the neighboring state's decision to attack the civilian population of South Ossetia.

The result of this mutual crisis of perceptions has been an unwillingness on the part of either Russia or the United States to see the other as just another powerful state pursuing a limited series of national interests. Both Moscow and Washington are caught to a large extent in the Manichaean images and categories of the Cold War, suspecting the other of expansionist designs and responding in ways that contribute to mutual distrust. The influence of such thinking has meant that neither side has adapted effectively to the new security challenges resulting from the breakdown of the bipolar world order and the emergence of new transnational threats such as terrorism and environmental degradation. Instead, actions by both sides contribute to a vicious circle in which each attributes the worst possible motives to the other's actions. In many ways, the U.S. has found it easier to cooperate with China, a larger, more militarily potent (in the conventional sphere), less democratic, and potentially more threatening state than Russia, in large part because of the perception that China is a rational and reasonably stable status quo power.

Still, even the mistrust and misperceptions that have dogged the relationship for much of the past decade have their hopeful aspect. By dashing hopes for seamless cooperation that emerged in the first years after the Soviet collapse, the difficult period in U.S.-Russian relations that has ensued has forced leaders in both countries to take stock of the long-term prospects and trends that will continue to shape ties between the two countries in the future. The Russian Ministry of Foreign Affairs argued in its annual 2007 foreign policy review that crises in U.S.-Russian relations have emerged when "the Americans embark on a quest to build [relations with Russia] on the basis of a leader and a follower." It nonetheless claimed that, despite the pitfalls of the past several years, relations with Washington "are taking on a generally positive dynamic."[14] Such an assessment was a reasonably good description of the contours of the U.S.-Russian relationship—at least up until the outbreak of hostilities between Moscow and Tbilisi in August 2008.

THE UNITED STATES IN RUSSIAN FOREIGN
POLICY THINKING

For Moscow, the state of relations with Washington at a given moment says a vast amount about the assumptions and capabilities underlying Russia's international behavior more generally. The debate between the various ideological groups among the Russian elite centers to a great extent on the nature of Russia's policy toward the United States, while Russia's actions in much of the rest of the world—from Iran to China to Africa—can be understood only in the context of Moscow's strategy for dealing with Washington.[15]

Though relations between the United States and Russia have gone through a range of peaks and troughs since 1991, what is notable has been the degree to which Russia's priorities in the relationship have remained essentially stable for the past decade or more. To be sure, the debate between Eurasianists and Westernizers over Russia's U.S. policy is real enough, but its impact on the actual conduct of Russian foreign policy in this particular area is less than might be expected. The *derzhavnost'* consensus has its greatest hold precisely on this aspect of foreign policy primarily because it is the U.S.—the remaining *sverkhderzhava* (superpower)—of which Russian *derzhavnost'* is a mirror. Russia's need to act like and be accepted as a major power in its own right is a legacy of the country's historical international role, principally (though not entirely) during the course of the Cold War, when Soviet foreign policy was essentially Soviet policy toward the U.S. writ large. Hence, even today, Russia's ability to match the U.S. is a critical gauge of its international standing, even though the bipolar confrontation between capitalism and Communism is no more.[16]

At the same time, Russian statesmen have repeatedly argued that the very idea of a superpower as it existed during the Cold War no longer has any meaning (given the transnational nature of most major security threats and the emergence of new power centers in the modern world).[17] For this reason, instead of one or two states dominating the rest of the world and shaping its choices, the dominant Russian paradigm at the start of the twenty-first century emphasizes the responsibility of all the leading states to uphold global security, working through Great Power clubs such as the UN Security Council and the G8.[18] For Russia, the proliferation of security threats to the east and south means that Russia itself is condemned to pursue a multivectoral foreign policy, in the context of the emerging multipolar world order. Relations with the U.S. are one major vector, but Russia's security situation is such that the country cannot afford to rely on its relationship with Washington alone to defend it. This recognition is the foundation of a strategy that Russian foreign minister Lavrov is fond of calling "network diplomacy [*setovaya diplomatiya*]," eschewing formal alliances and the ideologizing of foreign policy in favor of pragmatic, issue-based cooperation with all interested states.[19]

In terms of the actual relationship between the United States and Russia, Moscow's approach since the mid-1990s has emphasized selective cooperation in keeping with the preservation of Russia's role as an independent Great Power; this framework remains central to Medvedev's thinking about the United States as well. Even during the days of Primakov and the conflict over Kosovo or the war in Georgia, Russian policy has rarely, despite what many U.S. strategists are wont to perceive, been directed at countering U.S. interests as such.

As some observers noted even when Primakov decided to turn his plane around over the Atlantic and cancel a meeting with president Bill Clinton after the commencement of NATO's bombing of Serbia, such occasional shows of truculence have tended to improve U.S.-Russian relations. After all, they remind Washington of Moscow's concerns and red lines in ways that have made the U.S. government take them seriously. Similarly, the press of both countries recognized, following Putin's notorious 2007 speech to the Munich Security Conference—where he accused the U.S. of "overstepping all bounds" and seeking to impose itself on the world—that the speech's main consequence had been to clear the air between Moscow and Washington, reminding the U.S. that Russian patience was not limitless.[20] European leaders, feeling more vulnerable to Russian pressure, were less sanguine.[21]

To be sure, most Russian policy makers and intellectuals are smart enough to realize that their country has little to gain from an openly antagonistic stance toward Washington—though domestic criticism for seeking accommodation at the expense of Russian interests has at times driven more confrontational rhetoric. Rather, they lament Washington's penchant for ignoring Russia and not reciprocating gestures of cooperation.[22] Even during the war in Georgia, which represented a post–Cold War nadir for U.S.-Russian relations, Moscow appeared eager to wall off the impact of its intervention from the broader scope of bilateral relations (or, seen differently, hoped to force the U.S. to abandon Georgia as the price of preserving its relationship with Moscow).

The crisis of perceptions and unfulfilled expectations on both sides represent the greatest challenge for U.S.-Russian relations. On the American side, unmet expectations have mostly to do with Russia's transformation into a democratic state with a Western-oriented security posture. In 2005, Thomas Graham, then-director for Russian affairs on the U.S. National Security Council, listed six priorities for the United States in its relationship with Moscow:

- Russian integration in both the Euro-Atlantic and Northeast Asian security-economic zones
- Russia acting as "a key partner" in counterterrorism and counterproliferation efforts
- Russia contributing to "international coalitions for regional stability and humanitarian assistance"
- Russia becoming "a reliable supplier of energy on commercial terms to global markets"
- Russian cooperation in space exploration and technological development
- Russia becoming "a consolidated free-market democracy"[23]

Of these six aims, by the end of the Bush and Putin administrations it appeared only the second and fifth had been realized to a significant extent (and even here, with reservations). The first and third goals listed by Graham had not been attained, at least not yet. Russian integration into the Euro-Atlantic and Northeast Asian regions in particular is a generation-long project. The dream of Russia becoming a reliable supplier of energy, freeing the U.S. and its allies from dependence on the Middle East, has been no less problematic—with both technical limitations and political constraints interfering with Russia's development as a "reliable supplier" of energy. The failure to achieve the sixth of Graham's goals—free-market democracy in Russia—has been the most visible failure and the one that has probably done the most to shape U.S. perceptions of Putin and of Russia itself. As Bush himself lamented, "We have lost Putin. . . . [He] fears democracy more than anything else."[24] As an indicator of U.S. expectations, Graham's checklist gives some idea of where and why the U.S. government feels Russia has failed and a clear sense of the hurdles that remain.

On the Russian side, the unmet expectations in the relationship with Washington are just as real and have largely been about the absence of reciprocity—financial as well as diplomatic—in exchange for making painful and unpopular decisions for the sake of cooperation with the U.S. Certainly the lack of such reciprocity contributed to Russians' disaffection with the aid they received from the U.S. in the first years after the end of the Cold War. Yet even today the perception lives on that Washington failed to adequately compensate Moscow for the sacrifices it has made in the name of cooperation.[25] For instance, although Russia agreed to provide the U.S. with valuable intelligence on terrorist groups in Central Asia and Afghanistan in 2001, as late as 2009, Washington still had not even gotten around to graduating Russia from the provisions of the Jackson-Vanik amendment, passed in the 1970s to punish the Communist countries for their refusal to allow their citizens freedom of movement.

A more serious instance of this unwillingness to reciprocate is the United

States' unilateral overhaul of the foundations of the nuclear relationship between the two countries—refusing to ratify the START II agreement, the Bush administration's discussions of allowing START I to lapse, its withdrawal from the ABM Treaty, and its decision to place antimissile sites in Eastern Europe. The various nuclear agreements between Moscow and Washington are, like Russia's membership on the UN Security Council, part of the country's superpower legacy that Russian leaders value precisely because they symbolize a relationship of equality with the United States, and Washington's cavalier attitude toward them in the Bush years was seen as an attempt to remove Russia from the top rank of global powers.[26]

To many Russians, cooperation with the U.S. has been dangerously one-sided. Russian leaders have frequently made clear that they feel taken for granted and expect greater reciprocity on the part of the U.S.[27] On the whole, Putin succeeded in managing expectations by downplaying the actual danger posed by the U.S. and by voicing displeasure over the United States' tendency to overlook Russian concerns only selectively. In his emphasis on cooperative relations with the U.S.—to the extent that Russian *derzhavnost'* and sovereignty received their due—Putin was somewhat exceptional in the Russian security establishment.

For this reason, it is in relations with the U.S. that the Russian presidential transition in 2008 has the potential to alter Russian foreign policy behavior the most. To be sure, Dmitry Medvedev has always been seen as a relative liberal in the Russian context and, lacking a background in the security services, has never been associated with the more overt anti-Westernism of many *siloviki*. Precisely for that reason, however, his authority as president remains open to question—especially with Putin's continuing presence in the prime minister's office.[28] Indeed, the war in Georgia offered a clear indication of the limits on Medvedev's authority; the Russian president announced the cease-fire and withdrawal of Russian troops from Georgia proper only to be overruled by the prime minister and military command. As the crisis in Georgia dragged on, Medvedev's statements became increasingly bellicose and sprinkled with the aggressive language that was long Putin's personal trademark, much as Medvedev's first annual address to the Federal Assembly was notable especially for its call to station short-range missiles in Kaliningrad *oblast* on the Polish border in response to Poland's agreement to host the U.S.-sponsored antiballistic missile system.[29]

STRATEGIC PARTNERSHIP RENEWED? 2000–2004

In 2000–2001, when Vladimir Putin and George W. Bush were both settling into office, U.S.-Russian relations appeared to be headed for improvement. The dangerous drift in both domestic and foreign policy of the late Yeltsin years had done much to damage relations with Washington—despite the close personal relations that existed between Yeltsin and then-U.S. president Bill Clinton and the repeated, if vague, invocations of a U.S.-Russian strategic partnership dating from the mid-1990s. The Clinton administration had tried to institutionalize the partnership through a variety of mechanisms, including a strategic stability group and joint commission headed by U.S. vice president Al Gore and Russian prime minister Viktor Chernomyrdin, whose writ gradually expanded from energy and space to cover a whole range of bilateral problems. Initially there were a number of successes, including agreement on removing nuclear weapons from Belarus, Ukraine, and Kazakhstan and the withdrawal of Russian troops from the Baltic states.[30]

Despite the rhetoric of partnership and U.S. support for Russia's inclusion in the Group of Eight, difficulties continued to amass as Russia's transition away from Communism proved complicated and the U.S. found itself confronting other problems that put it at odds with Moscow. U.S. support for NATO expansion, the first wave of which culminated in the admission of the Czech Republic, Hungary, and Poland to the alliance in 1999, was a major impediment to closer relations with Moscow, as the Russians continued to see NATO as a fundamentally hostile force whose only justification could be to limit Russian influence in Europe. Meanwhile, U.S. interest in ending the bloodshed engulfing the former Yugoslavia, first in Bosnia and then in Kosovo, clashed with Russian support for the regime of Slobodan Milošević in Serbia, while the first war in Chechnya fed worries about Russia's potential disintegration.[31]

In fall 1998, a financial collapse of epic proportions left Russia impoverished and unstable at a moment when the United States was beginning to adopt an increasingly forceful policy toward Serbia, a country seen by many in both Moscow and Belgrade as a Russian client. Clinton's decision to launch airstrikes against Serbia, which led to then-foreign minister Primakov's notorious decision to turn his plane around over the Atlantic.[32] For the first time since the Cold War, the prospect of U.S. and Russian soldiers shooting at one another seemed possible when, without authorization from NATO, a detachment of Russian soldiers seized and held the Priština airport.

On the most basic level, four years before the start of the Iraq war, the Russian security establishment saw that the U.S., even under a committed internationalist like then-president Clinton, would not hesitate to act outside the framework of international law or the United Nations if doing so were deemed to be in the United States' national interest. This resort to the unilateral use of force (against a close Russian ally, no less) was evidence to many in Russia that, the end of the Cold War notwithstanding, international politics continued to be based on national interest and power rather than on multinational cooperation, and Russia's relative lack of power prevented it from making good on its support for a country it considered a close ally.[33] As a country that aspired to play a global role analogous to that of the United States, Russia had little choice, its security establishment believed, but to equip itself to survive in such an anarchic world order and be ready to respond forcefully when challenged.[34]

Nonetheless, the importance of the strategic partnership with Washington remained. Such a seemingly privileged relationship allowed Moscow to continue thinking of itself as central to U.S. security concerns (although Washington used the term *strategic partnership* to describe its relations with a number of countries of varying size and importance). Indeed, in the midst of the U.S.-Russian disagreement over Kosovo, Foreign Minister Igor Ivanov pressed U.S. Secretary of State Madeleine Albright to reaffirm that Washington remained committed to its strategic partnership with Russia.[35] Describing the relationship in these terms mattered to Russia precisely because of the country's post–Cold War decline, which made Russian pretensions to a global role increasingly tenuous. Since U.S. unipolarity appeared the dominant paradigm in international relations at the end of the 1990s, it flattered Russian amour propre and enhanced Russian influence to be considered a strategic partner of the lone superpower. This dynamic would continue to inform Russian policy toward the United States after the September 11 attacks, when the decision to move closer to Washington was taken in large measure to enhance Russia's role as one of the principal states in the reshaped global order.

While the Kosovo crisis remained unresolved and civil war stalked the North Caucasus, a series of suspicious bombings across the country led Russian leaders to authorize a new invasion of Chechnya, from which they had exited in 1996, starting the second Chechen War, drawing international condemnation for their lack of restraint, and catapulting new prime minister Vladimir Putin into the political limelight.[36] Putin's ascension to the presidency following Yeltsin's retirement at the end of 1999 held out the promise of a more pragmatic relationship with Washington, despite mounting U.S. unease over events in Chechnya.

In contrast to the ill and increasingly erratic Yeltsin, Putin was perceived in the U.S. as a sober, responsible leader who could be expected to conduct foreign policy on the basis of Russian national interests rather than the extremes of emotion that had characterized Yeltsin's diplomacy in the last years of his rule. Putin appeared to recognize early on that the major danger to Russia's security originated from instability around its borders and the threat of being sucked into futile small wars (akin to the USSR's disastrous Afghan adventure). By focusing on the threats from terrorism and small wars rather than on a large-scale conflict between Russia and NATO, Putin contributed substantially to reducing tensions with the United States.

One area where Putin's attempts at rapprochement had real results was in the field of arms control. Almost immediately after becoming president and in the face of strong opposition from the General Staff, Putin cancelled plans to upgrade the Strategic Rocket Forces and persuaded the Duma to conditionally ratify the START II agreement, which had been languishing in the Duma since its signing in 1997. Soon thereafter, and again over the military's objections, Putin signed a new, if limited, arms control pact with Washington, the Strategic Offensive Reductions Treaty (SORT), that also contained language committing the two sides to the establishment of a "new strategic relationship."[37]

Besides reducing tensions with the United States, the decisions to ratify START II and sign SORT also strengthened Russia's bargaining position in future arms control negotiations. By 2001, Bush had made clear his interest in withdrawing the United States from the ABM Treaty. For that reason, the Duma's ratification of START II was made conditional on Washington's continued adherence to the ABM agreement and ratification of an additional protocol to START II reaffirming the ban on antiballistic missile systems. Since Washington pulled out of the ABM agreement shortly thereafter and never did ratify the additional protocol, Moscow's affirmation of START II had few practical consequences apart from casting U.S. policy in a negative light.[38]

The dual effect of Russia's arms control policy in 2001–2002—lowering tensions with Washington while enhancing Russian bargaining power—was typical of Putin's approach to dealing with the United States in the first half of his presidency. Russia's arms control initiatives were not merely symbolic, as the opposition of the country's General Staff shows. At the same time, they were hardly a unilateral concession to the United States either. Since the size of the Russian arsenal had dropped precipitously since the end of the Cold War anyway (mainly due to budget constraints), SORT in effect ensured the maintenance of rough strategic parity by limiting the United States' ability to build new offensive weapons.[39] Meanwhile, START II ratification gave Moscow a card to play should Washington become serious about building an ABM system. In general, Putin's early appetite for arms control both put pressure on the U.S. to follow suit and, if successful, would have allowed Russia to cut back spending on its nuclear arsenal to focus on local threats.

These actions, while improving for a time U.S.-Russian relations, also helped promote Russia's global role and influence, which had long been a central goal of Russian foreign policy under Yeltsin. The main difference was that now, cooperation with the United States, rather than confrontation with it, was the most effective way for Russia to assert its global relevance since fighting fruitless battles with Washington over, for instance, the ABM Treaty would have done little for Russia's image as a powerful, responsible member of the global community.[40] At the same time, the emphasis on avoiding conflict with the United States allowed Putin to focus on his domestic agenda, which remained the central component of his strategy for reviving Russia as a major global power.[41]

Initially, the Bush administration responded with cautious optimism to the Russian push for cooperation. After meeting Putin at a summit in Ljubljana, Slovenia, in June 2001, Bush famously and inopportunely remarked that he had "looked [Putin] in the eye. . . . I got a sense of his soul."[42] Despite this positive appraisal of Putin and his soul, in the first years of his presidency, Bush downplayed the overall importance of relations with Moscow.[43] National security adviser (and later secretary of state) Condoleezza Rice, an old Russia hand, had been particularly critical of the way the Clinton administration had dealt with Russia. She argued that Clinton had been too quick to rush to the aid of Yeltsin and Russia on account of Clinton's friendship with the Russian president and out of a now-misplaced fear of a Communist revival. Rice firmly believed that the Clinton team had turned a blind eye to Russian malfeasance—in Chechnya and elsewhere—while pandering to Yeltsin's vanity by pressing for Russian inclusion in the G8 despite its economic weakness and lack of democratic credentials.[44]

Under Rice's guidance, Bush came into office determined to recast the United States' policy on Russia, rejecting what he saw as the naïve optimism of the Clinton administration in favor of a skeptical realism. Of course, given the legacy of the financial collapse and Russia's apparent international weakness, a policy of realism was easy to turn into a policy of neglect. To many Russians, the U.S. interest in abrogating the ABM Treaty and continuing to expand NATO was merely proof that Washington had decided it could proceed without taking Russian preferences into consideration, even on issues Russia deemed central to its international security.

Russia's leaders also remained cautious regarding the degree of intimacy with Washington they were willing to accept. Moscow might have been ready to see Washington as an ally but not to fall in line behind it. As early as mid-2001, then-foreign minister Igor Ivanov warned that Russia would "[combine] the firm protection of national interests with a consistent search for mutually acceptable solutions through dialogue and cooperation with the West."[45] On a more fundamental level, while Russia might have an interest in seeking cooperation with the U.S. on a range of issues where their interests overlapped, what was lacking, in 2001 and later, was an overriding interest on the part of either country in seeking deeper integration.

In the past, issues such as a common external threat (e.g., Nazism), mutually assured destruction, or (in the mid-1990s when Boris Yeltsin was casting around for legitimacy) domestic politics pushed the two countries closer. By the start of the twenty-first century, though, no such overwhelming imperative existed, and so cooperation, while real, was doomed to remain sporadic unless the underlying needs of both states changed.[46] The underlying needs of the United States did appear to change fundamentally after the September 11, 2001, attacks, though Russia's needs did not change to nearly the same extent, either on that day or since.

The attacks seemed at the time to provide a major impetus for refashioning U.S.-Russian relations, in part thanks to the genuine and public outpouring of sympathy in Russia for the victims of the attacks.[47] The rapprochement between Moscow and Washington that followed 9/11 resulted from the convergence of interests between the two countries, both of which had suffered egregiously from Islamic terrorism and hoped to rid themselves of the Taliban regime in Afghanistan, which, along with its al Qaeda confederates, was playing an increasingly prominent role in aiding and training Chechen rebels and spreading Islamic radicalism throughout Central Asia.[48]

Aware of Russia's own history of confronting terrorism as well as its continuing problems with ensuring the security of its nuclear arsenal, Putin noted in late 2003 that terrorism—especially nuclear terrorism—is "the main threat to peace in the twenty-first century."[49] This position represented an important departure in Russian foreign policy, both for downplaying the threat of conventional military assaults against Russia (on the part of NATO, for instance) and for recognizing that Russia and the United States found themselves on the same side of an important historical watershed. This issue has continued to unite the U.S. and Russia throughout the Bush-Putin era, with the two countries announcing at the 2006 G8 summit in St. Petersburg (a meeting otherwise notable for the other countries' criticism of Russia's human rights record) the formation of the new Global Initiative to Combat Nuclear Terrorism.[50] Cooperation in the sphere of counterterrorism continued even after the start of hostilities between Russia and Georgia in August 2008.

Because of the war in Chechnya, Moscow had in practice focused its attention on terrorism, especially Islamic terrorism, as the most immediate security challenge facing the country long before September 11, 2001. Previously, the U.S. had roundly condemned what it termed Russia's use of excessive force in waging what was essentially a counterinsurgency campaign, while Moscow responded that Washington lacked a proper frame of reference because it did not face the terrorist threat directly. With the attacks in New York and Washington, Islamic terrorism suddenly became the top security threat for the United States as well. To many Russians, September 11 had proven that Moscow had been right about terrorism all along and that now the U.S. would come to see the problem in the same light. As Igor

Ivanov put it, the September 11 attacks "opened many people's eyes about the reality of terrorism [and] forced a rethinking of approaches to international cooperation . . . in the struggle against this evil."[51]

In the weeks and months after the attacks, Russian hopes were not to be disappointed. Dealing with Afghanistan had already been a major concern of U.S.-Russian negotiations in the months before the September 11 attacks, though some U.S. observers were skeptical about the substance behind Moscow's professed hostility to the Taliban.[52] Four months before 9/11, a delegation to Moscow led by U.S. Deputy Secretary of State Richard Armitage agreed with its Russian hosts that the main issue in Afghanistan was that "the Taliban regime continues to sponsor terrorism, which has spread beyond the frontiers of Afghanistan."[53] When Armitage returned to Moscow a week after the attacks in September, he asked the Russians directly for assistance in fighting the Taliban and al Qaeda, including the possibility of Russian military intervention in Afghanistan.

While deciding to avoid direct military intervention, Putin was receptive to the American request for aid, offering intelligence cooperation, overflight of Russian territory, diplomatic pressure on the Central Asian states to cooperate with the antiterrorist campaign, participation in search-and-rescue missions, and military aid to the anti-Taliban Northern Alliance in Afghanistan, as well as (eventually) agreement to the placement of U.S. bases in Central Asia.[54] Russian leaders realized that, for perhaps the first time since the end of the Cold War a decade earlier, the United States needed Russian help. With its extensive ties to Central Asia (including a large intelligence presence) and experience in Afghanistan dating to the Soviet invasion of that country in 1979, Russia was ideally positioned to help the U.S. mission.

Moscow had also been a long-standing patron of the Northern Alliance, the predominantly Uzbek and Tajik force of former mujahideen now struggling to keep Afghanistan from falling to the mostly Pashtun Taliban. In addition to bringing about the demise of the Taliban and muting U.S. criticism of its activities in Chechnya, Putin—like British prime minister Tony Blair—hoped that by becoming an indispensable partner in the newly proclaimed war on terror, Russia could position itself as a crucial player in the postwar reconstruction of the world while also directly influencing how the United States conducted its campaign against the Afghans and al Qaeda.[55] This campaign, after all, could result in serious consequences for Russia (with a Muslim population of around twenty million), not to mention its immediate neighbors in Central Asia.

Russian aid in the campaign was significant. It included detailed intelligence sharing on the part of both civilian and military intelligence agencies as well as acquiescence to Bush's request to station American troops in Central Asia (Uzbekistan and Kyrgyzstan).[56] Yet despite the alacrity with which

Putin offered to aid the U.S. mission, the Russian security establishment—the military in particular—remained uneasy about turning over Russian secrets to the Americans and, even more, to countenancing the presence of U.S. troops on the territory of the former Soviet Union. To prevent the U.S. from becoming too established in the region, the Russian military urged the anti-Taliban Northern Alliance to drive the Taliban out of Kabul before U.S. forces arrived, and attempted to establish its own presence in Afghanistan ahead of the Americans.[57]

At the same time, Moscow had to worry about how its own Muslim population would react to the campaign against Islamic radicalism in and around Afghanistan. The political leadership in Muslim regions of Russia generally supported the campaign against the Taliban and Russia's participation in it. Muslim spiritual leaders, though, were mostly opposed to what one influential mufti called "the destruction of [Afghanistan's] peaceful population and the division of the world by the global gendarme."[58]

Even Putin was clear that the presence of U.S. troops in Central Asia would have to be temporary. Since the Russian leadership remained convinced that the U.S. still operated according to the same geopolitical categories as the Kremlin, it saw a U.S. presence in Central Asia as a step in expanding Washington's sphere of influence uncomfortably close to Russian borders. For the time being, a U.S. presence in Uzbekistan and Kyrgyzstan was the price to be paid for giving Russia a central position in the unfolding war on terror and for finishing off the Taliban. Once these aims were achieved and the usual wariness crept back into U.S.-Russian relations, the U.S. forces in Central Asia would come to represent a check on Russian power in its own neighborhood. This fear was especially pronounced because of how the September 11 attacks altered the fundamental assumptions underlying U.S. foreign policy. Washington's newfound readiness to use force and its willingness to act without seeking agreement among its allies renewed the criticisms emanating from Russia during the Kosovo war in 1999.[59] The United States may have considered Russia an ally in 2001–2002, but for the time being, Washington was not in the mood to defer to even its closest allies' sensibilities.

Russian leaders in any event continued to worry about the impact of an expanded U.S. presence in Central Asia. With the U.S. ensconced in the region, Moscow feared losing its ability to dictate the routes for new oil and gas pipelines running from Central Asia and the Caspian region to global markets.[60] Consequently, when Uzbek president Islam Karimov, with the backing of China and the Shanghai Cooperation Organization, ordered the U.S. troops to leave in mid-2005 after Washington had criticized his indiscriminate use of force against a popular uprising in the city of Andijon, the Kremlin stood firmly behind him. Immediately after the departure of U.S. troops in September 2005, Russia conducted its first ever joint exercises with Uzbek forces as a show of solidarity.[61] This opportunistic rush to embrace Karimov after the U.S. had rejected him is typical of the way Moscow, until the invasion of Georgia, had generally avoided initiating disputes but not hesitated to take advantage of Washington's difficulties to advance its own geopolitical agenda.

The Kremlin's decision to aid the U.S. in Afghanistan was the central piece of its new policy of cooperation with Washington, whose high point came in 2001–2002. In the eighteen months after the September 11 attacks, Moscow proved largely supportive of U.S. initiatives against the Iranian and North Korean nuclear programs and agreed to the launch of a "strategic energy dialogue" with the U.S. and EU in June 2002. Even in mid-2004, Russia signed on to the U.S.-devised Proliferation Security Initiative (PSI) to combat the spread of fissile material and other components of weapons of mass destruction.[62] All of these developments helped change the general climate in U.S.-Russian relations and created expectations for ongoing cooperation.[63]

The accumulation of good feeling that resulted overshadowed two fundamental realities, however. First, cooperation on problems like the Iranian and North Korean nuclear programs was easy to achieve because, as with Afghanistan, Washington and Moscow had largely the same aims. Cooperation between the two countries has remained strongest precisely on issues connected to nuclear proliferation, including the Iranian and North Korean weapons programs, as well as dismantling Russia's treaty-limited weapons stockpile under the aegis of the Cooperative Threat Reduction (Nunn-Lugar) program and interdiction efforts in the context of the PSI accord.[64] Second, it was relatively easy for Washington to reach agreement with Moscow on a whole range of issues when Russia's position in the global balance of power remained in eclipse, and significantly harder once a much strengthened Russia began aggressively promoting its own interests.

The strategic energy dialogue, for instance, foundered as the Kremlin moved to consolidate its hold on the energy sector (starting with the arrest of Mikhail Khodorkovsky in November 2003) and use its control of energy to underpin the country's more assertive foreign policy course.[65] This pattern would soon come to be repeated across a range of issues in the U.S.-Russian relationship. Even though Putin's post–September 11 cooperation with the United States altered expectations in the bilateral relationship, it did not change the underlying dynamic that for several years had been driving Russian foreign policy, which aimed primarily at enhancing Russia's global role. Neither did it represent a fundamental Russian capitulation to the United States, nor a civilizational watershed in which Russia chose once and for all to throw in its lot with the West.

For the Russians, the goals of cooperating with the U.S. in the Afghan campaign were clear: elimination of Afghanistan as a source of Islamic radicalism, enhancement of Russia's claim to a role as a global power, and a free hand in Chechnya. Unfortunately, many in the U.S. misunderstood the nature of Russia's cooperation. Rather than perceiving a calculated diplomatic maneuver, U.S. observers, including some in the Bush administration, saw Putin's decision to back the Afghan campaign as a signal that the Kremlin had made a fundamental strategic, even civilizational, choice to ally with the West.[66] Thus in his first meeting with Putin after the attacks, Bush thanked the Russian leader for the constructive role his nation was playing in the Afghan campaign and called for the establishment of a "new relationship with Russia based on cooperation and mutual interests."[67]

To be sure, Putin's decision to aid the United States in Afghanistan was a major decision, one that took substantial political courage to make in the face of real opposition from the Russian military and security services. Yet it was only one piece of a larger and more complex Russian diplomatic strategy and was basically instrumental in nature. Russian rhetoric at the time was notably devoid of the kind of sweeping, epochal language used by many American observers keen to praise Putin's willingness to make common cause with the West. In his first address to the Federal Assembly following the September 11 attacks, Putin noted that, while the era of confrontation with the U.S. was over, the post-9/11 world order was still based on "fierce competition—for markets, for investment, for political and economic influence," and that Russia had to be "strong and competitive" in this world.[68]

The attacks of September 11 provided an opportunity for Putin to achieve several long-standing aims of Russian foreign policy. His decision to ally with the United States was not just a tactical shift. Nor was it an enduring civilizational choice. Rather it was a strategic gamble that partnership with Washington would strengthen Russia internationally. Putin was sincere in wanting partnership with the United States in 2001, but not partnership at any price.

GROWING DISILLUSIONMENT

The strategic partnership between Russia and the United States, which was reaffirmed in a joint declaration by Putin and Bush in 2002, came under increasing pressure on both sides almost immediately afterward. By the middle of the decade, the relationship had degenerated into "a troubled partnership in drift" as a result of Russia's increasingly assertive international behavior, Putin's progressively more authoritarian leadership, and the continued U.S. inclination to make major strategic decisions that were at odds with Russia's professed national interests.[69] The partnership— always more the variety of an entente than a true alliance—came into being primarily because the two sides shared a common interest in Afghanistan and because Putin realized that overt opposition to the West (which at times had been the defining characteristic of Primakov's diplomacy) was counterproductive to his aim of restoring Russia's international credibility and influence.

The partnership began to crumble because Washington and Moscow perceived themselves to have widely diverging interests in parts of the world other than Afghanistan and because the post–September 11 understanding between the two sides was never formal enough to manage their diverging strategic priorities the way NATO, for example, can iron out differences between its members. It may well be true that Putin made a fundamental decision early in his term to seek good relations with Washington as a major element of his foreign policy.[70] Nonetheless, the vagaries of politics and the persistence of national interests have meant that cooperation with the U.S. has been only one component of Russian foreign policy, and often not the decisive one. Some of the signal moments in the downturn in came with the U.S.-led invasion of Iraq in March 2003 and then the admission of the Baltic states into NATO and the so-called Orange Revolution in Ukraine the following year, which revived fears of a U.S.-Russian struggle for influence on Russia's periphery. As Medvedev eased into the presidency, Washington pressed (successfully) for the independence of Kosovo and (unsuccessfully, so far) for NATO to extend invitations to Georgia and Ukraine, failing to devise an inducement for Medvedev to halt the growing drift toward confrontation.

Already by 2003, influential voices in Moscow were arguing that the partnership with the U.S. had gone off track. Although Congress and the White House had expressed their gratitude for Russian aid in Afghanistan, concrete concessions were few; restrictions on economic and technical cooperation as well as stringent visa requirements for travel to the United States remained in place, while Washington gave no indication it was willing to reconsider its opposition to the existing arms control regime. Putin's September 2003 visit to the United States, when the Russian president's advisers urged him to agree on a formula for an enduring alliance with Washington, was a kind of symbolic turning point. Two years after the September 11 attacks, it was clear to observers in both countries that the strategic partnership was not living up to expectations, yet enough warm feelings lingered on both sides to recognize that the partnership framework itself appeared savable.

The problem was to define what such a partnership really meant. Russian politicians and diplomats eager to preserve good relations with Washington began arguing that the partnership had hitherto been far too one sided and that the U.S. would have to start making concessions to Russian *derzhavnost'* in order to preserve Russian support for the partnership arrangement. Russia's decision to close overseas military facilities in Cuba and Vietnam, acceptance of U.S. military installations in Central Asia, and muted response to both the demise of the ABM Treaty and NATO expansion were justified to a skeptical elite as a kind of down payment on the strategic partnership with the U.S.[71] That down payment, however, ended up buying Moscow little in the way of enhanced influence with the Bush administration. As Russian ambassador to the U.S., Yury Ushakov, argued much of the difficulty in bilateral relations stems from the fact that Washington believes "Russia can be used when it is needed and discarded or even abused when it is not relevant to American objectives."[72]

A crucial report drafted by a group of pro-Kremlin analysts for Putin before his September 2003 Camp David summit meeting with Bush argued, "It is the American approach to formulating and manipulating the bilateral agenda in the U.S. interest that continues to dominate."[73] The report suggested that Russia dedicate itself to establishing a full alliance relationship with the United States, urging Putin to pledge his cooperation in building the liberal-democratic world order at the heart of the Bush doctrine and promise active assistance in resolving such major issues as the Israeli-Palestinian conflict and the Korean nuclear standoff.[74] As a privileged ally of the U.S., Russia would request a special responsibility for protecting the post-Soviet space from terrorism and instability. Putin took the proposal seriously and apparently raised the issue of a special U.S.-Russian partnership verging on an alliance with Bush at Camp David.[75]

The proponents of such an alliance stressed that, in exchange for Russia's friendship, the U.S. would have to accept Moscow's right to police its own neighborhood, albeit on the basis of a shared commitment to liberal-democratic values. Even in late 2003, however, Putin's commitment to liberal-democratic values appeared shaky at best, and the idea of Russia acting as a gendarme within the CIS looked, from Washington, too much like accepting Russia's claim to an exclusive sphere of influence—although the idea of a full alliance had its supporters in the United States as well.[76] In his statement to reporters after the Camp David summit, Bush called the U.S. and Russia "allies in the war on terror" and stressed their growing cooperation on arms control and in bringing stability to Afghanistan but made no mention of the proposal for a generalized U.S.-Russian alliance.[77]

The Camp David summit in September 2003 represented perhaps the last serious attempt to create a substantive foundation for the U.S.-Russian strategic partnership. In the succeeding twelve months, U.S.-Russian relations entered a period of significant tension from which they have yet to recover. Electoral campaigns in both countries in 2004 encouraged nationalistic posturing. In Russia, this posturing was accompanied by turnover in Putin's team of advisers, with the replacement of pro-U.S. liberals by Eurasianists and *siloviki* in a number of key positions.[78] The campaign to seize control

of Yukos, which began in the summer of 2003, threatened planned investment in the Russian energy sector on the part of several U.S. firms and fed
mounting skepticism in the U.S. about Putin's commitment to the rule of
law. The Yukos drama also heralded the beginning of a much more nationalistic approach to Russia's energy riches on the part of the Kremlin, one
that imperiled vast amounts of foreign investment in the energy sector,
much of it dating from the early 1990s.[79] By the end of 2004, the Orange
Revolution in Kyiv had found the U.S. and Russia on opposite sides in a
struggle for the soul of the most important state in the CIS after Russia
itself. Polarization, not partnership, had become the dominant theme in
U.S.-Russian relations.

A new, albeit more restrained attempt at defining the exact nature of the
U.S.-Russian partnership emerged during the final Bush-Putin summit in
Sochi in April 2008, when Washington and Moscow signed a new "Strategic
Framework Declaration." The document defined areas of strategic cooperation between Moscow and Washington with an eye toward the presidential
transitions in both countries. It aimed at filtering out the disagreements that
had long complicated the bilateral relationship and focusing on the numerous areas where U.S.-Russian cooperation was both possible and desirable.
At the top of the list was arms control, with Moscow and Washington
pledging to seek a legally binding successor to the START I agreement, continue cooperating on nonproliferation, and continue seeking agreement on
missile defense. The agreement also focused on economic cooperation, the
other area where common interests continued to prevail. Most notably, it
committed both sides in concrete terms to overcome the barriers to Russia's
WTO ascension.[80] At the time, the "Strategic Framework Declaration" was
heralded as an important recognition that despite their mistakes, both sides
recognized the importance of getting U.S.-Russian relations back on track.
That assumption would be sorely tested a few months later when war broke
out between Russia and close U.S. ally Georgia.

At Camp David in 2003, Bush had downplayed the significance of a
whole series of other U.S.-Russian disagreements: over the war in Iraq, over
oil supplies, and over U.S. missile defense plans. All of these issues
remained unresolved and made the attainment of the kind of close U.S.-
Russian cooperation many Russian elites still envisioned nearly impossible.
This accumulation of disputes is evidence that the strategic partnership
between Moscow and Washington was always based more on hope than on
a realistic assessment of the two sides' interests. It grew out of their common interests connected to the conflict in Afghanistan, but it did not
account for the facts that their long-term strategic priorities in other parts
of the world often diverged and that Moscow often came to believe the U.S.
was unwilling to offer it any quid pro quo for making the difficult choices
it was demanding.

Since even in 2001 Moscow was not willing to accept the post-1945 German or Japanese model of restraining its strategic ambitions in exchange for full participation in a Western security system, the fundamental nature of the relationship between Washington and Moscow remained more competitive than cooperative. While the weaknesses of the U.S.-Russian strategic partnership were to a large degree structural, it took a series of disputes, each manageable on its own, to undermine the edifice of cooperation, setting the stage for the more confrontational relationship between the two countries.

RUSSIA AND THE UNITED STATES IN THE MIDDLE EAST

If the U.S. remains Russia's top foreign policy priority, in Washington it is the Middle East that has occupied the most attention in the years since the 2001 terrorist attacks. Compared with the United States, Russia is something of a bit player in the Middle East—though Putin has often expressed an interest in Russia's having a larger role in resolving problems such as the Israeli-Palestinian quarrel. Nonetheless, as a large country with long-standing ties to the region (many of the Middle East's secular dictatorships were onetime Soviet clients and continue to be major buyers of Russian weapons) and increasing importance as an energy producer, Russia's role has proven a significant factor in U.S. policy in the region, especially with regard to Iraq and Iran.

Russian opposition to an assault on Saddam Hussein was hardly a surprise in Washington, and indeed, the Bush administration went out of its way to downplay the seriousness of the disagreements. The real problem was that, while Moscow had even less reason to defend Saddam Hussein than it did Slobodan Milošević in Serbia in 1999, it continued to stand for a concert-style model of international politics in which the UN Security Council was the ultimate repository of legality and legitimacy. As with the Kosovo war, the Kremlin was alarmed by the alacrity with which the United States was willing to go to war in contravention of international opinion and the interests of the other members of the Security Council.[81] Washington understood that Russia and the major EU states (apart from Britain) were going to oppose the decision to go to war, and in the words of then-national security adviser Rice, famously decided to "punish France, ignore Germany, and forgive Russia."[82] In U.S. discussions, though, the focus was on the degree of Russia's financial stake in Iraq rather than the larger issue of authorization and legitimation of the decision to go to war. To be sure, the Iraqi regime owed Russia billions of dollars, much of it Soviet-era debts for weapons purchased by Saddam's government during Iraq's war with

Iran in the 1980s.[83] Because Russia's opposition was seen in such primarily economic terms, and because Russia continued to be helpful in Afghanistan, the U.S. found it relatively easy to "forgive" Moscow while taking out its wrath on Paris and Berlin.

On the Russian side, though, while Saddam's debts were hardly a negligible issue, the real problem was that—as in Kosovo four years earlier—the U.S. was prepared to upset the international status quo in a way that portended uncertain consequences for Russia and its allies. Most fundamentally, Moscow objected to the sidelining of the UN Security Council as the supreme arbiter of war and peace. Given Russia's position as a permanent member of the council, inherited from the Soviet Union, upholding the primacy of the Security Council was simultaneously a defense of Russia's prerogative to have a hand in making key international decisions. The United States' unilateral decision to go to war in Iraq in the face of serious opposition in the international community (even from longtime U.S. allies like Germany) confirmed Russian fears about the country's marginalization. As one leading official in the Foreign Ministry described the problem, U.S. unilateralism "merely inflames the situation, making it less subject to resolution. . . . As recent experience demonstrates, states must turn to the collective wisdom and will of the United Nations."[84] Putin himself has sounded the same theme, most notably in his February 2007 Munich speech.

If U.S.-Russian relations are to be put back on a generally cooperative path even as Russia grows in wealth and confidence, the Kremlin argues, Washington will have to limit its claims to a privileged international role and accept the constraints imposed by a multilateral power configuration symbolized above all by the UN Security Council. Paradoxically, many Russian observers think that in the long run, the war in Iraq has helped move the U.S. away from its more unilateralist impulses by demonstrating the inability of even a country as large and powerful as the United States to act against the will of the international community. It is largely for this reason that Russian observers are inclined to argue that while the U.S. may still at times pursue unilateralist policies, the world in which it operates is no longer a unipolar one. As a result, in the words of Russia's 2007 foreign policy review, "In the [U.S.] administration's transition to a more sober evaluation of its capacities lies the potential for new and expanded cooperation with the USA within the framework of multilateral institutions— above all the UN."[85]

On the question of Iran, the U.S. and Russian positions are not as diametrically opposed as might seem at first glance, even after the war in Georgia strained U.S.-Russian cooperation generally. Russia has strongly resisted American pressure to cease its involvement in the Iranian nuclear program, above all in constructing a nuclear reactor for the Iranians at Bushehr that

Moscow and Tehran argue is for purely civilian purposes and meets Iran's obligations under the Nuclear Nonproliferation Treaty. Then again, Russian officials, including Putin himself, have made it clear that they share Washington's aversion to a nuclear-armed Iran.[86] As in Iraq, part of the equation is financial. The Bushehr reactor itself is set to bring Russia (mainly the state-owned firm Atomstroieksport) around $1 billion.[87] At the same time, completing the Bushehr facility would undoubtedly serve as an effective advertisement for the Russian nuclear industry, which has struggled badly since the fall of the Soviet Union and the drying up of state contracts at home. For this reason, and because of its general unwillingness to bow to foreign diktat (allowing Putin to demonstrate to his domestic audience that he is standing up to the U.S.), Moscow has resisted calls from the United States to cease work at Bushehr.

Nonetheless, the Russian government continues to regard nuclear proliferation as one of the major threats to the country's own security and opposes Iran obtaining nuclear weapons. Bushehr was a point of contention between Russia and the United States even during the Yeltsin era. Like Putin, Yeltsin could not be seen to capitulate to U.S. pressure. Moreover, Russia had its own reasons for seeking good relations with Tehran. Iran remains one of Moscow's major customers for industrial goods as well as conventional weaponry. Iran's diplomacy in the region has also largely coincided with Russia's. The two countries worked together to end the civil war in Tajikistan in the 1990s, and Moscow has appreciated Iranian restraint in Central Asia.[88] Such restraint extends as well to Iran's dealings with the Muslim populations around Russia's border. In contrast to its behavior during the first Chechen war (1994–1996), Tehran largely refrained from supporting the Chechen rebels during the war that began in 1999.[89] Moscow thus has a range of interests at stake in its relationship to Iran that transcend the nuclear issue and that it is loath to abandon needlessly.

With the insertion of U.S. troops into Iraq in early 2003 and the resulting expansion of U.S. influence in the Middle East, Moscow moved to accommodate the U.S. position on Iran. Putin argued in June 2003, after talks with Bush, that an Iranian nuclear capability could actually engage in competition with Russian companies on the world market and joined Bush in calling for International Atomic Energy Agency (IAEA) oversight of Iran's nuclear program.[90] Once the IAEA had forced Iran to report on its activities, Russia generally stayed on the sidelines of the unfolding diplomatic spat between Tehran and Washington, though Russian abstention on most IAEA votes allowed the organization to adopt a series of progressively more stringent resolutions on the Iranian issue, culminating in a vote in September 2005 that found Iran out of compliance with its obligations under the Nonproliferation Treaty.[91]

At the same time, Moscow benefits strategically from a situation in which, because of its pariah status, Iran cannot sell its oil and gas to Europe, thereby reinforcing Russia's dominant position and greatly complicating U.S. and EU efforts to construct an energy corridor bypassing Russia. For this reason, Moscow is generally happy to perpetuate a status quo in which Tehran is isolated, dependent on Moscow for its engagement with the outside world, and in no position to compete with Russia as an energy supplier.[92]

From late 2005, Russia's attitude toward Iran gradually hardened, moving it closer to the United States on the nuclear question while still seeking the economic benefits from cooperating with Iran elsewhere.[93] Shortly after the IAEA vote, Moscow announced that it would not supply nuclear fuel to Bushehr before construction had been completed.[94] Then the Russian government decided to stop construction on the reactor facility, citing Iran's failure to pay for the work completed up to that point.[95] When the U.S. at last succeeded in bringing Iran's nuclear program before the UN Security Council in December 2006, Russia, to the surprise of many observers, voted to support the Security Council's resolution imposing limited economic sanctions on Iran for its refusal to suspend uranium enrichment at sites around the country (not including the unfinished Bushehr reactor). Moscow's decision to support sanctions resulted above all from its commitment to uphold the nonproliferation regime that came into place during the Cold War, not out of any desire to curry favor with the United States.[96] Russia's UN ambassador Vitaly Churkin explained that Iran had to accept "more active and open cooperation with IAEA" in order to allay Russian concerns, even though Russia continued to reject the U.S. characterization of Iran as a rogue state, in line with the idea of "network diplomacy" and the de-ideologizing of foreign policy stressed by Putin and Lavrov.[97]

Russian participation in the construction of the Bushehr reactor appears in this light to be undertaken with some reluctance. The financial benefits of Bushehr, plus the need for generally cooperative relations with a close neighbor and the domestic need to resist U.S. pressure, have kept up Russian interest in the Bushehr project, regardless of various instances of Iranian malfeasance. Then again, it is clear Moscow has no desire to see the emergence of a nuclear-armed Iran, and Russian work at Bushehr has remained conditioned on verifiable guarantees that the facility not be used for the production of weapons components. Until being ruled out by Tehran, Moscow's suggestion that it could supply the uranium for Bushehr and then take possession of the spent nuclear fuel appeared to offer a way out of the crisis, allowing all sides to save face.

TENSION IN THE CIS

If U.S. and Russian priorities dovetailed in Iran, they diverged sharply in the republics of the former Soviet Union, even before the Russo-Georgian war. In this region, Russia has found the United States' unilateral inclinations especially threatening because of what Moscow sees as a U.S. strategic offensive in Russia's own backyard. Moscow continues to view the U.S. as a rival within the former Soviet space, regardless of joint initiatives in Afghanistan and elsewhere. It thus sees political developments within these countries primarily through the prism of relations with Washington. The ouster of authoritarian post-Soviet governments in Georgia (2003) and Ukraine (2004) by pro-Western forces has revived Russian fears of both strategic encirclement and domestic instability.[98] Even respectable political circles in Moscow have at times been wont to attribute the Rose and Orange Revolutions to U.S.-led machinations, while more extremist politicians have voiced concern that events in Tbilisi and Kyiv were merely a rehearsal for U.S. plans to implant a pro-American regime in Moscow itself.[99]

The invasion of Georgia, which was loudly condemned in the United States, was Russia's most overt attempt at undermining Western (especially U.S.) influence in the region. Even without ousting Georgian president Saakashvili, the Kremlin demonstrated the limits of Washington's reach and placed other wayward CIS members on notice about the costs of ignoring Russian interests. The Kremlin also gambled that the United States would judge its relationship with Russia too important to jeopardize over a small country in the South Caucasus. With uncharacteristic bluntness, Lavrov informed Washington that it had to "choose between defending its prestige over a virtual project [i.e., Saakashvili] or real partnership which requires joint action."[100] In the short run at least, the Kremlin's gamble appeared to pay off; despite tough words, on the bilateral level, the U.S. response was effectively limited to canceling a pending civilian nuclear cooperation agreement. The worsening situation in Afghanistan, mounting worries about Iran's nuclear program, and the United States' own economic troubles all limited U.S. leverage. Despite being appalled by the Russian invasion and recognition of South Ossetia and Abkhazia, the Bush administration in its waning days had no desire to pick a fight with Moscow, and indeed tempered its support for rushing Ukraine and Georgia into NATO after the summer 2008 war.

The invasion was in large part designed to counter what appeared to be mounting U.S. influence in the CIS. U.S. efforts at promoting democracy have been viewed with particular suspicion, allegedly as part of a U.S. scheme to install friendly governments in countries vital to Russian security. The fact that the postrevolutionary governments in Kyiv and Tbilisi have sought NATO membership feeds into Russian fears that the U.S. is intent on undermining Russia's own security zone in the CIS and pushing Russian influence out of Europe entirely, especially since Washington has expressed its qualified support for these ambitions.[101] In Moscow, the assumption is that postrevolutionary states will adopt an anti-Russian political orientation, as the Baltic countries did in the 1990s and as Saakashvili's Georgia did more recently.[102] Some Russian officials see the downfall of Soviet-era leaders as resulting from Western, particularly U.S., conspiracies conducted through democracy-promoting NGOs (whose activities, to be fair, have often been less than evenhanded).[103] On the fringes of Russian politics, the fear of U.S. intentions on this score is still more pronounced.

The old regimes in both Georgia and Ukraine were deeply corrupt and illegitimate but had close ties to powerful Kremlin-connected oligarchs. Washington largely supported the rise of Mikheil Saakashvili and Viktor Yushchenko as a step in the "right" (i.e., liberal and democratic) direction. At the same time, however, the new regimes were welcomed for their presumed foreign policy priorities as well, since both Saakashvili and Yushchenko portrayed their movements in anti-Russian, pro-Western terms—unsurprisingly, given Moscow's determination to maintain the old regime in power in the face of massive street demonstrations. Whatever the initial foreign policy orientation of their movements, in other words, Saakashvili and Yushchenko were forced by the revolutionary dynamic that brought them to power to look to the West for support, primarily as a result of Russia's clumsy attempts to keep them out of office in the first place (which, in Yushchenko's case, involved an assassination attempt in which the Russian security services may have been complicit).

As the promise of the Orange and Rose Revolutions has been undermined to varying degrees by corruption and paralysis, U.S. support for the regimes in Kyiv and Tbilisi came to depend almost entirely on their foreign policy orientation, a fact that has not been lost on the Ukrainian and Georgian leadership—not to mention Moscow.[104] Russia has consequently increasingly condemned U.S. support for the Saakashvili and Yushchenko regimes (not to mention authoritarian governments in key countries such as Azerbaijan and Kazakhstan) in the name of democratic legitimacy as embodying a double standard, especially as U.S. criticism of Russia's own antidemocratic behavior has increased.

Russian opposition has been further increased by the presence of U.S. troops on CIS territory as part of the war on terror. Although Putin himself authorized the deployment of U.S. forces in Uzbekistan and Kyrgyzstan in late 2001, Moscow has clashed repeatedly with Washington over the duration of the U.S. presence. Even in 2001, the Kremlin was keen to insist that while the U.S. had legitimate reasons for stationing troops in Uzbekistan and Kyrgyzstan, they could only stay for a fixed amount of time. When

Tashkent ordered the U.S. troops to leave following calls for an investigation into the massacre of demonstrators in Andijon, the Russians stood solidly behind the Uzbeks, as did the Shanghai Cooperation Organization, which is dominated by Moscow and Beijing.

The struggle over the status of U.S. troops in Central Asia and Russia's participation in that struggle are symptomatic of how the U.S.-Russian relationship continues in important ways to be driven by the traditional language of geopolitics. Certainly, in the aftermath of September 11, the United States has been more willing than in the previous decade to actively engage in balance-of-power politics, especially in a region as critical to the war on terror as Central Asia, while Russia has never ceased viewing the entirety of the former Soviet Union as its own sphere of influence.

Yet taken by themselves, these observations are insufficient to account for the increasingly bitter struggle between Washington and Moscow for influence in Central Asia, not to mention Georgia and Ukraine. Rather, this struggle for influence reflects the reality that Washington and Moscow continue to see each other as at least potentially rival powers. The good feeling of 2001–2002, in essence, was insufficient to change the underlying perceptions motivating either country's foreign policy. At the same time, the tension between Washington and Moscow in the CIS has only deepened the two sides' mutual suspicions in a kind of vicious circle. While continuing to insist even after the invasion of Georgia that the Cold War was over and that Russia was not a threat to peace and security, Washington pursued initiatives—including its role in the Georgian and Ukrainian revolutions, support for the anti-Russian GU(U)AM coalition, and a policy of building energy pipelines from production centers in the Caspian and Central Asia that bypass Russian (as well as Iranian) territory—that Moscow suspects have the at least tacit aim of containing Russian power. Washington's commitment to rebuild Georgia after the Russian invasion also looks in Moscow like an attempt at containment.

As a result of the growing importance of the CIS as a contested zone, it seems destined to play an increasingly prominent role in the agenda for U.S.-Russian relations.[105] As the war in Georgia showed, Moscow remains exceedingly sensitive to any diminution of its influence in the former Soviet space, while Washington has exacerbated tensions through its vacillation between two incompatible approaches to the region. On the one hand, the U.S. maintains a relatively traditional geopolitical view that seeks to win several of the post-Soviet states as allies for U.S. initiatives in Iraq and elsewhere. Such a policy, which has been largely successful with the former Soviet satellites in Eastern Europe, continues to compete with a more posthistorical desire to integrate the former Soviet republics into Western institutions as a means of cementing their adherence to liberal democratic principles. It is largely for this reason, as well as from fears of a colored revolution in Russia itself, that the Kremlin is skeptical of U.S. democracy promotion efforts and foreign-funded NGOs, which since April 2007 have been required to register their activities with the Kremlin.[106]

This inability on the part of the U.S. to settle on a single consistent framework for assessing the importance of the post-Soviet space, along with Russia's own insistence on treating the region as its own backyard, created a volatile situation that finally boiled over in Georgia in August 2008. In many ways, the future of the CIS is the most contested issue between Russia and the U.S. and the one where the partnership between Washington and Moscow is most likely to ultimately falter. The non-Russian members of the CIS have their own reasons for remaining wary of Moscow's intentions and for seeking U.S. support for their policy of keeping the Kremlin at arm's length. As long as Washington remains unclear about the underlying rationale for its involvement in the region, however, it continues to risk misunderstandings with Russia that could spill over to affect the broader relationship between the two countries. It also risks allowing itself to be manipulated by leaders like Saakashvili, who believe that U.S. interest in their independence from Russia gives them carte blanche to engage in provocative diplomacy toward their larger neighbor or, like Kazakh president Nursultan Nazarbaev, to merely pay lip service to democratic principles.

THE ENERGY EQUATION

For the United States, the real problem in the region, and the reason for this inability to articulate clearly the reasons for its involvement in the internal politics of the CIS countries, remains uncertainty about Russia itself. Specifically, the inability to decide once and for all whether Russia remains a threat to peace and stability in Europe has led the U.S. at different times to rationalize its approach to Russia and the other post-Soviet republics in different, contradictory ways. One major example of this contradictory approach can be found on the question of energy supplies. Washington's strategy for making use of energy resources from the major producing areas in the Caspian basin and Western Siberia has long been hampered by continued uncertainty about Russia's own political and economic role, namely, whether Russia itself can become a reliable energy supplier to the world or whether the subordination of economic rationality to the demands of Great Power politics means that Moscow will use its resources to blackmail and intimidate customers.[107] Additionally, as a major player in the Middle East, the United States has to walk a cautious line. As much as it would be in the U.S. national interest to limit its dependence on the Middle East for energy supplies, it also cannot afford to alienate its allies in Saudi Arabia, Kuwait, and elsewhere in the Gulf.[108]

On the one hand, Washington has been eager to secure contracts for delivery with Russian companies and to promote the participation of American companies in the Russian energy sector (including the right to invest directly in Gazprom). On the other, the U.S. has continually promoted the construction of pipelines from the Caspian and Central Asia that bypass Russian territory. And in a more general sense, the very fact that Russia is an energy producer while the United States is primarily a consumer means that the U.S. and Russia are, in the words of the Duma's Foreign Affairs Committee chairman Mikhail Margelov, "partners as well as bitter rivals" for the fruits of Russian energy production.[109] The 2006 St. Petersburg G8 summit did make some progress, with Russia agreeing to a statement calling for greater openness and competition in the energy sphere and giving official imprimatur to Russian calls for recognition of the principle of "security of demand."[110] Putin afterward vowed that Russia would strictly observe its obligations as a supplier, recognizing that Moscow is as dependent on having reliable customers for its oil and gas as its customers are on Russian deliveries.[111] Still, the basic dilemma remains and was only exacerbated by the fighting in Georgia, which called into question the viability of resting the West's energy security on pipelines through the volatile Caucasus.

As has been widely noted, Russia's conception of energy security is based on the idea of "security of demand," or having guaranteed customers for Russian energy paying a (preferably high) guaranteed price, while the West's notion of energy security revolves around having uninterrupted access to oil and gas from multiple sources at the lowest possible price.[112] Despite their best efforts, U.S. energy companies have made little headway in the Russian market, especially while energy prices were rising and Moscow saw more profit to be made from taking direct control of oil and gas production.[113] This push to expand state control coincided with slowing output from most of Russia's established oil and gas production sites. Increased investment in exploration and development of new sources (many in inaccessible locations like the Barents Sea) is needed, but like many energy producers, Russia remains reluctant to cede control of its assets to foreign firms or to invest the money itself.

Besides the resultant difficulties encountered by U.S. companies in their quest to acquire a stake in Russian energy production, Russia's use of energy supplies to put pressure on its neighbors has contributed to U.S. efforts to gain access to oil supplies from other former Soviet states (Azerbaijan and Kazakhstan in particular) and bring it to market without transiting Russian territory. This strategy has been most evident in the construction of the Baku-Tbilisi-Ceyhan (BTC) pipeline, a proposal that originated during the Clinton years as a way to ensure access to Caspian oil without having to rely on the goodwill of Moscow (or Tehran). Connecting the oil fields around the Azeri capital of Baku on the Caspian with the Turkish Mediterranean port of Ceyhan, BTC tied two key pro-U.S. countries (Azerbaijan and Georgia) to Turkey's growing market for energy as well as the broader world market. In the mid-1990s when the project was first proposed, low global oil prices meant that few analysts believed BTC could be profitable given the vast distances involved and a price tag that eventually ran to $4 billion (much of it provided out of European and American public funds).[114] Only the political logic of cutting Russia and Iran out of Western attempts to secure Caspian oil pushed the project forward, as political leaders in Baku and Tbilisi openly acknowledged.[115]

With the higher oil prices prevailing since 2000, BTC has proven profitable without overturning the original political subtext. If anything, Russia's increasingly open attempts to assert its hegemony in the former Soviet Union helped reinforce the original logic behind the pipeline's construction. In the aftermath of the January 2006 Ukrainian gas crisis, the European Union in particular shored up its support for alternative transit routes for Caspian energy to reduce its dependence on Russia. Moreover, thanks to the economic security accruing to Georgia and Azerbaijan from BTC, the pipeline strengthened those countries' ability to stand up to the kind of economic pressure Russia brought to bear against Georgia beginning in 2006.[116] For this reason, the United States and the European Union have backed a proposal to link Kazakhstan to the Baku-Ceyhan line as a means of freeing Astana of its dependence on Russia, and a separate proposal for a new gas pipeline dubbed Nabucco, designed to bring natural gas from the Caspian to Europe while skirting Russian (and Iranian) territory.[117]

Some Russian analysts even see a strategic offensive purpose behind the pipeline, speculating that BTC and future branch pipelines are designed to spur the outbreak of colored revolutions throughout the southern tier of the former Soviet Union.[118] On the Russian side, BTC (as well as Nabucco) is often held up as an example of the zero-sum logic underpinning U.S. policy toward Russia and in turn justifying the same sort of geopolitical approach on Moscow's part.[119] When the BTC project was first conceived, Russia's political and economic turmoil was cited as a compelling reason for building a pipeline in a way that minimized political risks. With Putin's consolidation of power after 2000, this justification would appear to make less sense unless the risk being hedged against is not generalized chaos but rather a renewed Russian imperial drive against its neighbors.

Of course, the construction of BTC, while inserting the United States into the struggle for control of export routes, has not eliminated Russia's own influence in what is sometimes termed the "new Great Game." Moscow has responded by building a series of its own gas and oil pipelines (notably the Blue Stream gas pipeline to Turkey and another major pipeline from Kazakhstan's Tengiz field to Novorossiisk in which Russia owns a controlling stake), ensuring that it, too, will continue to have a major say in the marketing of energy from the region.[120] Its proposed South Stream pipeline (see chapter 4) likewise appears designed above all to undermine the case for Nabucco. Pipelines, moreover, are central to the mounting competition between Russia and the Western powers for influence in the Caspian littoral states.

The invasion of Georgia in 2008 raised further concerns about the energy corridor strategy embodied by BTC. While the actual fighting did not damage the pipeline, British Petroleum was forced to shut down operations for over two weeks as a result of the generalized chaos (including Russia's bombing of a key rail link from Azerbaijan) as well as an explosion along the Turkish section of the line blamed on Kurdish rebels. Even though BTC was pumping again by the end of August, the war fed concerns about the potential for future disruptions. More broadly, it made the tasks of convincing companies to invest in new pipelines and convincing upstream countries to entrust their oil to such non-Russian pipelines substantially harder.[121]

RUSSIAN AUTHORITARIANISM AND
U.S. FOREIGN POLICY

Another major factor contributing to the worsening of U.S.-Russian relations during the Putin years has been the increasingly authoritarian nature of the Russian government itself. As the Putin government rolled back limitations on the power of the state—cracking down on independent journalists, NGOs, political parties, even big business—the U.S. grew increasingly wary of Russia's future intentions. U.S. unease flowed from a number of sources. First, Russia's authoritarian turn empowered, more than any other groups, the security services (the successor organizations to the KGB), home to some of the most intransigent anti-Western and above all anti-American thinking among the Russian political elite.[122]

Second, Russia's abandonment of democratic principles (however flawed in practice during the 1990s) is important as a symbolic indication of Russia's adherence to the general compendium of values comprising "the West." From the perspective of the United States, there is another consideration as well, namely, the commitment made in the 1990s to the success of Russian democratization. Given the level of activity and funding on the part of the U.S. government and nonprofits in the 1990s to promote democratic governance in Russia, the U.S. as a whole has a kind of vested interest in the success of Russia's democratic experiment.

For Russians themselves, the issue of democracy is extraordinarily complex. The "democratic" 1990s were, for most ordinary Russians, a time of personal as well as national insecurity. As in Weimar Germany in the 1920s, the notion of democratic government itself became tarnished by its association with an era many would like to forget. In the Russian case, it is therefore hardly surprising that many people associate the very idea of democracy with the chaos, corruption, and poverty of the Yeltsin era and look back fondly on the days of Leonid Brezhnev or even Josef Stalin, who nearly won a widely publicized poll to select history's most notable Russian.[123]

The irony, of course, is that by most objective measures, the Russia of the 1990s was not a paragon of democratic virtue either. Yeltsin's re-election in 1996 was secured through a corrupt bargain with the oligarchs that involved the massive violation of election rules, kickbacks, and the wholesale transfer of wealth to private hands through the now-infamous loans-for-shares scheme devised by Anatoly Chubais. The Russian press in the 1990s was free of the state control under which it now languishes but was instead a tool of the oligarchs, with most influential print and electronic outlets in the hands of a small number of individuals who used them to promote personal political and economic agendas.[124]

Saying that Russia under Putin retreated from democracy is perhaps misleading. It is indisputable that the Russia of 2009 is a less free and open society than was the Russia of a decade earlier, and this change has had important consequences for Russia's relationship to the United States.[125] Still, much of the problem is connected merely with the way the two countries perceive each other. For a U.S. public still accustomed, on some level, to the stereotypes of Russia that existed during the Cold War, it has been easy enough to see Putin's Russia in the guise of the Soviet Union, a development that the Kremlin's decision to consciously appropriate symbols of the Soviet era—not to mention invading a neighboring country—only feeds. Of course, Russia's leaders often have a point when they charge Washington with a kind of democratic double standard. Shortly after Vice President Cheney condemned Russia's retreat from democracy at an appearance in Vilnius, he traveled to Astana, where he praised the democratic bona fides of Kazakhstan's authoritarian president Nursultan Nazarbaev, a situation whose irony was not lost on Russian observers.[126]

The language of democracy and authoritarianism has dominated public discourse in the U.S. about developments in Russia, with real consequences for U.S.-Russian relations. For the U.S., democracy has become increasingly prominent as a factor in foreign relations since the end of the Cold War.[127] The salience of democracy in U.S. foreign policy was dramatically increased by the promulgation of the so-called Bush doctrine, glimpsed in Iraq and proclaimed in George W. Bush's second inaugural address, where he called on the United States to actively promote the spread of democracy around the world. For this reason, Russia's rejection of even the veneer of democratic values and practices is therefore a statement, too, about Russia's position in the international order of the twenty-first century, particularly, its position relative to the United States.

With some prominent exceptions (mainly in the Greater Middle East), those countries with which the U.S. maintains the closest relations in the twenty-first century are established or consolidating democracies. In the post-Soviet space, U.S. sympathy for Ukraine and Georgia following their colored revolutions was in large part connected to the (at least seeming) democratization promised by their new regimes. Besides, given the role that the U.S. itself played in the establishment of the Yeltsin-era Russian political system, the transformation of that system into something qualitatively different highlights the failure of Washington's investment (through the work of groups such as USAID, the Open Society Institute, NDI/IRI, and others) in creating a Russia in its own image. Regardless of Washington's normative judgment of the new Russia, the very fact that this Russia is not the one Washington sought to build in the 1990s gives individuals and groups connected with that earlier Russia a reason to dislike and distrust the Russia that has replaced it, however naïve may have been the expectation that outsiders could effectively shape the political culture of a country as large and diverse as Russia.

Given the continued emphasis on democracy and democratization in U.S. foreign policy, Russia's authoritarian turn will in all likelihood remain a source of contention and disagreement in relations between Washington and Moscow. Still, the growing divergence between the Russian and U.S. political systems does not change the fact that the two countries continue to have a range of common interests that can be addressed regardless of disputes over the state of Russian democracy. The challenge, of course, will lie in squaring the necessity of cooperating on such issues with the demands of domestic politics in both countries—especially the mounting revulsion in the U.S. at Russia's assault on the institutions of democracy and civil society and the still complex legacy of the war in Georgia.

On the Russian side, too, the deliberate cultivation of anti-U.S. sentiment in the media—alongside the general mistrust of the U.S. stemming from the abandonment of the ABM Treaty, support for NATO expansion and Kosovo's independence, and other provocative actions—has made the climate less hospitable to cooperation with Washington.[128] Indeed, in a roundabout way, the Kremlin's domination of the media and cultivation of anti-U.S. sentiment as a strategy for mobilizing public opinion may be the most consequential element in the country's Putin-era political development for relations with the United States. Even as Putin himself mostly sought to keep disagreements with the U.S. circumscribed, the repetition of tendentious stories in the Russian press shrinks the constituency within Russia for expanding U.S.-Russian cooperation. Increasingly, good U.S.-

Russian relations seem to be a pet issue of the liberal elite, whose influence diminished sharply under Putin.

THE SEARCH FOR STABILITY

On the whole, relations between Russia and the United States worsened throughout the period of Putin's presidency (which, of course, largely coincided with George W. Bush's presidency in the United States). This downturn is to a great extent the result of larger forces that neither Putin nor Bush could control. The very fact that Russia in 2008 had (at least until the fallout of its war with Georgia became evident) one of the world's most rapidly growing economies, had paid down its foreign debt, and was rebuilding its military from the chaos into which it fell during the 1990s means that today's Russia is a more uncomfortable partner for the U.S. than was the weak, cowed Russia of the 1990s.

Overt confrontation with Washington never appeared to be a goal of Putin—or of Medvedev, whose 2008 Foreign Policy Concept placed even greater emphasis on cooperation with the U.S. than its predecessor, calling for a renewal of the U.S.-Russian strategic partnership and joint efforts "to overcome obstacles [created by] strategic principles of the past."[129] In his speech on the basic principles of Russian foreign policy in the aftermath of the Georgian war, Medvedev sounded a very Putinist tone, condemning U.S. unipolarity but emphasizing Russia's interest in friendly relations with all countries—including the U.S.—as long as they recognize Russia's place as a major power and its special role in the CIS.

Still, the transition from Putin to a Putin-Medvedev diarchy and the dramatic events of summer 2008—war and the Russian stock market's collapse—helped re-expose the fissure in the Russian elite between Eurasianists and others about how to deal with a U.S. suffering from its own period of uncertainty. Elements within the Russian bureaucracy used the transition period to question the importance of relations with Washington.[130] The military, busy formulating a strategic doctrine that identifies the U.S. as the most significant threat to Russian security, stepped up its air- and seaborne patrols even while cozying up to American bête noire Hugo Chávez and threatening to sell advanced hardware to Syria.

In Georgia and elsewhere, Russian policy toward the United States has aimed since the mid-1990s above all at ensuring that Washington takes Russian interests into consideration. Russian opposition to U.S. foreign policy—in Iraq as in the former Soviet Union—has for the most part been connected to this larger strategy of promoting Russia's re-emergence as a Great Power and autonomous player on the international stage, rather than opposition to U.S. policy as such in the manner of the USSR. Much of the seemingly perpetual concern in the U.S. about the outbreak of a new Cold War, especially in the aftermath of the war between Russia and Georgia, thus misses the point. The first Cold War was a disaster for Russia, and no sane Russian would want to repeat the experience.

Thanks to the original Cold War, however, the United States is still central to Russian thinking, and hence Russian policy toward the U.S. remains the prism through which foreign policy more generally is filtered. When Russian statesmen talk about multipolarity and a multivector foreign policy, they really are making an argument about Moscow's position with regard to Washington. Consequently, those Russian actions that have fed worries about a new Cold War (Putin's Munich speech, gas cutoffs that affect Western Europe, the invasion of Georgia) seem above all predicated on a desire to remind the United States that Russia still matters. The point is not confrontation for the sake of confrontation, or even challenging U.S. hegemony, but not allowing Washington to get away with ignoring Russia. For that reason, despite the unquestioned notes of tension that crept into the U.S.-Russian relationship during Putin's presidency and boiled over at the start of Medvedev's, achieving a kind of stability in the relationship is not out of the question—at least if Moscow takes active steps to defuse the confrontation over Georgia and Washington under President Barack Obama makes a greater diplomatic effort to reach out to Russia.

Putin, of course, spurned his closest advisers on multiple occasions to ensure that tensions with the U.S. did not spiral out of control, whether over the issue of American troops in Central Asia or over the Baltic states' inclusion in NATO. That rejection of the zero-sum mentality that has so long dominated U.S.-Russian relations meant that when Putin lashed out at the United States (for instance, in the February 2007 Munich speech), his words got Washington's attention.[131] Whether Russian outbursts will have the same effect after the war in Georgia is open to doubt. More likely, filtering intemperate words through the prism of Georgia will only sharpen American mistrust of Russia's intentions. Russian leverage with the U.S. benefited as long as Moscow could credibly threaten its neighbors; the paradox is that following through on those threats damaged Russian leverage by reducing Washington's appetite for compromise and throwing Medvedev's credibility into doubt (not to mention helping weaken Russia's economic clout).

Still, Moscow has been at pains to portray actions with anti-U.S. overtones as a reaction to Washington's own policy choices, and for that reason, President Obama will have some leeway to rethink the nature of the U.S.-Russian relationship. Particularly in the sphere of arms control, Moscow has sought to portray itself as the defender of the status quo and its abrogation of existing obligations as merely a response to unfriendly actions by the United States.

Moscow's decision in late 2002 to withdraw from START II, for example, was depicted as a response to Bush's decision to withdraw the United States from the ABM Treaty.[132] When the Russian Duma first ratified START II back in 2000, Moscow's participation in the accord was made conditional on U.S. ratification of the 1997 additional protocol as well as on Washington's continued adherence to the ABM Treaty. With the Senate never ratifying the additional protocol and the U.S. pulling out of the ABM Treaty in 2002, Putin argued that Russia was no longer bound to respect the provisions of START II.[133] Likewise, when Putin suspended Russian participation in the CFE Treaty in July 2007, his decision was depicted by the Kremlin as a response to Washington's refusal to abandon its plans for antimissile systems in Eastern Europe.[134] Even the invasion of Georgia and recognition of South Ossetia and Abkhazia were depicted as a response to the West's decision to recognize Kosovo, a decision that Moscow insisted set a precedent for separatist conflicts elsewhere. This focus on reciprocity and equal treatment is one major legacy of the Cold War and the centrality of U.S.-Soviet bilateral relations, not only to Soviet foreign policy but to international security generally.

Russia's overall strategy has long been to seek cooperation with the United States to the extent that doing so does not conflict with its Great Power ambitions. What Moscow intends to do when those two elements of its grand strategy do conflict has not been adequately answered. The U.S. finds itself in a similar position, unable (or unwilling) to resolve the tension between its distrust of the newly assertive, active Russia and its hope that Russia can become a reliable partner at a minimum in promoting energy security and bringing stability to Afghanistan. Especially after the conflict in Georgia, this mutual uncertainty, along with a shrinking field of shared interests, remains the biggest obstacle to better relations between Russia and the United States.

NOTES

1. On the meaning of *strategic partnership* in U.S.-Russian relations, see Sean Kay, "What Is a Strategic Partnership?" *Problems of Post-Communism*, May–Jun 2000, 47(3): 15–24. Kay argues that the framework of a strategic partnership enabled the U.S. to manage Russia's decade-long decline, giving Moscow a forum for expressing its discontent without breaking the tie binding it to the West.

2. V. Putin, "Poslanie federal'nomu sobraniyu Rossiiskoi Federatsii," 10 May 2006, http://www.kremlin.ru/appears/2006/05/10/1357_type63372type63374type82634—105546.shtml.

3. R. Cheney, "Vice President's Remarks at the 2006 Vilnius Conference," 4 May 2006, http://www.whitehouse.gov/news/releases/2006/05/20060504-1.html. Vilnius was the site of bloody clashes between the Soviet army and pro-independence

demonstrators in early 1991, after Soviet president Mikhail Gorbachev ordered troops to retake a television tower from the demonstrators.

4. V. Putin, "Vystuplenie i diskussiya na Myunkhenskoi konferentsii po voprosam politiki bezopasnosti," 10 Feb 2007, http://www.kremlin.ru/appears/2007/02/10/1737_type63374type63376type63377t yp e63381type82634_118097.shtml.

5. See "Putin Attacks 'Very Dangerous' US," BBC News, 10 Feb 2007, http://news.bbc.co.uk/go/pr/fr/-/2/europe/6349287.stm; Steven Lee Myers, "No Cold War, Perhaps, but Surely a Lukewarm Peace," *New York Times*, 18 Feb 2007. In fact, the official response in the United States to these remarks was quite muted, perhaps because they cut through the pretense of partnership and rapprochement that is still invoked rhetorically in discussions of U.S.-Russian relations, despite the chill that has set in since around 2004. See Fedor [sic] Lukyanov, "Putin Munich Speech Seen Ending Post–Cold War Pretense," *Gazeta.ru, JRL #46*, 24 Feb 2007.

6. Daniel Fried, "Remarks before the U.S. Senate Foreign Relations Committee," 21 Jun 2007.

7. Thomas Graham, statement to "Russia: Today, Tomorrow—and in 2008" Conference, American Enterprise Institute, 14 Oct 2005, http://www.aei.org/events/eventID.1119,filter.all/event_detail.asp.

8. Sergei Rogov, "Strategicheskoe partnerstvo vse eshche vozmozhno," *Nezavisimaya Gazeta*, 19 Mar 2007.

9. See the discussion in Neil Malcolm and others, *Internal Factors in Russian Foreign Policy* (Oxford: Clarendon, 1996).

10. Revelations of pervasive corruption and double-dealing, for example, on the part of the Harvard Institute for International Development (HIID), which was successfully sued by the U.S. government and then shut down in response to the scandal, did nothing to allay Russian suspicion of U.S. motives in aiding the transition from Communism. On the HIID scandal, see David McClintick, "How Harvard Lost Russia," *Institutional Investor*, Feb 2006, http://www.dailyii.com/article.asp?ArticleID=1020662.

11. "Gosdep SShA prosit Rossiyu ne obol'shchat'sya svoei voennoi mosh'yu," *Izvestiya*, 20 Apr 2007. U.S. diplomats are of course aware of how U.S. actions are perceived in Russia but have had less success in changing those perceptions. See William J. Burns, "Coffee Break at the State Department: U.S. Ambassador to Russia," *JRL #8*, 12 Jan 2007.

12. Dmitry Zamyatin, "Nado zabyt' Evraziyu!" Agenstvo Politicheskoi Novosti, 1 Jun 2007, http://www.apn.ru/publications/article17194.htm.

13. See Council on Foreign Relations, "Russia's Wrong Direction; What the United States Can and Should Do," Independent Task Force Report #57, Mar 2006.

14. Russian Ministry of Foreign Affairs, "Obzor vneshnei politiki Rossiiskoi Federatsii," Mar 2007: 48–49, http://www.mid.ru/brp_4.nsf/sps.

15. See Irina Isakova, *Russian Governance in the Twenty-First Century: Geo-strategy, Geopolitics and Governance* (London: Frank Cass, 2005), 87–89.

16. See Andrew Monaghan, "'Calmly Critical': Evolving Russian Views of US Hegemony," *Journal of Strategic Studies*, Dec 2006, 29(6): 987–1013.

17. Yevgeny Primakov, "Superderzhavy perestali sushchestvovat' s okonchaniem 'kholodnoi voiny,'" interview with *Rossiiskaya Gazeta*, 20 Oct 2006.

18. See, for instance, Sergei Lavrov, "Rossiya i SShA: Mezhdu proshlym i budush-chim," *Mezhdunarodnik.ru*, 26 Sep 2006, http://www.mezhdunarodnik.ru/magazin/5308.html.

19. "Lavrov prokommentiroval otnosheniya Rossii s SShA," *Izvestiya*, 21 May 2007.

20. See Ted Hopf, *Social Construction of International Politics: Identities and Foreign Policies: Moscow 1955 and 1999* (Ithaca, NY: Cornell University Press, 2002), 245. Hopf cites a *Washington Post* editorial from the middle of the Kosovo crisis arguing that the "Russians have won the Kosovo conflict." Washington's restrained response to the Munich speech was similarly indicative of the fact that Putin's pique was at least partially justified. Putin had emphasized that his remarks merely reflected what many in the international community longed to tell Washington—that is, Russia was not interested in acting like a rogue state, but merely demanded that the U.S. take notice of its interests. See Andrew Tully, "Russia: Washington Reacts to Putin's Munich Speech," *RFE/RL Newsline*, 13 Feb 2007.

21. Judy Dempsey, "Putin's Harsh Speech Is Seen as Falling Flat in Europe," *International Herald Tribune*, 15 Feb 2007.

22. Alex Pravda, "Putin's Foreign Policy after 11 September: Radical or Revolutionary?" in *Russia between East and West: Russian Foreign Policy on the Threshold of the Twenty-First Century*, ed. Gabriel Gorodetsky (London: Frank Cass, 2003), 50–51.

23. Thomas Graham, statement to "Russia: Today, Tomorrow—and in 2008" Conference, American Enterprise Institute, 14 Oct 2005, http://www.aei.org/events/eventID.1119,filter.all/event_detail.asp.

24. Jim Hoagland, "Don't Give Up on Russia," *Washington Post*, 17 Nov 2006.

25. On this point see especially Dmitri Simes, "Losing Russia," *Foreign Affairs*, Nov–Dec 2007, 86(6).

26. Yevgeny Gal'tsov, "Kosmicheskaya oborona dlya zemnogo shara," *Nezavisimaya Gazeta*, 21 Mar 2003; Petr Polkovnikov, "Okno uyazvimosti," *Nezavisimaya Gazeta*, 21 Feb 2003.

27. See, for example, Lavrov, "Rossiya i SShA"; V. Putin, "Vystuplenie i diskussiya na Myunkhenskoi konferentsii po voprosam politiki bezopasnosti," 10 Feb 2007, http://www.kremlin.ru/appears/2007/02/10/1737_type63374type63377type633 81type82634_118109.shtml.

28. Olga Kryshtanovskaya and Stephen White, "Inside the Putin Court: A Research Note," *Europe-Asia Studies*, Nov 2005, 57(7): 1065–75.

29. Dmitry Medvedev, "Poslanie Federal'nomu Sobraniyu Rossiiskoi Federatsii," 5 Nov 2008, http://www.kremlin.ru/appears/2008/11/05/1349_type63372type 63374type63381t yp e82634_208749.shtml.

30. See especially James M. Goldgeier and Michael McFaul, *Power and Purpose: U.S. Policy toward Russia after the Cold War* (Washington, DC: Brookings, 2003), 157–60.

31. Goldgeier and McFaul, *Power and Purpose*, 158–59.

32. Yevgeni Primakov, "Turning Back over the Atlantic," *International Affairs: A Russian Journal of World Politics, Diplomacy and International Relations*, 2002, 48(6): 65–74.

33. Alan Russo, "Mir v Yugoslavii: Komu eto vygodno?" Carnegie Moscow Cen-

ter Briefing, Jun 1999, 1(6), http://www.carnegie.ru/ru/print/48347-print.htm. True, the bombing of Serbia was not technically unilateral since Washington's NATO allies were involved. Still accustomed to thinking in terms of power blocs, though, Moscow perceived the attack as a fundamentally U.S. policy in which the Western Europeans acquiesced.

34. Yevgeny Bazhanov, *Sovremennyi mir* (Moscow: Izvestiya, 2004), 134; Monaghan, "Evolving Russian Views," 996.

35. Sean Kay, "What Is a Strategic Partnership?" *Problems of Post-Communism*, May–Jun 2000, 47(3): 15–24.

36. On the international response to the October 1999 invasion of Chechnya, see Strobe Talbott, *The Russia Hand: A Memoir of Presidential Diplomacy* (New York: Random House, 2002); "EU Calls for Dialogue between Moscow, Grozny," *RFE/RL Newsline*, 8 Oct 1999.

37. On SORT and opposition to it, see Anatoly Dyakov and others, "Ratifitsirovat' nel'zya otklonit': Chto delat' s Dogovorom o strategicheskikh nastupatel'nykh potentsialakh Rossii i SShA?" *Nezavisimoe voennoe obozrenie*, 20 Sep 2002. Lacking verification measures and not mandating the destruction of decommissioned warheads, SORT has been criticized by arms control advocates as lacking substance. Precisely this feature induced the Bush administration to submit it to the Senate for ratification. See Donald Rumsfeld, "Prepared Statement to Senate Foreign Relations Committee," 17 Jul 2002, http://www.defenselink.mil/speeches/speech.aspx?speechid=269.

38. Amy F. Wolf and Stuart D. Goldman, "Arms Control after START-II: Next Steps on the U.S.-Russian Agenda," Congressional Research Service Report for Congress, 22 Jun 2001.

39. Wolf and Goldman, "Arms Control."

40. Pavel K. Baev, "The Trajectory of the Russian Military," in *The Russian Military*, ed. Steven E. Miller and Dmitri V. Trenin (Cambridge, MA: American Academy of Arts and Sciences, 2004), 57–59; Robert H. Donaldson and Joseph L. Nogee, *The Foreign Policy of Russia: Changing Systems, Enduring Interests*, 2nd ed. (Armonk, NY: M. E. Sharpe, 2002), 333–37.

41. This connection was made explicit, for instance, in Putin's 2003 address to the Federal Assembly. Putin, "Poslanie Federal'nomu Sobraniyu Rossiiskoi Federatsii," 16 May 2003, http://www.kremlin.ru/appears/2003/05/16/1259_type63372 type63374type82634 ... 44623.shtml.

42. See "Bush and Putin: Best of Friends," BBC News, 16 Jun 2001, http://news.bbc.co.uk/2/hi/europe/1392791.stm.

43. Dmitri K. Simes, "A View from Russia: Grading the President," *Foreign Policy*, Jul–Aug 2003 (137): 36.

44. Condoleezza Rice, "Campaign 2000: Promoting the National Interest," *Foreign Affairs*, Jan–Feb 2000, 79(1).

45. Igor Ivanov, "The New Russian Identity: Innovation and Continuity in Russian Foreign Policy," *Washington Quarterly*, Sum 2001, 24(3): 7–13.

46. See James M. Goldgeier, "The United States and Russia: Keeping Expectations Realistic," *Policy Review*, Oct–Nov 2001: 47–65.

47. Timothy J. Colton and Michael McFaul, "America's Real Russian Allies," *Foreign Affairs*, Nov–Dec 2001, 80(6): 46–58.

48. Paul J. Murphy, *Wolves of Islam: Russia and the Faces of Chechen Terror* (Washington, DC: Brassey's, 2004), 89–91; Dale Herspring and Peter Rutland, "Putin and Russian Foreign Policy," in *Putin's Russia: Past Imperfect, Future Uncertain*, ed. Dale Herspring (Lanham, MD: Rowman & Littlefield, 2005), 272–73.

49. Vladimir Putin, "Vstupiel'noe slovo na zasedanii Soveta bezopasnosti," 3 Dec 2003, http://www.kremlin.ru/appears/2003/12/03/1821_type63374type63 378_56602.shtml.

50. "Joint Statement by U.S. President George Bush and Russian Federation President V. V. Putin Announcing the Global Initiative to Combat Nuclear Terrorism," *Joint Communiqué of 2006 G8 Summit*, http://en.g8russia.ru/docs/5.html. See also Daniel Fried, "Statement before Senate Foreign Relations Committee," 21 Jun 2007.

51. Igor Ivanov interview, "Otvety Ministra inostrannykh del Rossiiskoi Federatsii I. S. Ivanova na voprosy zhurnala 'Kosmopolis,'" *Kosmopolis*, Aut 2002 (1).

52. See James Sherr, "Russia's Current Trajectory," *Russia in the International System*, Conference Report of the U.S. National Intelligence Council, 1 Jun 2001, http://www.dni.gov/nic/confreports_russiainter.html. Sherr believed in 2001 that Russian saber rattling in Afghanistan was in reality designed to intimidate Uzbekistan, which had recently joined the anti-Russian GUUAM grouping, into returning to the Russian fold.

53. Gennady Charodeev, "My raskroem amerikantsam afganskie tainy," *Izvestiya*, 14 Sep 2001.

54. Vladimir Putin, "Zayavlenie Prezidenta Rossii," statement to the press, 24 Sep 2001, http://www.kremlin.ru/appears/2001/09/24/0002_type63374type 63377_28639.shtml.

55. Vladimir Mukhin, "Vashington i Moskva uzhe planiruyut poslevoennoe ustroistvo mira," *Nezavisimaya Gazeta*, 21 Sep 2001.

56. Vladimir Mukhin, "SShA ishchut voennye bazy v SNG," *Nezavisimaya Gazeta*, 15 Sep 2001. His choices were also constrained by the willingness of Central Asia's leaders (especially Islam Karimov of Uzbekistan) to grant the U.S. basing rights regardless of Russian sensibilities.

57. Bobo Lo, *Vladimir Putin and the Evolution of Russian Foreign Policy* (London: Royal Institute of International Affairs, 2003), 118–20; Herspring and Rutland, "Putin and Russian Foreign Policy," 273–74. On Russian aid to the Northern Alliance, see Igor Korotchenko, "Lend-liz ot Sergeya Ivanova," *Nezavisimaya Gazeta*, 4 Oct 2001. On the other hand, the strategy of supporting the U.S. in Afghanistan also proved popular with the Russian public, as even Putin's opponents acknowledged. Grigory Yavlinsky, "Domestic and Foreign Policy Challenges in Russia," speech to Carnegie Endowment for International Peace, 31 Jan 2002, http://www.cdi.org/rus sia/johnson/6061-1.cfm.

58. Milrad Fatullaev, "Voina idet v Rossiyu," *Nezavisimaya Gazeta*, 11 Oct 2001.

59. See the roundtable discussion "Russia's Place in the World after September 11," *International Affairs: A Russian Journal of World Politics, Diplomacy, and International Relations*, 2002, 48(2): 78–91.

60. Yevgeny Primakov, "Is the Russia-U.S. Rapprochement Here to Stay?" *International Affairs: A Russian Journal of World Politics, Diplomacy, and International Relations*, 2002, 48(6): 87–88.

61. Karimov's demand was made in the name of the Shanghai Cooperation Organization, in which Russia (as well as China) plays a key role. See Lionel Beehner, "Severing of U.S.-Uzbek Ties over Counterterrorism," *Council on Foreign Relations Backgrounder*, 30 Sep 2005, http://www.cfr.org/publication/8940/severing _of_usuzbek_ties_over_counterterrorism.html.

62. Andrew C. Winner, "The Proliferation Security Initiative: The New Face of Interdiction," *Washington Quarterly*, Spr 2005, 28(2): 129–43.

63. Council on Foreign Relations, "Russia's Wrong Direction," 24–25.

64. Daniel Fried, "Remarks before the U.S. Senate Foreign Relations Committee," 21 Jun 2007.

65. "A Confusing Turn in Russia: Does Khodorkovsky's Arrest Signal a Retreat from Economic Reform?" Brookings Institution panel discussion, 25 Nov 2003, http://www.brookings.edu/comm/events/20031125.pdf.

66. See especially Thomas Nichols, "Russia's Turn West," *World Policy Journal*, Win 2002–2003, 19(4): 13–22.

67. George W. Bush and Vladimir Putin, "President Bush and Russian President Putin Discuss Progress," press conference, 21 Oct 2001, http://www.whitehouse .gov/news/releases/2001/10/20011021-3.html.

68. Vladimir Putin, "Poslanie Federal'nomu sobraniyu," 18 Apr 2002, http:// www.kremlin.ru/appears/2002/04/18/0000_type63372type63374type82634_28 876.shtml.

69. James M. Goldgeier and Michael McFaul, "What to Do about Russia," *Policy Review*, Oct–Nov 2005 (133): 46.

70. See Tor Bukkvoll, "Putin's Strategic Partnership with the West: The Domestic Politics of Russian Foreign Policy," *Comparative Strategy* (23): 222–42.

71. Andrew Kuchins, "A Turning Point in US-Russian Relations?" Carnegie Endowment for International Peace (originally published in *Vedomosti*, 20 Nov 2006), http://www.carnegiendowment.org/publications/index.cfm?fa = view&id = 18872&prog = zru.

72. Yuri Ushakov, "From Russia with Like," *Los Angeles Times*, 1 Feb 2007.

73. "Doktrina formirovaniya Strategicheskogo Soyuza Rossii i SShA," *Nezavisi-maya Gazeta*, 29 Oct 2003.

74. Nikita Ivanov and Vladimir Frolov, "Dogovor o strategicheskoi druzhbe," *Izvestiya*, 11 Sep 2003.

75. Yevgeny Verlin, "Vashingtonu predlozhili strategicheskii soyuz," *Nezavisi-maya Gazeta*, 29 Sep 2003.

76. Robert Legvold, "All the Way: Crafting a U.S.-Russian Alliance," *The National Interest*, Win 2002–2003: 21–31; Robert MacFarlane, "What's Good for Russia Is Good for America," *New York Times*, 26 Sep 2003.

77. "Remarks by the President and Russian President Putin in Press Availability Camp David," 27 Sep 2003, http://moscow.usembassy.gov/bilateral/transcript .php?record_id = 18.

78. Roderic Lyne, Strobe Talbott, and Koji Watanabe, "Engaging with Russia: The Next Phase," report to the Trilateral Commission, Triangle Papers 59, 2006: 40–44.

79. Janusz Bugajski, "Russia's New Europe," *The National Interest*, Win 2003–2004 (74): 84–91.

80. "Fact Sheet: U.S.-Russia Strategic Framework Declaration," 6 Apr 2008, http://www.whitehouse.gov/news/releases/2008/04/20080406-5.html.

81. Even in the immediate aftermath of the September 11 attacks, Russian diplomats were warning that the unfolding war on terror had to be conducted within the framework of international law and the supremacy of the Security Council. See Igor Ivanov interview, "Otvety"; A. E. Safonov, "Neobkhodima global'naya sistema protivodeistviya terrorizmu," *Mezhdunarodnaya zhizn'*, Jan 2003 (1).

82. Robin Wright and Keith B. Richburg, "Rice Reaches Out to Europe: Paris Speech Urges 'New Chapter' in U.S. Alliance," *Washington Post*, 9 Feb 2005.

83. Ariel Cohen, "Bringing Russia into an Anti-Saddam Coalition," Heritage Foundation Executive Memorandum #812, 29 Apr 2002, http://www.heritage.org/Research/RussiaandEurasia/EM812.cfm.

84. A. V. Konuzin, "Sil'naya OON—osnova zdorovykh mezhdunarodnykh otnoshenii," *Mezhdunarodnaya zhizn'*, 2006 (11).

85. Russian Ministry of Foreign Affairs, "Obzor vneshnei politiki," 49.

86. Putin, "Intervyu zhurnalistam pechatnykh sredstv massovoi informatsii iz stran-chlenov 'uppy vos'mi,' Jun 2007, http://www.kremlin.ru/text/appears/2007/06/132615.shtml.

87. David Holley, "Russia Losing Patience with Iran over Its Nuclear Stance," *Los Angeles Times*, 13 Mar 2007.

88. Ray Takeyh and Nicolas Gvosdev, "Why Rice's Moscow Visit Failed," *Moscow Times*, 20 Oct 2005.

89. Robert O. Freedman, "Putin, Iran, and the Nuclear Weapons Issue," *Problems of Post-Communism*, Mar–Apr 2006, 53(2): 39–48.

90. Simon Saradzhyan, "Russia Needs Iran Proof of Incentives," *Moscow Times*, 3 Jun 2003.

91. Freedman, "Putin, Iran, and the Nuclear Weapons Issue."

92. See Ray Takeyh and Nicholas Gvosdev, "Russia Goes Its Own Way," *International Herald Tribune*, 1 Jan 2008.

93. Alla Kassianova, "Russian Weapons Sales to Iran: Why They Are Unlikely to Stop," PONARS Policy Memo No. 427, Dec 2006, http://www.csis.org/media/csis/pubs/pm_0427.pdf.

94. "Bushehr-Iran Nuclear Reactor," GlobalSecurity.Org Report, http://www.globalsecurity.org/wmd/world/iran/bushehr.htm. In February 2005, Moscow had agreed to supply nuclear fuel to Tehran with the understanding that the spent fuel would be returned to Russia for reprocessing.

95. Ivan Groshkov, "Tegeran khochet sudit'sya s Moskvoi," *Nezavisimaya Gazeta*, 13 Aug 2007.

96. Dmitry Peskov, "On Iran and Energy, According to Russia," interview with *The National Interest* online, 28 Dec 2006, *JRL* #4, 5 Jan 2007.

97. "Security Council Imposes Sanctions on Iran for Failure to Halt Uranium Enrichment, Unanimously Adopting Resolution 737 (2006)," United Nations press release, 23 Dec 2006, http://www.un.org/News/Press/docs/2006/sc8928.doc.htm.

98. Andrei Ryabov, "Moskva prinimaet vyzov 'tsvetnykh revolyutsii,'" *Pro et Contra*, Jul–Aug 2005, 9(1).

99. Most notably, this charge was leveled by former Communist Party central

committee secretary and Soviet ambassador to West Germany Valentin Falin and retired Lt. General Gennady Yevstafiev of the SVR in a report leaked to the press in December 2006. The report was designed in part to discredit former prime minister Mikhail Kasyanov, who had become a leading critic of Putin, by charging him with being a U.S. agent and the likely beneficiary of a Russian colored revolution. See Yulia Petrovskaya, "Izolyatziya i revolyutsiya: V Vashingtone rasschityvayut na prikhod k vlasti v Moskve levogo politika, podderzhannogo liberal'nymi silami," *Nezavisimaya Gazeta*, 21 Sep 2006. Also see "Der Kalte Krieg ist nicht zu Ende," interview with Valentin Falin, *Russland.ru*, http://russland.ru/kapitulation1/more news.php?iditem = 39.

100. "Russia's Lavrov Slams Bush Statement on S. Ossetia," RIA-Novosti, 13 Aug 2008, http://en.rian.ru/russia/20080813/116020741.html.

101. See S. Oznobishchev, "Russia and the United States: Is 'Cold Peace' Possible?" *International Affairs: A Russian Journal of World Politics, Diplomacy, and International Relations*, 2004, 50(4): 55.

102. Of course, one should be careful about generalizing from these cases. The Baltic states never accepted their incorporation in the USSR at the start of World War II, while Georgia's anti-Russian inclinations are being strengthened by Moscow's encouragement of separatists in Abkhazia and South Ossetia. The recent history of Ukraine, where democratic opening has resulted in cohabitation between a pro-Western president and a pro-Russian prime minister, complicates the facile equation between democracy and hostility to Russia posited by the Kremlin. It might be more accurate to say that Russian meddling in the domestic politics of these states strengthens anti-Russian sentiment (such was the case in Ukraine leading up to the 2004 Orange Revolution). It is also worth noting that Saakashvili's Georgia has hardly turned into a paragon of democracy, though Saakashvili has maintained a pro-Western foreign policy orientation and expressed serious interest in bringing Georgia into NATO.

103. Thomas Carothers, "The Backlash against Democracy Promotion," *Foreign Affairs*, Mar–Apr 2006, 85(2): 55–68.

104. "Crisis in Georgia: Frozen Conflicts and U.S.-Russian Relations," Carnegie Endowment for International Peace meeting summary, 11 Oct 2006, *JRL* #237.

105. Stephen Sestanovich, testimony to U.S. Senate Committee on Foreign Relations, 29 Jun 2006, http://www.cfr.org/publications/11019/testimony_to_com mittee_on_foreign_relations_us_senate.html?breadcrumb = default.

106. "Russia: NGOs Uneasy as Deadline Passes," *RFE/RL Newsline*, 19 Apr 2007.

107. For a breakdown of Russian oil production by region, see Vladimir Milov, presentation to "Whither Russia's Oil?" Conference, American Enterprise Institute, 19 May 2006, http://www.aei.org/events/eventID.1314,filter.all/event_detail.asp. A similar breakdown of gas production can be found in Nikolai Dobretsov and others, "The 'Altai' Trunk Gas Pipeline and Prospects of Russia's Outlet to the Fuel-and-Energy Market of the Asia-Pacific Region and the Development of Transit Regions," *Far Eastern Affairs*, 2007, 35(2): 75.

108. See Edward L. Morse and James Richard, "The Battle for Energy," *Foreign Affairs*, Mar–Apr 2002, 81(2).

109. Mikhail Margelov, "Russia and the U.S.: Priorities Real and Artificial," *Inter-*

national Affairs: A Russian Journal of World Politics, Diplomacy, and International Relations, 2006, 52(1): 26.

110. Claire Bigg, "Russia: Energy Security, Nuclear Proliferation Top G8 Agenda," *RFE/RL Newsline*, 13 Jul 2006.

111. Vladimir Putin, "Vystuplenie na Balkanskom sammite po energeticheskoi bezopasnosti," 24 Jun 2007, http://www.kremlin.ru/appears/2007/06/24/1200_type63374type63377_135699.shtml.

112. "The Russian Federation," Brookings Institution Energy Security Series Report, Oct 2006: 28–29.

113. "Russian Federation," 20.

114. Manana Kochladze, "The BTC Pipeline: Botched, Tardy, and Chilling," *Transitions Online*, 7 Feb 2005.

115. Iusuf Osmanov, "Kaspiiskii uglevodorody protekut po koridoram mimo Rossii," *Kommersant*, 26 May 2005; Jon Gorvett, "End of the Line for Baku-Ceyhan?" *Middle East*, May 2001 (312).

116. Azerbaijan has already moved aggressively to reduce the amount of oil it exports through Russia, though Moscow continues attempting to bring Baku back into the fold. See Paul Kubicek, "Russian Energy Policy in the Caspian Basin," *World Affairs*, Spr 2004, 166(4).

117. Fred Weir, "Big Powers Jockey for Oil in Central Asia," *Christian Science Monitor*, 28 Mar 2007; Sergei Kulikov, "Kazakhstanskaia neft' poplyvet v obkhod," *Nezavisimaya Gazeta*, 9 Aug 2007. Astana signed a deal to send oil through the BTC pipeline in June 2006.

118. Emin Makhmudov and Mikhail Zigar, "S goriuchim revoliutsionnym privetom: Kaspiiskaia neft' vypolniaet truboprovod Baku-Dzheijkhan," *Kommersant*, 25 May 2005. When the BTC pipeline came online in 2006, Kazakh president Nursultan Nazarbaev was present, after having expressed interest in building an extension of BTC from his country across the Caspian Sea.

119. V. I. Kalyuzhny, "Energetika dolzhna imet' politicheskuyu sostavlyaushchuyu," *Izvestiya*, 7 Apr 2004; "Moscow Remains Opposed to Baku-Ceyhan Pipeline," *RFE/RL Newsline*, 12 Jan 2004.

120. Kubicek, "Russian Energy Policy."

121. Kazakhstan, for instance, considered diverting oil from BTC to Russian-controlled pipelines out of security concerns. See "Kazakhstan Considers to Divert [sic] Oil Export Route from BTC to Russia," *Hürriyet*, 10 Sep 2008, http://www.hurriyet.com.tr/english/finance/9714319.asp?scr=1.

122. Brian D. Taylor, "Power Surge? Russia's Power Ministries from Yeltsin to Putin and Beyond," PONARS Policy Memo No. 414, Dec 2006.

123. Richard Pipes, "Flight from Freedom: What Russians Think and Want," *Foreign Affairs*, May–Jun 2004, 83(3); Sarah E. Mendelson and Theodore P. Gerber, "Failing the Stalin Test," *Foreign Affairs*, Jan–Feb 2006, 85(1). For the "Imya Rossii [Name of Russia]" poll, see http://www.nameofrussia.ru/rating.html?all=1. Stalin finished in third place, with the thirteenth-century military hero Aleksandr Nevsky winning.

124. Dmitri Trenin, "Russia: Back to the Future?" statement to U.S. Senate Foreign Relations Committee, 29 Jun 2006.

125. Evgeni Kiselev, "The Future of Russian Politics: What the West Perceives and Misperceives," lecture to Carnegie Endowment for International Peace, 14 Nov 2006, http://www.carnegieendowment.org/events/index.cfm?fa = eventDetail& id = 934&&prog = zru.

126. Mikhail Zigar, "Dik Cheini proshchupal dno Kaspii," *Kommersant*, 6 May 2006.

127. Vladimir Shlapentokh, "The Dying Russian Democracy as a Victim of Corrupt Bureaucrats," *JRL* #126, 18 May 2007.

128. William Zimmerman, *The Russian People and Foreign Policy: Russian Elite and Mass Perspectives, 1993–2000* (Princeton, NJ: Princeton University Press, 2002); Pipes, "Flight from Freedom." The amount and depth of anti-American sentiment in Russia's state-controlled press increased sharply in early 2007. While most likely a ploy to promote an atmosphere of crisis and strengthen support for the Kremlin in advance of the 2008 presidential elections, some analysts have argued that the surge in hostile rhetoric in fact marks a new period in Russia's foreign policy history in which cooperation with Washington has been all but abandoned as an element of national strategy. See Leon Aron, "Putin-3," *AEI Russia Outlook*, 16 Jan 2008, http://www.aei.org/publications/filter.all,pubID.27367/pub_detail.asp.

129. "Kontseptsiya vneshnei politiki Rossiiskoi Federatsii," 2008.

130. Ilya Azar and Aleksandr Artemeyev, "Zaryadka mirovoi napryazhennosti," *Gazeta.ru*, 29 Jul 2008.

131. Andrew E. Kramer, "Putin Likens U.S. Foreign Policy to That of Third Reich," *International Herald Tribune*, 9 May 2007.

132. "Russia: START II Overview," Nuclear Threat Initiative NIS Nuclear and Missile Database, 4 Dec 2002, http://www.nti.org/db/nisprofs/russia/treaties/s2des-cr.htm.

133. Amy F. Wolf and Stuart D. Goldman, "Arms Control after START-II: Next Steps on the U.S.-Russian Agenda," Congressional Research Service Report for Congress, 22 Jun 2001. Of course, the fact that Washington was unlikely to meet the conditions necessary for Russia's ratification of START II to take effect helped Putin persuade the Duma to proceed with the ratification back in 2000.

134. "Russia Suspends Arms Control Pact," BBC News, 14 Jul 2007, http://news.bbc.co.uk/2/hi/europe/6898690.stm; "NATO Hopes Russia Remains in CFE Treaty," RIA-Novosti, 26 Jun 2007, http://en.rian.ru/world/20070626/67863 762.html.

4

Europe

Between Integration and Confrontation

If notes of tension have increasingly crept into Russia's relationship with the United States since the middle of the decade, by the last years of Putin's presidency Russo-European relations seemingly went into a free fall. More than a year before the outbreak of hostilities between Russia and Georgia, European Union Trade Commissioner (and one-time top foreign policy adviser to British prime minister Tony Blair) Peter Mandelson warned in April 2007 that "relations between the EU and Russia . . . contain a level of misunderstanding or even mistrust we have not seen since the end of the Cold War."[1] The reasons for the Russian estrangement from Europe are numerous: Russia's authoritarian drift, tensions over the expansion of the EU and NATO, Moscow's interference in the affairs of its neighbors, and disputes over Russian energy supplies to Europe. The U.S. has expressed concern about all of these issues as well, but given Europe's proximity and greater economic dependence on Russia, the consequences of the Kremlin's more assertive foreign policy course have on the whole been felt more immediately in Europe. Nonetheless, several European countries, notably Germany, Italy, and (to a slightly lesser degree) France, have been at the forefront of a push for rapprochement with Russia, often in opposition to the U.S. as well as to many of their European neighbors and the EU itself.

Europe continues to hold an anomalous position in Russia's foreign policy strategy. On the one hand, Europe, like the United States, is part of the broad coalition of democracies comprising the West. Yet despite this shared identity and shared commitment to democratic values, the Kremlin has often approached the U.S. and Europe on the basis of quite different calculations. For Russia, the U.S. remains important principally as the strongest political and military force in the post–Cold War world, one that often conducts diplomacy on the basis of the same geopolitical considerations underlying Russian foreign policy itself.

Besides being a geographic expression, Europe of course also implies the web of institutions and shared values that sprang up in the aftermath of World War II. Since the end of the Cold War, these institutions—above all the European Union and North Atlantic Treaty Organization (NATO)—have expanded into Europe's east, taking in countries that had long been in the Russian/Soviet sphere of influence. Europe's dense web of institutions, with their effects on the national sovereignty of their members, has no analogue elsewhere in the world. For this reason, Russia's relationship to Europe operates simultaneously on two levels: that of Moscow's bilateral ties with countries like Germany, France, and the United Kingdom, as well as that of its ties with the institutional structures of the EU, NATO, the Organization for Security and Cooperation in Europe (OSCE), and other regional organizations. With its preference for bilateral relations and distrust of institutions, Russia has often given the impression of playing off individual European countries—especially larger Western European powers—against the institutional center, even while at times also using Europe collectively as a counterweight against the United States.

Much of the difficulty in the relationship stems in one form or another from the evolving political identity of both Russia itself and of the structures comprising Europe. During the 1980s, Russia began a strategic retreat from Eastern Europe. Into the resulting vacuum stepped the institutional web of Europe. By 2007, both the EU and NATO had expanded to include most of the former Warsaw Pact states (apart from Russia and the non-Baltic former Soviet republics).[2] While Europe does not possess a military potential comparable to that of the United States, the expansion of both NATO and the EU has nonetheless substantially changed Russia's security landscape and fed into Russia's postimperial anxieties. Expansion has deprived Russia of the strategic glacis it acquired at the end of World War II and made Russia and Europe close, if somewhat uncomfortable, neighbors. The EU's continued expansion, particularly if it comes to include Turkey or additional post-Soviet states (such as Ukraine), also raises fundamental questions about Russia's identity and role in Europe's security architecture.[3]

So, too, does the quest for ever closer union among the states already in the EU. The halting steps that Brussels took toward the creation of an integrated European Security and Defense Policy (ESDP) and Common Foreign Policy (CFP) unsettled the Russians further, forcing Moscow to confront the sudden appearance of a new, at least potentially powerful security actor right on its border.[4] Besides aspiring to play a greater international role, the new, larger EU has been more assertive toward Russia than the old European Community or the original fifteen-member EU of the 1990s ever were.

European states that traditionally maintained close relations with Russia—such as (West) Germany, with its tradition of *Ostpolitik*—have looked on uncomfortably as states in the new Europe such as Poland pushed the EU in a more confrontational direction, often at the expense of the EU's own cohesiveness. Negotiations on a new Partnership and Cooperation Agreement (PCA) between Russia and the EU were held up for a year and a half by Poland and Lithuania, which were engaged in a dispute with the Russians over meat exports and oil deliveries, respectively.[5] By the time Moscow and Brussels finally began talks on a new PCA in late June 2008, it was only weeks until the Russians invaded Georgia, leading the EU—under pressure from its newer members—to convene an emergency summit and decide once again to postpone negotiations on a new agreement.

Like the EU, NATO's expansion to the East has affected Russia's security calculations while also buttressing Cold War–era anxieties about Russia's strategic isolation and encirclement. Given that NATO was created precisely to counter Soviet geopolitical ambitions in Europe, many Russians continue to view the alliance with substantial mistrust. With the Cold War over and the Warsaw Pact relegated to Trotsky's proverbial dustbin of history, from Russia's perspective NATO often seems equally outmoded. During the 1990s, while NATO struggled to identify a new mission for itself, Primakov and others called for the alliance to be disbanded altogether, or at least subordinated to some kind of pan-European security structure like the OSCE.[6] Putin and Medvedev have similarly suggested forming some sort of new pan-European security organization that would largely supplant NATO.

While NATO's continued existence was at times a source of frustration in Moscow, the alliance's decision to take in the former Warsaw Pact states of Eastern Europe was particularly unwelcome, especially as the Kremlin believed former U.S. president George H. W. Bush and his European counterparts had given their word that, in exchange for Russia tolerating the presence of a united Germany in NATO, the alliance would not expand any further.[7] Instead, NATO moved to include Russia's former satellites in Eastern Europe (including the Baltic states), openly discussed the possibility of bringing in Georgia and Ukraine, and greatly expanded its capacity for out-of-area operations near Russia's borders.[8] While Moscow had many reasons for sending troops into Georgia, concern about Tbilisi's NATO ambitions was among the most critical.

As in the 1990s, the scope and role of NATO remain central to the dispute between Russia and the Europeans. This expansion of NATO's reach has only in small part been offset by the alliance's growing political, in contrast to military-security, role. Dealing with a vastly expanded NATO whose security operations have become increasingly expansive in scope, alongside a European Union that is itself increasingly an actor in the field of international security, exacerbated Russian concerns about the country's vulnerability and fed suspicions that the West as a whole had not given up the idea of seeing Russia as a rival center of power to be confronted and contained, a reflex that the conflict in Georgia seems only to have strengthened.

Despite such fears, the Kremlin leadership has often emphasized the necessity of good relations with Europe, given Russia's proximity and the two sides' interdependence. The imperative for good relations is particularly evident in the realm of economics, since Europe, especially Eastern Europe, remains a major market for Russian exports (with the expansion of the European Union, the Russian government projected that over 50 percent of the country's exports would subsequently be directed to EU states).[9] Russia's dependence on Europe as a customer is matched by Europe's dependence on Russia as a supplier, especially of oil and gas—precisely those resources that remain at the heart of Russia's increasingly assertive foreign policy. For this reason, Russia cannot afford, at least in the short run, anything like complete estrangement from Europe without at the same time entirely undermining its own political and economic interests.

While long desirous of good relations with the EU, Russia has remained firmly opposed to joining the Union, much less NATO (though Russian membership in both organizations has been mooted at various times since 1991).[10] Even though Putin repeatedly stressed that Russia is "an integral part of European civilization," Russia's insistence on remaining outside the institutional framework of Europe has meant that Russia approached in particular the normative foundations of Europe cautiously.[11] As Europe's identity increasingly comes to be based on a consensus about values and institutions, the Great Power ambitions that have motivated Russian foreign policy for most of the country's post-Soviet history have put it at odds with the postmodern and postimperial Europe taking shape on its borders. Despite the very different ambitions of Russia and the EU, Putin insisted that Russia aspires to not only increased cooperation, but also increased integration, at least in the fields of economics and trade, which Moscow hopes will be the centerpiece of a new PCA.

Most Western European leaders have sought to stress the economic side of their relationship with Russia, at the expense of the traditional security relations that have dominated the U.S.-Russian agenda—even after the war in Georgia.[12] Still, as Russian foreign policy, especially under Putin, adapted economic tools to long-standing geopolitical ends, the security consequences for Europe became increasingly evident.

European fears have been exacerbated by the facts that Russia is the continent's largest supplier of oil and gas and that Europe's dependence will grow rapidly over the next two decades.[13] The experiences of January 2006 and January 2007, when Russia substantially reduced gas deliveries to Ukraine and Belarus, respectively, pushed the EU to reduce Russia's monopoly on supplying the continent's energy by promoting ties with alternative suppliers in North Africa and Central Asia. This search for alternate suppliers coupled with the fact that Russian oil and gas production are likely running at close to their peak, with little scope for further increases in the short run, clearly demonstrate the limitations inherent in this, Russia's seemingly most potent foreign policy tool.

At the same time, though, fears of Russia's monopoly power have succeeded in undermining European solidarity, with some large states such as Italy and Germany seeking direct agreements with Moscow over the head of Brussels (not to mention Warsaw or Vilnius).[14] The EU's own crisis of confidence, culminating in the rejection of both a proposed constitution and the Lisbon Treaty designed to replace it, only make it easier for Moscow to pursue selective cooperation with favored partners within Europe at the expense of accommodating itself to the demands of Brussels.

Nor, given the centrality of the United States to Russian foreign policy thinking, is it possible to ignore the impact of the U.S. on relations between Russia and Europe. Ever since the early years of the Cold War, Moscow has attempted to take advantage of the differences between Europe and the United States for its own ends. The end of the Cold War has done little to change this pattern, and the cooling of U.S.-European ties over the war in Iraq promoted Russian attempts to maneuver between Washington and Brussels. Similarly, the Georgian conflict exposed a continuing rift between the U.S. and at least the Western Europeans over the nature of the Russian challenge and the appropriate response to it. Medvedev's call for a new European security architecture likewise was interpreted, especially in the U.S., as a ploy to pry Europe from its strategic alignment with the United States.

Shortly after the September 11 attacks, Moscow pursued rapprochement with the U.S. on the basis of a shared commitment to fight terrorism, enlisting U.S. support for its campaign in Chechnya in the face of European opposition. During the run-up to the war in Iraq, Russia pursued a mirror image of this strategy, banding together with France and Germany to oppose a U.S.-led attack on Saddam Hussein. Since the start of the war in Iraq, Russia's maneuvering between Washington and Brussels has been more sophisticated, as the Russian leadership has come to the realization that at the end of the day, the EU will not jeopardize its relationship with the United States for the uncertain prospect of Russia's friendship. Instead of openly playing the U.S. and EU off against each other, Russian diplomacy after 2003 promoted the emergence of a strategic triangle of the U.S., EU, and Russia. In part, the idea of a strategic triangle with the U.S. and the EU was part of Russia's broader strategy of, in the words of Foreign Minister Lavrov, "restoring manageability to world affairs in accord with other centers of power."[15] In other words, a trilateral U.S.-EU-Russian partnership could take the place of the abortive special relationship with the U.S. as a means of returning Russia to a position as a key pillar of the new international order. This approach was also part of Putin's and Lavrov's network diplomacy strategy, which emphasizes Russia's ability to work out partnerships with important countries all around its borders, activating each partnership as appropriate to resolve particular issues in preference to maintaining fixed alliances. Such an approach is designed to maximize Russian flexibility and influence while minimizing the normative aspect that could prove particularly troubling in the context of relations with the EU.

Given Russia's proximity to Europe and the importance of Europe's markets for Russian goods (largely but not exclusively energy), economic integration continued even as political relations between the two sides deteriorated. Putin, and the Russian elite more generally, did much to promote ties to Europe as a critical driver in the recovery and growth of the Russian economy. Yet the economic benefits Russia derives from Europe have been imperiled to a certain extent by Moscow's geopolitical maneuverings, above all its attempts to use energy supplies as a means of obtaining political leverage over both post-Soviet Ukraine and Belarus and the countries of the EU themselves. A fundamental tension thus exists in Russia's policy toward Europe, between the desire for economic cooperation, even integration, and the power-political imperatives that have become a more visible element in Russian foreign policy during the Putin years.

This tension is especially pronounced since it is precisely Russia's economic recovery in the years since 2000—largely driven by high oil and gas prices—that has enabled the country to play the more active foreign policy role to which its elite aspires. In the short run at least, Russia has little alternative to exporting its oil and gas resources to Europe (pipelines and LNG terminals that would allow Russia to reroute supplies to Asia or North America have not yet been built on any scale). As a result, Moscow cannot afford to alienate its principal customer and jeopardize its own prosperity through actions like its decisions to cut off supplies to Ukraine and Belarus. Yet the expansive logic underlying Russian foreign policy has meant that the Kremlin will not moderate its ambitions to keep Belarus and Ukraine in its own orbit, to keep NATO assets away from its borders, or to prevent European Union moralizing from influencing its own political development. The larger Europe that has come into being in the past decade has increasingly complicated Russia's ability to achieve these and related aims. Despite Putin's rhetoric about Russia's European choice, both Russia and Europe's expanded ambitions and the deepening political-moral divide between the two sides have increasingly imperiled the economically driven rapprochement Moscow and Brussels have both pursued over the past two decades, even as Moscow's bilateral ties with Berlin, Paris, and Rome have deepened.

RUSSIA AND THE EUROPEAN UNION

The most salient factor in the evolution of Russia's foreign policy in Europe has been the transformation of the European Union itself. From 1992, when the Maastricht Treaty brought the EU into being and laid the foundation for ever closer union among its members, the EU has increasingly become an important international actor in its own right. The EU's emergence from the American shadow has forced Moscow to increasingly differentiate its approaches to Europe and the U.S. Putin's Russia initially sought to cooperate with the EU while emphasizing that Russia "does not set itself the task of becoming a member of the EU."[16]

This cooperation, however, remained troubled by European distrust of Russia's overall direction and an ongoing tug-of-war over the borderlands between Russia and Europe. At the same time, because the EU must reflect the position of the states it comprises, Brussels had had significant difficulty articulating a coherent approach to dealing with Russia. Significant disputes exist within Europe—between old and new members of the EU and between large and small countries—leaving the EU unable to agree on any sort of comprehensive strategy for relations with Russia.

Instead, EU members have resorted to bilateral arrangements with Moscow when it serves their interests to do so (especially on the question of energy supplies).[17] The growth of bilateral arrangements has on the whole increased Russian bargaining leverage, allowing the Kremlin to play different European states off against one another and limiting the range of issues where Russia finds itself confronting a solid European bloc. Meanwhile, countries like Poland and the Baltic states that have little leverage with Russia have at times sought to push the EU as a whole into a more confrontational posture, to the discomfort of states like Germany that have long had cozier arrangements with the Kremlin. As a result of the EU's internal divisions, its goals for policy toward Russia are fairly modest. According to the European Commission:

> The main interests of the EU in Russia lie in fostering the political and economic stability of the [Russian] Federation; in maintaining a stable supply of energy; in further co-operation in the fields of justice and home affairs, the environment and nuclear safety in order to combat "soft" security threats; and in stepping up cooperation with Russia in the Southern Caucasus and the Western NIS for the geopolitical stability of the CIS region, including for the resolution of frozen conflicts.[18]

Despite the EU's embrace of the formerly Communist states of Eastern Europe and Russia's aspirations to a larger international security role, Russia's most important interests in Europe remain economic. The economic linkages between Moscow and the EU create a kind of interdependence, which has at times both ameliorated and exacerbated the distrust between the two sides. While Europe's dependence on Russia for its energy imports has been much discussed, Russia's economy is heavily reliant on Europe as well. The resulting economic interdependence means that at least in the short run, the scope for broader geopolitical conflicts between the two is limited by the mutual need to avoid economic disruptions—creating what the German analyst Heinrich Vogel terms "mutually assured dependence."[19] In the long run, however, the EU's attempts to locate other sources of energy coupled with Russia's avowed interest in building the infrastructure necessary to bring its oil and gas to Asia or the U.S. may portend a partial decoupling of the economic, and hence political, fates of Russia and Europe.

The EU, of course, began its life as an economic organization, growing out of Franco-German heavy industrial cooperation in the early 1950s. Given the economic focus of the resulting European Economic Community (EEC), even during the height of the Cold War Moscow was willing to forge economic links with Western Europe, though without necessarily accepting the legitimacy of the EEC as a political actor.[20] With the end of the Cold War and the consolidation of the EEC into the more integrated, more explicitly political EU, Russia continued to value the Western Europeans as trading partners while also forging direct links to the EU as an institution. In the 1990s, even as Moscow consistently opposed the expansion of NATO into Eastern Europe, it supported the growth of the EU as a means of satisfying the Eastern Europeans' desire to anchor themselves in the West while not threatening Russia's own security.[21]

Yet, as with the United States, relations between the EU and Russia suffered from unfulfilled expectations on both sides. At the end of the Cold War, Moscow expected to be greeted, like West Germany in the 1950s, with an influx of foreign aid and investment as well as rapid integration into the institutional web of the new Europe. Brussels, meanwhile, assumed that Russia would rapidly adopt Western (or, more precisely, European) values regarding human rights, democracy, and free markets.[22]

Both were to be disappointed. Even as Russia and the EU signed the Partnership and Cooperation Agreement in 1994, they regarded each other warily. Primakov, as foreign minister, revived the Soviet-era practice of trying to split Europe from the United States, particularly during the conflicts in the Balkans at the end of the 1990s.[23] Beginning in 1994, Russia was also engaged in a vicious civil war in Chechnya, where its troops' employment of brute force against the civilian population brought stiff objections from the EU, including calls that Russia be expelled from the Council of Europe for its brazen violation of the council's human rights norms.[24]

Russia's growing authoritarianism has been a major source of contention with Europe, even more so than in Moscow's relationship with the United States. Especially since the start of the war on terror, Washington has been willing to overlook to a significant extent the antidemocratic trends under way in Putin's Russia. The most withering U.S. criticism of Russia has been directed at Moscow's foreign policy (e.g., Vice President Cheney's charge that Moscow was using energy as a weapon against its neighbors or condemnation of its invasion of Georgia). Washington has been less vocal about the Kremlin's crackdown on dissent and other human rights violations than has Brussels. Russian behavior in Chechnya and the North Caucasus more generally provides the most salient example of the differences between the European and U.S. approaches. The degree of Russia's acceptance into the European family will largely depend on the extent to which Moscow is willing and able to adopt European norms in fields like rule of law, freedom of the press, electoral transparency, and the like, all of which deteriorated during the years of Putin's presidency. Since the U.S. is more interested in Russian cooperation on a geopolitical level, the question of values, while not irrelevant, remains by comparison a secondary concern.

If democracy and all its attributes remain an area of deep disagreement between Russians and Europeans, a certain wariness about American hegemony has at times served to bring Moscow and Brussels closer. In 1999, Moscow elaborated its approach to relations with the EU in a document known as the "Medium-Term Strategy for the Development of Relations between the Russian Federation and the European Union (2000–2010) [*Strategiya razvitii otnoshenii Rossiiskoi federatsii s Evropeiskim soyuzom na srednesrochnuyu perspektivu (2000–2010 gody)*]," which Putin, as prime minister, had helped to draft.[25] This strategy document, presented by the Russians to their EU counterparts at the Helsinki summit in October 1999, was designed to govern Russian policy toward the EU until 2010. Like the roughly contemporaneous Russian Foreign Policy Concept, the Medium-Term Strategy emphasized Russia's interest in the creation of a multipolar world order, where international law constrained the ability of any single state to impose its will through force—precisely as Moscow argued the United States had just done in Kosovo. It praised Europe as Russia's strategic partner in this endeavor to establish a multipolar order and a system of collective security in Europe. The document did make clear that Russia's leadership viewed the country as a Euro-Asian state that by virtue of its size and history was not interested in any kind of formal association with—much less eventual membership in—the EU. At the same time, it held out the possibility of Russia playing a greater role in pan-European security, perhaps by way of the OSCE, which Moscow held out as a way to check what the Medium-Term Strategy termed "NATO-centrism in Europe."[26]

While the Medium-Term Strategy was designed to shape Russian relations with the EU for a full decade, in recent years Russia has been less sanguine about the EU than that document would indicate. One major factor
contributing to the recent estrangement has been the rapprochement with
the United States in the first years of Putin's presidency, which altered how
the Kremlin approached its goal of promoting multipolarity. By 2001,
bandwagoning with Washington, rather than balancing against it, appeared
the most effective way to promote Russia's role as a major actor in world
affairs. The September 11 attacks only reinforced Putin's strategy of promoting better ties with the U.S. while approaching the EU cautiously. The
attacks brought the U.S. and Russia together in advocating a muscular
approach to Islamic terrorism. Both meanwhile frequently found themselves in opposition to Brussels (not to mention Berlin and Paris), which
remained skeptical of the forceful methods advocated by the Bush and
Putin governments.[27] Unlike the United States, following September 11 the
EU and its members did not moderate their criticism of Russian behavior
in Chechnya or of the Kremlin's conduct during the 2003 parliamentary
and 2004 presidential elections. More generally, the EU largely rejected the
kind of power-driven geopolitical thinking common to both Russia and the
U.S., focusing on the need for better policing and improved international
cooperation rather than military force as the keys to defeating the terrorist
menace in Afghanistan, Chechnya, and elsewhere.[28]

While the U.S.-Russian rapprochement of 2002–2003 had the effect of
sidelining Europe, the EU's own development as an actor in international
affairs has limited the Union's ability to cooperate with Russia. Somewhat
paradoxically, while the EU's emphasis on the "soft" aspects of security in
response to the September 11 attacks put it at odds with a Kremlin still
employing massive force in its own antiterrorist campaign in Chechnya, the
potential development of the EU as a more effective wielder of "hard"
power has had a similar effect.

The Russian dilemma is now more complicated on account of the fact
that, with the (albeit temporary) parting of ways between Europe and the
United States over the war in Iraq, the EU accelerated the process of developing its own military capabilities to go alongside the impressive array of
economic, legal, and technical resources available to member states. In the
wake of the terrorist attacks on the United States and conscious of the EU's
tepid response to mass killing in Bosnia and Rwanda in the 1990s, the
Council of Europe adopted the first comprehensive EU security strategy in
December 2003.[29] The following year, the EU established an integrated
European Defense Agency to coordinate the strategic planning of member
states, while the EU also took over policing and peacekeeping responsibilities in Macedonia and Bosnia, respectively, and launched its first major out-

of-area operation in the Democratic Republic of Congo (DRC).[30] By 2004, the EU, NATO, and several European national governments all had authority over troops in the field, in theaters ranging from Kosovo to Iraq to the DRC, even if Brussels has continued to fall behind on its plans to upgrade (and fund) the EU's security capabilities.

The increased willingness and ability of both the EU collectively and its member states individually to deploy troops outside the long-established framework of NATO has had important implications for the way the Kremlin has approached its relationship with the EU. The sharp distinction Russian leaders in the 1990s made between the "good" EU and "bad" NATO is no longer quite so clear cut. Moscow no longer sees the two organizations' roles as being fundamentally distinct—particularly with the appointment of former NATO secretary-general Javier Solana as the EU's top foreign policy figure and the folding of the old Western European Union (WEU) with its close ties to NATO into the EU itself.[31]

The EU's capacity in the fields of security and defense may well increase in the future if member states commit more troops to the joint forces (Eurocorps and European Rapid Reaction Force) set up under the auspices of the ESDP and the process of defense integration continues. All of these developments would mean that the EU is no longer the *quantité négligeable* that Russian planners took it to be in the 1990s. And because of the existence of a formal mechanism for Russia's participation in NATO decision making (the NATO-Russia Council), Moscow is better placed to influence the deliberations of that organization than it is the deliberations of the EU, where it does not have any formal representation.

In addition to fears about the growing securitization of the EU, Moscow has worried about the effects of EU expansion and the impact of the Eastern European countries—which tend to be more skeptical of Russia's foreign policy—on the workings of the EU as a whole. Russia's worries on this score are also linked to the consolidation of the ESDP and the EU's expanded security role. After all, thanks to the simultaneous processes of expansion and defense integration within the EU, Russia now finds Europe right on its borders and on the borders of unstable states like Moldova and Ukraine that Russia continues to consider part of its own security zone.[32] In contrast to its opposition to further NATO expansion, Russia has not raised any objections to the prospect of Ukraine's membership in the EU (and for economic reasons, might even prove supportive), though increased momentum toward strengthening EU defense capacity might risk replaying the debate over NATO membership for the former Soviet republics.[33] In any case, the failure of the EU constitution and the Lisbon Treaty, which Irish voters rejected in a 2008 referendum, imposed at least a temporary pause on the further institutionalization of the EU's security role.

The cooling of relations between Moscow and Brussels that took place in the first years of Putin's presidency coincided with the first major wave of EU expansion to the East and the host of complications—technical as well as political—that ensued for Moscow.[34] By the time of the 2002 EU-Russia summit in Moscow, as a result of seemingly insoluble disputes over migration and access to Kaliningrad, relations with the EU had reached their (then-) nadir, even as the newly created NATO-Russia Council had led to a marked improvement in Russia's attitude toward the North Atlantic Alliance.[35]

Indeed, Russian observers have identified a trend toward Brussels devaluing the supposedly objective criteria for EU membership in favor of political criteria linked to the EU's international security role. In the Russian view, only the predominance of geopolitical criteria over the EU's historic emphasis on economic development, shared values, and democracy can explain the interest in admitting the countries of the Western Balkans or Turkey—much less the South Caucasus—into the EU.[36] Given the Russian proclivity to view the world in traditional balance-of-power terms, it is hardly surprising that many Russians see the EU's continued expansion— like NATO's—as part of a process of re-establishing containment of Russia.

As a result of its mounting skepticism of the EU as an organization, Russia has increasingly emphasized bilateral relations with states in Europe as an alternative to working through Brussels. This approach has several advantages from the Russian perspective. For one, it fits more neatly with Moscow's belief in the supremacy of states and distrust of international organizations and norms. States, so the reasoning goes, can at least be expected to act in their national interest and to be less moralistic about democracy, human rights, and so on than the EU as a whole.[37]

Moreover, the member states of the EU have long had diverging views of Russia as an actor in the international system. Germany under Gerhard Schröder and Italy under Silvio Berlusconi were on particularly good terms with Putin's Kremlin, and thus it made sense for the Kremlin to seek a privileged partnership with these states parallel to its relationship with the EU as a whole.[38] Schröder in particular was perceived to be close to the Russian president and at times even under his influence—an impression that Schröder's decision at the end of his term as chancellor to take a position with the joint concern building a gas pipeline from Russia to Germany did nothing to alleviate.[39] Even since Schröder's departure from office and replacement by the Christian Democrat (and onetime citizen of the German Democratic Republic) Angela Merkel, Berlin's fundamental interest in close relations with Russia has not changed, regardless of events in Brussels or Warsaw. Even Merkel, much warier of Putin than her predecessor, has maintained a high level of Russo-German engagement, embodied now in the slogan "*Wandel durch Verpflechtung,*" or "change through engagement."[40] Germany, like France, was also at the forefront of the campaign to relaunch relations with Russia in the messy aftermath of the war in Georgia.

Notably, all of the EU member states with which Russia has sought improved bilateral relations are in Western Europe. Russia's 2007 Foreign Policy Review listed improved bilateral relations with Germany, France, Spain, and Italy as priorities for Russian diplomacy. It also advocated the creation of a special French-German-Russian "trilateral political dialogue" as part of its strategy for enhancing Russia's role as a "stabilizing factor in the Eurasian space."[41] Disagreement between Eastern and Western Europe as well as among the various institutions the EU comprises (the European Parliament with its emphasis on democracy and the rule of law has often found itself at odds with the more realpolitik-inclined Commission and Council) has significantly inhibited the EU's ability to pursue a coherent policy toward Russia.

The Kremlin's preference for promoting special partnerships with selected European countries has nowhere been clearer than in the energy sphere.[42] The Kremlin's plans to build two new undersea bypass pipelines, Nord Stream and South Stream, would be especially beneficial to the two EU countries with which Russia enjoys the closest political ties, Germany and Italy, respectively. Nord Stream, which is to be built by a consortium including Gazprom and the German firms BASF and E.ON (as well as a Dutch company), will run under the Baltic Sea to Greifswald in Mecklenburg-Vorpommern. By cutting out current transit countries Poland, Belarus, and Ukraine, Nord Stream will turn Germany into a hub for Russian gas sales to Europe and a recipient of transit fees. Similarly, South Stream, which will run under the Black Sea and up the Balkan Peninsula to Italy and Austria, will benefit those countries (as well as the Italian gas company Eni, which is building the pipeline alongside Gazprom) financially and will tie them closer to Moscow while reducing their dependence on gas transited across Ukraine. The political importance of the two bypass pipelines is reflected in the fact that former German chancellor Schröder accepted a position as head of the shareholders' committee of Nord Stream AG, while former Italian prime minister Romano Prodi was offered, but declined, a similar position with South Stream AG.

Even as the Kremlin has sought closer ties with the major Western European powers, it has been engaged in a series of quarrels with its former satellites in Eastern Europe, most of which have been EU members since 2004. Such disputes have centered on the question of ethnic Russian minorities in the Baltic states, the adherence of the new members to the Conventional Forces in Europe Treaty, tariffs, border controls and inspections, visa requirements, access to Kaliningrad, energy, ties to opposition groups in Belarus and Ukraine, the stationing of NATO assets in Eastern Europe, and even the status of a memorial to World War II Red Army soldiers in Estonia.

The very process of specially cultivating Berlin, Paris, and Rome has also sown division within the EU. This development became particularly significant in the aftermath of the 2006 and 2007 energy crises when Germany rushed to approve the construction of Nord Stream, which Polish defense minister Radosław Sikorski likened to the notorious 1939 Molotov-Ribbentrop Pact in its consequences for Poland.[43]

The crisis in Georgia further exposed the deep fault line within Europe over how to deal with Moscow. The Western Europeans—France and Germany—blocked U.S. president Bush's proposal to extend NATO membership action plans to Georgia and Ukraine during the February 2008 NATO summit in Bucharest. After fighting broke out six months later during France's EU presidency, French president Nicolas Sarkozy was instrumental in negotiating a cease-fire, and without assigning blame, called for both Russia and Georgia to resume negotiations for a political solution to the conflict.[44] As the Russian occupation of Georgian territory beyond what was allowed by the cease-fire continued, Sarkozy and German chancellor Merkel attempted to increase the pressure on Moscow to comply without simultaneously jeopardizing broader EU-Russian cooperation, while Silvio Berlusconi's Italy remained firmly in Moscow's camp.[45] The Eastern Europeans, with Poland in the forefront, called on the EU to take a much firmer line with the Russians from the beginning, demanding sanctions in response to the Russian invasion. Other European countries with neither strong economic ties to Russia nor a history of confrontation with Moscow (such as Spain) were less interested in any action at all.[46] Such divisions in Europe made it easier for Moscow to ignore pressure to complete its withdrawal from Georgia, firm in the belief that the EU would prove unable to adopt a common position with any teeth.

Given their history of occupation and domination by Russia, the presence of the formerly Communist states of Eastern Europe inside the EU has been a matter of special concern for the Kremlin. Moscow has long sought to influence the process of expansion to ensure that its own security interests remain protected. The Russian government has insisted that the EU's new members adhere to the 1994 PCA governing relations between Russia and the EU. Agreement on this point was not reached until the EU-Russia Luxembourg summit in April 2004, when the new members pledged to abide by the PCA and met Russian objections on the issues of transit between the Kaliningrad exclave and Russia proper as well as the protection of Russian-speaking minorities in the Baltic states.[47] While the PCA, initially scheduled to expire at the end of 2007, was extended until negotiations are completed on a replacement, talks on a new agreement were held up first by Russia's disputes with Poland and Lithuania, and then by the war in Georgia.

The PCA, which was signed in 1994 but only came into effect in December 1997, was designed to regulate the evolution of relations between Russia and the EU. It emphasized political dialogue leading to the "gradual integration between Russia and a wider area of cooperation in Europe," as well as promoting Russia's transition to democracy and laying the foundation for deepening economic cooperation.[48] The PCA created a series of interlocking arenas for the Russians and Europeans to discuss their concerns, including semiannual summits at the head of state/government level, a permanent partnership council at the ministerial level, the so-called foreign ministers' troika, and regular consultations between working groups covering a series of common concerns. This series of consultative bodies and the regular schedule of meetings occurring under their auspices make the EU-Russian relationship unique in its level of institutionalization.[49] The dense institutional framework established by the PCA gives the EU-Russia relationship a degree of predictability and practicality lacking in the relationship between Moscow and Washington.

Yet as the long period between the document's signing and entry into force indicates, its provisions proved controversial, especially on the Russian side. The 2000 Russian Foreign Policy Concept argued that the PCA, while laying the foundation for more productive relations between Russia and the EU, was deficient in two principal ways: it did not allow Russia enough say in the process of EU expansion to the East, and it contained inadequate safeguards for Russian interests against the growth of EU competencies in the fields of defense and security.[50] The joint communiqué adopted at the 2004 Luxembourg summit largely disposed of Russia's objections on the question of EU expansion, but the issue of the EU's international security role remains an area of disagreement. Negotiations on prolonging or replacing it have to contend with this issue as well a series of additional disputes that have broken out over the course of the original PCA's existence.

Following the creation of the EU's European Neighborhood Policy (ENP) in 2003, Russia found itself in an anomalous position. Designed to bring coherence to the series of PCAs existing between Brussels and neighboring countries, the ENP aimed at creating between the EU and nearby states "privileged relationship[s], building upon a mutual commitment to common values" (mainly through bringing partner states' legislation in line with the EU *acquis communautaire*).[51] Russia rejected inclusion in the ENP because it saw the demand to coordinate its legislation with the principles contained in the *acquis communautaire* as interference in its internal affairs and because it objected to being given the same status as the smaller states covered by the ENP. While continuing to seek cooperation with Brussels on a range of issues, the Kremlin remained unwilling to surrender any of its sovereignty to the multinational EU. EU Enlargement Commissioner

Romano Prodi expressed the nature of EU-Russian cooperation as "anything but institutions," a formula Putin also came to endorse.[52]

Instead of participating in the ENP, Russia agreed to the creation of the so-called Four Common Spaces at the May 2003 St. Petersburg summit. The Common Spaces—economics; freedom, security, and justice; external security; and research, education, and culture—provided a framework for bringing Russia and the EU closer without the formalities of integration, allowing Russia to maintain its position that it merited a special status on account of its size and importance.[53] Russia's insistence on this special status was particularly important on account of the normative aspect of the ENP. By urging its neighbors to adhere to the provisions of the *acquis communautaire*, Brussels was, in the Russian view, essentially attempting to export its own value system and laws that had been made without Russian participation.

Putin and his advisers made clear by 2003 that as a large state with its own political traditions and claim to an independent position in world politics, Russia was not prepared to accept foreign interference in the workings of its own political system. For this reason, the Road Map for the Four Common Spaces contains much less discussion of common values—particularly of concrete steps to bring Russian practice in line with EU standards—and more emphasis on pursuing common interests.[54] Russian observers praised the creation of the Four Common Spaces as an important step in filling in the gaps of the PCA and a promising first step on the road to implementing a new agreement providing a legal and conceptual foundation for the strategic partnership between Brussels and Moscow.[55]

Agreeing on the shape of a new agreement to replace the 1994 PCA has also proven difficult. New Russian president Medvedev argued for replacing the PCA with an essentially technical agreement focusing primarily on economic cooperation, while the Europeans favor a more detailed arrangement with special emphasis on energy and security issues. Many Eastern Europeans also want the new agreement to focus on human rights and Russia's relations with neighboring (non-EU) states such as Georgia, inserting a clause into the EU negotiators' instructions that resolving the "frozen conflicts" around Russia's borders should be a priority in EU-Russia relations.[56] The first round of talks on crafting a new agreement, held in July 2008 in Khanty-Mansiisk, did little to resolve this basic difference. The second round, scheduled for September 2008, was postponed by the EU to punish Moscow for its recognition of South Ossetia and Abkhazia and its failure to completely withdraw its troops from Georgian territory.[57]

All the same, the EU continues to envision the Common Spaces themselves as growing out of existing European practice (for example, the Common Economic Space will be founded on the principles governing the EU's internal market in fields including customs inspections and standardization).[58] In this way, the Road Map, too, contains an element of exporting European values, albeit less explicitly than agreements like the ENP. This aspect of the Road Map has consequently encountered some resistance in Moscow, even though as president Putin was careful to at least pay lip service to shared values in his public statements on Russian-EU relations.[59] With the balance of power between Russia and the EU having changed substantially since the signing of the original PCA in 1994 (thanks to Russia's rapid growth and the crisis of confidence in the EU resulting from the failure of its constitutional project and the Lisbon Treaty), this particular part of the framework for EU-Russian relations will no doubt take on a new aspect when the PCA is eventually renegotiated.

The Road Map for the Four Common Spaces led to some tangible achievements in terms of improving ties between Brussels and Moscow, albeit primarily on the level of technical agreements. Long-running negotiations in the context of the Common Space of Freedom, Justice, and Security led to the signing, at the 2006 Sochi summit, of an EU-Russian agreement on visa facilitation and readmission, addressing Russian concerns about the difficulty of travel to the EU and of crossing between Russia proper and Kaliningrad *oblast*.[60] Still, the Road Map has not been able to arrest the continuing deterioration in relations between Russia and the EU. It is also rather technocratic, a feature which, while allowing the two sides to reach agreement more easily, ignores many of the broader conceptual and strategic issues affecting Russia's relationship to the EU.[61]

The need to renegotiate the PCA, under whose auspices the Four Common Spaces were elaborated, provides a major test of both the existing agreements and the changes that have taken place since the original PCA was signed in 1994. Putin and then-European Commission president José Manuel Barroso first discussed the possibility of replacing the PCA with a broader, legally binding treaty in April 2005. On the Russian side, both liberal Westernizers and many in Putin's inner circle called for the signing of a new treaty with the EU. For Westernizers, of course, a treaty relationship with the EU is attractive because of the influence it would have on Russia's domestic development and foreign policy orientation. For *derzhavniki* and *siloviki* in the Kremlin, conversely, such a formalized relationship would confirm Russia's position as a major power, giving it a special status in terms of its relationship to Europe and confirming its special responsibility for upholding order in its backyard.[62] Medvedev also supported a new agreement with Europe despite the fallout created by the war in Georgia. Indeed, a new PCA with Europe would allow Medvedev to contain the damage done by the war to Russia's international position.

Negotiations on extending or replacing the PCA have been held up by objections on both sides. One of the major disputes centers on the question of energy supplies, which both Moscow and Brussels acknowledge have become an increasingly central part of the relationship since the signing of the original PCA. Moscow's decision to cut off gas supplies to Ukraine in January 2006 and Belarus in January 2007 shocked European leaders into recognizing the degree of their dependence on Russia for their own energy supplies.[63] In the West, the gas cutoffs, especially to Ukraine, were generally interpreted in light of Russia's allegedly neo-imperial foreign policy rather than as a dispute over pricing. As a result, European leaders whose own economies depended on Russian gas (and who were affected directly when Kyiv and Minsk decided to siphon off EU-bound gas to make up for the shortfall caused by the Kremlin's actions) became acutely aware of their own vulnerability to the whims of Gazprom and its patrons in the Kremlin—and to the sometimes unpredictable governments in Minsk and Kyiv with their stack of unpaid debts to Gazprom.

This sense of vulnerability was reinforced by a series of Russian attempts to acquire "downstream" (i.e., distribution) assets inside the European Union, even while taking a hard line against foreign acquisitions of energy sector assets inside Russia itself. In order to secure Europe against the consequences of any future attempts to blackmail neighboring states with the prospect of oil and gas cutoffs, Brussels for a time insisted that a new PCA with Russia include Russia's adherence to the so-called Energy Charter Treaty, which came into effect in 1997 without Russian participation and which lays out a series of principles governing the trade, investment in, and transit of energy resources. In essence, the charter would ensure that WTO rules on nondiscrimination apply to the trade in energy between Russia and the EU while also laying out a set of rules for cross-border investment in the energy sector.[64]

With Moscow refusing to accept the charter, the EU has instead insisted on the unbundling of ownership between production and transit in order to prevent monopolistic practices by companies operating inside Europe. Given opposition to unbundling from European energy companies and the European parliament, Brussels has weakened its demands but continues to insist on the so-called Gazprom clause that would force foreign firms operating inside the EU to unbundle their operations. Naturally, Gazprom and the Kremlin are opposed to such demands, which, they argue, create a double standard.[65]

Negotiations on extending or renegotiating the PCA have also been held up on account of a series of disputes between Russia and its neighbors in Eastern Europe. Warsaw held up negotiations for over two years in order to pressure Russia to lift a ban on the import of meat from Poland, first imposed in November 2005, while Vilnius also objected to a new agreement as long as Russia held up oil deliveries through the Druzhba pipeline (a dispute arising out of Lithuania's decision to sell a refinery to a Polish rather than Russian company).[66] The seemingly minor issue of veterinary inspections and meat quality turned into a major stumbling block largely because it served as a proxy for the larger series of disagreements between Russia and its neighbors in Eastern Europe. Because the EU negotiates on the basis of consensus among members, Warsaw's insistence on a resolution of the meat dispute effectively prevented the rest of the EU from moving forward with negotiations. While EU officials publicly backed the Poles (and Lithuanians) and expressed frustration with what they considered Russia's use of the meat issue for political ends, in private, many officials in Brussels condemned Poland's intransigence.[67] In this way, the meat dispute was symptomatic of the lingering East-West divide within the EU over dealing with Russia, which has also manifested itself over the basing of NATO antimissile systems, energy pipelines, and other issues.

European leaders have been skeptical of Moscow's request to enshrine the EU-Russian relationship in a legally binding treaty, especially one that does not include Russian pledges to abide by the Energy Charter and adhere to European standards for human rights and democracy.[68] Unsurprisingly, though, the Europeans themselves have not been united on this question. Leaders of the Western European states have been rather more receptive to Putin and Medvedev's request for a more political treaty (emphasizing the strategic partnership between Russia and Europe) to replace the existing PCA. In part, their support for this proposal is predicated on the notion that such a treaty would bring Russia deeper into the web of European institutions and cement Russia's association with a European rather than Eurasian identity. The Eastern Europeans, led by the Poles, have been more skeptical regarding Russia's future intentions and capabilities and, apart from the ongoing dispute over meat imports, have largely favored extending the existing PCA and keeping Russia at arm's length, outside of Europe per se.[69]

Moscow, consequently, argues that a revised PCA or a new agreement governing EU-Russian relations will have to address the "anti-Russian syndrome" from which it claims several of the Eastern European governments suffer. At the Khanty-Mansiisk summit in June 2008, Medvedev expressed frustration that Lithuania could throw up obstacles to a new agreement through its appeals to European solidarity. Indeed, still smarting from the dispute over oil deliveries, Vilnius managed to force the EU to adopt a much tougher position in the course of its internal preparations for negotiations on replacing the PCA, inserting benchmarks on the oil dispute, Russia's justice system, and intervention in the Near Abroad that Moscow will have to meet before the EU accepts a new agreement.[70]

RUSSIA AND NATO

If expansion has been a major stumbling block in relations between Russia and the EU, the inclusion of new members has come close to completely derailing relations between Russia and NATO on a number of occasions. NATO, after all, remains a military alliance devoted above all to issues of "hard" security and for many Russians still carries the associations of the Cold War, when its very raison d'être was to check Russian power. Given the built-in hostility between NATO and the Soviet Union, statesmen on both sides recognized in the early 1990s that achieving some kind of reconciliation between the alliance and post-Soviet Russia was going to be a critical, if quite difficult task. Yet Yeltsin and Kozyrev believed reconciliation was a realistic goal, one they could sell to the Russian establishment on the basis of the conviction that with the end of the Cold War, NATO no longer posed a threat to Russian interests despite the crumbling of the Warsaw Pact and the implosion of the Soviet military machine. In particular, Yeltsin and Kozyrev were able to take solace in a seeming promise they had extracted from the major Western powers (above all, the U.S.), that NATO would not seek to expand to fill the power vacuum resulting from the dissolution of the Warsaw Pact and the collapse of the Soviet Union. Yet as the Russian crisis deepened during the latter part of the 1990s, this understanding unraveled, and the North Atlantic Alliance embarked on the largest campaign of expansion in its history while simultaneously modernizing and upgrading its military capacity in a way Moscow saw as provocative.

As president, Putin initially sought to manage tensions with NATO while taking advantage of the repercussions from expansion to assert Russia's own agenda with the alliance. Putin gave some hints that he did not regard NATO, even in its expanded form, as a major problem. Indeed, as president he pursued more wide-ranging and durable cooperation with NATO—in Afghanistan and elsewhere—than Yeltsin ever did. In the early part of Putin's presidency, he also tried to vocally downplay the impact of NATO expansion on Russian security as part of his larger strategy of making Russia an indispensable partner for the West. As relations between Russia and its erstwhile partners in the West frayed, NATO's geographical and technical growth revived old Russian fears about the purpose and scope of the alliance and led Moscow to take steps to limit the impact of the new NATO on its own security. The prospect of NATO taking in Ukraine and Georgia, which the 2008 Bucharest summit affirmed would happen at some unspecified future date, coupled with Russia's own political-military revival was instrumental in precipitating the conflict between Russia and Georgia. With its invasion, Moscow sought both to force the alliance to reconsider its interest in expanding up to Russia's borders and to instruct the leaders in Kyiv, Tbilisi, and elsewhere in the former Soviet Union about the limitations of Western power in the region.

While expansion has provided the backdrop for the most serious quarrels between Russia and NATO, tensions stretched back to the first years of the 1990s, when the end of the Cold War called into question the purpose, and indeed the very existence, of the North Atlantic Alliance. The leaders of Central and Eastern European states who had been members of the defunct Warsaw Pact pressed to be admitted into NATO both as a way to anchor their own societies to the secure democracies of the West and to provide a level of insurance against the possibility of renewed Russian aggression. NATO leaders' own desire to assure the Eastern Europeans that their Cold War–era estrangement from the mainstream of European development was not permanent often clashed with their ambition to promote the consolidation of democracy in Russia itself—since talk of NATO expansion empowered revanchist, anti-Western forces in Moscow and undermined those like Kozyrev arguing for a close partnership with the West.

Western leaders sought to mollify the Russians by assuring them that NATO expansion was not designed to confront or isolate them and by suggesting that a new European collective security mechanism could not function without Russia. Moscow continues to make this argument long after the prospect of Russian NATO membership has gone by the wayside, suggesting, for instance, the creation of a new pan-European security organization to displace NATO and the OSCE as remnants of an outdated "bloc mentality."[71] The very fact that the security rules for the new Europe were being written without Russian participation necessarily created resentment in Moscow and reinforced the tendency toward zero-sum thinking on the part of Russian politicians, generals, and diplomats.[72] Since NATO appeared to be extending its geographical reach into an area Moscow had long regarded as an area of special concern, Russian leaders claimed they had a justification for trying to wall off other such areas—especially the territory of the former Soviet Union—from Western interference. In this way, the bipolar logic of the Cold War reasserted itself in a new form even as the lines dividing Europe were being redrawn further to the east.

Yeltsin's Kremlin consequently opposed any expansion of NATO that did not include a path to membership for Russia itself (as Yeltsin suggested to Bill Clinton in September 1992)—though soon realizing it had little leverage to prevent such an eventuality.[73] With some trepidation, the Yeltsin administration approved Russian membership in the NATO Partnership for Peace (PfP) program in 1994, as did most of the former Soviet republics. Partnership for Peace, the result of a bureaucratic compromise between supporters and opponents of NATO expansion in the United States, functioned both as a halfway house on the road to full NATO membership and an alternative form of partnership for countries that would not or could not aspire to full membership. While calling on members to uphold NATO's commitment to democracy and transparency in their own governance, the framework agreement establishing PfP provided for a loose form of association, with individual members free to choose the level of cooperation with NATO with which they felt comfortable (with an emphasis on defense reform).[74] In terms of NATO's relationship with Russia, the role of PfP was mostly about reducing tensions and building cooperative intermilitary relationships rather than preparing a path for political integration. On this limited basis, the Russian Duma agreed to accept the invitation for Russian participation in PfP in June 1994.

Before the year was out, however, the thaw in relations that PfP was supposed to have produced had been overtaken by NATO's decision to take in new members in Central and Eastern Europe (Poland, the Czech Republic, and Hungary in the first round). The Russian elite was stunned by this reversal, which had occurred as a result of strong pressure from the United States. Yeltsin and Foreign Minister Kozyrev warned that expansion could derail the wary rapprochement between Russia and the West that had taken place since the end of the Cold War. NATO's commitment to expand, which it undertook at a ministerial meeting in December 1994, undermined hopes among Russian liberals in particular that PfP could serve as a kind of bridge to more general agreement between Russia and NATO. Yeltsin himself cautioned that NATO expansion would bring in its wake a new era of "cold peace."[75]

While the alliance's leadership justified expansion on the basis of new security threats originating in the chaos of the Balkans and the spread of Islamic fanaticism, to Moscow NATO remained the NATO of the Cold War and its expansion a sign that the West still sought to contain Russia. When the final decision to expand was made in July 1997, then-Russian foreign minister Primakov characterized it as "a big mistake, possibly the biggest mistake since the end of the Second World War."[76] This assessment was shared by many in the U.S. establishment as well, including such major figures as former defense secretary Robert McNamara, former senators Gary Hart, Sam Nunn, and Bill Bradley, former national security adviser Adm. Stansfield Turner, and Paul Nitze, architect of President Truman's containment strategy, who all argued in an open letter to President Clinton that U.S.-led efforts to expand NATO not only jeopardized the future of the arms control regime but would also "bring Russians to question the entire post–Cold War settlement."[77] Even liberal Russians like Anatoly Chubais argued against NATO expansion, fearing it would lead to Russia's isolation and the empowerment of hard-line, anti-Western forces and the marginalization of those, like Kozyrev, who had sought Russia's integration with Western institutions.[78]

Yet despite his firm opposition to NATO expansion, Yeltsin sought both to ameliorate domestic hostility and seek compensation from the Western powers for doing so. With its nuclear arsenal still intact, Russia's own security was not directly endangered by the expansion of NATO, a fact Yeltsin understood quite well. Yet the alliance's expansion in the face of what Moscow believed were promises to the contrary from George H. W. Bush, Secretary of State James Baker, German foreign minister Hans-Dietrich Genscher, and others deepened the gulf between Russia and its neighbors in Europe as well as the United States.[79] NATO realized the nature of the dilemma created by expansion and spent much of the time between the announcement that Poland, the Czech Republic, and Hungary would be admitted (in 1994) until the actual induction ceremony (in 1999) trying to come up with a way to proceed without causing a rupture with Moscow.[80]

At least until Putin's ascension to power, this circle could not be squared. The firestorm of criticism that broke out in Moscow when NATO announced its plans for expansion played a major role in discrediting Kozyrev's strategy of partnership with the West. If the West was not going to accept Russia into its clubs but would take advantage of Russian weakness to advance its own military frontiers at Russia's expense, then Kozyrev's quest for partnership seemed to have been a fool's errand, as the hapless foreign minister himself well understood.[81]

The appointment of Primakov as foreign minister was in large part an attempt by Yeltsin to co-opt the nationalist opposition that had grown up around the issue of NATO's expansion. Primakov portrayed himself as an implacable foe of NATO, particularly in its expanded form. Yet like Yeltsin, he was realistic enough to understand that expansion was going to proceed regardless of Russia's actions and that the best Moscow could do under the circumstances was to accommodate itself to the new reality and attempt to extract some kind of quid pro quo for not making unnecessary trouble. Despite his belief that NATO expansion was a mistake of historic proportions, Primakov admitted that "the expansion of NATO is not a military problem; it is a psychological one," and sought to adjust Russian perceptions of the alliance to the extent possible, a task for which the ex-spymaster had much more credibility with hard-liners in the Duma than did the liberal intellectual Kozyrev.[82]

It was under Primakov's stewardship that Russia participated in the creation of the first organization designed to integrate Russia into NATO's decision-making structure, the so-called Permanent Joint Council (PJC), which was established under the NATO-Russia Founding Act signed in Paris in May 1997.[83] The Founding Act was a kind of declaration of principles governing the interactions between Russia and the expanded alliance, though in large part it served merely as a concession to Moscow for having to accept NATO's decision to expand. It declared unambiguously that "NATO and Russia do not consider each other as adversaries" and have a "shared commitment to build a stable, peaceful and undivided Europe, whole and free, to the benefit of all its peoples."[84] The PJC provided for the presence of a Russian representative at NATO headquarters and for regular meetings at the ministerial level to discuss issues of common concern. At the time, the PJC was heralded as marking a real watershed in relations between a Russia no longer committed to expanding its territorial reach and a West that had abandoned containment as a principle of its foreign policy (Polish, Czech, and Hungarian membership in the alliance notwithstanding).

By signing the Founding Act and agreeing to participation in the PJC, Primakov recognized at least tacitly that the NATO of the late 1990s was a fundamentally different organization from the NATO of the Cold War and that the alliance's newer incarnation did not pose a direct threat to Russia. This recognition, however, continued to come up against the ingrained hostility of the Russian political and military elite to NATO as such and to NATO's expansion into Eastern Europe in particular. NATO's bombing campaign against Yugoslavia in 1999 deepened Russian hostility toward the alliance, and Moscow responded in part by suspending its participation in the Permanent Joint Council and withdrawing its representative from NATO headquarters in Brussels. The PJC's ineffectiveness was glaring.[85]

Primakov, of course, gave vent to the sentiments of many Russians who were disenchanted with the way NATO had pushed them aside. The Russian foreign minister responded by breaking off relations with the alliance and even threatening to aid Serbia directly. The Serbian campaign also coincided with the renewal of hostilities in Chechnya. With NATO expressing support for Kosovo's independence from Serbia, many in the Russian elite saw worrying parallels with Chechnya and blamed NATO for supplying, or at least inspiring, Chechen separatism as part of a larger strategy of encircling and weakening Russia. Fear of NATO involvement with the rebels played at least some role in the Kremlin's decision to embark on a full-scale military campaign in response to the rebels' incursion across the Chechen border into Dagestan in August 1999.[86]

One major consequence of the second Chechen war, of course, was the emergence of then-prime minister Vladimir Putin as the most popular figure in Russia, the only man seen as capable of finishing off the Chechens and standing up to NATO's alleged anti-Russian intrigues. Putin's approach to NATO was on the whole similar to Primakov's, though with an even greater emphasis on ameliorating the consequences of expansion. Putin sought to limit Russian opposition to the alliance and its activities, realizing that Moscow had a weak hand when it came to influencing NATO strategy. Putin acknowledged in October 2001 that Russia could live with even an expanded NATO, as long as NATO itself became more of a political organization and less of a traditional military alliance. He moreover emphasized that Russia would not repeat its at times hysterical denunciations if NATO should decide to expand again in the future.[87] The new Russian president soon gave a more concrete demonstration of his determination to improve NATO-Russia relations. The NATO secretary-general, Lord George Robertson, was among the first foreign dignitaries scheduled to come to Moscow after Putin's inauguration. Over the objections of his generals, Putin refused to cancel Robertson's visit in response to the crisis in Kosovo. Instead, Putin met personally with Robertson, and their talks led to the restoration of full relations between NATO and Russia.[88] In their joint communiqué, Putin and Robertson agreed that:

> Russia and NATO would pursue a vigorous dialogue on a wide range of security issues that will enable NATO and Russia to address the challenges that lie ahead and to make their mutual cooperation a cornerstone of European security.[89]

Robertson's visit was particularly important in that it laid the foundation for the establishment in 2002 of the NATO-Russia Council (NRC), which was designed to supplant the PJC and address Russian worries that the existing institutions for cooperation failed to give enough weight to Russian concerns. The establishment of the NATO-Russia Council gave Moscow a greater degree of influence with the alliance but was also more generally one component of Putin's policy of cooperation with the West adopted in the aftermath of September 11.[90]

Under the previous arrangement, NATO members would negotiate an agreed position among themselves before bringing the matter to Russian attention in the context of the PJC. Moscow complained that this procedure forced it to accept a series of faits accomplis and left it little opportunity to influence actual decision making. Instead of this "16 + 1" format, the NRC was designed to operate on the basis of consensus, with Russian representatives involved in all phases of the negotiating process (though without the ability to veto decisions that had been accepted by all the NATO member states).[91] Under the NRC, Russia created the post of ambassador to NATO, who participates in monthly meetings of the council.

The presence of a permanent Russian representative at NATO headquarters did much to alter the dynamic of the relationship, encouraging cooperation and collaboration on a day-to-day basis and building trust between the two sides.[92] Observers noted a qualitative change in the way representatives from Russia and NATO dealt with each other in the framework of the NRC, compared with the old PJC. Most fundamentally, it appeared for much of the 2000s that "the parties not only want to limit damages, but to achieve something in common."[93] Still, the war in Iraq and NATO's continuing commitment to expansion have exposed the limits of even this more formalized arrangement. Putin's appointment of the outspoken nationalist and former head of the Rodina Party Dmitry Rogozin as ambassador to

NATO (where he once hung a portrait of Stalin on his office wall) in January 2008 signaled a move away from accommodation on the part of Moscow, which was increasingly frustrated with its inability to shape NATO decision making.[94]

Rogozin's theatrics aside, NATO-Russia cooperation within the NRC remained pronounced in the area of counterterrorism—at least until the council was suspended by the Western powers in September 2008 to punish Moscow for its invasion of Georgia. Given that like Russia, NATO members including the United States, the United Kingdom, and Spain have all suffered major attacks by Islamic terrorists since 2001 and that NATO has made counterterrorism one of its key missions, cooperation with Moscow on this issue has been relatively straightforward. Russia and NATO have conducted joint naval patrols in the Mediterranean Sea to prevent the smuggling of unconventional weapons (Operation Active Endeavor, the only time a non-NATO member has participated in alliance activities under the auspices of Article 5 of the North Atlantic Treaty on self-defense), have staged joint training drills (especially in order to prepare civil defense personnel for dealing with a terrorist attack), and have even conducted joint exercises on theater missile defense.[95] The NRC has also been instrumental in bringing together Russian and Western intelligence analysts to assess the development of al Qaeda and the emerging terrorist threat to Central Asia.[96]

Despite the existence of the NRC, the second round of NATO expansion set off a firestorm among the Russian elite comparable to that of the mid-1990s. This time, Russia's objections centered not just on the fact of continued NATO expansion but also on the fact that it was the Baltic states specifically—formerly constituent parts of the Soviet Union and strategically located across from St. Petersburg—that were being invited into the alliance. Among the conditions Moscow had seemingly extracted from the Western powers in exchange for putting up with the initial round of NATO expansion in the 1990s was a promise that no further expansion would take place, especially with regard to the Baltic states, with Yeltsin even declaring in May 1998 that the inclusion of the Baltics in NATO was a redline for Moscow.[97] As in the days of Primakov, though, once NATO indicated it would invite the Balts into the alliance regardless of Russian opposition, Putin's Kremlin scrambled to salvage what it could from the relationship and secured approval of the NRC as a kind of compensation for swallowing the inclusion of Lithuania, Latvia, and Estonia in NATO.

Besides the problems resulting from the presence of NATO assets close to Russia's borders, the second round of NATO expansion has also posed a dilemma for the Kremlin because the Baltic states and Slovenia (unlike the other NATO member states) did not sign onto the CFE Treaty. This agreement, initially signed in 1990, aimed at limiting the number and type of military units stationed on the territory of the signatories ("from the Atlantic to the Urals") in order to head off the possibility of a blitzkrieg-type conventional offensive by either NATO or the old Warsaw Pact.

An updated version of the CFE Treaty was signed in Istanbul in 1999, replacing the original treaty's outdated emphasis on arms limitation by bloc (NATO and Warsaw Pact) with new national limits. However, NATO expansion complicated the implementation of the new Adapted CFE Treaty. The Western signatories have refused to ratify the treaty until Russia withdraws its forces from Georgia (which Putin agreed to do—excepting one base in Ajaria—by 2008) and Moldova/Transdniestria.[98] Russia refused the demand to withdraw from Transdniestria in large part because of the perception of increased vulnerability resulting from the expansion of NATO up to the border of what Russia perceives as its exclusive security zone, and because its interference in the CIS's "frozen conflicts" gives it an important mechanism for exerting influence over its neighbors, while the financial benefits from smuggling across Transdniestria's porous borders provided another inducement for Russian units to stay.[99]

Meanwhile, Moscow complained that its own Western frontier—and only slightly more realistically, the frontiers of Belarus and Ukraine—were exposed to a large-scale invasion mustered in the new members' territory.[100] The presence of Russian troops in Moldova and Georgia gave the Kremlin the ability to sow chaos in these countries if necessary, and hence a kind of insurance against any "aggressive actions" on the part of NATO.[101] The alliance's decision in principle to offer membership action plans to Tbilisi and Kyiv was perceived in Moscow as just such an action and provided an excuse to dispatch troops to limit Georgia's drift into the West's orbit.

While Western leaders were initially hopeful that the uproar over NATO's expansion would eventually pass, Moscow's response has, if anything, become more neuralgic in recent years (even before NATO agreed to the eventual membership of Georgia and Ukraine), once NATO members began discussing the possibility of placing significant military assets on the territory of new member states. Lavrov warned NATO in September 2007 that the presence of antimissile facilities in the former Warsaw Pact states (as well as the independence of Kosovo) was a critical issue where Moscow would not engage in "horse trading."[102] When, in response to the invasion of Georgia, Warsaw announced it had at least reached agreement with Washington to station parts of a planned antiballistic missile interceptor system (as well as an advanced air defense battery to defend the interceptors) on Polish territory, a leading Russian general responded by claiming Poland had opened itself up to the possibility of nuclear retaliation.[103]

Russia also protested against agreements signed in 2005 allowing the U.S. to establish military bases in Romania and Bulgaria (in part to replace the Karshi-Khanabad facility in Uzbekistan from which it was evicted) as violating the terms of the CFE Treaty—and justifying its own military pres-

ence in Transdniestria.[104] Russian fears for the future of the CFE regime
became even more evident once the United States announced it would station antimissile batteries on the territory of the new members. After a series
of sharp exchanges on the subject in the spring of 2007, the Kremlin
announced it was suspending its participation in the CFE Treaty altogether.[105]

Putin's own reaction to the potential inclusion of the Baltic states in
NATO was initially rather muted—or in the words of the Foreign Ministry,
"calmly negative [*spokoino negativnoe*]."[106] Yet while Putin worked to ameliorate Russian hostility to NATO's second round of expansion, the
response among the Russian elite as a whole has been, and remains, more
hostile. Perhaps unsurprisingly, it is the Russian military that has led the
bureaucratic opposition in Moscow to working more closely with NATO.
To be sure, Putin initially removed some of the most vocal opponents of
NATO per se and NATO-Russian cooperation in particular from their positions in order to facilitate greater cooperation; the two most notable victims
of this purge are former defense minister Igor Sergeev and head of the
Defense Ministry's international department Col.-Gen. Leonid Ivashov.[107]
While Putin for the most part succeeded in using the NRC to defuse tensions and in maintaining a good working relationship with NATO, this area
is one where the former president was significantly out of touch with the
general run of elite opinion. The appointment of Rogozin as NATO ambassador and the invasion of Georgia thus constituted something of a recognition by Moscow that its attempts to minimize conflicts with NATO were
not bringing results.

Apart from Putin himself, the Russian elite remains vocally hostile to
NATO and to the prospect of further expansion, while the general public is
at least skeptical of NATO's intentions. Despite its general subservience to
the Kremlin, the Duma in 2004 saw fit to formally condemn the Baltic
states' inclusion in NATO and adopted a resolution suggesting Moscow
might reconsider its strategic approach toward the alliance as a result.[108]
This warning was echoed initially by the Foreign Ministry as well. Even
while Putin authorized renewal of contacts with NATO following the September 11 attacks, Russian diplomats cautioned that the alliance's further
expansion, to include the Baltic states, could derail the whole framework of
cooperation. Deputy Foreign Minister Yevgeny Gusarov warned that Russia
would take "adequate measures of a military and political nature" should
NATO decide to bring Lithuania, Latvia, and Estonia into the alliance.[109] As
for the public, opinion polls taken in mid-2007 showed that fully 56 percent of Russian citizens believe that NATO remains hostile to Russia, twelve
percentage points higher than in a similar survey conducted in 1997.[110]

In 2001, Putin himself suggested that Russia would be open to deepening
cooperation with a NATO that saw its mission more as promoting stability

and democracy among its new members rather than functioning as a traditional military bloc.[111] Continued expansion, however, undermined Russian faith that the organization had adapted itself to a new mission that no longer required seeing Russia as a threat, as did the robust out-of-area operations undertaken by NATO in the Balkans, Afghanistan, and elsewhere, as well as the alliance's commitment to further expansion.[112] By 2007, the Russian Foreign Ministry lamented that the transformation of NATO had "frozen." It cautioned:

> NATO's real adaptation to the new conditions of [international] security can only succeed if it is willing to engage in equal partnership with other countries and regional organizations. . . . Our relationship to the transformation of NATO will depend . . . on the degree to which it observes international law, including the prerogatives of the UN Security Council, and takes account in deed rather than in word Russia's security interests.[113]

Even the creation of the NRC did not suffice to overcome Russian fears about being unable to prevent the alliance from lessening its own security—since even with the consensual principle embodied in the NRC, Moscow cannot prevent the twenty-five current NATO members from making a decision with which Russia vehemently disagrees, such as that to leave the door open to Georgian and Ukrainian membership. Besides, for all the cooperation and trust building that took place within the framework of the NRC, Russian observers charged that while the council promotes superficial or working-level interactions, it has demonstrably failed to address the major political problems that continue to bedevil the relationship between Russia and NATO, mainly those stemming from Moscow's sense of insecurity in part growing out of its opposition to NATO expansion.[114]

Despite ongoing cooperation between NATO and Russia in areas like counterterrorism and stability operations in Afghanistan, the impact of NATO expansion has hardly been forgotten in Moscow. Medvedev captured Russian objections succinctly in an exchange with Western academics in the so-called Valdai Club in September 2008, dismissing Western attempts to claim that NATO's expansion was not directed against Russia. Pointing to the alliance's interest in stationing an antiballistic missile system in Eastern Europe, Medvedev said, "Of course it's [directed] against us. No other variant is possible."[115]

One aspect of Moscow's strategy for dealing with NATO that is often overlooked in the West is the Russian attempt to re-create at least the façade of a bipolar relationship through the promotion of its own security alliances paralleling and counterbalancing NATO. The Shanghai Cooperation Organization, or SCO, is seen in some quarters as a replacement for the old Warsaw Pact, a counterhegemonic bloc of large states dedicated to checking the expansion of American influence around the world.[116] While the role and geographic scope of the SCO remains somewhat in flux (see chapter 5), Moscow has been more successful in organizing at least a small-scale analogue to NATO under the auspices of the Collective Security Treaty Organization (CSTO, in Russian *Organizatsiya Dogovora o Kollektivnoi Bezopasnosti*, or ODKB). Established on the basis of the 1992 Tashkent Treaty, the CSTO is essentially the international security arm of the CIS (comprising Russia, Belarus, Armenia, Kazakhstan, Uzbekistan, Kyrgyzstan, and Tajikistan). Part of the importance of the CSTO to Russia lies in the fact that the agreement establishing the organization prohibits members from joining any other international security bloc (i.e., NATO). In this way, the existence of the CSTO helps ameliorate Russia's fear of encirclement, insofar as the organization remains intact.

Russian leaders have sought to establish the CSTO as a kind of Eurasian counterpart to NATO and have advocated the creation of security arrangements based on the cooperation and integration of NATO and the CSTO. Foreign Minister Lavrov raised the possibility of NATO-CSTO cooperation to bring stability to postconflict Afghanistan.[117] Likewise, Medvedev suggested the establishment of a new pan-European security alliance including Russia that would render NATO in its current form obsolete. Moscow has also suggested the creation of joint rapid-reaction forces for stability operations inside the CIS, though Western leaders have not paid much attention to such suggestions on Russia's part. In general, Russian officials complain that while they are forced to deal with NATO collectively, NATO and its members refuse to approach the CSTO in the same light. Instead, they see Western attempts to negotiate with Russia and the other CSTO members on a bilateral basis as an attempt to undermine the organization's solidarity and weaken Russia's influence over its neighbors in the CIS, particularly since NATO continues to moot plans for expansion further into Eurasia.[118]

The essential bargain Putin offered NATO at the beginning of his term in office—a reasonably phlegmatic response to then-current plans for expansion in exchange for the alliance's transformation into a more political organization—has not been realized. In the long run, it is precisely Moscow's opposition to NATO expansion that may prove to be the most significant obstacle to achieving a durable partnership between Russia and the West. Already, the war in Georgia has highlighted the potentially explosive role of NATO. Western leaders' affirmation that, despite the war, Georgia and Ukraine remain on track for eventual membership is a clear signal that Russia's invasion did not (for the moment) succeed in stabilizing the relationship by putting an end to either the former Soviet republics' NATO aspirations or the alliance's willingness to continue expanding.

The years since September 11 have seen a series of crises in the relationship that, while relatively minor individually, have collectively undermined hopes for an end to the divisions and polarization of the Cold War. As Lavrov argued in February 2005, NATO expansion "does not address a single one of the real challenges that the European states confront today."[119] Instead, the zero-sum logic of the past continues to be powerfully felt in relations between Russia and NATO.

The various crises marring the relationship have resulted not so much from the malevolence or bad faith of either side as from differing understandings of the security challenges facing each country and the appropriate responses. For a Russia seeking to halt and reverse its post–Cold War decline and a West seeking to expand the reach of its underlying values, the perceptions, challenges, and opportunities are quite different. NATO itself remains an organization in transition, struggling to adapt to the realities of the post–Cold War, post–September 11 world. As long as NATO remains uncertain about its exact role and final boundaries, it will have serious difficulties dealing with a Russia intent on holding the line against any further diminution of its international standing or the security margin on its borders, and may well prove to be the spark igniting further conflicts.

EUROPEAN AND RUSSIAN
ENERGY DIPLOMACY

While global energy prices remained at historically high levels, the implications of oil and gas for the relationship between Russia and Europe became increasingly problematic. Much more than the United States, which gets the bulk of its imported energy from North America and the Middle East, the EU is heavily dependent on Russia for deliveries of both oil and gas. Russia's role as an energy supplier to Europe encompasses not only direct production for the European market but also its role as a transit corridor, particularly for gas originating in the Caspian basin and Central Asia. Russia's role as an energy supplier has, not surprisingly, raised alarms in much of Europe about the dangers of overdependence. These fears were stoked by Gazprom's decision to cut off supplies to Ukraine and Belarus, disputes over Russian purchases of transit infrastructure inside the EU, concerns over declining output inside Russia, and the war in Georgia, which threatened Europe's principal non-Russian pipeline corridor. Despite Europe's fears, the Russian leadership argues that dependence is a two-way street and that while Europe may have little choice but to import oil and gas from Russia, Russia itself has equally little choice of customers, given the absence of pipelines capable of delivering energy to Russia's neighbors in Asia and the expense of liquefying gas to be carried by tanker to the United States and the rest of the world.

Still, Russia's position on this issue is slightly ingenuous, insofar as the

Kremlin has been actively courting alternative customers for its energy riches, particularly in East Asia. Pipeline diplomacy has been an important component of Russian foreign policy for much of the past decade as the Kremlin has sought to maneuver between the demands of Europe, Asia, and the former Soviet states in a way that maximizes both profit and influence. The consolidation of state control over the energy sector that took place under Putin has for this reason been a key element in the projection of Russian power abroad. The displacement of Khodorkovsky, state-owned oil company Rosneft's (heavily discounted) purchase of Yukos, and the state's increased stake in national champions Gazprom and Rosneft have all made it easier for the Kremlin to take advantage of the country's mineral riches as a way of promoting its foreign policy goals, as Putin has advocated since the 1990s.[120] In this way, changes in the domestic ownership and control of energy resources have had significant effects on the conduct of foreign policy. The Kremlin's ability to make decisions about the distribution of Russia's energy riches coupled with the dominant position enjoyed by Russian gas (and, to a lesser extent, oil) in the European market has played a major role in the success of Putin's strategy for making Russia again one of the major pillars of the global order.

Europe's dependence on Russian energy dates back to the Cold War, when, despite ideological differences and the standoff between NATO and the Warsaw Pact, the Kremlin built pipelines to Europe as a way of earning hard currency and creating a wedge between Europe and the United States (which opposed increased Soviet energy sales to its European allies). Of course, for Russian energy to reach Western Europe, it had to cross the territory of Moscow's Eastern European allies, who received oil and gas from Russia at subsidized prices as a means of ensuring their loyalty to the Soviet Union. With the end of the Cold War, this pipeline infrastructure has largely remained in place. Despite globalization and technological improvements, Europe continues to receive by far the largest amount of its oil and natural gas from Russian suppliers. In 2007, roughly 30 percent of Europe's oil imports and 50 percent of its gas imports came from Russia; the figures were even higher in Eastern Europe, with some states entirely dependent on Moscow for their gas supplies.[121]

So far, Russia's leadership has generally refrained from directly threatening energy cutoffs as a means of influencing EU foreign policy. Yet the very state of dependence in which Europe finds itself has limited the EU's options in dealing with Russia—whether muting its objections on antimonopoly grounds to Gazprom's swallowing up of competitors or opposing serious sanctions in response to the invasion of Georgia.[122] Of course, the Kremlin has gone beyond threats in dealing with former Soviet republics, including the three Baltic states that are now members of the EU and NATO; state-owned oil pipeline operator Transneft cut deliveries to Lithuania and Latvia when those states sold a major refinery and an oil terminal, respectively, to non-Russian companies.

Most notorious, though, was the decision to stop sending gas to Ukraine in January 2006 until Kyiv agreed to pay a substantially higher rate—a dispute the Kremlin attributed to its insistence on ending subsidies and implementing market principles in relations with its neighbors, but which many in the West saw as a dangerous game of brinksmanship designed to force Kyiv to abandon its pro-European, pro-NATO foreign policy line. The Ukrainian gas crisis and its sequel a year later in Belarus forced downstream countries (whose own deliveries suffered when Kyiv and Minsk began siphoning off Europe-bound gas to counteract the effects of the Russian cutoff) to confront the reality of their own dependence on Moscow.

In part, the result has been an intensified competition to locate new sources of energy for the continent and build new pipelines to bring oil and gas to Europe while bypassing Russia. The most well known example of this approach has been the Baku-Tbilisi-Ceyhan (BTC) oil pipeline from the Caspian Sea to Turkey's Mediterranean coast (a roughly parallel gas pipeline from Baku to Erzurum also opened in late 2006). BTC is hardly the only example of this new pipeline diplomacy, with Europe and the United States actively engaged in construction or negotiations for the construction of a range of pipelines from the Caspian and Central Asia through the Caucasus on to Turkey and the EU, the most important of which is the so-called Nabucco gas pipeline from Erzurum in Turkey to Southern Europe—a project the Kremlin has strongly opposed and whose prospects were dealt a serious blow by the war in Georgia.[123]

Russia, meanwhile, has been playing the same game, promoting the Nord and South Stream pipelines as a means of undermining support for U.S.-backed alternatives such as Nabucco. Moscow accuses the Europeans (with some justification) of adopting a double standard by condemning Russian attempts to translate energy and pipelines into leverage while in fact pursuing an identical calculation itself.[124] Russia has also been attempting to lock up large amounts of oil and gas production outside its borders (especially in Turkmenistan, Kazakhstan, Azerbaijan, and Uzbekistan) as well as the infrastructure for transporting it to the outside world.

The Blue Stream pipeline under the Black Sea to Turkey, which Moscow completed in 2002, was motivated both by a desire to undermine the rationale for a competing American-backed project (the so-called Transcaspian pipeline connecting Kazakhstan to BTC) that would have bypassed Russia, and by an interest in increasing Russian influence in Ankara in the face of the EU's apparent rejection of Turkey's bid for membership.[125] On the other hand, Blue Stream also highlighted the interdependency that limits Russia's ability to use its energy resources for geopolitical ends. Following a serious contraction in the Turkish economy, Ankara suspended the long-term contract it had signed with Moscow for gas deliveries through Blue Stream. Russia was forced to swallow the construction costs, having already built the pipeline infrastructure (which, of course, cannot be rerouted once put in place).[126]

For the time being, the bulk of Russia's existing pipeline infrastructure leads to Europe, which has had the somewhat paradoxical effect of making Moscow dependent on the Europeans as consumers of their energy as much as it has left Europe little choice but to turn to Russia as a supplier. As Putin noted in 2006, two-thirds of Russia's gas exports go to Europe, and because of the sunk costs associated with the construction of pipelines, Moscow has little choice in the short run but to continue sending its energy westward.[127] In the long run, of course, Moscow has the option of constructing new pipelines (as well as liquid natural gas, or LNG, refineries) that would open up opportunities for diverting supplies to Asia or, in the case of LNG, to the United States—although the associated costs will be high and the wait long until alternate routes are in place. Indeed, this threat has been one the Russians have not been hesitant to make in their dealings with the Europeans, although both pipelines to Asia and LNG refineries have their own sets of logistical, financial, and political complications.[128]

The mutual dependence between Russia and Europe that exists for the time being has meant that Russia's energy weapon has, in actuality, turned out to be less potent than some in the Kremlin may have hoped and than many Europeans feared. In part as a way to overcome this limitation, Russia has sought to enhance its leverage over Europe through the construction of new pipelines. Not only will new pipelines increase the sheer quantity of oil and gas Russia can export and hence increase Europe's dependence on Russia for its energy (absent the construction of new alternative pipelines), they will also change the economic geography of the relationship by differentiating between European states' access and ability to profit from Russian energy—unless the EU succeeds in creating an integrated gas market among its members.

Blue Stream, which aimed at bringing Russian energy to Turkey and thence to southern Italy, was in part designed to play such a role. This element of the Russian strategy has been most notable, though, in the quest to build Nord Stream, which, when built, will tie Germany directly to Russia, bypassing Poland and the Baltic states, and South Stream, which will supply southern and central Europe while bypassing Ukraine (across which 80 percent of the gas currently sold by Russia to the EU passes). For the time being, it remains unclear whether Nord Stream will lead to reductions in the amount of gas Russia sends to Europe through the existing pipelines. Nord Stream's planned annual capacity is fifty-five billion cubic meters (bcm), about 20 percent of the total amount of gas currently shipped by Russia to the EU. Given Moscow's lack of investment in boosting production and lack of clarity regarding its ultimate intentions, many Europeans worry that Nord Stream (and South Stream, designed to carry an additional thirty bcm) will not increase Russia's overall deliveries but will merely reroute existing volumes in ways that benefit some EU members (Germany and Italy) at the expense of others (Poland and the Baltic states) as well the EU as a whole. Until Nord Stream comes online, Russia cannot cut off energy supplies to the Poles and Balts without imperiling deliveries to countries further downstream, since Poland and the Baltic countries could still siphon off gas as Ukraine did in 2006. When constructed, Nord Stream will drastically reduce the economic as well as political influence wielded by the countries located between Germany and Russia, who, along with the United States, have been strongly opposed to the deal.[129]

Moscow's calculation appears similar with regard to South Stream.[130] South Stream was announced in June 2007 and appears designed in large part to undermine support for the U.S.-sponsored Nabucco pipeline between the Caspian gas fields in Azerbaijan and southeastern Europe (Bulgaria, Hungary, and Romania—in all of which the U.S. would like to limit Russian influence—as well as Austria).[131] Thanks to Gazprom's close links with the Kremlin and ability to make decisions without the complicated attempts at coordination that often bedevil the Europeans, it has been able to move rapidly to secure bilateral deals with the states along the route of South Stream, as well as a new oil pipeline (Burgas-Alexandroupolis) across Greece and Bulgaria.[132]

Nord and South Stream thus dovetail with Russia's strategy of seeking privileged relationships with the established Western European powers, especially its two largest customers (by volume), Germany and Italy, while reducing the leverage countries like Poland have on the overall foreign policy of the EU. The construction of Nord Stream would deprive current transit countries—including Poland, the Baltic states, Hungary, Slovakia, and the Czech Republic—of the revenue they collect for allowing Russian gas to cross their territory. On the other hand, Nord Stream would benefit Germany by lowering the price Berlin pays for deliveries of Russian gas and creating an opportunity for Germany to profit as the primary agent for redistribution of Russian energy throughout the EU.[133] Likewise, South Stream would give Gazprom another option for routing its gas supplies to Europe without having to rely on the good offices of neighboring states it continues to mistrust, particularly Ukraine.

Moscow argues that the bypass pipelines are both justified on purely economic grounds and will prove beneficial to Europe as well as to Russia. Gazprom's largest operating expense is the transit fees it pays to the countries its pipelines cross. With so many states taking a cut, the price consumers in (for instance) Germany pay for Russian gas is substantially higher than the price they would pay for gas that transited only the Baltic Sea.[134]

Moreover, several of the transit countries—especially Ukraine—are unstable politically and chronically behind on repaying their debts to Gazprom. The Ukrainian government paid Gazprom more than $1 billion in arrears in February 2008 but still owed more than $600 million for past deliveries, contributing to an ongoing cycle of threats and counterthreats.[135] Given Ukraine's poor record in discharging its debts, Kyiv could well find itself facing another cutoff in the future (indeed, Gazprom had cut supplies to Ukraine on several occasions before January 2006 without significant EU protest). For the EU to stake its energy security on the Ukrainians' fiscal probity and the stability of Russo-Ukrainian relations is a substantial risk.

Apart from pipelines, the EU has another energy-related concern, namely, the Kremlin's and Gazprom's attempts to extend their reach in Europe through the acquisition of downstream assets (pipelines, refineries, and other infrastructure) inside EU member countries. Thanks to the legacy of Soviet infrastructure, the distribution networks in the Baltic states have long been in Russian hands. More recently, Gazprom has signed deals with major corporations in Italy, Germany, the Netherlands, and France to acquire a stake in their infrastructure for energy distribution to Europe. Coupled with its already dominant control over the transit routes bringing gas to Europe, Russia's acquisition of downstream assets has increased European fears about Moscow's ability to shape Europe's foreign policy. From the European perspective, this danger is especially acute because of what Brussels sees as Russia's lack of reciprocity—while Gazprom is in theory at least free to buy up assets in downstream EU countries, Putin's Russia for the most part refused to allow European companies to buy Russian upstream assets or to establish a legal framework governing Russian energy sales to Europe and shielding Europe from the potential vagaries of Russian foreign policy.[136]

Ownership questions also bedevil energy production. Contracts signed in the 1990s allowing European oil majors, including British Petroleum (BP), Total, and others to acquire a stake in Russia's production sector, usually in the form of so-called production sharing agreements, or PSAs, have come under attack. The PSAs were a particular arrangement granting foreign energy companies the right to develop and profit from underdeveloped Russian reserves, with Moscow maintaining overall ownership of the assets. Mostly signed in the mid-1990s when Russia was at its weakest economically and politically, PSAs covering major deposits typically specified that foreign companies would invest a set amount in developing the resources in exchange for receiving a fixed percentage of the profits.

Under Putin, PSAs covering major deposits, including Shell's concession for Sakhalin-2 and British Petroleum's for Kovykta (in Irkutsk *oblast*), were invalidated by the Russian government and taken over by the state. In both the Sakhalin-2 and Kovykta cases, state pressure forced foreign companies to sell out to Gazprom at significantly below-market prices to avoid losing their investments entirely. Given Gazprom's control of the export facilities needed to move oil and gas from production sites to markets as well as the Kremlin's ability to use other forms of pressure (including environmental and tax inspections), even major European companies like Shell and BP have found themselves trapped in a corner, despite their PSAs with the Kremlin and despite the Russian energy sector's continued reliance on foreign capital for development.

The major underlying factor in the seizure of Sakhalin-2 and Kovykta appears to have been a desire on the part of the Kremlin to take control of these increasingly valuable resources both for the rent-seeking opportunities they present and as a lever for conducting foreign policy.[137] Legislation adopted by the Duma between 2006 and 2008 strengthened this trend toward state control of strategic industries (above all, energy) and limited opportunities for foreign investment despite Russia's very clear need for outside investors to inject capital into the production of oil and gas to promote long-term growth.[138]

In the 1990s when Russia was relatively weak and indebted, the influx of foreign cash from the PSA arrangements was seen as a sufficiently attractive inducement to allow extensive foreign participation in the exploitation of major oil and gas deposits such as Sakhalin-2. As Russia came out of its economic doldrums, in large part thanks to the sustained rise in global energy prices, the potential gains from foreign investment in oil and gas production appeared outweighed by the geopolitical possibilities available to a country controlling some of the largest oil and gas deposits in the world.

A similar calculus, as well as the inherent limitations in the Russian approach, is evident in Gazprom's desire to spurn outside assistance in developing the massive Shtokman gas field in the Barents Sea. For much of the past decade, Gazprom expressed an interest in attracting foreign partners to assist it in extracting gas from Shtokman. In late 2006, Gazprom suddenly announced it would develop the huge Shtokman field on its own. The announcement was in part the result of Gazprom's inability to find an outside partner willing to meet its demands for downstream assets in exchange for access to Shtokman, but also due to the company's (and presumably the Kremlin's) desire to keep the strategic resource represented by the Shtokman reserves in Russian hands.[139] In July 2007, though, Gazprom suddenly announced that it was in fact open to foreign participation in the development of Shtokman and that France's Total and Norway's Statoil Hydro had been tapped to participate in the project, albeit in the capacity of contractors rather than equity holders. This reversal apparently resulted from Gazprom's recognition of its own limits, especially in the realm of LNG refining. The participation of Total and Statoil (and potentially other European companies in future stages of development) also means that when production from Shtokman is finally brought online, it may well have a significant impact on Russia's economic and political relations with Europe, especially if Moscow follows through on its 2006 decision to route the bulk of Shtokman gas to Europe by way of Nord Stream.[140]

CONCLUSION

Russia's approach to dealing with Europe remains caught between mutual dependence and mutual fear. Moscow and Brussels need each other economically, yet Russia's energy policy, authoritarianism, and involvement in the affairs of its neighbors have all limited its ability to seek fuller integration with the evolving institutional web of Europe. Of course, in comparison with Russo-U.S. relations, which remain dominated by yardsticks of traditional security, the relationship between Russia and Europe operates simultaneously on a range of levels. The very complexity of ties between Moscow and Brussels (not to mention Berlin, Rome, Warsaw, and so on) has on the whole meant that the relationship has not been subjected to the drastic swings that have at times characterized interactions between Russia and the United States. Geographical proximity and the resulting economic interdependence have to a significant degree insulated Russia and Europe from such shocks. At the same time, of course, Europe has never posed a security threat to Russia on par with that of the United States. Even NATO, whose expansion Russia has consistently opposed, is seen as dangerous mostly on account of its U.S. component. Europe's own halting securitization has only partially changed this calculus on the part of the Kremlin.

Yet Peter Mandelson's observation that Russia-Europe relations reached a new low in 2007 was quite accurate at the time, even if the independence of Kosovo and conflict in Georgia a year later damaged the relationship still further. Whatever Putin and other Russian leaders have said about their country's "European choice," the fact remains that Russia as it exists almost two decades after the end of the Cold War looks quite different from its neighbors to the West in some very fundamental ways. Since Europe has come to mean a series of values and institutions, for Russia to truly be European would require that it accept the supremacy of these values and institutions over the naked pursuit of geopolitical advantage. Russia remains too wedded to traditional measures of power and sovereignty to be a full participant in the still-unfolding project of creating a united Europe. And since the members of the European club have all pledged themselves to act according to an agreed set of rules (in terms of democratic legitimacy, open societies, rule of law, nonaggression, and so on), the gap in behavior between European states—even former Soviet satellites—and Russia itself remains wide. As Russia has again sought to take on a major international role for itself, it has come increasingly into conflict with a Europe that sees in Moscow's behavior an uncomfortable reminder of its own past.

To a much greater extent than most Europeans, the Kremlin's worldview remains dominated by traditional security concerns. Even though Europe itself is not generally seen as a first-order threat to the security of the Russian Federation, the relationship between Moscow and Brussels has at times suffered on account of the very different approaches to international affairs adopted by the two sides. The pattern is most evident when it comes to discussions about the expansion of both the EU and NATO. For most European countries, especially Western European countries, the value of these institutions lies above all in their ability to reconcile former enemies and expand the realm of democracy and open societies into new regions. To Russia, though, both the EU and NATO are tokens of an expanded, aggressive West that has not yet broken with the Cold War–era logic of containment and continues to see Russia as a potential danger that must be hedged against. The issues of energy and energy security provide yet another example of this divergence. The Kremlin's and Gazprom's interest in acquiring downstream assets is an outgrowth of the policy of using control of oil and gas supplies as a means of exerting foreign policy leverage over neighboring countries.

The past few years have seen Russia simultaneously pursue European integration, especially in the sphere of economics, even while taking steps to assert its geopolitical weight against a neighbor moving uncomfortably close to its borders. The war in Georgia was, if nothing else, a signal from the Kremlin that it had had enough of the West's encroachment and that it would begin pushing back, at least around the fringes of Europe. Europe, in other words, has been a key vector for Russia's multivectoral foreign policy, one that is only partially separable from the more general notion of "the West." Lavrov's idea of a Russia-U.S.-Europe strategic triangle makes sense only if the United States and Europe really are distinct poles in the international system.

Despite the legacy of bipolarity and the periodic crises that continue to plague U.S.-Russian relations, in many ways Europe is a more difficult partner for the Kremlin than is the United States. Unlike the U.S., which is at least an old, familiar rival, for Russia the new Europe remains something of an unknown quantity, and it is precisely on account of the resulting uncertainty that Russia's policy toward Europe in all its institutional embodiments has been so complex and contradictory. Europe, as much as Russia itself, remains in search of a stable identity for the long term. Until those identities can fully coalesce, the nature of relations between Russia and Europe will remain at once interdependent and confrontational, especially on the fundamental political values at the core of the new Europe.

NOTES

1. "EU-Russia Relations 'at Low Ebb,'" BBC, 20 Apr 2007, http://news.bbc.co.uk/2/hi/europe/6574615.stm.

2. As of 2007, of the non-USSR former Warsaw Pact states, only Albania—which left the Pact in 1968—remained outside the EU. Albania was also the only ex-Warsaw Pact country not to be a NATO member in 2007. NATO has also signed membership action plans with Albania, Croatia, and Macedonia. Thanks to the Tito-Stalin rift, Communist Yugoslavia never joined the Warsaw Pact. By 2007 only Slovenia of the former Yugoslav republics had joined the EU and NATO. Croatia and Albania were invited to join NATO in 2008. The former Soviet republics of Lithuania, Latvia, and Estonia are all members of both organizations.

3. Fiona Hill and Omer Taspinar, "Turkey and Russia: Axis of the Excluded?" *Survival*, Mar 2006, 48(1): 81–92.

4. See Dov Lynch, "Russia's Strategic Partnership with Europe," *Washington Quarterly*, Spr 2004, 27(2): 100.

5. Yelena Shesternina, "Polyaki oshiblis' v terminologii," *Izvestiya*, 1 May 2007. In private, many Western European diplomats were exasperated by the Poles' stance, which they were obliged to support in public in order to maintain EU solidarity.

6. Yevgeny Primakov, "Intervention," speech to North Atlantic Cooperation Council ministerial session, 11 Dec 1996, http://www.nato.int/docu/speech/1996/s9612115.htm.

7. Putin mentioned this promise in his widely covered 2007 Munich Security Conference speech. Vladimir Putin, "Vystuplenie i diskussiya na Myunkhenskoi konferentsii po voprosam politiki bezopasnosti," 10 Feb 2007, http://www.kremlin.ru/appears/2007/02/10/1737_type63374type63377type63381type82634_118 10 97.shtml.

8. Daniel Fried, "The Future of NATO: How Valuable an Asset?" testimony to House of Representatives Committee on Foreign Affairs, 22 Jun 2007, http://foreign affairs.house.gov/110/fri062207.htm.

9. Russian Ministry of Foreign Affairs, "Ekonomicheskaya diplomatiya Rossii v 2003 godu," http://www.mid.ru/ns-dipecon.nsf/41786e3b4b21362343256a0c003 fb87c/8baf813b08faa5fac3256e52001fd204?OpenDocument.

10. On discussions concerning Russian membership in the EU, see Vitaly Merkushev, "Relations between Russia and the EU: The View from across the Atlantic," *Perspectives on European Politics and Society*, 2005, 6(2): 360–62. On NATO, see Yevgeny Grigoriev, "Prizrak Rossii v NATO brodit po Evrope," *Nezavisimaya Gazeta*, 2 Oct 2001.

11. Vladimir Putin, "50 Years of the [sic] European Integration and Russia," *JRL* #72, 26 Mar 2007. See also Putin, "Poslanie Federal'nomu sobraniyu," 16 May

2003, http://www.kremlin.ru/appears/2003/05/16/1259_type63372type63374type 82634_44623.shtml.

12. Merkushev, "Relations between Russia and the EU," 366.

13. Doug Saunders, "Fear of Russia Marks Europe's Green Policy," *Globe and Mail*, 11 Jan 2007. Some estimates place Europe's dependence on Russian gas even higher. Jonathan P. Stern, *The Future of Russian Gas and Gazprom* (Oxford: Oxford University Press, 2005), 143. The projected increase in dependence on Russian gas is due to the likely depletion of existing British and Norwegian reserves in the North Sea.

14. Marc Champion, "Russian Energy Grip Splits EU," *Wall Street Journal*, 13 Nov 2006.

15. "Ministr inostrannykh del Rossii Sergei Lavrov: 'Setovaya diplomatiya' sei-chas vostrebovana kak nikogda," *Izvestiya*, 28 Dec 2006.

16. Vladimir Putin, "Vystuplenie na soveshchanii rukovodyashchego sostava sotrudnikov diplomaticheskoi sluzhby Rossii," 26 Jan 2001, http://www.kremlin .ru/appears/2001/01/26/0000_type63374type63377type63378_28464.shtml.

17. Angela Stent, "Berlin's Russia Challenge," *The National Interest*, Mar–Apr 2007: 47.

18. European Union External Relations Directorate-General, "Russia: Country Strategy Paper, 2007–2013," 7 Mar 2007, http://ec.europa.eu/external_relations/ russia/csp/index.htm. The "frozen conflicts" refer to the unresolved disputes between Georgia and Abkhazia/South Ossetia, between Moldova and Trans-dniestria, and the three-way dispute among Armenia, Azerbaijan, and the Nagorno-Karabakh enclave.

19. Heinrich Vogel, "Prospects for Coordination of Western Policies," in *Russia versus the United States and Europe—or 'Strategic Triangle': Developments in Russian Domestic and Foreign Policy, Western Responses, and Prospects for Policy Coordination*, ed. Hannes Adomeit and Anders Åslund (Berlin: SWP Berlin, 2005), 92.

20. Russia did not sign any agreements with the EC proper until 1988. See Mer-kushev, "Relations between Russia and the EU," 357–58.

21. Despite the general downturn in relations between Moscow and Brussels, Russians continue to see the EU in a generally favorable light. According to the Lev-ada Center's monthly polls, during 2007 around two-thirds of Russian citizens gen-erally regarded the EU favorably. (While high, this figure was down substantially from previous years.) See "Rossiya i mir," Levada Center Poll, Aug 2007, http:// www.levada.ru/press/2007081001.html.

22. Nadezhda Arbatova, "L'échéance de 2007 et l'état des relations politiques entre la Russie et l'UE," Institut Français des Relations Internationales (IFRI), Rus-sie.Nei.Visions (20): 7.

23. Mette Skak, "The Mismatch of Russia and the EU as Actors in a Globalized World," presentation to the "Russia and the European Union after Enlargement: New Prospects and Problems" Conference, *JRL* #9265, 11 Oct 2005.

24. During the Second Chechen War, the Council of Europe's Parliamentary Assembly (PACE) briefly suspended Russia's voting rights in April 2000.

25. Russian Ministry of Foreign Affairs, "Medium-term Strategy for Development of Relations between the Russian Federation and the EU," 22 Oct 1999, http:// presidency.finland.fi/netcomm/News/showarticle1610.html.

26. Ibid.

27. Angela Stent and Lilia Shevtsova, "America, Russia, and Europe: A Realignment?" *Survival*, Win 2002–2003, 44(4): 121–34.

28. European Council, "Conclusions and Plan of Action of the Extraordinary European Council Meeting on 21 September 2001," http://www.eurunion.org/partner/EUUSTerror/ExtrEurCounc.pdf.

29. European Council, "A Secure Europe in a Better World," 12 Dec 2003, http://www.consilium.europa.eu/uedocs/cms_data/docs/2004/4/29/European%20Security%20Strategy.pdf.

30. On the European Union's expanded defense capability, see Bastian Giegerich and William Wallace, "Not Such a Soft Power: The External Deployment of European Forces," *Survival*, Sum 2004, 46(2): 163–82.

31. Alexander Nikitin, "Russian Perceptions of the CFSP/ESDP," European Institute for Security Studies Analysis, May 2006, www.iss-eu.org/new/analysis/analy145.pdf.

32. "Russia Warns EU over Ex-Soviet Sphere of Influence," *JRL* #30, 7 Feb 2007.

33. "EU Must Give Kiev Ascension Hope," *Financial Times*, 28 Aug 2008.

34. Vladimir Avdonin, "Rossiiskaya transformatsiya i partnerstvo s Evropoi," *Kosmopolis*, Win 2003–2004, 4(6).

35. Nataliya Alekseeva, "'My nikogda ne smozhem zasedat' v odnom parlamente,'" *Izvestiya*, 29 May 2002.

36. Nikitin, "Russian Perceptions," 7.

37. Celeste A. Wallander, "The Challenge of Russia for U.S. Policy," testimony to Senate Committee on Foreign Relations, 21 Jun 2005. See also Jeffrey Mankoff, "Russian Foreign Policy in the Putin Era," Yale University International Security Studies Working Papers, Jan 2007, http://www.yale.edu/macmillan/iac/mankoff.pdf.

38. Uwe Klussmann, Christian Neef, and Matthias Schepp, "Russland: Annähern und verflechten," *Der Spiegel*, 2 Oct 2006; Stent, "Berlin's Russia Challenge."

39. Katrin Bastian and Roland Götz, "Deutsch-russische Beziehungen im europäisschen Kontext: Zwischen Interessenallianz und strategischer Partnerschaft," Stiftungs Wissenschaft und Politik Berlin (SWP-Berlin) Diskussionspapiere, May 2005: 5–6.

40. This policy has been associated in particular with Merkel's foreign minister, Frank-Walter Steinmeier, a Social Democrat who was also a close adviser to Schröder. See Stent, "Berlin's Russia Challenge."

41. Ministerstvo Inostrannykh Del, "Obzor vneshnei politiki Rossiiskoi Federatsii," 27 Mar 2007: 45.

42. See Jeffrey Mankoff, "Energy Security in Eurasia," Council on Foreign Relations Special Report, Dec 2008.

43. Stent, "Berlin's Russia Challenge."

44. "Declaration by the Presidency on Behalf of the European Union on the Deterioration of the Situation in South Ossetia (Georgia)," 11 Aug 2008, http://europa.eu/rapid/pressReleasesAction.do?reference = PESC/08/99&format = HTML&aged = 0&language = EN&guiLanguage = en.

45. Steven Erlanger, "E.U. Treads Gingerly in Georgia Crisis," *New York Times*, 25

Aug 2008; Judy Dempsey, "Diplomatic Memo—A Role for Merkel as Bridge to Russia," *New York Times*, 24 Aug 2008.

46. "EU Must Be United and Firm on Russia," *Financial Times*, 31 Aug 2008.

47. V. A. Chizhov, "Rossiya-EC: Strategiya partnerstvo," *Mezhdunarodnaya zhizn'*, Sep 2004 (9).

48. "Russia-EU Agreement on Partnership and Cooperation," 1 Dec 1997, http://eur-lex.europa.eu / LexUriServ / LexUriServ.do?uri = CELEX:21997A1128(01):EN:HTML. Although signed in 1994, the PCA was not ratified until 1997—for a period of ten years.

49. Katrin Bastian and Rolf Schuette, "The Specific Character of EU-Russia Relations," in *Russia versus the United States and Europe*, ed. Hannes Adomeit and Anders Åslund (Berlin: SWP Berlin, 2005), 85–88.

50. "Kontseptsiya vneshnei politiki Rossiiskoi Federatsii," 28 Jun 2000, http://www.mid.ru/ns-osndoc.nsf/0e9272befa34209743256c630042d1aa/fd86620b37 1b0cf7432569fb004872a7?OpenDocument.

51. European Commission, "The Policy: What Is the European Neighborhood Policy?" http://ec.europa.eu/world/enp/policy_en.htm.

52. Putin, "50 Years."

53. Thomas Gomart, "Predstavlenie pri polupustovom zale," *Nezavisimaya Gazeta*, 11 May 2005; Adonin, "Rossiiskaya transformatsiya."

54. Sabine Fischer, "Die EU und Russland: Konflikte und Potentiale einer schwierigen Partnerschaft," SWP-Berlin Diskussionspapiere, Dec 2006: 16.

55. V. Likhachev, "Russia and the European Union," *International Affairs: A Russian Journal of World Politics, Diplomacy, and International Relations*, 2006, 52(2): 111.

56. "EU, Russia Hold First Talks on New Partnership Pact," Deutsche-Welle, 27 May 2008, http://www.dw-world.de/dw/article/0,2144,3459034,00.html.

57. Stephen Castle and Steven Erlanger, "European Leaders Agree on New Warning to Russia," *New York Times*, 2 Sep 2008.

58. Timofeï Bordatchev, "L'UE en crise: des opportunités à saisir pour la Russie?" IFRI Russie.Nei.Visions, Oct 2005 (7).

59. Bastian and Schuette, "The Specific Character of EU-Russian Relations," 88.

60. Andrei Terekhov, "Partnery na vse vremena," interview with EU Commissioner for External Relations Benita Ferrero-Waldner, *Nezavisimaya Gazeta*, 16 May 2007.

61. Arbatova, "L'échéance de 2007," 9.

62. Nadezhda Arbatova, "'Problema-2007': Chto dal'she?" *Rossiya v global'noi politike*, Jan–Feb 2006 (1).

63. Ariel Cohen, "The North European Gas Pipeline Threatens Europe's Energy Security," Heritage Foundation Backgrounder #1980, 26 Oct 2006: 2.

64. T. A. Romanova, "Rossiya i ES: Dialog na raznykh yazykakh," *Rossiya v global'-noi politike*, Nov–Dec 2006 (6).

65. Mankoff, "Energy Security in Eurasia." Also see "European Union: Quick Deal Undermines Unbundling Plan," *Oxford Analytica*, 9 Jun 2008; Vladimir Milov, "Fussing about Pipelines Won't Help Russia Solve Its Crisis in Gas Production," *Gazeta.ru*, 17 Mar 2008.

66. According to the Russians, lax quality control and inspections in Poland have

allowed substandard meat to enter the Russian market, including Indian buffalo that was labeled as beef. See George Parker, "EU-Russia Meat Talks End in Deadlock," *Financial Times*, 22 Apr 2007.

67. Ahto Lobjakas, "EU Suspects Political Motives in Russia-Poland Meat Row," *RFE/RL Newsline*, 22 May 2007; Champion, "Russia Energy Grip Splits EU."

68. "Truba Dostoevskogo," *Vedomosti*, 26 Mar 2007.

69. Arbatova, "L'échéance de 2007," 9; Arbatova, "Problema-2007."

70. Vladimir Socor, "EU-Russia Summit Targets New Partnership Agreement," *Eurasia Daily Monitor*, 2 Jul 2008.

71. Judy Dempsey, "Russian Proposal Calls for Broader Security Pact," *New York Times*, 28 Jul 2008.

72. Robert E. Hunter, "Solving Russia: Final Piece in NATO's Puzzle," *Washington Quarterly*, Win 2000, 23(1): 118–23.

73. James M. Goldgeier, "NATO Expansion: The Anatomy of a Decision," *Washington Quarterly*, Win 1998, 21(1): 88.

74. NATO Topics, "The Partnership for Peace," http://www.nato.int/issues/pfp. On the political background to the development of PfP, see Goldgeier, "NATO Expansion," 86–92.

75. Sergei Oznobishchev, "Rossiya-NATO: Realisticheskoe partnerstvo ili virtual' noe protivostoyanie?" *Mirovaya ekonomika i mezhdunarodnye otnosheniya*, Jan 2006 (1): 15–16.

76. John Vinocur, "Historic Expansion Is Approved with Some Discord at Summit: Alliance Votes to Accept Poland, Hungary and Czech Republic," *International Herald Tribune*, 9 Jul 1997; Gary Hart and Gordon Humphrey, "Creating a Cold Peace by Expanding NATO," Cato Institute brief, 20 Mar 1998, http://www.cato.org/pub_display.php?pub_id=5929.

77. "Opposition to NATO Expansion," open letter to Bill Clinton signed by fifty leading figures in U.S. foreign policy, 26 Jun 1997, http://www.armscontrol.org/act/1997_06-07/natolet.asp.

78. James M. Goldgeier and Michael McFaul, *Power and Purpose: U.S. Policy toward Russia after the Cold War* (Washington, DC: Brookings, 2003), 183–85.

79. Ibid.

80. Hunter, "Solving Russia," 123.

81. Andrei Kozyrev, "The Lagging Partnership," *Foreign Affairs*, May–Jun 1994, 73(3).

82. Quoted in Andrei P. Tsygankov, *Russia's Foreign Policy: Change and Continuity in National Identity* (Lanham, MD: Rowman & Littlefield, 2006), 100–101.

83. Russian representatives had participated in NATO activities since 1991 as part of the North Atlantic Cooperation Council, and since 1994 in the context of the Partnership for Peace. The PJC for the first time institutionalized relations at the political level and provided a regular schedule for discussion.

84. "Founding Act on Mutual Relations, Cooperation and Security between NATO and the Russian Federation," 27 May 1997, http://www.nato.int/docu/basic-txt/fndact-a.htm.

85. Goldgeier and McFaul, *Power and Purpose*, 247–48.

86. Ira Straus, "NATO: The Only West Russia Has?" *Demokratizatsiya*, Spr 2003, 11(2).

87. Dmitri Trenin, "Russia's Foreign and Security Policy under Putin," Carnegie Moscow Center, 24 Jun 2005, http://www.carnegie.ru/en/pubs/media/72804.htm.

88. Dmitri Trenin and Bobo Lo, *The Landscape of Russian Foreign Policy Decision Making* (Moscow: Carnegie Moscow Center, 2005), 4.

89. "Joint Statement on the Occasion of the Visit of the Secretary General of NATO, Lord Robertson, in Moscow on 16 February 2000," http://www.nato.int/docu/review/2000/0001-0c.htm.

90. A. I. Voronin, "Russia-NATO Strategic Partnership: Problems, Prospects," *Military Thought*, 2005, 14(4): 20–21.

91. "NATO-Russia Relations: A New Quality," declaration by Heads of State and Government of NATO Member States and the Russian Federation, 28 May 2002, http://www.nato-russia-council.info/htm/EN/documents28may02_1.shtml.

92. Jaap de Hoop Schaeffer, "Opening Statement by the Secretary General [to] Informal Meeting of the NATO-Russia Council and the Level of Foreign Ministers," 26 Apr 2007, http://www.nato-russia-council.info/htm/EN/documents26apr07.shtml.

93. Tuomas Forsberg, "Russia's Relationship with NATO: A Qualitative Change or Old Wine in New Bottles?" *Journal of Communist Studies and Transition Politics*, Sep 2005, 21(3): 342.

94. Clifford J. Levy, "Russia Adopts Blustery Tone Set by Envoy," *New York Times*, 27 Aug 2008.

95. "NATO Riga Summit Declaration," 29 Nov 2006, http://www.nato.int/docu/pr/2006/p06-150e.htm#eapc_pfp.

96. R. Nicholas Burns, "The NATO-Russia Council: A Vital Partnership in the War on Terror," speech in Moscow, 4 Nov 2004, http://www.state.gov/p/eur/rls/rm/38244.htm.

97. Forsberg, "Russia's Relationship with NATO," 337.

98. Besides the question of Russian soldiers stationed in Georgia and Moldova, the dispute has to do with the large quantities of heavy weapons Moscow provided to separatist groups in these countries. The CFE Treaty places limitations on the possession of such weaponry by states; at issue is whether the agreement also covers weapons in the possession of nonstate actors with political ties to a state (in this case, Russia). See Vladimir Socor, "Moscow Confronts the West over CFE Treaty at OSCE," *Jamestown Foundation Eurasia Daily Monitor*, 25 May 2007.

99. Sergei Ivanov, "Speech at the 42nd Munich Conference on Security Policy," 5 Feb 2006, http://www.securityconference.de/konferenzen/rede.php?id=171&sprache=en&.

100. Dmitrij Polikanov, "U-Turns in Russia-NATO Relations," *Perspectives*, 2001 (17): 73.

101. Voronin, "Russia-NATO," 21–22; Irina Isakova, *Russian Governance in the Twenty-First Century: Geo-strategy, Geopolitics and Governance* (London: Frank Cass, 2005), 47–52. The Russian government suspended participation in the CFE Treaty in July 2007 in protest at U.S. plans to build antimissile systems in Eastern Europe.

102. Sergei Lavrov, "Speech at MGIMO University, Moscow, 3 Sep 2007," *JRL* #188, 4 Sep 2007.

103. Isabel Gorst and Jan Cienski, "Missile Shield Accord Draws Russian Fire," *Financial Times*, 15 Aug 2008.

104. Andrew Tully, "US: What Is Strategy for Bases in Former Soviet Bloc?" *RFE/RL Newsline*, 7 Dec 2005.

105. It also, however, suggested it would be willing to establish a joint antimissile system based on existing Russian advance warning radar sites in Azerbaijan. Though obviously in part a tactical ploy to undermine support for the Czech-Polish system, Putin's offer also reflects the underlying logic of his approach to dealing with the United States—seeking cooperation within the constraints imposed by Russia's Great Power ambitions. For a persuasive argument that Putin's offer should be taken seriously as a basis for further cooperation, see Henry A. Kissinger, "Don't Rule Out Putin's Initiative," *International Herald Tribune*, 9 Aug 2007.

106. Charles Grant, "A More Political NATO, a More European Russia," in *Europe after September 11*, ed. Howard Bannerman and others (London: Centre for European Reform, 2001), 50; A. V. Kelin, "Spokoino negativnoe otnoshenie k rasshireniyu NATO," *Mezhdunarodnaya zhizn'*, 31 Dec 2003.

107. Forsberg, "Russia's Relationship with NATO," 345.

108. "Russia Condemns NATO's Expansion," BBC News, 1 Apr 2004, http://news.bbc.co.uk/2/hi/europe/3587717.stm.

109. Yulia Petrovskaya and Lyudmila Romanova, "Sblizhenie—da, smyagchenie—nyet," *Nezavisimaya Gazeta*, 3 Oct 2001.

110. "Russians Consider NATO as Hostile," *JRL* #186, 31 Aug 2007.

111. "Putin Says Moscow May Change View of NATO Expansion if NATO Changes Itself," *RFE/RL Report*, 4 Oct 2001, http://www.rferl.org/newsline/2001/10/041001.asp.

112. On the expansion of NATO's role, see especially Ivo Daalder and James Goldgeier, "Global NATO," *Foreign Affairs*, Sep–Oct 2006, 85(5): 105–13.

113. Ministerstvo Inostrannykh Del, "Obzor vneshnei politiki," 44–45.

114. Oznobishchev, "Rossiya-NATO," 18–19.

115. Dmitry Medvedev, "Stenograficheskii otchet o vstreche s uchastnikami mezhdunarodnogo kluba Valdai," 12 Sep 2008, http://www.kremlin.ru/text/appears/2008/09/206408.

116. Vadim Solov'ev and Vladimir Ivanov, "Shankhaiskii dogovor vmesto Varshavskogo," *Nezavisimaya Gazeta*, 10 Aug 2007.

117. Sergei Lavrov, "Ministr inostrannykh del Rossii Sergei Lavrov: 'Setovaya diplomatiya' seichas vostrebovana kak nikogda," interview with Yevgeny Umerenkov, *Izvestiya*, 28 Dec 2006. Also see Polikanov, "U-Turns," 78.

118. Nikitin, "Russian Perceptions," 2, 8–9.

119. Sergei Lavrov, "Arkhitektura zavtrashnego mira," *Rossiiskaya Gazeta*, 11 Feb 2005.

120. Yevlaliya Samedova and Oksana Gavshina, "Neft' i gaz iz odnikh ruk," *Nezavisimaya Gazeta*, 22 Nov 2005; Martha Olcott, "Vladimir Putin i neftyanaya politika Rossii," Carnegie Moscow Center Working Paper, 2005 (1): 10–13.

121. Zeyno Baran, "EU Energy Security: Time to End Russian Leverage," *Washington Quarterly*, Aut 2007, 30(4): 132. Also see British Petroleum, "Statistical Review of World Energy 2007," http://www.bp.com/productlanding.do?categoryId=6848&contentId=7033471.

122. Baran, "EU Energy Security," 130–31; Lionel Beehner, "Energy's Impact on

EU-Russian Relations," Council on Foreign Relations Backgrounder, Jan 2006, http://www.cfr.org/publication/9535/energys_impact_on_eurussian_relations.html.

123. Nabucco would essentially be an extension of the existing Baku-Tbilisi-Erzurum (BTE) gas pipeline; it is designed to run roughly parallel to Russia's planned South Stream pipeline. For more on the competition between these two projects, see Mankoff, "Energy Security in Eurasia."

124. Paul Reynolds, "G8 Summit: It's Really about Russia," BBC News, 10 Jul 2006, http://news.bbc.co.uk/go/em/fr/-/2/hi/europe/5147948.stm.

125. Oksana Gavshina, "Turetskii gambit," *Nezavisimaya Gazeta*, 18 Nov 2005; Mamuka Tsereteli, "The Blue Stream Pipeline and Geopolitics of Natural Gas in Eurasia," *Central Asia-Caucasus Analyst*, 30 Nov 2005. On Russia's wary embrace of Turkey, see also Hill and Taspinar, "Turkey and Russia."

126. Fiona Hill, "Beyond Co-Dependency: European Reliance on Russian Energy," Brookings Institution U.S.-Europe Analysis Series, Jul 2005: 4–5.

127. V. Putin, "Initsiativa ukhudsheniya otnoshenii iskhodit ne ot rossiiskoi storony," interview with Ekaterina Grigorieva, *Izvestiya*, 26 Oct 2006.

128. At a press conference with Finnish prime Minister Matti Vanhanen in November 2008, Putin responded to European attempts at blocking Nord Stream by threatening to cancel the project and instead building LNG facilities that would result in both higher end-user prices and reduced European leverage. Putin, "Presedatel' Pravitel'stvo Rossiiskoi Federatsii V. V. Putin provel peregovory s Prem'er-Ministrom Finlyandii Matti Vankhanenom," 12 Nov 2008, http://www.government .ru/content/rfgovernment/rfgovernmentchairman/chronicle /a rchive/2008/11/12/ 5856287.htm.

129. Fidelius Schmid, Wolfgang Proissl, and Daniel Dombey, "US Uneasy at Germany's Pipeline Deal with Russia," *Financial Times*, 29 Oct 2006.

130. Roland Götz, "Europa und das Erdgas des kaspischen Raums," SWP-Berlin Diskussionspapiere, Aug 2007: 10.

131. Nikolai Scevola and Dmitry Zhdannikov, "Corrected—Gazprom, Eni Plan Big Gas Pipeline Bypassing Turkey," Reuters, 23 Jun 2007.

132. Baran, "EU Energy Security," 138–39. Russia had initially asked to be allowed to participate in the consortium to build Nabucco. After its offer was refused, presumably because of U.S. opposition, Gazprom moved forward with negotiations on building South Stream.

133. Cohen, "The North European Gas Pipeline," 7.

134. Stern, *The Future of Russian Gas*, 139.

135. "Putin Says Ukraine Must Repay Debt to Receive Gas Directly," RIA-Novosti, 23 May 2008.

136. In mid-2007, the EU began discussing new regulations limiting the ability of companies from countries that impose their own restrictions on foreign ownership to acquire pieces of the energy distribution networks inside the EU—hence the so-called Gazprom clause. See Wolfgang Proissl and Ed Crooks, "Russian Energy Faces EU Barriers," *Financial Times*, 30 Aug 2007.

137. On Sakhalin-2, see Andrew E. Kramer, "Shell Cedes Control of Sakhalin-2 to Gazprom," *International Herald Tribune*, 21 Dec 2006. The PSA granting Shell and its partners a stake in Sakhalin-2 was signed in 1994.

138. Vladimir Milov, "Can Russia Become an Energy Superpower?" *Social Sciences,* 2007, 38(1): 27–28.

139. Romanova, "Rossiya i ES."

140. Roman Kupchinsky, "Russia: Gazprom Looks to a LNG Future," *RFE/RL Newsline,* 16 Jul 2007.

5

Rising China and Russia's Asian Vector

The emergence of China represents a different kind of challenge for Russian foreign policy than dealing with the West. Russia's post-Soviet decline coincided with China's rapid emergence as an economic and geopolitical powerhouse that, unlike the United States or the major European powers, shares a long land border with Russia and is not necessarily a satiated, status quo power, despite its oft-professed commitment to a "peaceful rise." Despite the uncertainty surrounding Chinese intentions and the inherent difficulty for a relatively diminished power like Russia to reconcile itself to the rise of another, Russo-Chinese relations over the past decade have continued a warming trend that began in the late 1980s. Despite the basically Western focus of Russian foreign policy and even though many Russian officials fear China's growing strength, relations between Moscow and Beijing continue to develop rapidly. This development in part stems from a mutual desire to overcome the legacy of the old Sino-Soviet split, which led to a series of serious border clashes and war scares. However, it also reflects a shared uneasiness with the way the international order has developed since the end of the Cold War. As Great Powers in a world dominated by the U.S. hyperpower, Russia and China have found themselves on the same side of many of the most critical issues in global politics.

As in relations with the United States, Russia's approach to China has been characterized by a geopolitical understanding of the world, a preference for bilateral interaction between Great Powers, and a willingness to make short-run compromises in order to avoid being dragged into fruitless quarrels.[1] Sino-Russian cooperation has become significantly more visible and substantive in recent years. Trade and investment have increased rapidly. Moscow and Beijing have joined together to oppose U.S. action in Iraq and to call for the withdrawal of NATO forces from Central Asia. They have institutionalized their relationship through regular summit and working-level meetings and through security cooperation in the Shanghai Coopera-tion Organization (SCO). The so-called Year of Russia in China (2005) and Year of China in Russia (2006) helped expand economic opportunities for Russian and Chinese companies across the border in addition to promoting person-to-person and cultural exchanges.[2]

China is a key regional partner but also a country whose support is nec-essary in order for Russia to play the geopolitical role to which its elites aspire. Russia's interest in promoting a multipolar world order is heavily dependent on the cooperation of China, since Russia by itself is no longer rich, powerful, or influential enough to consistently stand against the United States or shape the international order on its own. Cooperation with China provides Moscow with a kind of diplomatic force multiplier and an alternative to pursuing integration with the powers of the West.

China is at the same time critical to Russia's economic recovery. The value of trade between the two countries quintupled in the decade between 1996 and 2006, to $33.4 billion per year, making China Russia's fourth-largest trading partner.[3] China remains a crucial source of labor for Russia's underdeveloped Far East, where the mass exodus of Russian workers after the fall of the Soviet Union led to the collapse of the local economy. In recent years, migrants from China (often from the primarily Muslim, Tur-kic-speaking population of Xinjiang province) have been central to both retail trade and agriculture in Siberia and the Far East, despite hostility from much of the local population and the Kremlin's own ambiguous attitude toward migrants. China's importance for the Russian economy also extends to the energy sector. Construction of pipelines to Asia is one strategy Rus-sian energy producers have adopted as a means of reducing their own dependence on Europe (with its troublesome eastern fringe) as a purchaser of Russian oil and gas.

Beijing was long an important customer for the Russian military-indus-trial complex, which for much of the past two decades relied on Chinese purchases to remain profitable while Russia's own military was in a period of retrenchment. Finally, China remains for many Russians an attractive model of a country that has achieved rapid economic growth without sacri-ficing extensive state control over society.[4] It is precisely this success in achieving development without liberalization that has made China an attractive partner for those Russian elites uncomfortable with the West's conditions (especially relating to democratization) for achieving a real stra-tegic partnership.

Yet Russia's courtship of China remains constrained by Beijing's desire to pursue integration into the currently Western-dominated political and economic order. Unlike rising powers from previous centuries, China appears content to accept the rules of the existing international system and to be a responsible stakeholder within that system. While Russia hesitates between autarky and integration, China has rushed into the global economy, pursuing wholesale deregulation and opening its doors to foreign investment. Beijing has been one of the biggest winners in the post–Cold War realignment, and its success has made it wary of Russian attempts to upset the balance. Despite a shared commitment to multipolarity, Beijing and Moscow often have radically divergent understandings of their respective interests, limiting China's receptiveness to Russian overtures even as it welcomes improved relations with Moscow.

Like his immediate predecessors, Putin gave special attention to this partnership, promoting border agreements and a deepening of economic ties while moving farther down the road of security cooperation. Deepening the partnership with China and extending it to new areas remains one of Putin's major accomplishments in foreign policy. Putin told a Chinese newspaper of his satisfaction that "we have overcome all the tensions and disagreements [between Russia and China] that existed in the past. Today there is not a single problem we cannot openly and in an absolutely friendly manner discuss and find a mutually acceptable solution."[5] Medvedev's first trip abroad as president took him to China (and Kazakhstan), where he praised Russia's relationship with China for its "dynamism, mutual trust, and progress toward a stronger strategic partnership."[6]

All the same, China remains something of an uncomfortable neighbor. Many Russian officials continue to believe that China represents at least a potential rival. China's attractiveness as an ally is offset in the minds of many officials by the fear that Russia itself is not safe from the growing power and influence of its giant neighbor; as one Russian analyst described it, the Russo-Chinese partnership is really an "alliance of a rabbit and a boa constrictor."[7] The rapidity of China's economic growth, during an era when Russia itself was going through a series of convulsions and crises following the demise of the Soviet Union, has increased the power disparity between the two countries.

Though the volume of trade between Russia and China continues to skyrocket, Russian analysts worry their country is becoming locked in a kind of neocolonial economic relationship, exporting primary commodities (energy, timber, minerals) and importing Chinese finished goods. Many Russians likewise question the construction of oil and gas pipelines to China because of the danger of increasing Moscow's dependence on Beijing (an alternate proposal to build a pipeline across the Far East with a terminus across from Japan has found support primarily for this reason, despite far higher costs). Worried about the implications for its own quest to stamp out separatism in Tibet (not to mention Taiwan), China quietly but firmly

opposed Russia's 2008 incursion into Georgia and recognition of the separatist regimes in South Ossetia and Abkhazia.

Meanwhile, China's military modernization has been something of a
double-edged sword for Russia. While Chinese weapons purchases and tactical innovations are focused primarily on the possibility of a conflict across
the Taiwan Straits, the long history of Russo-Chinese border disputes has
given Russian strategists pause, despite the signing of a series of border treaties between the two countries over the past fifteen years. The Russian
Defense Ministry continues to consider China a potential adversary, even
though China was long the Russian military-industrial complex's best customer. Russia's own military modernization started comparatively late and
has been heavily focused on overcoming years of neglect and decay rather
than on enhancing the country's conventional strength. While Russia's
stockpile of nuclear weapons continues to shrink in line with various arms
control agreements between Moscow and Washington, China, which is not
a signatory to START I, SORT, or other major nuclear limitation treaties,
continues to expand its own nuclear arsenal.[8]

The mounting disparity in economic and military weight between China
and Russia continues to have important strategic consequences, even as
Moscow and Beijing have moved to resolve their disputes. Most notably,
China has taken advantage of its newfound economic and political power
to expand its influence in Russia's traditional sphere of influence in Central
Asia. The result has been an intensified struggle for influence and resources
in the Central Asian states, with both Moscow and Beijing seeking to lock
up energy and pipelines for economic as well as geopolitical reasons.[9] The
result has been a net loss of influence by Moscow, as the Central Asian leaders have increasingly realized their ability to pursue an independent foreign
policy on the basis of balancing among Russia, China, and the West.

Russia has sponsored the creation of regional organizations to provide an
institutional framework for its influence and to contain the rivalry between
Moscow and Beijing. Such regional groupings, above all the Shanghai
Cooperation Organization (SCO), have gone some way toward ameliorating the Russo-Chinese rivalry in Central Asia. The SCO has benefited China
by institutionalizing its presence in Central Asia both economically and in
security terms.[10] For Russia, the SCO provides an additional means of
maintaining Russian influence in the former Soviet Union (along with the
CIS, the CSTO, and a series of bilateral agreements) and for keeping an eye
on Beijing's activities in the region. The SCO itself, however, has also
become the subject of its two leading members' ambitions.

Russia and China have articulated rather different strategies for the future
development of the SCO and the limits of its eventual membership. Some
Russian thinkers in particular have advocated using the SCO as a kind of
replacement for the old Warsaw Pact, that is, as a kind of geopolitical coun-

terweight against the U.S. and a NATO that has increasingly committed itself to conducting out-of-area operations and drawing Russia's neighbors into its orbit.[11] China prefers using the SCO to combat militant Islamist organizations threatening the Central Asian republics as well as Chinese Xinjiang.[12] The continuing tug-of-war between Beijing and Moscow over the future of the SCO is one of the principal reasons the organization is unlikely to become a major security player in the foreseeable future, despite the institution of regular joint exercises and other forms of coordination among its members.

Moscow's approach to the bilateral relationship has emphasized security concerns—balancing against the U.S. and NATO, extending the Russian sphere of influence in Central Asia, and maintaining a rough military balance—while Beijing has focused more on the economic components of the relationship. These competing perspectives and the competing goals underpinning them have contributed to the wariness with which the two powers regard each other, despite their cooperation. As in its relationship with the United States and Europe, Russia's distinct perspective on the nature of the post–Cold War world has shaped and constrained its interactions with a rising China that is undergoing its own process of modernization and development.

To a great extent, Russia's China policy is a function of its larger strategic vision of carving out an independent role for itself on the world stage. In this capacity, China is a useful ally, one whose economy (with its massive demand for energy) nicely complements Russia's own and which shares Moscow's commitment to a multipolar world order based on the principle of sovereign Great Powers. Of course, Moscow also continues to cultivate the Western powers (as well as other major Asian countries such as Japan and India), and given its closer proximity and history of participation in European security, few Russians are willing to embrace China at the expense of ties with the West. China's own interest in integration into the world economy also militates against the formation of an anti-Western bloc stretching from Moscow to Beijing. China is without doubt a close strategic partner for Russia. The Sino-Russian relationship, though, is heavily instrumental, based on overlapping interests and subject to future swings as Russia continues to define its overall position between Europe and Asia.

RUSSIA AND CHINA IN
A MULTIPOLAR WORLD

Much of China's attractiveness as a strategic partner for Russia stems from the fact that Moscow and Beijing have parallel understandings of international order in the twenty-first century. Both are profoundly uncomfortable in a world dominated by the United States where Western norms regarding democracy and human rights reign supreme. According to the Russian Foreign Ministry, Russo-Chinese cooperation is a result of "Russia's long-term national interests and the similarity of [our] approaches to the fundamental questions" of international politics.[13] The central Russian concept of *mnogo-polyarnost'*, or multipolarity, has a Chinese equivalent—*duojihua*—which is frequently employed in official documents describing the nature of the emerging world order.[14] Russo-Chinese cooperation at the United Nations, on arms control, and elsewhere is to a significant degree predicated on the fact that Beijing and Moscow both believe that a world dominated by a handful of Great Powers in which sovereignty and national interest provide the framework for conducting international relations is most conducive to their own well-being.

Consequently, Russian interest in a closer partnership with China is to a large degree a reflection of the state of Russia's relationship to the West. If Moscow perceives its interests being ignored by a hegemonic West, a partnership with China, itself a powerful outsider, enhances Moscow's ability to challenge the legitimacy of an international order based on Western norms. Like Russia, China's Communist government rejects the idea of universal standards for democracy and human rights and believes state sovereignty is absolute (even for post-Soviet republics like Georgia). China thus strongly opposed the bombing of Yugoslavia and Iraq, defended the right of Iran to establish its own nuclear program, and attacked U.S. democracy promotion efforts as unwonted interference in other countries' internal affairs. On all these issues, Beijing made common cause with Moscow, and the strategic partnership between the two grew closer each time.[15] China's lukewarm reaction to the war in Georgia was thus quite notable for showcasing the limits of Beijing's interest in closer ties with Russia.

Of course, basing its interactions with Beijing primarily in the context of its relationship to the United States has certain disadvantages from the standpoint of Moscow, too. Seeing Washington and Beijing as competing poles complicates Russian attempts to maintain good relations with Beijing and Washington at the same time and also prevents Russia from reaping the benefits of a more permanent, institutionalized presence in the Asia-Pacific region.[16] Despite the very real gains made in Russo-Chinese relations since the mid-1990s, China is at best a part-time ally of the Kremlin whose rush toward economic modernization can make Russia's postimperial bluster seem like a hopeless anachronism. China, of course, is not a passive object of Russian policy and has its own reasons for seeking cooperation with Moscow. The benefits to Beijing in seeking a closer partnership with Moscow are numerous: guaranteed supplies of oil and gas, diplomatic support in the UN Security Council and against the expansion of U.S. power in the Asia-Pacific region, military technology, and decreased tension along the Russo-Chinese frontier that allows Beijing to focus its attention on Taiwan and global challenges.

Many Russian observers, especially those with liberal, pro-Western tendencies, are therefore skeptical about what Russia stands to gain from its closer association with China. Former foreign minister Kozyrev argued against embracing Beijing because, as the stronger power, China would be more able to bend Russia to its ends than vice versa. Russian liberals continue to fear that Beijing is using the budding Russo-Chinese partnership to estrange Russia from its Western partners and force it into dependence on China for diplomatic support as well as economic development.[17] For Kozyrev, China and Russia were rivals for foreign investment, and the prospect of a Russo-Chinese rapprochement provided Beijing with a means of pressing the West to admit it to the World Trade Organization and back down over Taiwan.[18] Kozyrev's perspective is shared by many pro-Western Russians. To the extent that the West and China are competing poles in the struggle for Russian allegiance, seeking closer cooperation with Beijing implies a comparable distancing from the West. In this way, the Russian Westernizers and their opponents share a common outlook on the importance of China for Russian foreign policy as a possible counterweight (whether for good or ill) to the West.

This dichotomous approach of seeing the West and China as competing poles of attraction for Russian foreign policy is a somewhat recent development in Russian foreign policy thinking. Despite their emphasis on better relations with the Western world, Russian leaders in the early 1990s sought to simultaneously promote improved ties with China. Moscow's ability to seek improved relations with both Beijing and Washington stemmed largely from the belief that Cold War notions of power and interest were no longer relevant in the same way. By the middle of the 1990s, when NATO expansion and Western intervention in the Balkans had become a reality, the notion of a strategic partnership between Moscow and Beijing based on the idea of promoting a multipolar world and resisting the expansion of Western (i.e., American) power became more prominent in the rhetoric of both sides. The establishment of the Russo-Chinese strategic partnership in 1996 coincided with the downfall of Kozyrev and the emergence of a new, more assertive approach to diplomacy on the part of Yevgeny Primakov and his associates.

This partnership not only allowed Russia to more successfully resist the expansion of Western power and influence in its neighborhood but also provided an alternative concept of Russia's identity as a state and a civilization lying in Eurasia rather than Europe. If the faith of Kozyrev and his backers that Russia's historical destiny lay in the West was misplaced, then perhaps China would prove a more welcoming partner. Beijing was perfectly happy to stay silent about Russia's actions in Chechnya (indeed, the Chinese government consistently backed Russia's right to act as it sees fit in Chechnya, in return for Moscow's firm commitment to a "one China" policy) and made no demands for political or economic reform as a necessary condition for better relations.[19]

More generally, because China is a nation-state rather than a value-driven multilateral agglomeration like the West, the very nature of its relationship with Russia has been different. Unlike the West, China cannot offer Moscow the prospect of integration into multilateral institutions such as the G8, NATO, or the WTO. Instead of a relationship based on rules and values, the budding Russo-Chinese rapprochement looks much more like a traditional geopolitical partnership, where each side is out to maximize its national interest (however it chooses to define that amorphous concept). For a Russia that remains deeply protective of its own sovereignty, such a partnership is in many ways a more natural and comfortable fit, regardless of its cultural and historical affinity with the West. Such was the case even in the 1990s when Russia was more or less considered to be an emerging democracy. Since 2000, as Russia has become more authoritarian and moved increasingly to emulate the Chinese model of authoritarian capitalism, the mutual affinity between Beijing and Moscow has only increased, much to the discomfort of those who conceive of Russia as a fundamentally Western country.[20]

In Russia, this belief that China could balance the growing influence of the United States had to overcome not only the skepticism of those like Kozyrev, who saw a long-term partnership with the U.S. as a more promising route for Russia's development, but also the outright hostility of many nationalists and members of the military. After all, China had been a serious rival to the Soviet Union for leadership of the international Communist movement and had fought a series of serious border skirmishes with the Red Army. The fact that large swaths of the Russian military and nationalist right remain anti-American has not necessarily made them pro-Chinese (racial factors play a role, as does fear). Primakov, the most influential supporter of multipolarity as a Russian strategic goal—and hence of a rapprochement with Beijing—fought a bitter, though ultimately successful battle with parts of the defense establishment that continued to view China as a military rival and source of a "yellow peril" menacing the Russian Far East.[21]

BETWEEN RAPPROCHEMENT AND RIVALRY

The first hints of warming in the Sino-Soviet relationship came during the late 1980s, with Mikhail Gorbachev visiting Beijing in June 1989 and announcing the normalization of relations between the USSR and China, effectively putting an end to the Sino-Soviet split. Momentum toward rapprochement continued under Yeltsin, who issued a December 1992 declaration terming China a "friendly" state and announced the creation of a Russo-Chinese "strategic partnership" during a visit to China in April 1996.[22] In the unsettled 1990s, Russia's nascent rapprochement with China represented a major achievement for the country's foreign policy.[23] Nonetheless, as with other strategic partnerships undertaken by the Yeltsin administration (including that with the United States), the overall aim of the Russo-Chinese partnership remained somewhat vague, despite some real successes such as demarcating and demilitarizing the Russo-Chinese border, expanding trade ties, adopting a common perspective on the challenges facing the post–Cold War world, and institutionalizing ties through regular diplomatic contacts.[24]

In part, the impetus for better Russo-Chinese relations in the 1990s came from the United States, whose unilateral activities in the Balkans, commitment to NATO expansion, and questioning of established arms control regimes created unease in both countries. On the Russian side, this unease contributed to the elevation of Primakov to the Foreign Ministry and the proclamation of Russia's commitment to creating a multipolar world order. In April 1997, Yeltsin and Chinese leader Jiang Zemin signed the "Joint Declaration on a Multipolar World and the Establishment of a New World Order" during Yeltsin's state visit to Beijing. The declaration affirmed Moscow and Beijing's commitment to "respect for sovereignty and territorial integrity, mutual non-aggression, non-interference in each other's internal affairs, equality and mutual advantage, peaceful coexistence and other universally recognized principles of international law."[25] In essence, the declaration grew out of the desire of both sides to register their disapproval with the way the post–Cold War international security architecture had evolved, though it contained little in the way of a positive program for reversing developments that had taken place since the fall of the Soviet Union.

Primakov sought to give the budding geopolitical rapprochement with Beijing greater heft by using it as the foundation for a multilateral dialogue on the preservation of an international order based on state sovereignty and the leading role of the Great Powers. In 1999, Primakov put forward the idea of a strategic triangle comprising Russia, China, and India as a kind of counterhegemonic bloc comprising nearly half the world's inhabitants. Neither Beijing nor Delhi was particularly enthusiastic about the idea at the time (both were more subtle in expressing their discomfiture at U.S. foreign policy), but the logic underpinning such an approach has been evident in much Russian thinking about the future of the Shanghai Cooperation Organization.[26]

In May 1997, Primakov gave a major address to the Association of Southeast Asian Nations (ASEAN) Regional Forum, where Russia has observer status, suggesting that the Russo-Chinese agreement on forming a multipolar world could serve as a model for partnership agreements with other ASEAN states. He also cited the Shanghai Agreement (the document that would lay the foundation for the SCO) as another example of Russia's commitment to building a multipolar and, in his view, more stable and equitable world.[27] As Primakov took pains to point out, though, his support for closer relations with China was not based on the kind of visceral anti-Americanism associated with some in the neo-imperialist camp of Russian politics. Rather, as Primakov explained in 2005, Russia cannot afford to be dependent on any one country or group of countries for its stability and security. Instead, "only . . . diversification, rather than concentration on one foreign policy vector or another creates the possibility for building optimal conditions for securing Russia's external security."[28]

This thinking was also reflected in the network diplomacy strategy articulated by Putin and Lavrov during Putin's second term in office—positioning Russia at the center of a web of partnerships to be activated selectively as needed. To the extent that better relations with China were accompanied by a parallel effort to promote better cooperation with the West, they met with little overt opposition from the Russian elite. As former Russian diplomat Alexander Lukin noted, Communists welcomed the rapprochement between Moscow and Beijing for constraining U.S. power, while even some liberals welcomed the new climate of reduced Sino-Russian tensions, which could free Moscow to focus on getting its own house in order.[29]

Difficulties arose, however, because the Kremlin was somewhat inconsistent in its justification for seeking an opening to Beijing. Can Moscow function simultaneously as a strategic partner to both Beijing and Washington, given the complexities and contradictions inherent in the U.S.-China relationship? For network diplomacy to succeed, the Kremlin has to perform a delicate balancing act between its two most important partners. Initiatives such as the SCO have been variously described as growing out of the need to promote regional security and a desire to overturn U.S. hegemony. To the extent that Russian leaders continue to view the U.S. and China as competitors for Russia's affections, the choice will continue to appear zero sum. Such a perception is perilous both in the context of Russian domestic politics, where strong opposition exists to reliance on either Washington or Beijing, and internationally—above all in a U.S. that retains deep suspicions of both Russian and Chinese motives.

While the initial impetus for increased Russo-Chinese cooperation in the 1990s came from a desire to resolve old problems as well as a shared concern about a U.S. threat to international stability, once the process was under way, it took on a momentum of its own. This rapprochement came to encompass a wide variety of issues, from military cooperation to energy to intelligence sharing.[30] Much of the 1990s-era warming between Moscow and Beijing was based on energy, beginning with a 1996 agreement between the two governments on energy cooperation and continuing with the signing of a protocol in 1999 approving the construction of an oil pipeline from Siberia to China.[31] A much-discussed 2001 Treaty on Friendship and Cooperation also had an economic underpinning; the agreement opened the way for Moscow to begin negotiations with Beijing on the construction of this pipeline.[32]

The initial period of warming Russo-Chinese relations in the 1990s also encompassed defense cooperation, with a series of agreements on troop limitations and the promotion of high-level dialogue between the Russian and Chinese militaries. The improved climate in military relations between the two sides was the more significant because it laid the foundation for greater economic cooperation in the defense sector. China soon emerged as the largest customer for Russian weaponry and technology, which came to account for a substantial percentage of Russian export revenue.[33]

The improved relationship between Russia and China was embodied as well in a number of more concrete agreements. One of the first benefits of the new climate in relations was a resolution of literally thousands of outstanding border disputes between the two countries. Given the vast population disparity between Northern China and the Russian Far East, the series of border agreements signed in the 1990s (the first such agreement was actually signed by a dying Soviet government in 1991) benefited Russia in particular. It drastically reduced the likelihood of Chinese intervention in areas of the Russian Federation with substantial ethnic Chinese populations and secured Beijing's acceptance of changes to the frontier imposed in the nineteenth century on a weakened China. Negotiations on delimiting the entire 2,700-mile frontier continued piecemeal for over a decade. The two sides signed a treaty fully resolving their territorial disputes in October 2004, and the last pieces of disputed territory (two small islands in the Amur River) were finally disposed of during Lavrov's July 2008 visit to Beijing.[34]

In addition to establishing demarcation commissions to draw an agreed-upon frontier, Russo-Chinese border agreements attempted to finesse outstanding disputes, for example, by agreeing to the joint development of the once-disputed islands in the Amur and Ussuri rivers between the two countries.[35] While much of this work was of a technical nature, the continued momentum toward a full territorial settlement had a fundamentally political purpose (particularly given the long history of border skirmishes between China and the USSR) and benefited from the direct involvement of the political leadership in both countries—in sharp contrast to the still-festering territorial disputes between Russia and Japan. In Russia, the border agreements often set off sharp protests from regional officials and

nationalists concerned about the precedent of giving away Russian territory, while public opinion was also generally hostile.[36] Nonetheless, the
Kremlin's insistence on following through with the agreements (and pushing them through a sometimes skeptical Duma) while not seeking similar
accords with Japan is indicative of the importance Putin and his allies
placed on Beijing as a geopolitical partner.

Meanwhile, more active cooperation between Russia and China was
developing in the context of opposing the spread of Islamic radicalism, separatism, and terrorism in Central Asia. The explosion of Islamic radicalism
in the wake of the Afghan civil war posed a direct threat to both Russian
and Chinese interests in the region, even before September 11, 2001, and
the deployment of American forces to Afghanistan. Moscow had been confronting the specter of Islamic radicalism since the outbreak of hostilities
in Chechnya in the mid-1990s; though the Chechen rebels were motivated
largely by secular nationalist goals, foreign jihadist ideology became more
prominent as Chechnya spiraled further into chaos.[37] Violent Islamic radicalism was an even greater problem in large swaths of Central Asia, where
it posed a threat not only to local secular strongmen (generally Russophone
ex-Communist Party first secretaries) but also to Russian and Chinese
influence in the region.

China has had to worry about its Xinjiang province, where the restive
Turkic-speaking, Muslim Uyghur majority continues to chafe under Beijing's
rule and has the potential to become a fertile breeding ground for jihadist
groups. For Moscow, Beijing, and the Central Asian leaders, the Islamist
threat provided another rationale for seeking deeper regional integration
and multilateral cooperation. The consolidation of the SCO into a full-
fledged regional security organization (including Uzbekistan, which does
not even share a border with China) owed much to its participants' interest
in sharing information, resources, and experience in combating the perceived Islamist threat.[38]

In July 2001, Moscow and Beijing signed a Treaty of Friendship and
Cooperation, the first comprehensive agreement between the two countries
since before the outbreak of the Korean War in 1950. This accord was significant as well in that it encapsulated Russia and China's shared aversion
to the idea of a unipolar world. It grew out of the initiatives of leaders, especially in China, to ground the improved climate in relations in a concrete
agreement.[39] With demarcation of the Russo-Chinese border nearly completed, the potential for military confrontation drastically reduced on
account of the Russian military's decline, and the emergence of unilateral
action by the United States as a major irritant for leaders in both Beijing
and Moscow, the treaty both reflected how Russian and Chinese interests
had undergone a fundamental realignment in the decade since the collapse

of the Soviet Union and laid the foundation for more intensive Sino-Russian cooperation in the future.

The treaty called for Russia and China to stop aiming nuclear weapons at each other and to commit to the "no first strike" principle. It also affirmed the two sides' acceptance of each other's territorial integrity (i.e., Beijing agreed to give Moscow a free hand in Chechnya in exchange for a reaffirmation of Russia's commitment to the "one China" policy). On the level of geopolitics, the treaty enshrined Moscow and Beijing's commitment to eschew interference in the internal affairs of other countries and to strengthen the United Nations as the key forum for resolving international disputes.[40] Such language was far from meaningless, given both countries' worries about the role being played by the United States, particularly in the Balkans (the treaty was signed two months before the September 11 attacks), and about U.S. president George W. Bush's declared interest in withdrawing from the ABM Treaty.[41] In this way the Russo-Chinese agreement was as much an effort at coordinating against the perceived excesses of U.S. unilateralism as it was about overcoming the legacies of the past in Sino-Russian relations.

At the same time, of course, the treaty was vague enough to be open to multiple interpretations. Given the continued interest of both Russia and China in good relations with the United States, the agreement had to be couched in terms that, while indicating displeasure with Washington's actions, did not threaten either signatory's ability to cooperate with the U.S. (particularly the ability to trade). The actual agreement was largely free from specific commitments to act, and Moscow was at pains to deny that the treaty was directed against any outside power, especially the United States.[42] Deputy Russian Foreign Minister Aleksandr Losyukov declared after the signing, "To say that our partnership with China is directed against anyone in the West is entirely inaccurate. I think it must be understood in the West that there are boundaries beyond which neither Russia nor China is prepared to go."[43] Top U.S. officials also sought to downplay the importance of the treaty, arguing that given the volume of shared interests, it was perfectly logical for Moscow and Beijing to sign such an agreement.[44]

Under Putin, Russian diplomacy toward China continued to balance cautiously between promoting better relations with Beijing and complicating ties with the U.S. Despite the rise of China and despite the greater attention being paid to improved Russo-Chinese relations, it remains the case that Russian foreign policy is Western-centric, particularly in the aftermath of the September 11 attacks and the unleashing of Washington's global campaign against Islamic terrorism. Putin's approach was somewhat more subtle than that of Primakov and his associates, who were more overt about using China as a counterweight to the United States. Putin's repeated assertions that Russia's destiny is European appeared in part designed to mollify

Western critics who would see a Sino-Russian rapprochement as evidence that Russia was turning its back on the West. At the same time, the Kremlin has not hesitated to hold up a deeper Russo-Chinese partnership as a bogeyman to fend off Western hectoring, while China is happy to use Russia as a cat's-paw in its own quarrels with the West. Thus, in the aftermath of Russia's invasion of Georgia, Beijing (like Russia's other putative allies in the SCO) gave only reluctant backing to the invasion without accepting the independence of South Ossetia and Abkhazia. China was perfectly happy to see Russia deal a blow to the notion of colored revolutions—and to contrast Moscow's heavy-handed intervention with its own preference for soft power, a contrast not lost on the Central Asian states being courted by both Moscow and Beijing.[45]

To be sure, China shares Russia's discomfort at the colored revolutions and the more general expansion of Western influence in Eurasia. With the U.S. bogged down in Iraq, Russia and China began cooperating in opposing the U.S. drive to spread democracy. In both Beijing and Moscow, U.S. democracy promotion efforts often appear to be an attempt by Washington to expand its influence abroad by installing friendly regimes, with democracy as a fig leaf. In the face of this perceived threat, Russia and China united around a worldview that emphasizes each state's right to choose its own political system as well as, domestically, a preference for authoritarian politics and capitalist economics with a heavy dose of state intervention.[46] This so-called Beijing Consensus was a notable development of the Putin years, thanks to Russia's own increased skepticism regarding the virtues of democratic government and a perception that U.S. interest in democracy promotion is selective and driven by the needs of U.S. foreign policy rather than a moral commitment to democracy and human rights. The notion of sovereign democracy—Kremlin ideologist Vladislav Surkov's postulate that each country has a right to take its own path to democracy without foreign interference—is essentially the Russian contribution to the Beijing Consensus, which has played a major role in frustrating U.S. efforts to promote democracy in the CIS, the Middle East, and elsewhere.[47]

As Lavrov acknowledged, the Russo-Chinese partnership in the twenty-first century is based on the "congruence of Moscow and Beijing's approaches to . . . global problems [like] the future world order, strategic stability, the leading role of the UN and the like."[48] On concrete issues ranging from the U.S.-led conflict in Iraq, checking the proliferation of weapons of mass destruction, rogue states, and the role of the United Nations, Beijing and Moscow continue to find common language.[49] This shared understanding was most directly embodied in the so-called Joint Declaration on the International Order of the Twenty-First Century, signed in July 2005 during Chinese president Hu Jintao's visit to Moscow. This declaration, which the Russian Foreign Ministry terms a "most important document," affirms the two sides' shared commitment to "a just and rational world order" based on international law, multilateralism, state sovereignty, and the leading role of the UN in resolving global problems.[50]

While Russo-Chinese relations may lack the formal institutional apparatus of Russia's interactions with the West, the regular series of meetings between Putin and his Chinese counterparts (Jiang Zemin until 2003, then Hu Jintao) imparted a sense of predictability to the relationship it had hitherto lacked. Medvedev, who visited Hu in Beijing shortly after being inaugurated, looks set to continue this effort to foster regular high-level dialogue. The 2005 treaty was supplemented by an action plan on implementation that laid out a framework for deepening Sino-Russian cooperation in the years ahead, paying special attention not only to economics but also to increasing cooperation in the spheres of security and defense.[51] It is notable, too, that while praising the contributions made by the Sino-Russian Friendship and Cooperation Treaty, both Putin and Hu agreed that high-level contacts had played an especially valuable role in advancing the relationship. The two leaders committed themselves to "enhance existing structures while expanding other channels" for bilateral dialogue, particularly on security issues.[52]

Such interest in an enhanced Russo-Chinese dialogue was partly the result of the long-term trend toward closer cooperation between the two states, but interest was also boosted by the atmosphere of crisis surrounding the decision by the United States to go ahead with its attack on Iraq despite the UN Security Council's refusal to authorize the use of force. The U.S. decision for war revived Russian and Chinese fears about the dangers stemming from unipolarity and unilateralism on the part of the United States. Beijing and Moscow both opposed Security Council resolutions laying the groundwork for a U.S.-led invasion of Iraq and called for Washington to allow UN weapons inspectors to continue their work.[53] The standoff over Iraq, along with Washington's broader diplomatic assault on the states termed by President Bush the "axis of evil" (Iraq, Iran, and North Korea) reinforced both Russian and Chinese fears about the dangers of untrammeled American power and provided an impetus for greater coordination between Moscow and Beijing.[54]

At the same time, the tensions created by September 11 in some ways complicated Putin's task of trying to balance between the West and China. Since Washington's response to the attacks created substantial discomfort in Beijing, the Russian decision to support U.S. initiatives in Afghanistan was poorly received by the Chinese.[55] Moscow's decision to share intelligence with the United States and to authorize the deployment of U.S. troops in Central Asia as part of the campaign in Afghanistan was made over Chinese objections.[56] Yet after suggesting to Washington that he might be open to constructing a joint U.S.-EU-Russian theater missile defense system, Putin went out of his way to reassure Beijing that Russia, like China, remained fully committed to the ABM Treaty.[57]

More generally, the muscular U.S. response to the September 11 attacks, in Iraq as well as Afghanistan, increased Chinese worries about a potential future conflict with the United States, just as the development of the Chinese military and spectacular economic growth deepened American concerns about China. Russia, trying to maintain reasonably good relations with both Washington and Beijing in a rather polarized international order, has found itself in an increasingly uncomfortable position.[58] Of course, as relations between Moscow and Washington have worsened over the past few years and Russia's own geopolitical weight has increased along with its foreign currency reserves, "playing the China card" has come to seem like an increasingly attractive option—even if Russia has little interest in getting dragged into a conflict between the U.S. and China over Taiwan.[59] In concrete terms, the increasing warmth of Russo-Chinese relations since 2003 has been reflected primarily in deepening economic integration between the two countries and growing security cooperation—in the context of the SCO, arms sales, and preparations for joint operations.

RUSSO-CHINESE ECONOMIC TIES

Economic congruence has long been central to Russo-Chinese relations. China's rapidly growing demand for energy to feed its booming economy has coincided with the emergence of Russia as the world's leading producer of natural gas (and number two oil producer). Meanwhile, Beijing's modernization of the People's Liberation Army and Navy was initially accomplished to a great extent through the purchase of Russian weapons and the licenses to produce them domestically—in the process saving the Russian military-industrial complex from complete collapse during the lean years of the 1990s. This cooperation in the energy and military-industrial spheres has also benefited from and contributed to the political rapprochement between Russia and China, which has removed barriers to economic activity.

With the reduction in political tension between Moscow and Beijing, bilateral trade has boomed in recent years, especially in the border region, where a huge population disparity and the resolution of border disputes have created an opportunity for cross-border trade and migration on a large scale. For the Russian Far East in particular, China is a critical trading partner. Given the vast distances involved and the lack of communications infrastructure between the Far East and European Russia, the economies of many Far Eastern regions are more closely tied to China than to the rest of

Russia. This cross-border integration, which is most visible in the retail trade conducted by Chinese entrepreneurs in towns and cities along the border, is largely the result of market forces unleashed by the collapse of the Soviet Union. For the economically deprived Far East, the opportunity to build economic links to China offers the chance to participate in globalization without having to go through Moscow and represents the most promising opportunity for the region's economic recovery.[60]

The growth in trade between Russia and China is also a reflection of political developments, especially efforts on the part of Putin and his Chinese counterparts to boost bilateral trade and economic cooperation, as well as economic liberalization in both China and (to a lesser extent) Russia. Indeed, the rapprochement between Moscow and Beijing in the 1990s was most clearly visible in the deepening integration of the two economies. While the bulk of Russian exports to China consisted for most of the 1990s of natural resources (energy as well as minerals and timber), followed by military technology, over the past decade both the volume and range of goods being traded have expanded significantly, with aircraft and other vehicles, electronics, and machinery all contributing a significantly higher percentage of Russian exports to China than they had in the 1990s.[61] In aggregate terms, in 1999 the total value of Russo-Chinese trade was $5.5 billion.[62] By 2006, the total value of trade between the two countries exceeded $32 billion, with Russian officials at the time predicting it would reach as much as $80 billion per year in the near future.[63]

Bilateral negotiations between Russia and China increasingly focused on economic issues during the Putin years—especially Russian oil and gas exports, but also on gaining Chinese support for Russian membership in the WTO, arms sales, Chinese participation in the privatization of Russian companies, and the economic impact of Chinese immigration on the Russian Far East. Both Putin and Hu acknowledged that the full promise of Sino-Russian economic cooperation has yet to be realized.[64] One major impediment to improved economic relations remains high Russian tariffs on Chinese consumer goods as well as pervasive corruption in the Russian customs service. Chinese support for Russian membership in the WTO is in part based on the calculation that, when admitted, Russia will have to bring its tariff regime in line with WTO standards and make a real effort to crack down on corruption.[65] Still, fear of China's economic might and concern about Moscow's ability to maintain its hold over the Far East continue to impose obstacles to deeper regional economic integration.

Economics has been a bone of contention between Moscow and Beijing in other ways as well. As an energy supplier, Russia's desire for high prices and security of demand clash with China's interest in low prices and a diversity of supply. Moscow, not to mention Russian regional leaders, worries openly about the effects of Chinese investment in the Russian economy. Such worries are particularly acute in sectors the Russians consider strategically important (such as energy and defense), to the extent that the Kremlin openly blocked Chinese firms from participating in the auction for the Russian oil firm Slavneft.[66] Despite the growing variety of goods exported from Russia and Putin's own efforts at boosting Russian exports to China, bilateral trade continues to be dominated by Russian energy (54 percent of total exports to China), and Chinese finished consumer goods—largely because of the low quality of most Russian manufactures.[67] Between 1995 and 2002, energy as a percentage of the total value of Russian exports to China tripled, reinforcing Russian fears about becoming locked into a neocolonial economic relationship with a rapidly growing, globalizing China.[68]

Both the cooperative and competitive aspects of Russo-Chinese economic interaction are most clearly visible in the energy sector, which has come to play a central role in Russian foreign policy generally and Russo-Chinese relations in particular. Russia's development as a major supplier of oil and gas to world markets has been one of the principal reasons for the country's return as a major international actor. Since the bulk of Russian oil and gas is pumped from fields in Siberia and the Far East, Russian energy would theoretically enjoy a comparative advantage in Asian markets as a result of proximity and lower transportation costs relative to energy extracted from the Middle East or elsewhere.

Russian oil and gas are also attractive to China for a series of geopolitical reasons. Thanks to its rapid industrialization and economic growth exceeding 9 percent per year, China has rapidly become the world's third-largest oil consumer (after the United States and Japan). Its own reserves are inadequate to meet the needs of its economy. Meanwhile, China's growth and modernization have positioned it as a potential rival and strategic competitor to the U.S., and Washington has consequently sought ways of gaining influence and leverage over China.[69] Given U.S. naval supremacy, China's ability to import oil by tanker from the Middle East could be cut off relatively easily. Washington's interest in Central Asia—including its deployment of troops in Uzbekistan (since withdrawn) and Kyrgyzstan—is in part driven by similar geopolitical concerns. Under the circumstances, Russian oil and gas appear increasingly attractive: pipelines from the Russian Far East to China could not be disrupted by the U.S. Navy, and Moscow is less likely than its neighbors in Central Asia to accept U.S. diktat in the event of a clash between the U.S. and China. Of course, Russian oil companies, with strong backing from the Kremlin, are also busy trying to establish as much control as possible over the production and supply infrastructure in Central Asia, even as China attempts to peel off individual states by signing bilateral deals.[70]

On the Russian side, the construction of oil and gas pipelines to China is attractive as a way of achieving the security of demand that is central to Russian ideas of energy security (and which have been a major stumbling block in Moscow's negotiations with the EU). At the same time, boosting energy exports to China would fit into the larger Russian foreign policy strategy of achieving maximum influence through balancing. In 2006, Russia exported over 151 billion cubic meters of natural gas, almost all to Europe, while the former Soviet states collectively exported 353 million tons of oil, of which only 24.1 million tons went to China.[71] Not only does China represent a vast untapped market for the Russian energy industry, it also provides the Kremlin with an alternative to excessive reliance on Europe as a customer. As the crises over oil and gas deliveries to Ukraine and Belarus demonstrated, energy can be a double-edged sword. Having China (indeed, Asia more generally) as a significant consumer of Russian energy would provide the Kremlin with much greater foreign policy flexibility since it would no longer be dependent on the EU, with its own deeply ambiguous view of Russia, as a purchaser of its major source of export revenue. For the moment, Russian energy sales to China are minuscule, and major steps have to be taken before Russia becomes a significant supplier of energy to the Chinese economy. Infrastructure for transportation is badly lacking; current Russian oil exports to China go primarily by rail, which is a more expensive and less efficient means of transport than pipelines. Natural gas cannot even be shipped by rail unless first converted to LNG, adding another layer of expense to the process.

The potential of the Chinese market, along with the geopolitical advantages of balancing between East and West, were responsible for Russian interest in the construction of a major oil pipeline from Angarsk in Western Siberia to the Chinese industrial center of Daqing, a proposal fraught with complications for Russia's Asian strategy. Yet Russia's wariness about China and desire to balance between China and Japan within Asia, along with massive corruption and inefficiency in the Russian pipeline monopoly Transneft, continue to prevent completion of this Asia-Pacific Ocean pipeline. Transneft began mooting the idea of a pipeline to Daqing in the mid-1990s, but lack of capital and political uncertainty prevented construction from beginning. Moscow and Beijing at last reached a basic agreement on the scope of the project in July 2001. The project was to cost around $3 billion and be completed by 2005. In May 2003 the Chinese National Petroleum Company (CNPC) and Russia's Yukos signed an accord on the actual construction and operation of the Angarsk-Daqing pipeline. The agreement called for Russia to provide for the bulk of the cost, with China covering expenses for the section from the Chinese frontier to the terminus at Daqing.[72] The deal had broad support within the Kremlin, including from then-prime minister Mikhail Kasyanov. The Daqing pipeline promised Russia a major stimulus for developing new energy production sites in

Siberia as well as a guaranteed market for Russian energy and the prospect of greater economic integration between China and Russia's struggling Far East.[73]

In the end the agreement fell through, becoming both a catalyst for and a casualty of the Kremlin's assault on Yukos and its founder Mikhail Khodorkovsky as Putin and his *silovik* allies stepped in to prevent the consummation of the deal. For Putin, the proposed agreement with Beijing appeared to threaten Russia's national security and ability to make use of its most valuable resource. The state's takeover of Yukos was thus portrayed officially as part of Putin's campaign of "raising the effectiveness of the state for the successful development of the economy."[74] Above all, the construction of the proposed pipeline (especially by a privately held oil company like Yukos) seemed to imperil Moscow's aspiration to carve out a substantial international role by tying the Russian economy too tightly to China and reducing the country's ability to function as an independent actor in the international system. For similar reasons, the Kremlin blocked Chinese attempts to purchase Slavneft when it went on the block in December 2002, sought to establish control over energy transport routes from Central Asia at Chinese expense, and stepped up pressure on foreign energy firms working to develop new fields on Sakhalin Island, with Gazprom eventually seizing control of the most important projects.[75]

Russia insisted on maintaining control over the firms supplying energy through its pipelines, effectively giving the Kremlin a free hand to manipulate prices and supplies (much as it did to Ukraine and Belarus). Beijing, along with Yukos, unsurprisingly resisted Russian demands for full ownership of the pipeline, and the Kremlin decided that it could not accept such a strategically valuable piece of infrastructure in the hands of either the Chinese or the unreliable Khodorkovsky without sacrificing too much of its foreign policy autonomy.[76] Despite lobbying from Chinese premier Wen Jiabao and a loan of $6 billion from Chinese banks to finance the Kremlin's purchase of Yukos, Putin's intervention effectively killed the deal.[77]

With the idea of a pipeline to Daqing seemingly off the table, the Kremlin returned to an alternative proposal for a pipeline to East Asia that would remain entirely on Russian territory, with its terminus at the port of Nakhodka on the Sea of Japan. The cabinet of Prime Minister Mikhail Fradkov formally approved the building of a pipeline to Nakhodka in December 2004. This Japanese route was substantially more expensive than the Chinese variant, since the pipeline would have to snake its way for thousands of kilometers along the Russo-Chinese frontier (plans call for the pipeline's total length to reach 4,130 kilometers, versus 2,400 kilometers for the Daqing route) through remote wilderness where construction would be difficult and expensive. Transneft, which would be responsible for operating the pipeline, initially put the cost of the Nakhodka route at around $11.5 billion (the price went even higher when the route was altered in 2004 to avoid ecologically sensitive regions near Lake Baikal), or nearly quadruple the cost of building to Daqing.[78]

Despite the increased cost, Putin and his allies backed the Nakhodka route both because of financial incentives offered by Tokyo and because of the increased strategic flexibility it would provide to the Kremlin. The Japanese government, desperate to reduce its dependence on oil from the Middle East (currently 90 percent of Japanese oil imports originate in the Persian Gulf states), offered to provide as much as $14 billion for the construction of a pipeline to Nakhodka while allowing Transneft to maintain ownership of the completed pipeline. China, meanwhile, had offered only to pay for construction of a pipeline from Daqing to the Russian frontier and in exchange demanded ownership of the pipeline on Chinese territory.[79]

The Nakhodka route also provided Russia greater strategic flexibility, allowing it to avoid becoming overly reliant on any one country as a customer for its oil in the Far East (such as had happened with Turkey following construction of the Blue Stream gas pipeline, when Ankara had unilaterally reduced the price it was willing to pay for Russian gas, secure in the knowledge that the pipeline could not go anywhere else). Since the terminus at Nakhodka would be on Russian territory, the Kremlin would retain control over the ultimate destination of oil passing through the pipeline. Transporting oil from Nakhodka to Japan by ship would be relatively inexpensive, but unlike a pipeline that terminated on foreign territory, Moscow would still have the option of shipping oil from Nakhodka to China, Southeast Asia, or even North America. In this way, Russia would reduce its dependence on any one state (i.e., China), a consideration which fit well with Putin's emphasis on promoting Russia's foreign policy independence. Construction on the first segment, from Taishet (where the pipeline's upstream terminus was moved after protests over the environmental impact of building at Angarsk, which is located close to the shore of Lake Baikal), finally began in April 2006, several months late. Transneft officially hoped to complete the first stage from Taishet to Skovorodino by the end of 2008, though corruption and inefficiency have kept construction far behind schedule.[80]

Of course, the decision to build the pipeline to Nakhodka was bound to ruffle feathers in Beijing, and soon after the announcement that the Kremlin favored the Nakhodka route, it sought to address Chinese concerns. Even if Beijing's hoped-for oil pipeline did not materialize, the Russian government promised it would build a separate pipeline bringing natural gas to China (thereby also reducing Moscow's dependence on an increasingly wary EU to buy its gas).[81] With Yukos out of the way and the Kremlin again in a position to balance between China and Japan, Moscow also began openly suggesting in mid-2004 that it might be open to building a spur from the Taishet-Nakhodka pipeline to Daqing. During Putin's visit to China in October 2004, Economics and Trade Minister German Gref explicitly promised to begin construction on the spur route to Daqing by the end of the year.[82] Despite such promises, by mid-2007 construction had yet to begin, even though Beijing had agreed to finance construction of the spur between Skovorodino and Daqing. The actual feasibility of the dual pipeline remains uncertain. For one thing, current Russian oil production in Western Siberia (where the pipeline originates) is insufficient to supply both the Japanese and Chinese branches. New production sites in Eastern Siberia would have to be developed, adding substantially to the overall cost of the project. Some analysts speculate that talk of building both the Nakhodka and Daqing branches is merely a way for the Kremlin to promote uncertainty about its intentions for as long as possible.[83]

What was long Russia's second-largest export to China—weapons and military technology—reflects a similar duality. On the one hand, the Kremlin has been eager to sell Beijing everything from AK-47 assault rifles to advanced antiship missiles as a way of earning export revenue and promoting the Chinese military's dependence on Russian suppliers. On the other hand, the Russian brass continues to have profound misgivings about the nature of Chinese ambitions (present and future) and has expressed its opposition to selling Beijing top-of-the-line weapons systems out of fear that one day Russia could find itself attacked with its own weapons. This ongoing debate pitting the Kremlin and much of the military-industrial complex against the uniformed leadership speaks to the generally anomalous position China holds in Russian strategic calculations, at once a valued ally in the quest to promote a more balanced world alignment and perhaps the most dangerous potential foe.

The debate is particularly important because military technology is one of the few fields where Russia can compete on an equal basis with Western firms and because unlike U.S. or European defense contractors, the Russian military-industrial complex is willing to sell its wares indiscriminately, including to regimes Western firms and governments try to shun (e.g., Sudan, Venezuela, and Iran).[84] China, which the U.S. views as a strategic competitor, and which was cut off from U.S. and EU weapons deliveries following the 1989 Tiananmen Square massacre, is the supreme example of Moscow's mercantile (some might say mercenary) approach to weapons sales.

The list of Russian military technology that has found its way into Chinese hands is lengthy. It includes advanced Russian aircraft (forty-eight Su-27 Flanker interceptors and around eighty of the updated Su-30 MKK fighter-bombers), surface-to-air missiles (SAMs), up to ten *Varshavyanka* class (Kilo class in NATO nomenclature) diesel submarines, and four top-of-the-line *Sovremenny* class destroyers armed with *Moskit* (Mosquito) antiship missile batteries.[85] In addition to such advanced hardware, Beijing has acquired the licenses to produce many Russian platforms (including the Su-27) domestically and has employed thousands of Russian engineers and designers in its own military-industrial complex.[86]

Particularly during the 1990s, when Moscow's own spending on the military fell to historic lows, the ability to sell weapons abroad (particularly to China, whose army and navy were already using primarily Soviet-model weaponry) was a major factor in keeping the Russian defense industry afloat.[87] Chinese purchases of Russian arms reached $2 billion per year by 1999 (jumping significantly following NATO's intervention in Kosovo) and roughly $2.2 billion by 2003.[88] Meanwhile, even as the Russian Ministry of Defense allocated larger sums for arms purchases as well as research and development following Putin's ascension to power, Russian industrialists still generally preferred selling to the Chinese (and Indians, and anyone else who paid cash on time), since much of the money Moscow allocated for military procurement disappeared through corruption or wastage.[89]

During Putin's second term, though, arms sales to Beijing declined rapidly. By 2006, they were close to nil. The decline stemmed from a variety of sources, including the Russian military's increasing fear of China, Russia's own economic recovery (which made arms sales to China less critical), and resentment at Beijing's proclivity for re-engineering and reselling Russian technology. In response to the drying up of sales to China, Russia has increasingly turned to other customers for its weapons, notably (to China's intense dismay) India.[90]

Despite the recent decline in Russian weapons sales, many analysts predict that Moscow and Beijing will find reason to resume their trade in arms. Russian military experts complain of the existence of a strong China lobby in Moscow that encourages the Kremlin to continue selling weapons even as the Chinese leadership prepares for the possibility of an eventual conflict with Russia.[91] While some elements in the Russian military fear an actual conflict with China, a more general concern for maintaining the strategic balance in East Asia as well as worry about exacerbating tensions with the United States also drive opposition to sales of military equipment to China.[92] Russian interest in China as a customer for military technology generally increases at moments of tension with the United States, when Beijing's value as a potential counterweight appears to overshadow concern about the possibility of Chinese aggression against Russia itself or disruption to the balance of power in Asia.

The issue of arms sales to China in many ways pits two powerful elements in Russian foreign policy thinking against each other—a mercantile policy of enriching the state and seizing export markets versus expansion of Moscow's geopolitical influence, which China threatens. China was long a good customer, with a near limitless appetite for Russian weapons technology. At the same time, China remains a potential strategic competitor to Russia, despite the rhetoric of partnership that has prevailed on both sides since the mid-1990s. Given the influence of powerful economic interests that make up the so-called Kremlin, Inc., some in Moscow worry that the state may not be able to ensure that Russia's national interests are paramount in decisions regarding the sale of advanced weapons to the Chinese.[93]

THE SHANGHAI COOPERATION ORGANIZATION

From the early 1990s, the deepening of bilateral ties between Russia and China has been predicated to a considerable extent on the desire to balance against the dominant power of the United States. With its ability to project power and influence anywhere in the world, Washington provided an important impetus for many of the milestones in Sino-Russian relations. The 1997 declaration on the formation of a multipolar world was above all a warning to the U.S. that China and Russia would not accept an international order dominated by Washington. China's interest in buying advanced weaponry from Russia, and Russia's willingness to sell such weaponry despite its own concerns about Chinese intentions, was also linked to how Beijing and Moscow view Washington.

Perhaps no aspect of the Russo-Chinese rapprochement has caused more consternation in the West than the consolidation of the Shanghai Cooperation Organization (*Shankhaiskaya Organizatsiya Sotrudnichestva*, or ShOS) into a reasonably cohesive multilateral bloc founded on the principles of multipolarity and national sovereignty—precisely those values that U.S. intervention in the Balkans and Iraq challenged. While the contours and purpose of the SCO remain somewhat in flux, there can be little doubt that its principal members, Russia and China (other members are Kazakhstan, Kyrgyzstan, Uzbekistan, and Tajikistan, while Iran, Mongolia, India, and Pakistan are observers, and Turkmenistan and Afghanistan are often invited to participate in SCO activities), view the organization as something more than just a forum for resolving mutual difficulties. Many U.S. analysts consequently look on with great trepidation at an organization that unites Moscow and Beijing, opposes a U.S. military presence in Central Asia, overtly rejects the U.S. democratization agenda as unwarranted interference in countries' internal affairs, aspires to a larger regional security role, and has actively reached out to Iran—the country Washington considers the single greatest menace to peace in the world.[94]

Of course, the actual purpose and structure of the SCO remains somewhat unsettled. The organization was created only in 2001, on the basis of a treaty signed in 1996 by Russia, China, Kazakhstan, Kyrgyzstan, and Tajikistan. The original 1996 Shanghai Treaty (as well as a supplementary agreement signed in 1997) merely committed the signatory nations to undertake force reductions and confidence-building measures along their mutual borders. The driving force behind the initial agreement was the signatories' concerns about Islamic extremism (Kabul had just fallen to the Taliban, and Taliban-inspired movements were active throughout Central Asia and the Caucasus). These so-called Shanghai Five, along with Uzbekistan, signed the Declaration of the Shanghai Cooperation Organization in June 2001. According to the declaration, the SCO aimed at:

> strengthening mutual trust, friendship and good-neighborliness among member states; broadening effective cooperation among them in the political, economic/trade, scientific-technical, cultural, educational, energy, transportation, ecological, and other spheres; mutual striving to support and strengthen peace, security and stability in the region; and constructing a new democratic, just, and rational international order.[95]

The declaration, as well as subsequent documents adopted by the organization's members, was broad enough that its significance could be interpreted in a number of ways. On the one hand, the SCO's emphasis on resolving economic disputes and promoting mutual cooperation seemed fairly benign. Then again, the focus on "constructing a new democratic, just and rational international order" seemed to indicate that the SCO was really designed to act as a check on U.S. power in the region. Subsequent SCO statements, including those opposing U.S. missile defense plans and calling for U.S. troops to depart from Central Asia, indicate the extent of its members' discomfort with the United States' post–Cold War geopolitical role in Central Asia and elsewhere. A number of observers in the West see the SCO as a deliberate attempt on the part of China and Russia to weaken U.S. influence in the region and secure monopolistic control over energy resources, perhaps even as a nascent authoritarian rival to NATO.[96] To some extent, Washington's problem with the SCO is merely that the U.S. itself is not a member and has not been invited to participate.[97]

Much of the U.S. concern about the SCO is overblown; for all its talk of military cooperation and integration, the SCO has no standing force of its own, much less a general staff or any of the other attributes of a unified command structure. SCO members remain free to make their own decisions on security matters, including the right to join other blocs and alliances without consulting other member states.

Besides, the Central Asian members of the SCO also belong to NATO's Partnership for Peace program, and most have strong bilateral ties with the United States (which provides large amounts of military assistance to

Kazakhstan, Kyrgyzstan, and Tajikistan).[98] The aftermath of the September 11 attacks, when SCO members Kyrgyzstan and Uzbekistan signed bilateral agreements with Washington to permit the stationing of U.S. forces on their soil, was a clear example of the organization's limits as a tool for coordinating foreign policy.[99] So, too, was the 2008 war in Georgia, when an SCO summit refused to give Moscow more than equivocal support for its military intervention. Its members agreed merely to "express their deep concern in connection with the recent tension around the issue of South Ossetia, and call on the relevant parties to resolve existing problems in a peaceful way through dialogue, to make efforts for reconciliation and facilitation of negotiations."[100]

Moreover, the SCO member states face a variety of regional security threats, of which Islamic extremism and terrorism (whether in the guise of the Islamic Movement of Uzbekistan, Hizb-ut-Tahrir, or China's East Turkestan Islamic Movement) are the most prominent. Much of the SCO's security focus has in fact been directed at promoting cooperation among member states in intelligence sharing and joint law enforcement activities against such Islamic radicals. These include the 2001 Shanghai Convention on Terrorism, Extremism, and Separatism and the establishment in 2004 of the SCO's Regional Anti-Terrorist Structure (RATS).[101]

Apart from combating Islamic extremism, China and Russia continue to disagree about the proper role for the SCO and about how it should affect relations with the United States. As fairly traditional Great Powers, both China and Russia have emphasized bilateral ties rather than participation in overarching organizations (especially in the field of security). Besides, Russian and Chinese interests in a number of key areas diverge sharply. Most starkly, Russia is trying to hold onto the vestiges of its empire, while China is rapidly expanding its sphere of influence through investment and other forms of soft power in Russia's backyard.

For China, the SCO facilitates this expansion, while for Russia it is at best a means of ensuring Russian interests are not ignored entirely. The Central Asian leaders, meanwhile, see the SCO as a way to preserve the balance between their two giant neighbors in a way that maximizes their own autonomy. Thus the Central Asians are on the whole less categorical about the need for U.S. troops to depart the region (since the presence of even small numbers of American forces limits both Russian and Chinese influence), and they simultaneously court the West, Russia, and China as partners in developing their energy sectors.[102]

On balance, the SCO looks more like a forum for Beijing and Moscow to keep an eye on each other than a tool for mounting a joint challenge to the status quo. The SCO benefits China by allowing Beijing to boost its exports and providing a mechanism for the participation of the Chinese military in regional security issues.[103] While Beijing generally treats the SCO as a bridge for expanding its own role in Central Asia, Russia benefits from the institutionalization of its partnership with China and from coordination of members states' policies on dealing with terrorism, drug trafficking, and other regional security problems. The greatest benefit to Russia from the SCO, however, may be precisely that the organization gives Moscow some leverage over the expansion of Chinese power into Central Asia. Compared with the CSTO, the Eurasian Economic Association (EurAsEc), and the CIS, Russia's influence in the SCO is relatively limited; as a result, Moscow's approach has emphasized using the SCO to preserve its existing influence and provide a channel through which to shape Chinese thinking.[104]

To be sure, some Russian strategists (like Dugin) would like to see the SCO transformed into a kind of latter-day Warsaw Pact, using it to build a bloc of revisionist states to actively challenge post–Cold War U.S. hegemony.[105] Putin did not endorse this more global, more confrontational vision of what the SCO should be. Rather, he consistently denied that Beijing and Moscow had any ulterior motives for setting up the SCO. Putin argued in 2006 that the SCO emerged because "after the bipolar world collapsed there was a demand for other centres of power. We understand this great principle but we are not planning anything like that. The SCO has a good future. We are not going to turn this organization into [a] military-political bloc."[106] To the extent that the SCO has found itself in opposition to the United States on issues ranging from the presence of American troops in Central Asia to the supremacy of the UN Security Council in authorizing the use of force, it has generally been the result of incompatible visions about the nature of the international order and opposition to specific U.S. actions, rather than any kind of deep-seated anti-Americanism on the part of the SCO collectively or its members individually.[107]

To be sure, the most visible aspect of SCO activity has been in the security sphere, though the organization plays an increasingly prominent role in building economic (as well as cultural) links between its member states. In the field of economics, the 2003 Framework Agreement as well as a series of technical implementation accords signed in 2004 laid the foundation for expanded trade links within the SCO space. The signatories promised to create "conditions for the free movement of goods, capital, services and technology, developing necessary legal documents and coordinating relevant legislation," and to increase cooperation in the energy, mining, high-tech, and communications sectors.[108] The increased attention being paid to economic as well as cultural issues by the leadership of the SCO is an indication that the group, despite its shared commitment to multipolarity, is in fact an organization without a clearly defined mission. Beijing, Moscow, and the Central Asian states all have their reasons for wanting better mutual relations, though there is much less consensus on the long-range goals for their partnership.

Agreement on the SCO's role in hard security issues is even more elusive. In political-military terms, the SCO is a fairly loose partnership. Unlike NATO, it does not require members to spend a fixed percentage of their budget on its operations. In contrast to NATO—or even the CSTO—it does not have a mutual defense clause (something akin to NATO's Article 5) or any standing forces of its own. The degree of attention paid by the SCO to geopolitics has in any case varied over time. SCO members gave particular attention to this component of their relationship in the aftermath of the 2003–2005 colored revolutions in Georgia, Ukraine, and SCO member Kyrgyzstan, which appeared to provide a template for overturning the status quo throughout the post-Soviet space. Largely as a result, the SCO increasingly set itself up in opposition to the U.S.-led campaign for democratization. As Lavrov remarked following the 2007 SCO ministers' meeting in Kyrgyzstan:

> It is clear to everyone that one-sided approaches to solving regional and international problems, [those] not relying on international law, are out of place, and that ideological approaches to international affairs, including any kind of "democratization" schemes are ineffective because they do not account for the historical, cultural, and civilization peculiarities of the countries involved.[109]

Given the widespread belief among ruling elites in the CIS that the colored revolutions benefited from Western assistance, the SCO's growing focus on security in subsequent years at times took on, at least implicitly, an anti-Western tint. The SCO's 2005 Astana summit (in which Iran participated for the first time as an observer) adopted a declaration demanding the departure of U.S. troops from their bases in Uzbekistan and Kyrgyzstan, perhaps the high-water mark for the SCO's collective distrust of the West. Shortly thereafter, the SCO held its first large-scale joint exercises (dubbed "Peace Mission 2005") involving both the Russian and Chinese militaries. Despite the alarming (in the West) image of Russian and Chinese soldiers jointly conducting maneuvers euphemistically referred to as "antiterrorist operations," in fact the Peace Mission operation and its follow-up in August 2007 reflect all the ambiguities of Russo-Chinese relations and uncertainty over the precise role of the SCO.[110]

Peace Mission 2005 appeared designed primarily as a way for Russia to showcase new weapons systems it was eager to sell to China as well as to send a political signal to the United States, Taiwan, and perhaps the Koreas about China's and Russia's shared commitment to reducing U.S. influence in Eurasia.[111] Notably, though, Beijing had requested that the exercises take place in Southeastern China, directly across the Straits from Taiwan, as a way of intimidating the independence-minded Taiwanese government. Despite its firm support for the one China principle, Russia had little interest in being dragged into a conflict over the status of Taiwan and demanded a different venue for the maneuvers, ultimately settling on the Shandong Peninsula.

The 2007 Peace Mission exercises, held in Russia's Chelyabinsk *oblast* and paid for exclusively by Moscow, were a significantly smaller affair. Only 6,500 personnel took part (versus 10,000 in Peace Mission 2005), while tanks and naval forces were entirely lacking.[112] The scaled down nature of Peace Mission 2007 reflected in part a realization on the part of Moscow that such exercises' utility as a tool of foreign policy is somewhat limited. China made clear its opposition to transforming the SCO into a full-fledged security organization (in line with Beijing's commitment to a nonaligned foreign policy that seeks to avoid confrontation with the West). Consequently, the deterrence capacity of such maneuvers is not great. Meanwhile, Russia's uncertainty about Chinese intentions led many Russian officials to view the CSTO, of which China is not a member, as a better vehicle for promoting the integration of Central Asia into a Russian-led security architecture.[113]

Russia continues to express interest in a broadening of the SCO's responsibilities in the security sphere (and has even raised the possibility of India's participation in future military exercises). Still, Putin emphasized that the SCO's main contribution to security lies in its ability to address a variety of more local security threats, including terrorism, drug trafficking, and stabilization in Afghanistan.[114] Indeed, the rise of the Taliban provided one of the original impetuses for the formation of the SCO, and the worsening security situation in Afghanistan has led Moscow to press for a more active SCO role in containing potential instability. As the Taliban recuperated across the border in Pakistan in 2007–2008 and the government of Hamid Karzai saw its authority crumble, Russia increasingly turned to the SCO as a mechanism for institutionalizing a foreign presence in Afghanistan alongside NATO forces—even though China, and NATO itself, remain wary of a greater SCO role in Afghanistan.

The first SCO summit of Medvedev's presidency came shortly after the invasion of Georgia, in late August 2008 in the Tajik capital of Dushanbe. Besides seeking, with quite limited success, the organization's backing for the Russian invasion, Medvedev described the SCO's founding as resulting in particular from the "recognition of the necessity for coordinating efforts to promote regional security and stability," which, in his view, the organization had done following the recent war.[115] In spite of the other members' hesitance to accept the Russian position on Georgia, Medvedev laid out an ambitious agenda of other areas where Moscow hoped the SCO would be able to generate coordination, including combating terrorism and drug trafficking, policy toward the war in Afghanistan, and economic cooperation. He was also keen to give the SCO observer states a more substantive role in an effort to enhance the organization's influence. And while the Dushanbe summit echoed past Russian language on the importance of international law and the need to resolve disputes without resorting to force, Moscow's tortured effort to carve out an exception for its intervention in Georgia was a clear indication that the SCO remains less than the sum of its parts.

FAR EASTERN CHALLENGES

While Russo-Chinese military cooperation under the auspices of the SCO is often portrayed as signaling the consolidation of an anti-American bloc in Eurasia, less attention is paid to what may be the most intractable threat to the Russo-Chinese strategic partnership—the fate of Siberia and the Russian Far East. Eastern Siberia and the Far East are the most sparsely populated and economically deprived regions of the Russian Federation. Despite Putin's success in centralizing power in the Kremlin, the center's ability to control these regions remains limited by long distances, poor communications, and a lack of funding. Putin told the Security Council in December 2006 that the economic and demographic collapse of the Far East "poses a serious threat to our political and economic position in the Asia-Pacific region . . . and without any exaggeration, to Russia's national security in general."[116]

Meanwhile, economic pressures and a porous border have led to large-scale Chinese immigration to Siberia and the Far East. Chinese immigrants—initially small-scale traders, followed by farmers, laborers, and entrepreneurs—have transformed the landscape of the Russian East. While critical to the area's economic recovery, their presence has inflamed nationalist passions inside Russia, fueling talk of a creeping Chinese takeover, or at least the gradual sinicizing of Siberia and the Far East. Such nationalist discourse has become widespread in Russia and was not fully disavowed by Putin's Kremlin. While Russian fears of losing Siberia and the Far East to China are excessive, the growth of nationalist, anti-Chinese sentiment among a broad segment of the population (including in the military) could pose a significant challenge to continued Russo-Chinese cooperation.

In general, Russian public attitudes toward China are positive. A 2007 poll by the All-Russian Center for the Study of Public Opinion (VTsIOM) found that 52 percent of Russians believe Russia and China will be partners or allies in the twenty-first century, while only 4 percent thought they would be enemies. Then again, fully 62 percent felt that the presence of Chinese firms and workers in the Far East was dangerous to Russia.[117] Despite the fundamentally nondemocratic nature of Russian politics, such popular attitudes—fueled by racial prejudice and economic insecurity—

have the potential to undermine the ongoing rapprochement between Russia and China.

Russia's problems and perceived vulnerability in the Far East are both economic and demographic. Although Siberia and the Far East contain the vast majority of Russian oil and gas reserves, they are among the poorest, most sparsely populated, and most remote parts of the Russian Federation. Moreover, their importance is bound to increase as existing sources of oil and gas in Western Siberia and the Urals run out, even as Moscow commits itself to exporting larger quantities of oil and gas. Eastern Siberia alone is estimated to possess at least as much oil as the entire U.S. (around 20 billion barrels), along with vast quantities of natural gas. Developing the region and bringing its resources to market will cost up to $100 billion by 2020.[118]

Improving the parlous economic state of the Russian East will require more than injections of cash, however. It will need trade and economic integration, which in turn demand openness to outside goods and people. It will also need workers, since Russia's demographic collapse is particularly severe in Siberia and the Far East, which have experienced a massive population outflow since the end of the USSR. Because of the great distances and poor communications between the Far East and Western Russia, since the 1990s the regional economy has increasingly become integrated into an Asian exchange network, closer to Beijing than to Moscow, despite the Kremlin's attempts to limit the expansion of Chinese businesses. The Russian authorities have raised tariffs and lowered the threshold for importing Chinese goods tax free and nixed several Chinese proposals for building infrastructure linking the two countries (including a railway from northeastern China to the coast north of Vladivostok and cross-border special economic zones), while the impact in the Far East of Moscow's general crackdown on foreigners in the retail trade has most affected Chinese migrants.[119]

Much of the reason for Russia's reticence about the Far East's economic links with China has to do with fears that the region is moving inexorably into China's sphere of influence. The collapse of the Soviet border regime and the subsequent series of agreements with Beijing to demarcate the frontier have facilitated cross-border trade between the Russian Far East and China, leading to substantial Chinese immigration into Russia.[120] The Amur River divides the roughly seven million people of the Russian Far East from the thirty-eight million of China's Heilongjiang province (another 19.6 million Chinese citizens reside in the border province of Xinjiang). Many Russians fear that the population disparity, coupled with a porous border, will inevitably lead to massive Chinese migration into the Russian Far East, changing the region's ethnic makeup and perhaps laying the foundation for a political takeover by Beijing.

As Clifford Gaddy and Fiona Hill have argued, given its extreme climate and distance from major population centers, the Russian Far East is actually *overpopulated* relative to areas of the world with comparable climates, such as Alaska and Canada.[121] Still, given the Russian economy's reliance on resource extraction and the fact that most natural resource deposits are located in Siberia and the Far East, in the short run at least, maintaining a reasonably stable population is an economic necessity for Russia. Due to high mortality rates as well as massive out-migration by native-born inhabitants, the region's population is falling even more rapidly than that of Russia as a whole. The imbalance between the Russian and Chinese sides of the border, along with the opportunities for trade, farming, and the provision of services have already contributed to the migration (legal as well as illegal) of hundreds of thousands of Chinese into Russia. Officially, 35,000 Chinese nationals live in the Russian Federation, though even the Russian government acknowledges this figure to be much too low, with the head of the Foreign Ministry's Asian department, Konstantin Vnukov, estimating that the number of Chinese nationals in Russia fluctuates between about 150,000 and 200,000.[122]

While this Chinese immigration has succored the regional economy and offset to some degree the out-migration of the native population, it has at the same time stoked nationalist passions on the part of many, even highly placed Russians. It is certainly not uncommon to hear Russians in Moscow as well as in the Far East express unease at what is often portrayed as the creeping sinicizing of the border region. One mainstream journalist lamented in early 2007 that "China's annexation [of the Far East] has already begun."[123] Russian fears about the future of the Far East take a number of forms: fear that Moscow's neglect will feed regional separatist movements, fear that the center's weakening hold will leave the region vulnerable to Chinese aggression, or the fear of a more invidious invasion by Chinese migrants who will irrevocably transform the character of Siberia and the Far East, even if Beijing never exercises formal control. Russian alarmists point out that Beijing has never completely accepted the 1858 and 1860 unequal treaties by which Russia acquired vast areas of the Far East from a Qing Dynasty in terminal decline, and that modern Chinese textbooks do not acknowledge Russian sovereignty over the region.[124] Of course, many also see China's military buildup as creating a direct threat to Russia's possession of Siberia.

Even Putin expressed fears about Russia's tenuous grasp of Siberia and the Far East in the face of increasing demographic and economic pressure from Asia, calling for increased migration controls lest "the local population [of the Russian Far East] will in the future be speaking Japanese, Chinese and Korean."[125] Putin's government made it more difficult for Chinese entrepreneurs to import goods into Russia, banned foreigners (which, in the Far East, primarily meant Chinese) from working in the retail trade, and even imposed restrictions on the ability of Russian citizens to work or reside close to the frontier. Such steps represent one of the ways the Putin government fell in behind the nationalist rabble-rousing of groups like the DPNI, even at the cost of exacerbating tensions with China. For the time being, Beijing has been fairly tolerant of Russia's nationalist posturing; however, the Russo-Chinese strategic partnership will never develop into a true alliance as long as Russia's mistrust of China and deployment of xenophobic rhetoric remain prominent features of the Russian political landscape and as long as Moscow and Beijing continue to have divergent or competing interests in the Far East.

RUSSIA AS AN ASIAN POWER

China, of course, is hardly Russia's only major concern along the Asian vector of its foreign policy. Russian engagement with Asia more generally has expanded since the end of the Cold War and since the economic boom that transformed the "Asian Tigers" into economic powerhouses. Putin stepped up Russian participation in summits of ASEAN, while Russia joined ASEAN's regional forum (ARF) as an observer, in large part to ensure Russian access to the rapidly growing markets of Southeast Asia.[126] The same is true of the Asia-Pacific Economic Cooperation organization (APEC), which is becoming increasingly important as a source of investment for developing Russia's Far East. However, Russia's foreign policy in Asia and the Pacific focuses on creating "deepened and balanced relations with the countries of the region that guarantee its long-term stability."[127] This approach requires paying special attention to the major powers—a hallmark of Russian foreign policy globally, too. Apart from China, it is Japan and India that have received the most attention from Moscow in Asia.

As a close ally of the United States, a wary rival of China, and a potentially vast market for Russian energy, Japan is a key economic and security actor in the region, and one that Moscow must continue to balance cautiously against China. Lingering hostility between Japan and Russia dating from the end of World War II continues to complicate the relationship. Ownership of four small and sparsely populated islands remains a major thorn in relations between Moscow and Tokyo, largely because of domestic considerations in both countries. Russian nationalists have insisted the Kremlin take a hard line over these so-called Southern Kurile Islands (called the Northern Territories by Japan), while pragmatists eager to reach an accord with Tokyo see little point in dragging out a dispute over four sparsely populated rocks in the Pacific. Putin and then-Japanese premier Junichiro Koizumi signed a so-called action plan to advance bilateral relations in 2003, calling for increased contacts at both the official level and between business and citizen groups. Nonetheless, the inability to resolve the impasse over the Kuriles has remained a major impediment to deepening ties.[128] It is also a sharp contrast to the alacrity with which Moscow and Beijing moved over the past decade to resolve their territorial disputes.

Despite this failure, the Kremlin continues to view Japan as a useful counterweight against China and as another source of potential investment for reviving the Far East. Indeed, fear of becoming too closely intertwined with Beijing has been a major factor driving Russian officials to seek better relations with Tokyo. Of course, Japan is also a close ally of the United States, and relations with the U.S. are never far from Russian calculations on Japan. Moscow's decision to accommodate China as a counterweight to the U.S. has at least indirectly prevented a closer rapprochement with Japan. Conversely, concern about Chinese influence has at times led Russia to seek closer relations with Japan as a means of retaining a free hand.

The painstaking debate over the placement of Russia's pipeline to the Pacific coast is perhaps the starkest example of Moscow's desire to maneuver between China and Japan. The eventual construction of a pipeline to Nakhodka, if completed, would represent a major step forward in Russo-Japanese economic relations as well as a sign that economic factors are coming to play a more prominent position in Russia's foreign policy in Asia. For Japan, which is entirely reliant on imported energy to power its economy, the selection of Nakhodka as the terminus for Russia's Pacific pipeline is a matter of vital economic and political importance. Despite the depth of public hostility in Japan to any compromise over the Kuriles, the need to secure non-Middle Eastern sources of energy as well as a desire to prevent the emergence of a real partnership between Russia and China has led to greater flexibility on an eventual territorial settlement.[129]

On the other hand, Russia, whose negotiating position improved along with the country's economy, and which generally seems to believe it holds the cards on the question of routing the Pacific pipeline, appeared much less flexible on the future of the Kuriles during the Putin administration than previously. In the early 1990s, when the Russian economy was in a free fall, Moscow offered to return two of the disputed islands to Tokyo in exchange for Japanese investment in the Russian economy, a deal that Tokyo rejected under pressure from its own nationalists, who demanded all four islands.[130] In the subsequent decade, Russia's weight in the relationship increased, and Moscow has been less willing to discuss handing back even the southern islands—though Putin held out that possibility as late as December 2004 in negotiations with his Japanese counterpart. The larger context has been a factor, too; since Japan is a close ally of the United States, Moscow's decision to prioritize China over Japan is in part a reflection of the increased difficulties between Russia and the U.S.

The 2003 Russo-Japanese action plan dealt simultaneously with energy and the territorial dispute, with Japanese premier Koizumi stressing that while negotiations would proceed on both tracks, the two issues would have to be settled separately.[131] Putin meanwhile called for substantially increasing state investment in the economy of the Kuriles, a sign that Moscow intends to maintain control of the islands even as rapid economic growth in the Kuriles themselves has made the local population less receptive to Japanese overtures.[132] And given Japan's need for Russian oil and eagerness to secure the Pacific pipeline to Nakhodka, Moscow now has much less reason to enter into negotiations over the disputed islands in the first place.

Though the search for an eventual territorial settlement and official end to World War II have dominated the diplomatic agenda between Moscow and Tokyo, the changing dynamics of Asian politics have forced both sides to consider a much broader range of issues, particularly in the security realm. With Japan showing signs of loosening the post-1945 strictures on the deployment of its military, Russian strategists must also increasingly take into account Japan's role as a hard security actor with regard to China, the Korean Peninsula, and elsewhere. Moscow has been eager to prevent the outbreak of hostilities on the Korean Peninsula and has consequently worked, both through the six-party talks on North Korea's nuclear program and bilaterally with Pyongyang, to reduce tensions and head off the threat of outside intervention. In this regard, Japan and Russia have, for the most part, found themselves on the same page.[133]

Moreover, since Japan and Russia do not share a land border and since Japan's population is declining almost as precipitously as Russia's, the immigration issue has not roiled Russo-Japanese relations as it has done with ties between Moscow and Beijing. If Russia's relationship to China is in large part a function of its relationship to the United States, then it is equally true that relations with Japan are largely a function of relations with China. Moscow's ability and willingness to overcome its fraught history with Japan will thus depend to a great degree on how its strategic partnership with China develops in the twenty-first century.

The other Asian giant, India, presents a challenge of a different sort for Moscow. As a traditional partner of the Soviet Union, India continues to be a major purchaser of Russian weapons as well as various types of consumer goods—though the overall value of trade has fallen precipitously since the collapse of the Soviet Union. Then again, in the post–Cold War world, democratic India has found itself moving closer to the United States as it pursues its own calculations about resisting China's inexorable rise and pursuing its long-standing feud with Pakistan. India's close ties to the USSR were in large part the result of the Washington-Islamabad partnership. With the fall of the Soviet Union, Delhi lost its superpower patron, while India's own economic growth since the 1990s has significantly lessened the need for such a partnership. Still, Moscow and Delhi signed a friendship and cooperation treaty in 1993 and a joint declaration on creating a strategic partnership in 2003. Russia, of course, has signed such agreements with countries ranging from China to the U.S., and in practice, the depth of the partnership varies significantly.

Rhetoric aside, the relationship between India and Russia has suffered as China has become the major pole for Russia's Asian policy while India and the United States have moved to overcome their own legacy of mistrust. Instead of aligning itself with a seemingly unreliable Russia, India has generally found itself competing with Pakistan for the affections of the United States. By moving closer to Washington (a process symbolized above all by the U.S. decision to provide India with nuclear fuel for its civilian reactors despite Delhi's nuclear weapons tests and refusal to sign the Nonproliferation Treaty), India signaled its own desire for strategic independence.[134] Both Russia and India, in other words, have found reason to focus their attention elsewhere for much of the past decade.

As a major emerging economy, India (which is, along with Russia and China, one of the so-called BRICs) represents yet another potential customer for Russian energy and another potential lever to use as a means of limiting Chinese power in the region. For Russia, India remains valuable as a buyer of weapons (fully 70 percent of India's military equipment is Russian made) and India has provided firm support on Chechnya while keeping quiet about developments in Russian domestic politics that other democracies have criticized.[135] Trade turnover has risen recently, to an annual value of $4 billion—albeit from a low base. In political terms, India joined the SCO as an observer in 2005 and has subsequently participated in a variety of the organization's more substantive activities, including those of counterterrorism and counternarcotics, as well as the building of a transportation network linking Central and South Asia. Though it has so far declined full membership in the SCO, Indian prime minister Manmohan Singh and Putin issued a joint statement following their summit meeting in 2004 expressing support for multilateral approaches to international problems and rejecting unipolarity. Additionally, Russia has lobbied for Indian membership on the UN Security Council.[136]

On the whole, Russian policy toward India appears designed to compensate for a long period of neglect, beginning in the 1990s, when the emphasis on East Asia allowed the old Soviet-Indian partnership to shrivel and opened the way for the United States to successfully court Delhi. Russia's renewed attention to this relationship, however, cannot but complicate the task of deepening the strategic partnership with China, which itself has increasingly come to see in India a (democratic and increasingly pro-Western) rival for leadership in Asia. Moscow's courtship of Delhi will in all probability remain at most a mirror on the state of Russo-Chinese relations.

CONCLUSION

Russia's rapprochement with China over the past two decades has in many ways reflected the larger evolution of Russian foreign policy since the end of the Cold War. Although Gorbachev began the process in the late 1980s, the real warming of ties has come in the decade-plus since the installation of Primakov as foreign minister. For Primakov as well as his successors, China was useful as an alternative to the emphasis on Russia's European/ Western identity during the first post-Soviet years. In a larger sense, the Russo-Chinese rapprochement has fit in with Moscow's interest in returning to the world stage as an independent Great Power. Given that in many ways Russia itself is too weak and divided to represent a pole unto itself in a multipolar world, a true partnership with China allows Russia to pursue this preference more persistently. That calculation, indeed, seems to be one of the key principles underlying Primakov's and Putin's quest for better relations with Beijing. For pro-Western liberals, it is precisely because China represents an alternative model and pole of attraction for Russia that it is so dangerous a partner.

To be sure, there is a range of more mundane reasons why Russian leaders should seek good relations with a rapidly growing and developing China. Expanded trade offers the best chance to resurrect the economy of the Russian Far East. Reduced friction over border questions diminishes the likelihood of future clashes. Post-Soviet Russia has had similar incentives to pursue closer relations with many of its neighbors, including the EU and Japan. Yet relations with China have in many ways been better and more consistent than Russo-European or Russo-Japanese ties. Even though China's future path remains an issue of great concern in the Kremlin and in Russian academic circles, the fact remains that China has been a major foreign policy priority for more than a decade.

Indeed, if the real turning point in Russia's international behavior came around 1996 with the appointment of Primakov to the Foreign Ministry, it is tempting to see the signing of the Russo-Chinese strategic partnership and the subsequent development of that partnership as emblematic of this era in Russian foreign policy, the era in which the notion of Great Power-dom and a concert model of international relations have predominated. The West may still be the top priority for Russian policy makers, but relations with China are in a sense the true touchstone for understanding where Russian foreign policy is heading. As China enters the twenty-first century apparently poised to become a new superpower, the onetime superpower to its north will have little choice but to make China a priority in its own right, independent of Moscow's relationship with the West. China's emergence, then, is one of the principal forces driving Russia's adoption of a more Eurasian identity in the coming century.

NOTES

1. Igor Ivanov, *The New Russian Diplomacy* (Washington, DC: Nixon Center/ Brookings Institution Press, 2001), 122.

2. Aleksandr Alekseev, "Putin otkroet God Rossii v Kitae," *Nezavisimaya Gazeta*, 15 Mar 2006; Konstantin Vnukov, "The Year of Russia in China and Year of China in Russia: Two Halves of a Single Whole," *Far Eastern Affairs*, 2007, 34(1): 33–37.

3. "Cross-Border Bridge on Heilong River to Bring Russia Closer," *China Daily*, 28 Jun 2007. Beijing and Moscow are aiming to reach at least $60 billion in yearly traded turnover by 2010.

4. Scholars and commentators have increasingly seen Russia and China as exemplars of a new "authoritarian capitalism" that seeks to combine economic openness with tightly controlled political and social life. See Azar Gat, "The Return of Authoritarian Great Powers," *Foreign Affairs*, Jul–Aug 2007, 86(4); Andrew Kuchins, "État terrible," *The National Interest*, Sep–Oct 2007, (91); *Russia Profile* Weekly Experts Panel: "The Russian Model: Do Russia and China Provide an Alternative to Liberal Democracy?" 5 Oct 2007, http://www.russiaprofile.org/page.php?pageid = Experts%27 + Panel&articleid = a1191582534; Gordon G. Chang, "How China and Russia Threaten the World," *Commentary*, Dec 2006. For a more skeptical assessment, see Francis Fukuyama, "The Kings and I," *The American Interest*, Sep–Oct 2007, 3(1).

5. Vladimir Putin, interview with Wenmin Jiabao, 13 Oct 2004, http://www .kremlin.ru/text/appears/2004/10/77852.shtml.

6. Dmitry Medvedev and Hu Jintao, "Zayavleniya dlya pressy po itogam rossiisko-kitaiskikh peregovorov," 23 May 2008, http://www.kremlin.ru/appears/2008/ 05/23/1933_type63377type63380_201233.shtml.

7. Andrey Piontkovsky, "At the Edge of the Middle Kingdom," *Moscow Times*, 15 Aug 2005.

8. While Russia is cutting back its nuclear force in line with the START II accord with the U.S., China (which was not a party to the START negotiations) is rapidly modernizing and expanding its own nuclear forces and will likely reach parity with Russia within the next decade. Dmitri Trenin, *Russia's China Problem* (Washington, DC: Carnegie Endowment for International Peace, 1999) 9–10, 27–31.

9. The Chinese National Petroleum Company won a tender in August 2005 to take control of Petrokazakhstan, the largest oil company in Kazakhstan, by paying far above market price, following a pattern of "overpay[ing] for assets; it's more of a security issue for them than the absolute price." See Keith Bradsher and Christopher Pala, "China Ups the Ante in Its Bid for Oil," *New York Times*, 22 Aug 2005: C1.

10. E. Wayne Merry, "Moscow's Retreat and Beijing's Rise as Regional Great Power," *Problems of Post-Communism*, May–Jun 2003, 50(3): 25–26.

11. Vadim Solov'ev and Vladimir Ivanov, "Shankhaiskii dogovor vmesto varshavskogo," *Nezavisimaya Gazeta*, 10 Aug 2007. Also see "The Shanghai Cooperation Organization: Is It Undermining U.S. Interests in Central Asia?" U.S. Commission on Security and Cooperation in Europe hearing, 26 Sep 2006.

12. Alexei Bogaturov, "International Relations in Central-Eastern Asia: Geopolitical Challenges and Prospects for Political Cooperation," Brookings Institution Center for Northeast Asian Policy Studies (CNAPS), Jun 2004: 9.

13. Russian Ministry of Foreign Affairs, "Obzor vneshnei politiki Rossiiskoi Federatsii," Mar 2007: 53.

14. Li Jingjie, "From Good Neighbors to Strategic Partners," in *Rapprochement or Rivalry? Russia-China Relations in a Changing Asia*, ed. Sherman W. Garnett (Washington, DC: Carnegie Endowment, 2000), 94.

15. See Paradorn Rangsimaporn, "Russian Elite Perceptions of the Russo-Chinese 'Strategic Partnership' (1996–2001)," *Slovo*, Aut 2006, 18(2): 129–45.

16. *Mir vokrug Rossii: 2017. Kontury nedalekogo budushchego*, SVOP/State Higher School of Economics/RIO-Tsentr, 2007: 81.

17. Dmitri Trenin and Vitaly Tsygichko, "Kitai dlya Rossii: Tovarishch ili gospodin?" *Indeks bezopasnosti*, 82(2).

18. Andrei Kozyrev, "Riski svoi i chuzhie," *Moskovskie novosti*, 1 Aug 2000. See also Alexander Lukin, "Russia's Image of China and Russian-Chinese Relations," Brookings Institution CNAPS Working Paper, May 2001, http://www.brookings.edu/fp/cnaps/papers/lukinwp_01.pdf.

19. Dmitri Trenin, "Natsional'naya bezopasnost': Bol'shaya vostochnaya strategiya," *Vedomosti*, 14 Feb 2005.

20. For the most eloquent statement of this position, see Dmitri Trenin, *The End of Eurasia: Russia on the Border between Geopolitics and Globalization* (Washington, DC: Carnegie, 2002). See also Robert Kagan, *The Return of History and the End of Dreams* (Washington, DC: Knopf, 2008).

21. See Chandler Rosenberger, "Moscow's Multipolar Mission," *ISCIP Perspective*, Nov–Dec 1997, 8(2), http://www.bu.edu/iscip/vol8/Rosenberger.html. Primakov's victory culminated in the sacking of then-defense minister Igor Rodionov, who had publicly identified China as a common foe of the CIS states.

22. Jeanne L. Wilson, "Strategic Partners: Russian-Chinese Relations and the July 2001 Friendship Treaty," *Problems of Post-Communism*, May–Jun 2002, 49(3): 3–13.

23. Lo termed the warming of Russo-Chinese ties "arguably the greatest Russian foreign policy success of the post-Soviet era." See Bobo Lo, "The Long Sunset of Strategic Partnership: Russia's Evolving China Policy," *International Affairs*, 2004, 80(2): 296.

24. Sherman Garnett, "Limited Partnership," in *Rapprochement or Rivalry? Russia-China Relations in a Changing Asia*, ed. Sherman W. Garnett (Washington, DC: Carnegie Endowment, 2000), 7–15.

25. "Russian-Chinese Joint Declaration on a Multipolar World and the Establishment of a New International Order," 23 Apr 1997, http://www.fas.org/news/russia/1997/a52—153en.htm.

26. US Open Source Center Analysis, "Russia: Foreign Policy Thinkers Undaunted by Rising China," *JRL* #191, 7 Sep 2007.

27. Ye. Primakov, "Opening Statement by H. E. Mr. E. Primakov, Minister of Foreign Affairs of Russia," May 1997, http://www.shaps.hawaii.edu/security/arf/primakov-arf-9707.html.

28. Primakov, "Yevgeny Primakov: Nam nuzhny stabil'nost' i bezopasnost'," *Rossiiskaya Gazeta*, 19 Jan 2006.

29. Lukin, "Russia's Image."

30. Lanxin Xiang, "China's Eurasian Experiment," *Survival*, Sum 2004, 46(2): 112–13.

31. Lyle Goldstein and Vitaly Kozyrev, "China, Japan, and the Scramble for Siberia," *Washington Quarterly*, Spr 2006, 48(1): 168–69.

32. Sabrina Tavernise, "Gazprom Sees Room to Grow after Russian-Chinese Treaty," *New York Times*, 9 Aug 2001.

33. Sherman Garnett, "Challenges of the Sino-Russian Strategic Partnership," *Washington Quarterly*, Aut 2001, 24(4): 142–43. Garnett cites a figure of $3.3 billion for the value of Chinese purchases of Russian arms in the period 1995–1999.

34. "O peregovorakh Prezidenta Rossii V. V. Putina s Predsedatelem KNR Khu Tsintao," 21 Mar 2006, http://www.mid.ru/ns-rasia.nsf/1083b7937ae580ae432569 e7004199c2/432569d80021985fc3257139002ba25d?OpenDocument. In July 2008, Russia agreed to cede what it terms Tarabarov Island to China and divide Bolshoi Ussuriisky Island between the two countries. See "China, Russia: An End to an Island Dispute," Stratfor, 17 Jul 2008, http://www.stratfor.com/analysis/china _russia_end_island_dispute.

35. "Russia and China End 300 Year Old Border Dispute," BBC News, http:// news.bbc.co.uk/1/hi/world/analysis/29263.stm.

36. Vladimir Skosyrev, "Granitsa s Podnebesnoi yuridicheski oformlena," *Nezavisimaya Gazeta*, 25 Oct 2004; Sergei Blagov, "Russia Hails Border Agreement with China Despite Criticism," *Jamestown Foundation Weekly Monitor*, 25 May 2005, http://www.jamestown.org/publications_details.php?volume_id = 407&issueid = 3345&article_id = 2369795.

37. Miriam Lanskoy, Jessica Stern, and Monica Duffy Toft, "Russia's Struggle with Chechnya: Implications for the War on International Terrorism," Kennedy School of Government/Belfer Center Report, Caspian Studies Program, 26 Nov 2002. For the most comprehensive analysis of Islamism's role in the Chechen conflict, see Paul J. Murphy, *The Wolves of Islam: Russia and the Faces of Chechen Terror* (Washington, DC: Potomac, 2004).

38. Xiang, "China's Eurasian Experiment," 112; John Daly, "'Shanghai Five' Expands to Combat Islamic Radicals," *Jane's Terrorism & Security Monitor*, 19 June 2001; Ariel Cohen, "The Russia-China Friendship and Cooperation Treaty: A Strategic Shift in Eurasia?" 18 Jul 2001, Heritage Foundation Backgrounder #1459, http://www.heritage.org/Research/RussiaandEurasia/BG1459.cfm.

39. Garnett, "Challenges," 44–46. The initiative for the treaty came from the Chinese side, which was eager for a resolution of its outstanding disputes with Russia. See V. Putin, "Zayavlenie dlya pressy i otvety na voprosy na sovmestnoi press-konferentsii s Predsedatel'em Kitaiskoi Narodnoi Respubliki Jiang Zeminem," 16

Jul 2001, http://www.kremlin.ru/appears/2001/07/16/0003_type63377type63380_28588.shtml.

40. "China, Russia Sign Good-Neighborly Friendship, Cooperation Treaty," *People's Daily*, 17 Jul 2001, http://english.people.com.cn/english/200107/16/eng20010716_75105.html. The text of the treaty is available from the Chinese Foreign Ministry at http://www.fmprc.gov.cn/eng/wjdt/2649/t15771.htm.

41. Robert Marquand, Ilene Prusher, and Fred Weir, "US Quickens China, Russia Thaw," *Christian Science Monitor*, 3 May 2001, 93(111).

42. Svetlana Babaeva and Ekaterina Grigorieva, "Prostranstvo svobody," *Izvestiya*, 16 Jul 2001. The 2001 treaty was supplemented by a joint agreement on implementation signed by Putin and new Chinese leader Hu Jintao in May 2003.

43. Russian Ministry of Foreign Affairs, "Interv'yu zamestitel' Ministra inostrannykh del Rossii A. P. Losyukova agenstvu 'Interfaks' po rossiisko-kitaiskim otnosheniyam," 16 Jul 2001, http://www.mid.ru/ns-rasia.nsf/1083b7937ae580ae432569e7004199c2/432569d80021985f43256a8b00563c25?OpenDocument.

44. Patrick E. Tyler, "Russia and China Sign 'Friendship' Pact," *New York Times*, 17 Jul 2001.

45. "Russia's Isolation Plays into China's Hands," *International Herald Tribune*, 30 Aug 2008.

46. Kuchins, "État terrible."

47. On the origins and substance of this consensus, see Joshua Cooper Ramo, *The Beijing Consensus* (London: The Foreign Policy Centre, 2004).

48. Sergei Lavrov, "Rossiya-Kitai: Partnerstvo otkryvayushchee budushchee," 12 Oct 2004, http://www.mid.ru/ns-rasia.nsf/1083b7937ae580ae432569e7004199c2/432569d80021985fc3256f2c003bf774?OpenDocument.

49. See "Zayavleniya dlya pressy Prezidenta Rossii V. V. Putina i Predsedatelya Kitaiskoi Narodnoi Respubliki Khu Tsintao i otvety na voprosy zhurnalistov po okonchanii kitaisko-rossiiskikh peregovorov," 27 May 2003, http://www.ln.mid.ru/brp_4.nsf/sps/76C04FB86CB13A8F43256D340032EEFB.

50. "Stat'ya ofitsial'nogo predstavitelya MID Rossii A. V. Yakovenko po voprosam rossiisko-kitaiskikh otnoshenii," 29 Jun 2005, http://www.mid.ru/ns-rasia.nsf/1083b7937ae580ae432569e7004199c2/432569d80021985fc325702f001ca314?OpenDocument.

51. "Plan deistvii po realizatsii polozhenii o Dogovore o dobrososedstve, druzhbe i sotrudnichestve mezhdu Rossiiskoi Federatsiei i Kitaiskoi Narodnoi Respublikoi (2005–2008g.)," 14 Oct 2004, http://www.kremlin.ru/interdocs/2004/10/14/0000_type72067_78193.shtml?type=72067.

52. "Sovmestnaya deklaratsiya Rossiiskoi Federatsii i Kitaiskoi Narodnoi Respubliki," 27 May 2003, http://www.kremlin.ru/interdocs/2003/05/27/1649_type72067_46160.shtml?type=72067.

53. "Threats and Responses; In Their Words: The Security Council," *New York Times*, 6 Feb 2003.

54. An overview of Russian and Chinese interests in the "axis of evil" countries is available in Oleksandr Gladkyy, "American Foreign Policy and U.S. Relations with Russia and China after 11 September," *World Affairs*, Sum 2003, 166(1): 3–24.

55. Natalya Melikova, "Putinu pokazhut chudo sveta," *Nezavisimaya Gazeta*, 14 Oct 2004.

56. Dmitri Trenin, "After the Empire: Russia's Emerging International Identity," in *Russia between East and West: Russian Foreign Policy on the Threshold of the Twenty-First Century*, ed. Gabriel Gorodetsky (London: Frank Cass, 2003), 43–45.

57. Lukin, "Russia's Image."

58. Lo, "Long Sunset," 302; Denny Roy, "China's Reaction to American Predominance," *Survival*, Aut 2003, 45(3): 74.

59. In this regard, Ariel Cohen's concerns about the possibility of a secret codicil to the 2001 Russo-Chinese Treaty committing Moscow to assist Beijing in the event of a conflict in the Taiwan Strait seem quixotic at best. Cohen, "The Russia-China Friendship and Cooperation Treaty."

60. Mikhail Dmitriev, "Strategiya dlya nebol'shogo gosudarstva," *Kommersant*, 21 Nov 2006.

61. Richard Lotspeich, "Perspectives on the Economic Relations between China and Russia," *Journal of Contemporary Asia*, 2006, 36(1): 63.

62. Lotspeich, "Perspectives," 63.

63. "Russia-China Trade to Hit $32–34 bln in 2006—Ambassador," RIA-Novosti, 25 Oct 2006, http://en.rian.ru/russia/20061025/55110192.html; K. V. Vnukov, "Russkii s kitaitsem brat'ya navek?" *Mezhdunarodnaya zhizn'*, 2006 (1–2).

64. "President Hu Vows to Push Forward Sino-Russian Strategic Partnership," Xinhua Online, 20 Nov 2006, http://english.gov.cn/2006-11/19/content_446644.htm.

65. Chen Yun, "Kitai i Rossiya v sovremennom mire," *Svobodnaya Mysl'*, 2006 (3): 47.

66. Melikova, "Putinu pokazhut chudo sveta."

67. Melikova, "V Kitae pogonim ne tol'ko gaz, no i neft'," *Nezavisimaya Gazeta*, 23 Mar 2006.

68. Interview with K. V. Vnukov, 12 Mar 2007, http://www.mid.ru/ns-rasia.nsf/1083b7937ae580ae432569e7004199c2/432569d80021985fc325729c003a7971?OpenDocument.

69. Hsiu-Ling Wen and Chien-Hsun Chen, "The Prospects for Regional Economic Integration between China and the Five Central Asian Countries," *Europe-Asia Studies*, Nov 2004, 56(7): 1062–65.

70. Stephen J. Blank, "The Eurasian Energy Triangle: China, Russia, and the Central Asian States," *Brown Journal of World Affairs*, Win–Spr 2006, 12(2).

71. British Petroleum, "Statistical Review of World Energy, 2007," http://www.bp.com/productlanding.do?categoryId=6848&contentId=7033471. Figures for oil exports are for the former Soviet Union as a whole.

72. Goldstein and Kozyrev, "China, Japan, and the Scramble for Siberia," 169.

73. A thorough account of the Kremlin maneuvering over Yukos and the Daqing pipeline deal can be found in Leszek Buszynski, "Oil and Territory in Putin's Relations with China and Japan," *Pacific Review*, Sep 2006, 19(3): 289–93. See also Danila Bochkarev, *Russian Energy Policy during President Putin's Tenure: Trends and Strategies* (London: GMB, 2006).

74. Petr Netreba, "Prezident otmenil 'popravku Yukosa,'" *Kommersant*, 18 Nov 2003; Netreba, "Vladimir Putin rasshevelil biznes-soobshchestvo," *Kommersant*, 4 Oct 2003.

75. Khodorkovsky's fall resulted at least in part from his role in pushing for the construction of the Daqing pipeline. See Stephen Blank, "China Makes Policy Shift, Aiming to Widen Access to Central Asian Energy," EurasiaNet.org, 13 Mar 2006, http://www.eurasianet.org/departments/business/articles/eav031306.shtml. On Sakhalin, see James Brooke, "Russia Rattles Asia with Attack on Shell's Sakhalin-2," Bloomberg News, 19 Oct 2006, *JRL* #235.

76. Blank, "The Eurasian Energy Triangle."

77. Buszynski, "Oil and Territory," 290. See also Aleksandr Blinov, "Ven poprosil verit' Kitayu," *Nezavisimaya Gazeta*, 27 Sep 2004.

78. Under pressure from environmental groups and the Ministry of Environment, the Russian cabinet agreed to move the starting point of the pipeline from Angarsk (due west of Lake Baikal) to Taishet, some 500 kilometers farther north. The Taishet-Nakhodka route would pass well north of the lake rather than skirting along its shores as foreseen in the initial plan. Eventually the pipeline's endpoint was moved for environmental reasons as well, from Perevoznaya Bay to Kozmino Bay, several kilometers southeast of Nakhodka in Russia's Maritime Province (*Primorskii Krai*).

79. Sergei Blagov, "Russia's Pacific Pipeline Seen as Double Edged Sword," *Jamestown Foundation Eurasia Daily Monitor*, 12 Jan 2005, http://www.jamestown.org/edm/article.php?article_id=2369078.

80. U.S. Department of Energy, Russia Country Analysis Brief, Apr 2007, http://www.eia.doe.gov/emeu/cabs/Russia/Background.html.

81. Natalya Melikova, "Severo-Evropeiskii gazoprovod po-kitaiski," *Nezavisimaya Gazeta*, 22 Mar 2006.

82. Konstantin Simonov, "Vostochnyi ekspress pribudet po raspisaniyu," *Nezavisimaya Gazeta*, 18 Nov 2006.

83. "Putin Hints at China Oil Pipeline," BBC News, 22 Mar 2006, http://news.bbc.co.uk/2/hi/asia-pacific/4831624.stm.

84. Oliver Bullough, "Russian Arms Sales: A Rising Worry," *International Herald Tribune*, 21 Jun 2006.

85. For a breakdown of the hardware sold to China, see Alexander Shlyndov, "Military Technical Collaboration between Russia and China: Its Current Status, Problems, and Outlook," *Far Eastern Affairs*, 2005, 33(1): 2–6.

86. Cohen, "The Russia-China Friendship and Cooperation Treaty."

87. Chen Yun, "Kitai i Rossiya v sovremennom mire," 49.

88. Paradorn Rangsimaporn, "Russia's Debate on Military-Technological Cooperation with China: From Yeltsin to Putin," *Asian Survey*, May–Jun 2006, 46(3): 478. Figures taken from Center for Analysis of Strategies and Technologies, "Identified Contracts for Russian Arms Deliveries Signed in 2003," Moscow Defense Brief #2.

89. Pavel Felgenhauer, "Billions Down the Drain," *Moscow Times*, 1 Jun 2004. Felgenhauer points out that because military research and development is tax exempt in Russia, firms have an incentive to claim to be doing military research without ever producing anything.

90. David Lague, "Russia and China Rethink Arms Deals," *International Herald Tribune*, 2 Mar 2008.

91. OSC Analysis, "Russia: Foreign Policy Thinkers Undaunted by Rising China."

92. Part of the problem is that, like Yukos's advocacy of an oil pipeline to China, large defense contractors (rather than the Kremlin) have been the motor behind many arms deals. To be sure, this problem was more severe in the chaotic 1990s, when Sukhoi licensed production of the Su-27 to Beijing without seeking clearance from the Kremlin. While a similar scenario is all but unthinkable under Putin, in a sense, the damage has already been done. Rangsimaporn, "Russia's Debate," 479; Stephen J. Blank, "The Dynamics of Russian Weapons Sales to China," U.S. Army War College Strategic Studies Institute, 1997, http://www.fas.org/nuke/guide/china/doctrine/ruswep.pdf.

93. On the other hand, Putin's success in subordinating private economic interests to the state (via the arms export monopoly Rosoboroneksport) has meant that such concerns are likely less relevant today than in earlier phases of Russia's post-Soviet history. Putin has given Rosoboroneksport control over export decisions by individual firms. See Rangsimaporn, "Russia's Debate," 482–83.

94. Ariel Cohen, "Washington Ponders Ways to Counter the Rise of the Shanghai Cooperation Organization," *Eurasia Insight*, 15 Jun 2006, http://www.eurasianet.org/departments/insight/articles/eav061506_pr.shtml.

95. "Deklaratsiya o sozdanii Shankhaiskoi organizatsiya sotrudnichestva," 15 Jun 2001, http://www.sectsco.org/html/00651.html. The six countries who combined to form the SCO also signed the so-called Shanghai Convention on the Struggle against Terrorism, Separatism, and Extremism during the June 2001 Shanghai summit.

96. Analysts taking a particularly negative view of the SCO's intentions include Ariel Cohen and William Odom. Others, including Daniel Kimmage, Martha Brill Olcott, Carlos Pascual, and Stephen Blank are more sanguine, arguing that the SCO's focus is increasingly economic and that in any case, Russo-Chinese tensions remain too serious for the SCO to evolve into a real military-political bloc akin to NATO. For an overview, see Lionel Beehner, "The Rise of the Shanghai Cooperation Organization," Council on Foreign Relations Backgrounder, 12 Jul 2006, http://www.cfr.org/publication/10883/.

97. Carlos Pascual, "Russo-Chinese Ties Need Not Worry U.S.," Reuters, 27 Mar 2007, http://www.brookings.edu/interviews/2007/0327russia_pascual.aspx.

98. Evan A. Feigenbaum, "The Shanghai Cooperation Organization and the Future of Central Asia," speech at the Nixon Center, 6 Sep 2007, http://www.state.gov/p/sca/rls/rm/2007/91858.htm. Also see Caitlin B. Doherty, "Inside Track: The SCO and the Future of Central Asia," *The National Interest*, 7 Sep 2007.

99. Jao Huashen, "Kitai, Tsentral'naya Aziya i Shankhaiskaya Organizatsiya Sotrudnichestva," Carnegie Moscow Center Working Paper No. 5, 2005: 17.

100. "Dushanbe Declaration of Heads of SCO Member States," 28 Aug 2008, http://www.sectsco.org/news_detail.asp?id=2360&LanguageID=2.

101. "Here There Be Dragons: The Shanghai Cooperation Organization," Center for Defense Information China Report, 26 Sep 2006; Daly, "'Shanghai Five' Expands to Combat Islamic Radicals."

102. "The Limits of the Shanghai Cooperation Organization," *RFE/RL Press Release*, 7 Aug 2006.

103. Merry, "Moscow's Retreat," 25–26; Alexei Bogaturov, "International Rela-

tions in Central-Eastern Asia: Geopolitical Challenges and Prospects for Political Cooperation," Report of the Brookings Institution Center for Northeast Asian Policy Studies, Jun 2004: 9.

104. "Here There Be Dragons."

105. Aleksandr Dugin, "Zapad-Vostok: Velikii shans Rossii," *Vedomosti*, 13 Jul 2005.

106. Edited transcript of Putin remarks to Valdai Discussion Club, 9 Sep 2006, http://en.valday2006.rian.ru/materials/20060910/52329444.html.

107. Jao Huashen, "Kitai, Tsentral'naya Aziya i Shankhaiskaya Organizatsiya Sotrudnichestva," 11–12. Chinese general secretary Hu Jintao went out of his way to assure the U.S. that the SCO was not an anti-American bloc during a summit meeting with U.S. president Bush in April 2006. See "Predsedatel' KNR: ShOS ne yavlyaetsya antamerikanskoi organizatsiei," IBK.ru News, 21 Apr 2006, http://www.ibk.ru/news/predsedatel_knr_shos_ne_yavlyaetsya_antiamerikanskoi_organi zatsiei-16946/.

108. "Joint Communique of the Council of Governmental Heads (Prime Ministers) of Shanghai Cooperation Organization Member States," 23 Sep 2004, http://www.shaps.hawaii.edu/fp/russia/2004/20040923_sco_jc.html.

109. S. Lavrov, "Vystuplenie Ministra Inostrannykh Del Rossii S. V. Lavrova na zasedanii MID ShOS, Bishkek," 7 Jul 2007, http://www.mid.ru/ns-rasia.nsf/3a010 8443c964002432569e7004199c0/432569d80021985fc3257313002e5334?Open Document; V. Putin, "Otvety na voprosy rossiiskikh i inostrannykh zhurnalistov po okonchanii sammita Shankhaiskoi organizatsii sotrudnichestva," 16 Jun 2005, http://www.mid.ru/ns-rasia.nsf/1083b7937ae580ae432569e7004199c2/432569d 80021985fc325718f0028c259?OpenDocument.

110. Both Beijing and Moscow had previously conducted maneuvers with the militaries from the Central Asian states (in the Russian case, under the auspices of the CSTO as well as the SCO). Previous exercises, however, were much smaller in scale and more focused on specifically local threats. In contrast, Peace Mission 2005 was held on China's Shandong Peninsula and involved land, air, naval, and amphibious forces from both Russia and China. Though portrayed as providing operational training in antiterrorist tactics, the scale of the exercises and the use of heavy weaponry (including naval/amphibious forces and Russian Tu-22 strategic bombers) belied such claims.

111. "Exercise of Power," *Financial Times* editorial, 19 Aug 2005; Stephen Blank, testimony to U.S. Commission on Security and Cooperation in Europe, 26 Sep 2006; Dmitri Trenin, "ShOS i vybor za mir," *Ezhednevnyi zhurnal*, 29 Aug 2007.

112. Vladimir Mukhin, "Mirnaya missiya za dva milliarda," *Nezavisimaya Gazeta*, 7 Aug 2007.

113. Erica Marat, "Fissures in the Force: Multilateral Security Integration Can Only Go So Far," *Jane's Intelligence Review*, 12 May 2007.

114. Artur Blinov, "Vybor ShOS—dogovor o druzhbe," *Nezavisimaya Gazeta*, 15 Aug 2007.

115. Dmitry Medvedev, "Vystuplenie na zasedanii Soveta glav gosudarstv—chlenov Shankhaiskoi organizatsii sotrudnichestva," 28 Aug 2008, http://www .kremlin.ru/appears/2008/08/28/1418_type63377_205835.shtml.

116. V. Putin, "Vstupitel'noe slovo na zasedanii Soveta Bezopasnosti," 20 Dec 2006, http://president.kremlin.ru/appears/2006/12/20/1548_type63374type63378 type82634_115648.shtml.

117. "Rossiyane khotyat druzhit' s Kitaem, no na rasstoyanii," VTsIOM Press Release, 16 Apr 2007, http://wciom.ru/arkhiv/tematicheskii-arkhiv/item/single/ 4397.html.

118. Goldstein and Kozyrev, "China, Japan and the Scramble for Siberia," 168. Already the Kremlin has agreed to allocate $13.8 billion (358 billion rubles) for Far Eastern development until 2013. Sergei Blagov, "Balancing China in the Russian Far East," *JRL* #77, 2 Apr 2007.

119. Gabriel Gatehouse, "Russia's Far East Looks to China," BBC News, 5 Jun 2007, http://news.bbc.co.uk/2/hi/europe/6713509.stm; David Wall, "Kremlin Fears for Its Far East," *Japan Times*, 21 Dec 2006.

120. Rajan Menon, "The Sick Man of Asia: Russia's Endangered Far East," *The National Interest*, Aut 2003.

121. Clifford G. Gaddy, "As Russia Looks East: Can It Manage Resources, Space, and People?" *Gaiko Forum*, Jan 2007. Also see Clifford G. Gaddy and Fiona Hill, *The Siberian Curse: How Communist Planners Left Russia Out in the Cold* (Washington, DC: Brookings Institution, 2003).

122. Interview with K. V. Vnukov, 12 Mar 2007, http://www.mid.ru/ns-rasia.nsf/ 1083b7937ae580ae432569e7004199c2/432569d80021985fc325729c003a7971 ?OpenDocument.

123. Yulia Latynina, "Lyubov' k Dal'nemu," *Novaya Gazeta*, 11 Jan 2007.

124. Menon, "The Sick Man of Asia;" Trenin and Tsygichko, "Kitai dlya Rossii."

125. Quoted in "Ugroza po sosedstvu: Pered rossiiskim Dal'nem Vostokom vstaet real'naya ugroza 'polzuchei' kitaiskoi ekspansii," *Vzglyad*, 4 Aug 2005, http://www .vzglyad.ru/politics/2005/8/42962.html. On the whole, there is little discussion, polemical or otherwise, in the Russian press regarding the immigration of non-Chinese East Asians. Trenin has called for Moscow to encourage the immigration of a range of ethnicities to populate the Far East (including Koreans, Thais, and other Southeast Asians) precisely as a way to ensure that the region does not pass under Chinese hegemony.

126. For an overview of Russian participation in ASEAN structures, see Lavrov, "Vystuplenie Ministra Inostrannykh Del S. V. Lavrova na Postministerskoi Konferentsii Rossiya-ASEAN, Manila, 1 avgusta 2007 g.," http://www.mid.ru/ns-rasia.nsf/ 3a0108443c964002432569e7004199c0/432569d80021985fc325732a00310118 ?OpenDocument. Also see Natalya Melikova, "Zavoevanie Azii," *Nezavisimaya Gazeta*, 14 Dec 2004.

127. Russian Ministry of Foreign Affairs, "Obzor vneshnei politiki Rossiiskoi Federatsii," 51.

128. "Moscow Says Japan-Russia Diplomacy 'in a State of Catastrophe,'" AFP News, *JRL* #255, 13 Nov 2006. For a comprehensive history of the Kuriles dispute up to the mid-1990s, see James E. Goodby, Vladimir I. Ivanov, and Nobuo Shimotomai, eds., *"Northern Territories" and Beyond: Russian, Japanese, and American Perspectives* (Westport, CT: Praeger, 1995).

129. Jonathan Eyal, "Russia-Japan Relations Set to Improve with Visits," *Straits Times*, 26 Jan 2007.

130. In 1955, Moscow offered to return the southernmost Kuriles (the two Habomai islets and Shitokan) in exchange for an explicit statement by Tokyo that its alliance with the U.S. was not directed at any third power (i.e., the Soviet Union). Japanese vacillation, backed by pressure from Washington, scuttled the agreement. A 1956 Russo-Japanese joint declaration affirmed that the southern islands would be returned to Japanese sovereignty when a formal peace treaty between Japan and the USSR was signed. Subsequent Soviet—and Russian—offers to negotiate the status of the southern islands have often appeared to be attempts to wrong-foot the Japanese. See Gregory Clark, "Northern Territories Dispute Highlights Flawed Diplomacy," *Japan Times*, 24 Mar 2005.

131. Buszynski, "Oil and Territory," 293.

132. Robert Parsons, "Russia: Government Plans Major Investment in Disputed Kurile Islands," *RFE/RL Newsline*, 9 Aug 2006. Shingo Ito, "Islands Disputed with Japan Feel Russia's Boom," *China Post*, 14 Sep 2007.

133. For a comprehensive account of Russia's policy toward North Korea, see Alexander Vorontsov, "Current Russia-North Korea Relations: Challenges and Achievements," Brookings Institution, CNAPS Working Paper, Feb 2007.

134. Jo Johnson and Neil Buckley, "Russia and India Seek to Remodel Partnership," *Financial Times*, 25 Jan 2007.

135. "Ne otdeli Moskvu ot Deli," editorial, *Kommersant*, 25 Jan 2007.

136. For a list of achievements in the Russo-Indian relationship, see S. Lavrov, "Russia and India: Mutually Beneficial Cooperation and Strategic Partnership," *International Affairs: A Russian Journal of World Politics, Diplomacy, and International Relations*, 2007, 53(3): 24–29; A. Mantyskii and V. Khodzhaev, "New Vistas of Russia-India Cooperation," *International Affairs: A Russian Journal of World Politics, Diplomacy, and International Relations*, 2005, 51(1): 49–55.

6

Back on the Offensive?

The Former Soviet Union

Given the legacy of Soviet control and continued political, cultural, and economic linkages between Russia and its neighbors in the Commonwealth of Independent States (CIS, *Sodruzhestvo nezavisimykh gosudarstv,* or SNG), Russia's leadership has not consistently regarded its dealings with the CIS states as a branch of *foreign* policy.[1] Moscow's invasion of Georgia in the face of its pious declarations about the importance of international law and state sovereignty points to a certain disconnect in Russian thinking about the CIS. Since the collapse of the Soviet Union, the CIS has increasingly turned into a contested zone between the major powers: Russia, the United States, Europe, and, increasingly, China. The struggle for influence in the former Soviet republics has often come as a surprise to Moscow, which long regarded the entire region as its exclusive preserve but was too weak for much of the 1990s to enforce its claim to exclusivity.

Of course, much of the outside world's encroachment into this traditional sphere of Russian influence is a consequence of the larger process of globalization, for which Moscow's attachment to a worldview based on the predominance of a handful of Great Powers has left it somewhat ill prepared. Then again, the Kremlin and independent Russian observers often argue that outsiders' involvement in the CIS—whether in supervising Ukrainian and Georgian elections or seeking energy deals with countries like Kazakhstan and Turkmenistan—is predicated on precisely the same kind of geopolitical view of the world adhered to by much of the Russian elite and is designed to promote anti-Russian groups on Russia's borders.

As Russia's power and reach have grown over the past decade, Moscow has sought to reassert itself as the pivotal player inside the CIS, and to reverse the CIS states' drift from its orbit. The struggle for influence in the former Soviet Union provided a major test of Putin's generally pragmatic approach, since important constituencies in Russia (including much of the military and security services) continued to adhere to a kind of paternalistic view of Russia's relationship to its former dependencies. In some instances, Russia was able to maintain generally cooperative relations with foreign powers, as when it agreed to the stationing of U.S. forces in Central Asia following September 11, 2001. In other cases, the relationship took on more of a competitive, zero-sum dynamic, as in the multilateral struggle for control of Kazakhstan's energy resources, where Moscow, Beijing, and Washington all sought to advance their own interests at one another's expense. In a few instances, notably the political struggles in Georgia and Ukraine, the interactions among the major powers edged into downright hostility, with Russia's approach at times giving off a strong whiff of Eurasianist neo-imperialism.

The war in Georgia, which Western powers roundly condemned, appears to be something of a turning point in Russia's dealings with the CIS. After years of finding itself on the defensive as outside—principally Western—influence spread throughout the former USSR, Moscow decided on a sharp blow that would weaken or topple the West's most important outpost in the former Soviet Union and serve notice to others that they would have no choice but to reach some kind of accommodation with their former hegemon. While it remains too soon to assess the long-term consequences, it is clear that the relationship between Russia and the West in the borderlands between them will be much more competitive than in the past, and Western leaders will have to decide what risks they are willing to take to maintain their influence in the face of mounting Russian opposition.

Given the extent to which most of Russia's foreign policy attention is devoted to cultivating and balancing the Great Powers, its approach to the former Soviet Union—a region where there are no Great Powers (apart from Russia itself)—is in many ways sui generis. In general, Russia's leaders have seen the former USSR as an arena within which the complex interactions of the major powers play themselves out—as objects for diplomacy rather than subjects in their own right. For much of the post-1991 period, Russia's approach to dealing with its immediate neighbors was little more than an adjunct to its larger ambition of establishing itself as a major international player. Early in the 1990s, the non-Russian parts of the former Soviet Union (especially its Caucasian and Central Asian peripheries) were perceived as little better than dead weight, to be left behind as rapidly as possible so that Russia could rush ahead to join the developed West.[2] During the Primakov interlude, Moscow began paying more attention to the republics of the CIS.

At first, this attention took the form of imperial nostalgia. Under Putin, Russian policy in the CIS became more nuanced. Competition among the Great Powers remained an important element. The expansion of Europe to the east, along with the deployment of American troops to Central Asia and the increasingly intense struggle for energy and the infrastructure to transport it, have combined to enhance the strategic significance of the former Soviet Union for all of the major powers. Russia has been active in protecting friendly regimes and establishing its predominance in the energy sector throughout the territory of the former USSR.

At the same time, though, Russian policy has often been constrained by outside powers' renewed interest in the former Soviet states as well as Russia's own desire to have generally cooperative relations with all the Great Powers while exerting a dominant influence within the CIS. The paradox has been that the more Moscow seeks regional hegemony through military or other means, the more difficult it becomes for Moscow to be seen as a responsible pillar of the international system. For this reason, Russian policy in the region has been at times an uncomfortable mixture of bluster and accommodation of outside interests, as the CIS has often served as a sidebar to Russia's relations with the United States, Europe, and China. With its invasion of Georgia in the summer of 2008, Moscow demonstrated for the first time since the Soviet collapse that under some circumstances, it was willing to court real foreign opposition to assert what it perceived as its interests inside the CIS. Still wedded to a fairly traditional geopolitical view of international relations, the invasion was also about demonstrating Russia's continuing relevance as a major power.

The instrumental nature of Russia's approach to the former Soviet Union has resulted in variations over both time and space. The European republics (Belarus, Ukraine, and Moldova, plus the three Baltic states) have served as a buffer zone between Russia and the expanding Europe of the EU and NATO. The Caucasus and Central Asia, on the other hand, have been important to Moscow initially as a zone of instability and insecurity along Russia's vulnerable southern frontier. Since September 11, 2001, these states have taken on an added importance as the location of a complex diplomatic and economic struggle between Russia and its onetime superpower rival, which found itself pulled into Central Asia as part of the broader war on terror. Early in the U.S.-led campaign against the Taliban, U.S. troops were deployed to Uzbekistan and Kyrgyzstan, initially with Russian approval. Russian troops, meanwhile, remained in Tajikistan as a result of their role in ending that country's civil war, while Moscow deployed forces in Kyrgyzstan in 2003 in order to match the American presence and redeployed them to Georgia in 2008 in the course of an invasion largely designed to check the spread of Western influence.

Both the Caucasus and Central Asia have also been the object of outside attention as a result of their contribution to global energy security. Azerbaijan, Uzbekistan, Turkmenistan, and Kazakhstan are all major energy producers.[3] Meanwhile, the strategic location of the Caucasian republics (Azerbaijan, Armenia, and Georgia), Belarus, and Ukraine has made them all important pawns in the pipeline diplomacy of the major powers. Given the importance of energy and pipelines in Russian foreign policy more generally, the Kremlin's engagement with countries of the Caucasus and Central Asia has increasingly focused on the energy sector, with Russian companies (backed by the state) seeking to invest heavily in the production and transportation of energy reserves throughout the former Soviet Union.

In some ways, the growing focus on energy has come at the expense of other kinds of concerns. Russia's decision to cut off gas supplies to Belarus—long its closest ally among the CIS states—in January 2007 signaled the effective end of attempts to construct a so-called union state combining the two countries into a single entity.[4] The decision to embargo gas deliveries to Belarus caught most observers by surprise—both because Belarus had thitherto been reliably pro-Russian and because of the difficulties Moscow encountered a year previously when it had imposed a similar embargo on Ukraine. Yet the Belarusian imbroglio was perhaps the clearest example of Moscow choosing to prioritize narrowly national interests at the expense of a broader neo-imperial policy within the CIS. Put differently, Russian policy inside the CIS remains largely a stepping-stone in Moscow's quest to be taken seriously as a world power, even if its actions within the CIS at times lead other states to question its readiness to play a responsible international role.

The instrumental nature of Russia's approach to the post-Soviet world has given Russia a degree of flexibility in the region, which it has used to manage relations with the other major powers that have established a presence there. No doubt, the relationship between Moscow, Beijing, and Washington (and Brussels) remains competitive throughout much of the former Soviet Union: Ukraine is still torn between East and West, Georgia was in a state of perpetual chaos even before Russian troops marched in, while much of Central Asia remains a vast playing field for the ambitions of the Great Powers. Yet with some exceptions (especially Georgia), Russian policy in the region has been fairly sophisticated, with Russia using its residual influence in neighboring states as a way to leverage its return to major power status through control of energy transport routes, forward military deployments, economic linkages, and other forms of soft power.[5] As the invasion of Georgia showed, however, Russia retains hard power options in the CIS that it lacks elsewhere.

While Russia's residual influence remains strong in many, though not all, of the former Soviet states, a persistent pattern of bartering such interests for the sake of promoting Russia's global influence has been evident. Russia retains many levers for exerting control in what many Russians still term the Near Abroad, including the presence of Russian troops in some neighboring countries (Moldova, Kyrgyzstan, Tajikistan, Georgia, and Armenia), encouragement of regional separatists in the context of the so-called frozen conflicts, and control of oil and gas supplies in many CIS states.[6] In general, Moscow remains interested in preserving its influence in the former Soviet Union, ensuring access to the seas (especially the Baltic and Black) and transit rights for Russian gas and oil, and to a lesser degree protecting the rights of Russian speakers who found themselves living outside their homeland following the collapse of the USSR.[7] A combination of these factors has driven Russia's attempts to sustain the regimes of Aleksandr Lukashenko in Belarus (so far successful) and Askar Akaev in Kyrgyzstan (eventually failed), as well as Moscow's continuing intervention in the frozen conflicts in Transdniestria, South Ossetia, Abkhazia, and Nagorno-Karabakh.

Russia's usual willingness to seek accommodation with outside powers like the U.S. and China inside the boundaries of the CIS is both testament to Moscow's emphasis on Great Power relations as the driving force in international affairs and a recognition that Russia's national interests cannot be defined simplistically in terms of an imperial grab for territory. In strengthening the Russian Federation as an international actor and protecting its security interests, Moscow has largely accepted the fact that all politics is not zero sum.

Moscow's offer to let the United States use the Russian radar station at Gabala in Azerbaijan as part of the planned U.S. missile defense program (despite the increasingly frosty tone of exchanges between Washington and Moscow in 2006–2007) is one recent example of this approach to foreign policy inside the CIS. Given Moscow's general inclination to prioritize relations with the major powers (above all the U.S.), the decision to invite a U.S. presence in an area as strategically sensitive as the South Caucasus fits in with a pattern of seeing Russia's presence in the CIS as a resource to be exploited in the service of the country's broader foreign policy goals. The Georgian conflict fits this pattern as well: having failed to make outside powers take its interests seriously through other means, Moscow took advantage of its regional military preponderance to force the issue, all the while proclaiming its desire not to precipitate a break with the West—as long as the West proved willing to accept the fait accompli of its defeat in this conflict.

The United States' increasingly assertive role inside the Commonwealth of Independent States (including the deployment of U.S. military forces in Central Asia) represents a fundamental challenge to Russian amour propre and self-image as a Great Power. Consequently, the generally cooperative relationship that prevailed between Moscow and Washington within the

CIS at least until August 2008 was quite significant. Although rhetorical clashes occurred, the overall pattern was long similar to the conflict over NATO enlargement—Russia exerted firm opposition to the deployment of U.S. troops in Kyrgyzstan and Uzbekistan, to Western "meddling" in Ukrainian presidential elections, and to criticism of Russia's actions in Chechnya, but repeatedly backed down from the brink. The successful campaign to expel the U.S. from the Karshi-Khanabad base in Uzbekistan was an exception that proved the rule; only when relations between Washington and Tashkent were at their nadir (because of the Uzbek government's massacre of demonstrators in the city of Andijon in May 2005) and only after Tashkent and Beijing had seized the initiative did Moscow step up its pressure on Washington to withdraw its forces. In Georgia, Moscow appears to have made a calculated gamble that the damage to its relationship with the West can be contained; for the most part, it seems to have gambled correctly. On the whole, in this most sensitive of regions, Russian foreign policy has again demonstrated Moscow's geopolitical vision of the world and the concomitant recognition that managing relations with the Great Powers to promote Russia's re-emergence remains the centerpiece of Russian foreign policy.

THE EUROPEAN CIS:
SHADOWBOXING OVER UKRAINE

Russia's cautiously opportunistic approach to restoring its influence in the CIS has been on display throughout the former Soviet Union. In the European CIS states—Belarus, Ukraine, and Moldova—Russian policy has often seemed inconsistent. On the one hand, an interest in maintaining cooperative relations with the Western powers (including the EU, which now shares a border with the European members of the CIS) has meant that Moscow's more aggressively imperial impulses have been fairly restrained. On the other hand, though, the very proximity of the West has raised the stakes in the contest to influence Minsk, Kyiv, and Chisinău.

Russian influence in all three European CIS member states remained strong after the fall of the Soviet Union. In Moldova, Russian sponsorship of the Transdniestrian separatist regime and the presence of Russian peacekeepers have served throughout the post-Soviet period to check Chisinău's foreign policy autonomy. Belarus's dictatorial ruler Aleksandr Lukashenko has been forced to rely on Russia for diplomatic and economic support as a result of the West's hostility to his regime, even after the January 2007 spat over gas prices.

Ukraine is a more complicated case. Since the so-called Orange Revolution of 2004, Ukraine's complex identity as a state on the border (the word *Ukraina* means "borderland") between Russia and Europe exacerbated the split between Moscow and the West. Russia and the U.S./Europe backed different sides in the Orange Revolution, largely on the basis of the foreign policy visions articulated by the competing camps. The Orange Revolution highlighted a deep divide within Ukrainian society and also between Russia and its putative partners in the West. The new era in relations heralded by Putin's decision to back the U.S. in Afghanistan appeared to end in the flurry of charges and countercharges hurled by Moscow and Washington during the Ukrainian standoff.

On one level, the struggle for Ukraine highlighted just how much circumstances had changed since the end of the Cold War. The very idea that Ukraine could turn its back on Russia, seeking integration with the European Union—and more importantly, NATO—reflected the degree to which Russian power had collapsed since 1991. By 2004, that collapse was ending, and Russia's active participation in the struggle over Ukraine's future was a sign of things to come. Moscow's intent never appeared to be the reabsorption of Ukraine or the undermining of Ukrainian statehood—which it certainly had the capability to attempt, given Ukraine's limited historical existence as a state and the presence of a significant number of Russian speakers in the country (most importantly in the Crimean Peninsula).[8] Russian policy has surely borne a strong whiff of realpolitik, seeking to influence Kyiv's choices in ways congenial to Russian interests through economic pressure, bluff, and interference in Ukraine's domestic politics.

Before the Orange Revolution, Ukraine was for the most part content to balance between East and West. Participation in NATO's Partnership for Peace and the GU(U)AM (i.e., Georgia, Ukraine, Azerbaijan, and Moldova, joined for a time by Uzbekistan) organization of ex-Soviet republics seeking distance from Moscow were balanced against membership in the CIS and a friendship and cooperation treaty with Russia ratified by the Verkhovna Rada (the Ukrainian parliament) in 1998.[9] For the westward vector of Ukraine's foreign policy, GU(U)AM was particularly important in that it united members of the CIS who were both seeking energy independence from Russia and had (apart from Ukraine itself) endured Russian military intervention. The formation of GU(U)AM was thus intimately linked to the construction of the Baku-Tbilisi-Ceyhan oil pipeline, the construction of which would allow Ukraine to import oil by ship across the Black Sea from Ceyhan without relying on Russia. In this way, Ukraine would significantly reduce its dependence on Russian energy supplies and come into closer political alignment with Azerbaijan, Georgia, and Moldova, all of whom have sought to limit the reassertion of Russian influence in the CIS.[10] Participation in GU(U)AM, however, could easily be interpreted in Moscow as an unfriendly act, and former Ukrainian president Leonid Kuchma's government was unwilling to alienate Moscow entirely, especially as support for Kuchma within Ukraine dwindled as his government became bogged down in a series of scandals.

Still, Kyiv's stated interest in integration with the West continued for most of Kuchma's term in office (1994–2004).[11] By the eve of the Orange Revolution, however, corruption, the Kuchma government's involvement in arms smuggling to Saddam Hussein's Iraq, and its possible complicity in the murder of an investigative journalist had made it increasingly toxic to the West, deepening Ukraine's reliance on Russia.[12] The semi-rapprochement between Kyiv and Moscow in Putin's first term was reflected in increasingly frequent attempts to coordinate the two countries' integration into and participation in European structures such as the OSCE and the Council of Europe.[13] This approach, termed in Ukraine as "returning to Europe with Russia," was elaborated with the help of the Moscow-based Fund for Effective Politics (*Fond Effektivnoi Politiki*), headed by notorious Kremlin spin doctor Gleb Pavlovsky.[14]

Beset by scandal and increasingly unpopular, Kuchma sought to engineer with Russian help a transition to a reliable successor in 2004. The controlled transition got out of hand when manipulation by Kuchma and his allies in Moscow became too blatant to ignore. The fall of Kuchma and the contested succession that brought to power the pro-Western Viktor Yushchenko revealed deep underlying tensions among the Ukrainian political elites and opened Ukraine to the competing geopolitical ambitions of both Russia and the Western powers. For Moscow, the specter of a Yushchenko presidency was to be avoided at all cost. Russia's leaders had an opportunity to familiarize themselves with Yushchenko during his term as prime minister from 1999 to 2001. During this time, Yushchenko concentrated on reforming the Ukrainian economy, weakening the hold of oligarchs with close connections to Russia.[15] In addition, Yushchenko—whose wife held American citizenship—spoke of possible Ukrainian membership in NATO and was supported by various groups of Ukrainian nationalists whose activities have historically been perceived in Moscow as anti-Russian.

A series of underhanded maneuvers was undertaken to prevent Yushchenko from winning the 2004 Ukrainian presidential elections. These included at least two attempts to assassinate Yushchenko—including one that left him disfigured from severe dioxin poisoning, the employment of agents provocateurs who attempted to tar the Yushchenko campaign by associating it with neo-Nazi organizations (a maneuver not as bizarre as it might seem, given the existence of a vocal neo-Nazi fringe within the Ukrainian nationalist movement), and massive violations of campaign finance regulations. While much about the lead-up to the 2004 election remains murky, it is certain that Moscow was at least cognizant of many of the dirty tricks being employed, some at the behest of Pavlovsky and other Russian political technologists with good Kremlin connections.[16]

Apart from such attempts to sabotage the Yushchenko campaign before the election, the Russian government pushed hard in the November 21, 2004, runoff vote for its favored candidate, the former transportation manager (whose past also included jail time for robbery and assault) Viktor Yanukovych, to assume office despite widespread allegations of fraud in the conduct of the election.[17] Exit polls showed Yushchenko ahead by a comfortable margin (52 percent versus 43 percent for Yanukovych), but the official results gave Yanukovych a narrow victory, thanks to suspiciously high voter turnout levels in the Russian-speaking eastern part of Ukraine.

Moscow and Putin himself had been open in their support for Yanukovych during the campaign (making joint public appearances with the Ukrainian premier throughout the campaign), while the Kremlin openly helped Russian businesses channel money to the Yanukovych campaign.[18] The Kremlin, along with the Kuchma government, which was hoping for an orderly transition of power and protection against potential prosecution after leaving office, was also complicit in the activities of figures like Pavlovsky, who were responsible for devising and implementing various techniques to ensure a Yanukovych victory. Once the votes were in, moreover, the Kremlin urged international acceptance of Yanukovych's supposed victory, ignoring outside observers' conclusion that the results had been falsified.

Putin immediately declared the vote fair and strongly criticized both the Ukrainian opposition (led by Yushchenko) for its failure to accept the "results" of the election and, apparently unaware of the irony, outside powers for their willingness to intervene in Ukraine's internal affairs.[19] U.S. Secretary of State Colin Powell meanwhile declared unambiguously that because of widespread fraud and manipulation "we cannot accept this result as legitimate."[20] Many Ukrainians also rejected the results, and major protests soon broke out in Kyiv and cities in western Ukraine with heavy concentrations of Yushchenko voters. Even as the protests by orange-clad Yushchenko backers mounted, Russian leaders refused to back down from their support of Yanukovych until the Ukrainian Supreme Court stepped in and ordered the runoff between Yushchenko and Yanukovych to be held again. The whole process resulted in Yushchenko's eventual victory—and a Russian realization that continued resistance was jeopardizing both its influence in Kyiv and its relationship with the West.[21] Yushchenko was sworn in as Ukraine's new president on January 23, 2005.

The Kremlin had clearly botched its handling of the crisis that followed the Ukrainian presidential election and contributed directly to the outbreak of the Orange Revolution shortly thereafter. Moscow's overt support for Yanukovych during the campaign offended many Ukrainians, who saw it as a display of Russian paternalism (or worse). Repeated attempts to gain recognition for Yanukovych as president also damaged Russia's standing with the Western powers, which saw Russian intervention in Ukraine's politics as a form of renewed Russian imperialism. Russian leaders largely perceived the events in Ukraine through the lens of geopolitics, and hence interpreted the West's condemnation of the election as part of a broader campaign to undermine Russian influence across the former Soviet Union and contain Russia—a charge Moscow has leveled at a range of Western democracy promotion activities in the former Soviet Union and elsewhere.

Western officials, of course, denied trying to pull Ukraine out of Russia's sphere of influence. Instead, they generally portrayed their rejection of Yanukovych's victory as a consequence of insisting that democratic procedures be respected.[22] The United States did have something of a stake in the Ukrainian elections, since a wide range of official and semiofficial organizations (from USAID to the National Democratic Institute and International Republican Institute to George Soros's Open Society Foundation) provided money and expertise to the democratic opposition. Although this aid was designed to ensure a fair electoral process and was not given directly to any Ukrainian party or candidate, supporters of the Kuchma-Yanukovych regime objected, not without some justification, that U.S. policies favored Yushchenko in practice.[23]

Because Yanukovych's campaign emphasized deepening ties between Ukraine and Russia while Yushchenko's focused on integration with the West, the geopolitical implications of the election could not be ignored. The events surrounding the Orange Revolution fed worries of a new Cold War between Russia and the West (worries that have been renewed with each succeeding crisis on Russia's periphery). Yet precisely because of the potential geopolitical consequences, Moscow's subsequent handling of relations with Ukraine was somewhat more nuanced, shaped around its broader relationship with the United States and Europe. Its handling of Russo-Ukrainian relations since Yushchenko's eventual election has provided one fairly significant example of how Moscow was willing to endure what Trenin termed a "painful and humiliating" diplomatic defeat in order to avoid a full-blown diplomatic showdown with the United States, even in a country like Ukraine that it considers vital to its national interests, at least as long as it felt that the consolidation of power at home was not complete.[24]

The confrontation between Russia and the United States did not advance beyond the level of hostile rhetoric (U.S.-Russian cooperation in Afghanistan, for instance, continued largely unimpeded by the standoff in Ukraine).[25] Given Russia's still considerable leverage over Ukraine and the very real danger that a hostile Ukraine would pose to Russian interests, the most surprising aspect of Russia's response to the Orange Revolution was its restraint, a restraint that appears to be fraying in the aftermath of the Georgia conflict, with reports of Russian attempts to stir up nationalist passions in the Crimea. Furthermore, as the depth of the crisis in Ukraine as well as the U.S. and European commitment to upholding the rule of law became clear in Moscow, Putin took the lead in seeking a graceful exit based on Russian ambassador to Ukraine Viktor Chernomyrdin's recognition that "anybody who becomes Ukrainian president will be compelled to develop good-neighborly relations with Russia," and that future elections would provide new opportunities to influence Ukrainian politics.[26] Yushchenko's own attempts to mollify Russian concerns played an important role in the gradual Russian climb-down. The new president went out of his way to reassure Moscow of his good intentions, including holding a face-to-face meeting with Putin shortly after his inauguration.

While Ukraine's political scene has remained sharply divided since the Orange Revolution, with deep splits in particular between the largely industrial, Russian-speaking east (as well as the Crimea) and the more agrarian, Ukrainian-speaking west, for the most part Russia and the Western powers who opposed it in late 2004 achieved a kind of modus vivendi. In part, this reconciliation was driven by the mutual recognition that the tug-of-war over Ukraine that broke out in 2004–2005 was politically damaging and destabilizing. Russia's reported decision to issue passports to Russian-speaking inhabitants of the Crimea in late 2008 was a reminder that, if pressed, Moscow retains the ability to sow chaos in Ukraine.

Even Pavlovsky, the architect of the Kremlin plan to impose a managed transition from Kuchma to Yanukovych, recognized that Russian policy had gone too far and risked too much. In a frank review of Russian policy toward Ukraine and his own role in the disputed election, Pavlovsky suggested that in the future, Moscow would seek to exert influence on countries in the post-Soviet space, regardless of the composition of their governments and whether they were ultimately to join either the EU or NATO.[27] In this way, he argued, Russia would be able to move beyond the zero-sum mentality that characterized the Kremlin's role in the 2004 Ukrainian election and not risk a complete diplomatic defeat should pro-Western parties come to power elsewhere in the CIS. One high-ranking Kremlin official described the goal of Russia's post–Orange Revolution approach to the CIS as "imparting a civilized character to Moscow's relations with Washington and European structures on the territory of the former USSR."[28]

Putin's September 2005 visit to Western Europe, which focused primarily on energy, also laid the groundwork for a kind of détente over Ukraine, in part by focusing Western attention on the potentially destabilizing effects of continued polarization.[29] While political instability remains a fact of life in Ukraine, with the Yushchenko and Yanukovych (not to mention wildcards like the charismatic Yulia Tymoshenko) camps doing battle over the constitution, the powers of the Rada, the timing of new elections, and foreign policy, the proxy battle between Russia and the West over Ukraine largely abated, at least until 2008.[30] Then, Yushchenko's outspoken opposition to the invasion of Georgia and threats to ban ships from the Russian Black Sea Fleet from returning to their base at Sevastopol rekindled fears about Russian designs against Ukraine's integrity.

Even earlier, this détente in Ukraine was repeatedly tested, above all on the question of energy. Gazprom's decision to raise the price of gas supplied to Ukraine, first broached in March 2005, ended up badly shaking Russia's relations with Europe (and by extension the United States). Apart from Western interest in Ukraine for its own sake, the broader consequences of the gas dispute resulted from the fact that Western Europe itself is heavily dependent on Russian gas supplies, 80 percent of which reach Europe after transiting Ukrainian territory. Ukraine and Russia have quarreled since the breakup of the Soviet Union over the status and use of the pipelines that cross Ukrainian territory en route to Europe. Even during the Kuchma years, Kyiv sought to take advantage of Russia's dependence on Ukraine as a supply corridor to demand high tariffs for the use of pipelines on its territory. It also (along with Belarus) fiercely resisted Russian attempts to secure an ownership stake in its pipeline infrastructure as a means of paying off the country's debts to Russia. In 2000, Gazprom sought to undercut Ukraine's transport monopoly by mooting the prospect of a new pipeline (which eventually became Nord Stream) bypassing Ukrainian as well as Polish territory. Kuchma as well as his then-prime minister—Viktor Yushchenko—strongly opposed Gazprom's attempt to skirt Ukraine.[31]

Throughout Putin's presidency, the question of Ukraine's payments for Russian gas festered as a major impediment to improved Russo-Ukrainian relations. The dispute became a crisis when Gazprom cut off deliveries on January 1, 2006, over the still unresolved price dispute and Kyiv's unpaid bills. Gazprom had begun by demanding an increase in the price paid by Kyiv for gas deliveries from $50 per thousand cubic meters to $160, starting in January 2006 (even though the existing contract setting prices at $50 was set to run through 2009). Although Gazprom's initial demand for increased payments was made in the summer of 2005, Kyiv did not respond until Gazprom threatened in mid-December to cut off supplies at the start of the new year unless the Ukrainian government and its state-owned energy company Naftohaz Ukrayiny accepted the increased price. Ukraine refused to pay the higher rate and charged Russia with violating existing agreements on gas sales, whereupon Gazprom executives told Kyiv it now would have to pay $230 per thousand cubic meters instead of the originally proposed $160.[32] When the government of Prime Minister Yury Yekhanurov refused to sign an agreement on Gazprom's terms, the Russian gas monopoly stopped deliveries on January 1.[33]

Kyiv responded to the resulting shortages by announcing it would siphon off Europe-bound gas from pipelines crossing its territory. While the Ukrainian authorities represented their actions as a response to blatant imperialism on the part of Russia, Moscow claimed the entire affair was a simple commercial dispute, with Gazprom deputy chief executive Aleksandr Ryazanov arguing, "This isn't politics. Gazprom isn't under pressure from the government. This is simple economics."[34] The Yekhanurov government portrayed the siphoning of gas destined for Europe as a desperate measure by the Ukrainian state to preserve its independence. The Russian Foreign Ministry, in a press release on the first day of the crisis, termed Ukraine's actions "an attempt to blackmail the countries of Europe with the threat of the illegal confiscation" of gas for which the Europeans had already paid, as well as a desperate maneuver to enhance the ruling coalition's popularity in the run-up to parliamentary elections that the "orange" parties were predicted to lose.[35] After much acrimonious rhetoric on both sides, the dispute was (temporarily, at least) settled on January 4, when Gazprom and Naftohaz Ukrayiny signed an agreement setting the price for Ukraine's gas purchases at $95 per thousand cubic meters—payable in cash only rather than the mix of cash and barter theretofore prevailing.[36]

For many observers in the West, the whole dispute appeared a blatant attempt by the Kremlin, operating through state-controlled Gazprom, to punish Ukraine for the Orange Revolution and for its leaders' interest in seeking integration with Western institutions. The Ukrainian authorities sought consciously to encourage this perception. Yekhanurov told Western ambassadors that Russia was not only in violation of a commercial agreement but was actively threatening Ukrainian sovereignty. The significance of this line of reasoning lay in the fact that Britain and the United States had signed a commitment to defend Ukraine's political and economic sovereignty in 1994 in exchange for Kyiv's willingness to surrender the nuclear weapons that had been left on its territory by the Soviet military.[37]

The Western powers all called for a quick end to the crisis (particularly those European states whose own economies remained dependent on Russian gas). Still, the bulk of Western opinion, both public and official, seemed to assign blame for the crisis and the resulting gas shortages in Europe to Russia's neo-imperialist policies in the CIS rather than to either a legitimate commercial dispute or manipulation by the Ukrainian authorities.[38] While the gas dispute between Kyiv and Moscow did have a strong geopolitical undertone, the implications of the crisis were more complex than much of the alarmist commentary at the time acknowledged.

On one level, much of the problem was simply economic. Ukraine continues to heavily subsidize domestic gas sales (as does Russia itself), such that households pay only $27 per thousand cubic meters, while businesses pay between $60 and $80 for the same amount—well below even the price paid by Kyiv before the renegotiation in January 2006. These subsidized prices have been a disincentive to conservation, with the result that, like its neighbors in the former Soviet Union, Ukraine's gas consumption is profligate. Moreover, because Ukraine itself produces little gas, much of the cost of Ukrainian inefficiency has been borne by Gazprom, which, as a state-run company, is not subject to the full measure of market discipline affecting private companies.[39] And since Gazprom is for all intents and purposes an arm of the Kremlin (or, more cynically, vice versa), Moscow believed it had good reasons for subsidizing gas exports to Ukraine as long as it could gain noneconomic benefits from doing so.

Yushchenko's emphasis on seeking integration with the West, which of necessity implied reducing Russian influence in Ukraine, gave Moscow less reason to continue with these subsidies. In other words, Russia's decision to reduce its subsidies by demanding a higher price was more than anything a recognition that its attempts to keep Ukraine in its sphere of influence through economic incentives had failed. If Moscow was not gaining foreign policy benefits from its (expensive) subsidization of the Ukrainian economy, there remained little reason for Gazprom to keep throwing money at Ukraine. Incidentally, the Russian demand for higher prices reflected in a general way many of the demands that European governments had long been making: to reduce the role of barter in economic exchange among the post-Soviet states, to increase Gazprom's overall transparency, and, most importantly, to internalize the notion that the former Soviet republics had become fully sovereign states. Indeed, Moscow justified its demand that Kyiv pay more for its gas by pointing out the (much higher) price paid for Russian gas by consumers in Europe and suggesting that if Ukraine wanted to be a European state, it should pay its bills like one.[40] That said, Moscow was more than happy to have an excuse to cause mischief for Ukraine's pro-Western leadership.

Nor has the January 2006 agreement, which was heavily criticized in the Western press, succeeded in curbing Ukraine's drift out of Moscow's orbit. Moscow's strategy during the gas crisis appeared to aim much more at cutting its losses—financial as well as diplomatic—rather than seeking to capture Ukraine as a satellite. Ambassador Chernomyrdin (a former prime minister and Gazprom chief executive) affirmed that "Russia has a general approach for all states—we are moving to market [based] relations with absolutely every state," regardless of domestic political conditions.[41] Gazprom has in fact demanded—and received—higher payments from all of its downstream customers in the CIS over the past few years, though the steepness of the increase and the timing of its introduction have varied.

Moscow and Kyiv conducted another round of negotiations on gas prices in October 2006, more than two months after Yanukovych had become prime minister and after it had become clear that Ukraine's prospects for joining the EU or NATO in the immediate future were minuscule.[42] Yanukovych's return did not prevent Gazprom from demanding another price increase for 2007. The Russian media reported that Moscow was offering Kyiv gas for $130 per thousand cubic meters (in line with the prices outlined in the Yanukovych government's budget, rather than the $230 Gazprom had been demanding) in exchange for Ukraine holding a referendum on NATO membership and affirming its agreement to allow the Black Sea Fleet to keep its base at Sevastopol until 2017.[43] While the deal that was finally signed confirmed that Ukraine would pay only $130 per thousand cubic meters, the only conditionality discussed in the aftermath touched on coordinating Moscow and Kyiv's entry into the World Trade Organization.[44] By the middle of 2008, there had been no referendum on NATO; meanwhile, the Black Sea Fleet remains very much the subject of intensive maneuvering between Moscow and Kyiv (which announced in March 2007 its intention to take control of the fleet's ground-based navigation equipment in Sevastopol despite strong Russian protests, and which later threatened to cancel the lease altogether over the fleet's role in the Georgian war).[45] Whatever the other consequences of its gas dispute with Moscow, Ukraine remains fiercely defensive of its independence, while Russia's overriding interest in selling gas to Europe means the Kremlin cannot lightly repeat its decision to shut off the spigots to Ukraine, at least until the South Stream pipeline entirely bypassing Ukraine becomes a reality.

In January 2007, a year after the Ukrainian gas crisis and after Moscow and Kyiv had agreed on a new price structure for gas deliveries in 2007, Gazprom likewise sought higher prices from Belarus, which had long been Russia's closest ally among the states of the CIS. In the final analysis, the gas conflict with Ukraine seemingly had less to do with Russian revanchism than with a realization that the policy of subsidizing friendly regimes had outlived its usefulness in an age of record-high energy prices. In the words of Dmitri Simes, "Russia grudgingly accepts the Atlanticist choices of its neighbors but refuses to subsidize them."[46] Whether the war in Georgia heralds a new paradigm remains to be seen.

THE CAUCASUS: GEORGIA'S CHALLENGE

The Caucasus remains the most troubled of Russia's peripheries. Both the North Caucasus (republics of the Russian Federation including Chechnya, Dagestan, Ingushetia, North Ossetia-Alania, Adygea, Karachevo-Cherkessia, and Kabardino-Balkaria) and the South Caucasus (the independent states of Armenia, Azerbaijan, and Georgia plus the disputed provinces of South

Ossetia and Abkhazia that Russia seized from Georgia in the August 2008 war) are beset by a plethora of tribal, religious, and ethnic conflicts. Because of the close linkages between peoples on both sides of the Russian border, instability in the independent South Caucasian states has a direct impact on the security of the Russian Federation, and vice versa. For Moscow, the region has had a dual importance: on the one hand, as a source of instability, connected above all to the simmering conflict in Chechnya, and on the other, as a result of the competing geopolitical ambitions of the South Caucasus states.

Azerbaijan, and even more Georgia, have sought since the end of the Soviet Union to promote their independence from Russian hegemony. Their strategic location and—in the Azeri case—possession of significant oil and gas resources prompted outside powers to take an interest in the region, too. Russia has meanwhile sought, with mixed success, to keep the Caucasian states within its own sphere of influence, its invasion of Georgia a signal to Tbilisi and others that there is a large price for ignoring Moscow's interests.

Georgia was long a flashpoint, especially since the rise of President Mikheil Saakashvili, a U.S.-educated lawyer who came to power as result of the so-called Rose Revolution of 2003, the first colored revolution directed against a post-Soviet autocrat (in this case, the former Soviet foreign minister Eduard Shevardnadze, who had ruled Georgia for a decade). While Shevardnadze's Georgia had little affinity for Russia and was at times less than helpful in Moscow's campaign to restore its control over Chechnya, Russo-Georgian relations worsened dramatically under Saakashvili as Tbilisi pursued fast-track integration into Western structures, especially NATO.

The deterioration of relations since the Rose Revolution is evidence of the fundamentally geopolitical nature of Russian foreign policy around its borders. For Moscow, the problem with Saakashvili was in part that he came to power without Kremlin support, in part that he attempted to end the frozen conflicts on Georgia's territory that Moscow has done much to inflame, but mostly that he and his supporters saw Georgia as an aspiring outpost of the West. This worldview underpinned Georgia's open interest in NATO membership (it is the only CIS country to unambiguously court NATO), its decision to send troops to the U.S.-led Operation Iraqi Freedom, and the extensive financial and military assistance received from Western sources. The prospect of Georgian NATO membership in particular fed into Russian fears of encirclement by a hostile military alliance and provided the strategic rationale for Moscow's seizure of the breakaway provinces and attempts to oust Saakashvili.

Shevardnadze had also pursued a largely pro-Western foreign policy, which, along with his role in dismantling the Soviet Union (as Gorbachev's foreign minister) and ambivalent attitude toward the Chechen conflict, made him much disliked in Moscow.[47] Under Shevardnadze's leadership, the Georgian parliament in 2001 passed a resolution calling for CIS peacekeepers to depart Abkhazia and South Ossetia and calling on the UN to formally address the legality of their presence.[48] Still, Shevardnadze was a recognizable type of post-Soviet leader, and one whose cronies had strong financial and political links to Moscow. Consequently, while Moscow did little to help Shevardnadze restore Georgia's territorial integrity, it never approached him with the same degree of enmity it has shown toward Saakashvili.

For Russia, the Georgian rush into the Western embrace was seen as both an embarrassment and a threat. Like the subsequent Orange Revolution in Ukraine, the toppling of Shevardnadze fed Russian fears of the West's encroachment and the potential for a similar colored revolution to break out in Russia itself—despite the Kremlin's near-total control of the political process inside Russia.[49] Shevardnadze himself blamed U.S. financier and political activist George Soros for underwriting the Rose Revolution.[50] More importantly, the Rose Revolution also was portrayed in Moscow as an example of how the West's democracy-promotion efforts have in fact resulted in the capture of former Soviet republics in what Russian strategists see as the Eurasian geopolitical chess game among the Great Powers. Moscow saw Western support for routing the Baku-Tbilisi-Ceyhan pipeline through Georgia and receptiveness to the idea of Georgia joining NATO as inducements for Tbilisi to turn its back on Moscow.[51]

Moscow's undisguised rage at Saakashvili seems principally the result of the Georgian president's active attempts to undermine Russian influence through bringing Georgia into NATO, encouraging colored revolutions elsewhere in the CIS, and squeezing the pro-Russian enclaves of South Ossetia and Abkhazia.[52] While the Rose Revolution represented the first time public discontent had upset the orderly transfer of power from one oligarchic collective to another in the CIS, similar bouts of unrest soon broke out in Ukraine (the Orange Revolution), Kyrgyzstan (Tulip Revolution), and Uzbekistan (the bloody and abortive uprising in Andijon). Saakashvili thus seemed to represent the crest of a wave threatening the cozy and profitable status quo that benefited many powerful people in Moscow.

With the situation in Chechnya approaching a crisis point in early 2004, Saakashvili also had a potentially dangerous weapon in his hands in the Chechen rebels who moved back and forth across the Georgian frontier. In February 2004, Sergei Ivanov accused Tbilisi of providing sanctuary to the rebels, even issuing them passports. He then suggested Russia might withdraw from its commitments under the CFE Treaty and halt the withdrawal of Russian forces from Georgia if Tbilisi did not adopt a more cooperative approach to the conflict in Chechnya.[53]

Saakashvili himself appeared to be encouraging further unrest. In August

2005, he signed an agreement with Ukraine's "orange" prime minister, Yulia Tymoshenko, establishing the so-called Community of Democratic Choice (CDC) as a possible democratic, pro-Western alternative to the CIS. According to Saakashvili, "The CDC will support other democratic aspirants in the region by encouraging countries at various stages of integration with Euro-Atlantic institutions to advise and support states outside the Euro-Atlantic sphere."[54] This expansive vision of its mission, along with the CDC's stated interest in bringing civil society into the foreign policy process, has made it look in Moscow like a kind of democratic Holy Alliance aiming to spread colored revolutions throughout the post-Soviet space.

Moscow sought by a variety of means to counter the spread of colored revolutionary ideas and to keep Georgia in check. If the West's influence in Georgia was connected to the building of pipelines (principally BTC and the roughly parallel Baku-Tbilisi-Erzurum gas pipeline, designed in part to maintain Tbilisi's energy independence from Moscow) and the support of Saakashvili's backers, Russia's influence flowed largely from the frozen conflicts. The Kremlin posed as protector of South Ossetia and Abkhazia, two regions with independence-minded populations that sought to break away from Georgia in the first chaotic years after 1991 (as well as Ajaria, which sought to transform itself into an autonomous part of the Georgian state). Both the Ossetians and the Abkhaz have large numbers of coethnics living on the Russian side of the Russo-Georgian frontier, mainly in the regions of North Ossetia-Alania and Adygea, respectively. Destabilization and irredentism on the Georgian side of the border thus have potentially serious implications for Russian security in the North Caucasus, a fact supporters of Russia's intervention in the frozen conflicts often tout.[55]

At the same time, the Kremlin used the existence of the frozen conflicts (in Georgia as well as in Moldova and Azerbaijan) to keep a leash on post-Soviet states' ambitions of joining the EU or NATO, which are pledged to not admit member states with unresolved territorial disputes.[56] The existence of the breakaway provinces and the Kremlin's willingness to prop them up even while attempting to play the role of peacekeeper and mediator has poisoned Georgian attitudes toward Russia. Both Saakashvili and his political opponents were equally hostile to the continued Russian presence in the breakaway regions and to Moscow's interference in what they consider Georgia's internal affairs—a fact that greatly complicates Russian attempts to meddle in Georgian politics directly.

Both South Ossetia and Abkhazia experienced wars in the early 1990s as they sought to establish their independence from Georgia. The conflicts resulted in hundreds of thousands of refugees (largely ethnic Georgians, few of whom had returned home more than a decade later) and the fragmenting of the Georgian state.[57] The problems connected with such massive numbers of refugees, most of whom have been living away from their homes for a decade and a half, have bedeviled any attempt to impose a solution on the South Ossetian and Abkhaz conflicts, even though reaching a settlement on the refugee issue is absolutely critical if the breakaway provinces are to ever receive international recognition.

Yeltsin's Kremlin eventually sent peacekeepers to South Ossetia and Abkhazia in order to keep the warring sides apart and, in Tbilisi's view, to curb Georgian independence.[58] Under the protection of Russian soldiers, South Ossetia and Abkhazia increasingly integrated their political and economic lives with Russia. During the Putin years, residents of the breakaway regions received Russian passports, effectively turning them into citizens of the Russian Federation and de facto internationalizing their quarrel with Tbilisi. It was on the basis of protecting these Russian "citizens" that the Kremlin justified its invasion of Georgia and seizure of the breakaway provinces.

More than on almost any other issue, the frozen conflicts highlighted the contradictions inherent in Russia's foreign policy strategy. The Kremlin has struggled to square its backing for Abkhaz and South Ossetian separatists with its own broader geopolitical concerns and its rhetorical commitment to the principles of state sovereignty and international law. Russia's pious concern for the fate of civilian populations in the breakaway regions of Georgia has a hollow ring when compared with the devastation inflicted on Chechen civilians. Russia, of course, managed to conduct a referendum in Chechnya following the installation of a loyalist regime, and Putin at times proposed a similar solution to the frozen conflicts in Georgia. Yet Kremlin calls for referenda to decide the fate of South Ossetia and Abkhazia (as well as Transdniestria in Moldova) were quickly silenced when anyone suggested applying the same principle to Kosovo.[59]

As long as South Ossetia and Abkhazia were discontented bits of Georgia, they were useful tools for Russian diplomacy (as a means of keeping the pressure on Tbilisi and discouraging Western initiatives to promote the independence of Kosovo), though as constituent members of the Russian Federation they would be sources of instability to Russia itself. They also gave Moscow an excuse to keep its soldiers, in the guise of peacekeepers, stationed in Georgian territory while complying with the letter of an agreement reached between Putin and Saakashvili to withdraw Russian forces from Georgia. Russia thus hoped to keep the conflicts frozen in order to maintain its leverage and to sharply limit the possibility that Georgia will be accepted as a member of either the EU or (more crucially) NATO for the foreseeable future. The West's decision to move ahead with Kosovar independence and Saakashvili's misguided attempt to seize South Ossetia by force reduced Russia's incentives to keep the conflicts frozen.[60] In essence, the threat of Russian intervention in Georgia was insufficient to deter either Tbilisi or the West, and so Moscow decided it had to make good on its threats.

While Shevardnadze remained president of Georgia, Russia's patronage of Abkhazia and South Ossetia was largely perceived in Moscow as an inducement for Tbilisi to behave better. Russia saw Shevardnadze's government as not doing all it could to clamp down on Chechen fighters seeking refuge in Georgian territory (especially the poorly controlled Kodori Gorge) and was annoyed at Tbilisi's flirtations with the West, including its membership in GU(U)AM and participation in the BTC project. Abkhazia and South Ossetia were mainly bargaining chips the Kremlin was willing to trade for a more cooperative Georgian attitude, while Russian troops in the South Caucasus were an insurance policy against the further spread of ethnic unrest into Russia.[61] They were also profitable for many well-connected Russian officials and businessmen.

In late 2004 Russia threatened to use force against Abkhazia itself in response to elections in that province that appeared to result in the victory of a candidate—Sergei Bagapsh—who promised to clamp down on Abkhazia's widespread corruption, the tentacles of which reached back to Moscow. Bagapsh was no Russophobe (no Abkhaz politician could afford to alienate the region's only outside supporter), but his candidacy had developed outside the framework of the Kremlin patronage that sustained his rival, Raul Khajimba.[62] The Abkhaz crisis of 2004–2005 was thus a smaller version of the struggle for Ukraine going on at almost the same moment.

Saakashvili's ascension to power in January 2004 again placed the Abkhaz and South Ossetian conflicts in the limelight. Saakashvili had promised to restore Georgian territorial integrity, threatening in the process to deprive Russia of its most effective leverage against Tbilisi. Still, during his first meeting with Putin in February 2004, the new Georgian president expressed a willingness to look for joint solutions to a problem for which neither Putin nor he himself bore personal responsibility. While Saakashvili spoke of the need for dialogue with Russia, he also left no doubt about his commitment to restoring Georgian sovereignty over all of the republic's territory, or about his willingness to court Western assistance to do so.[63]

The new Georgian president staked much of his political legitimacy on resolving the frozen conflicts, confident that his close relationship with Western powers (above all the U.S.) would insulate him against Russian intervention. His confidence in Western backing at times led Saakashvili to act rashly. In a joint press conference with Putin in June 2006, Saakashvili declared of the frozen conflicts that "the reality is that the annexation of our territory is underway."[64] After his first bridge-building visit to Moscow, moreover, Saakashvili then went to Washington, where he pressed the Bush administration for additional security and economic assistance in order to lessen Georgia's dependence on Moscow.[65] During and immediately after the Rose Revolution, Saakashvili's government did receive substantial aid from the U.S., including $3 million to pay the salaries of Georgian military personnel and an agreement, signed in January 2004, to provide upward of $10 million in general financial assistance. Moscow perceived this aid, along with the construction of the BTC pipeline across Georgian territory soon after the installation of Saakashvili's overtly pro-Western government, as proof of the connection between the Rose Revolution and Western geopolitical designs in the Caucasus.[66]

Saakashvili also gave an indication of his approach to the frozen conflicts by moving rapidly and decisively to restore Tbilisi's authority in Ajaria in the spring of 2004. Saakashvili's success in Ajaria was the result of mounting frustration with regional strongman Aslan Abashidze's corrupt and deeply unpopular government and of Russia's disinclination to come to Abashidze's defense—despite the presence of a Russian military base in the restive province. In contrast to Abkhazia or South Ossetia, however, Ajaria was outside Tbilisi's grasp not because of an intractable civil conflict (its inhabitants are ethnic Georgians), but because its ruler had been a crony of ex-president Shevardnadze, who allowed him to run Ajaria as a private fief, free from state taxation or oversight. Consequently, Abashidze had little popular support. In late March 2004 Saakashvili declared a blockade of the rebel province.[67] When the Ajarian strongman refused to back down, Saakashvili threatened to use force. The Kremlin dispatched then-foreign minister Igor Ivanov to negotiate a settlement, but his efforts were overtaken by events. Remaining defiant, Abashidze ordered bridges between Ajaria and Georgia proper destroyed, only to flee when mass protests in the regional capital of Batumi and elsewhere demonstrated his lack of public backing.[68]

While Moscow intervened late and relatively ineffectively in the Ajarian crisis, the events of spring 2004 showed that Saakashvili was serious about regaining control over Georgia's breakaway regions. His success in Ajaria emboldened Saakashvili to take a harder line toward the frozen conflicts in Abkhazia and South Ossetia. In the summer of 2006, Tbilisi moved to reassert control over the upper portion of the Kodori Gorge, an area Moscow had long alleged to be a refuge and staging ground for Chechen rebels, and which cut across the boundary between Abkhazia and Georgia proper. The gorge had been demilitarized as a result of the 1994 Moscow Accords ending the Georgian-Abkhaz war, and in subsequent years it had remained a major flashpoint.[69]

In July 2006, Saakashvili sent troops from the Georgian Interior Ministry into the gorge to depose a local strongman. With this police operation completed, Tbilisi installed a loyalist Abkhaz government-in-exile in the area newly renamed "Upper Abkhazia." Tbilisi's intent was clearly to provide an alternative to the Abkhaz leadership in hope of reconciling Abkhazia as a whole to living under Georgian rule. Saakashvili's efforts in "Upper Abkhazia" disturbed the Abkhaz separatist regime in Tskhinvali as well as

Moscow, which saw its influence in the region threatened by a government in Tbilisi it had already come to despise.[70]

In South Ossetia, the Georgian authorities similarly tried to create a competing center of power in the fall of 2007. Tbilisi sponsored a presidential vote in those parts of South Ossetia inhabited principally by ethnic Georgians, which resulted in a victory for the pro-integrationist parties headed by Dmitry Sanakoev (a onetime Ossetian separatist). Russia, as well as the international community in the form of the OSCE, condemned the election for disrupting ongoing negotiations to ameliorate tensions on the ground.[71] For Tbilisi, of course, the point was not to reduce tensions in the breakaway regions, but to "unfreeze" the frozen conflicts altogether. In practice, Sanakoev had little authority, and South Ossetia as a whole remained outside Tbilisi's writ, setting the stage for Saakashvili's desperate gamble in August 2008 to retake the region by force.

The prewar nadir for Russo-Georgian relations came in late 2006, after Georgian security services arrested four Russian officers and accused them publicly of espionage and sabotage. In particular, Tbilisi charged that the arrested officials had coordinated a series of terrorist attacks on Georgian infrastructure with the aim of stirring up tensions between Georgia and the breakaway republics. In a television broadcast discussing the arrests, Georgian defense minister Irakly Okruashvili blamed Russia for fomenting the South Ossetian and Abkhaz conflicts and demanded the withdrawal of Russian peacekeepers from Georgian territory.[72] The Russians responded by alleging that Tbilisi was trying to provoke Russia to overreact in order to build Western sympathy and accelerate the process of NATO integration.[73]

Moscow responded to the arrests by recalling its ambassador and suspending the withdrawal of Russian troops from Georgia proper, even after Tbilisi agreed to deport the arrested agents. Russia also suspended transportation links between the two countries, banned Georgia's major exports (wine and bottled water), stopped issuing visas to Georgian citizens, and announced a crackdown on the large ethnic Georgian diaspora inside Russia, whose remittances were critical for the Georgian economy. The crackdown culminated in the deportation of around 700 ethnic Georgians from Russian territory, which Moscow claimed was an anticrime measure (though members of other nationalities, criminals or otherwise, were not rounded up in the same way).[74]

These measures were accompanied by a barrage of ferocious rhetoric from the Kremlin and its supporters in the press. Putin's close ally, Deputy Prime Minister Sergei Ivanov, declared that "in its insolence the Saakashvili regime has gone beyond any civilized boundaries" and charged the Georgian leadership with being in foreign pay.[75] Putin himself was hardly more restrained, calling the arrest of the alleged spies "an act of state terrorism" and "a legacy of [Stalin's secret police chief and Georgian native] Lavrenty Pavlovich Beria."[76]

The Russian response was strikingly disproportionate relative to the action of the Georgian authorities, most likely by design. Worried by Saakashvili's open courting of the West and his determination to restore Georgia's sovereignty in the breakaway republics, the Kremlin upped the ante in an attempt to make the cost of achieving Saakashvili's goals too high for the Georgian leadership to accept. In the event, Russian policy largely backfired. The disproportionate assault on a small, pro-Western country being considered for NATO membership merely fed U.S. and European perceptions that Putin's Russia had become a danger to the post-Soviet status quo. Moscow's approach did little to curb Saakashvili's appetite for integration with the West, either. Instead, it helped legitimate an ugly streak of xenophobia in Russian society to the benefit of rabid nationalist groups, some of whom remained opposed to the Putin government anyway.[77] If Moscow was going to teach Tbilisi a lesson, it would have to use other means.

For the subsequent two years, little was done to restore trust in Russo-Georgian relations. Even as Moscow withdrew the last of its troops from Georgia proper in the latter part of 2007 (where they had been based since the fall of the USSR), it ramped up its presence in the breakaway regions, especially Abkhazia. Tbilisi interpreted this move as preparation for war, though the Kremlin argued that it was Saakashvili who was bringing arms into the region.[78] The frozen conflicts remained frozen, while Saakashvili's decision to disperse antigovernment protesters with force in November 2007 damaged his democratic credentials in a West that had already begun reconsidering Georgia's suitability for NATO membership.

The dam finally broke in the summer of 2008, when with the world's attention focused on the opening of the Olympics in Beijing, Saakashvili responded to a new round of provocations by ordering his forces to retake South Ossetia. Starting on August 7, Georgian forces launched an artillery barrage against Tskhinvali and moved to seize control of the region's infrastructure from the separatist regime. If Saakashvili was counting on his friendship with the West to keep Moscow at bay, he miscalculated badly. The attempt to seize South Ossetia provided the Kremlin with the excuse it had been seeking to go after Saakashvili. The day after the Georgian incursion against Tskhinvali, massed Russian forces began crossing into South Ossetia through the Roki Tunnel, while the Russian air force carried out strikes on targets in both South Ossetia and Georgia proper.

Moscow charged the Georgian government with ethnic cleansing against the Ossetian population in Tskhinvali and other population centers and justified its decision to send troops on the basis of defending the civilian population (many of whom had been granted Russian passports) and the Russian peacekeepers that Georgia charged were now part of a hostile occupying army.[79] New Russian president Medvedev gave a terse announcement of the Russian invasion, arguing that the Georgian peacekeeping contingent in South Ossetia had opened fire on its Russian counterpart and claiming Tbilisi's "act of aggression" had resulted in the deaths of "civilians, women, children, the elderly, and the majority of them citizens of the Russian Federation."[80] Moscow initially claimed that the Georgian seizure of Tskhinvali had resulted in upward of 2,000 dead, though hospital records indicated that fewer than 100 civilians had been killed in the South Ossetian capital.

After driving the overmanned Georgians out of South Ossetia, Russian forces continued into Georgia proper, seizing the key city of Gori and Georgia's main east-west highway, blockading the Black Sea port of Poti, and systematically destroying Georgian military assets (as well as some other infrastructure). Russian troops also moved into Abkhazia, retaking the Kodori Gorge from the Georgians, who had redeployed all available troops (including their forces serving in Iraq) to defend Tbilisi. In South Ossetia, local militias rampaged behind Russian lines, looting, pillaging, and driving out the ethnic Georgian population, which fled en masse into Georgia proper.[81]

Despite agreeing to a cease-fire negotiated by French president Sarkozy on August 13, Russian troops remained in Georgia for several weeks thereafter, systematically destroying military assets in an attempt to weaken Georgia and prevent it from undertaking any further attempts at seizing the disputed regions.[82] After the tame Duma had voted in favor of recognizing South Ossetia and Abkhazia as independent states, Medvedev agreed, and Russia became the first (and apart from Nicaragua, the only) state to recognize the two breakaway regions' independence.

Following years of warning the Georgians that they were playing a dangerous game, Moscow's patience finally ran out. For essentially the first time since the collapse of the Soviet Union, Moscow undertook a major cross-border military operation in the face of the outside world's condemnation. The United States and Europe strongly protested Russian behavior and threatened Moscow with a range of punishments, some symbolic (expulsion from the G8), others real (the cancellation of a lucrative civilian nuclear cooperation accord with Washington). None of it mattered. The invasion of Georgia and recognition of the breakaway regions reflected a calculation in Moscow that the strategic pause—Gorchakov's *sosredotochenie* or Stolypin's *peredyshka*—following the collapse of the Soviet Union was over. It was a signal to the rest of the world that Russia continued to regard the CIS as its own sphere of influence, where it would not tolerate having its interests ignored.

CENTRAL ASIA

For much of the Soviet period, Central Asia was an imperial backwater, important mainly as a producer of primary goods such as cotton and as a dumping ground for political opponents. The early post-Soviet period did not see much change. The Central Asian leaders were not consulted about the eventual dissolution of the USSR and were notified that they had become rulers of independent states only after the fact. The five primarily Muslim republics of Central Asia came into the world in 1991 as inchoate entities, with a weak sense of national identity, and where loyalty to the newly created states and their Russian-speaking strongmen was tenuous at best.

Central Asia turned into a region of key strategic interest for both Russia and outside powers like the United States primarily for two reasons: Islamic fundamentalism and energy. The power vacuum that emerged following the Soviet withdrawal from Afghanistan and the subsequent collapse of Soviet rule in Central Asia provided fertile ground for the development of a new politics based on somewhat fictive tribal loyalties, even as veterans of the Afghan war introduced a new, puritanical strain of Islamic thought to a region that had traditionally worn its religion lightly. This nexus of tribalism and religion erupted into war in the newly independent state of Tajikistan in 1992, followed shortly thereafter by the redeployment of Russian troops outside the border of the Russian Federation to deal with the consequences of that war. The Tajik experience, itself following soon after the end of the Soviet Union's Afghan apotheosis, did much to color subsequent Russian perceptions of developments in Central Asia. Alongside other foreign ideological imports, radical Islam, at times manifesting itself in acts of terrorism, spread throughout parts of Central Asia in the 1990s, a combination that the secular, Russian-speaking apparatchiks who inherited power after the Soviet collapse perceived as a threat.[83] Moscow found itself pulled into Central Asia to protect these secular autocrats who, even when they made difficulties for Russia, remained preferable to the specter of rising Islamist governments along Russia's Muslim southern fringe. Greater Russian involvement in Central Asian affairs also helped compensate Moscow for its perceived neglect by the Western powers, who were at the same time busy expanding the reach of the European Union and NATO into the Soviet Union's former sphere of influence in Eastern Europe.[84]

This more active Russian approach was embodied in President Yeltsin's decree of September 1995 proclaiming the CIS a top foreign policy priority for Russia. This move was interpreted by some at the time as a signal of Moscow's ambitions to re-establish a state resembling the USSR and to restore some kind of bipolar global order, since it called for Russia to assume a "leading role" in the CIS as part of its broader quest for "a worthy place in world society."[85] Moscow essentially gave itself an exclusive right to manage the security of its neighbors throughout the CIS, though in practical terms, Russia's enhanced influence was at the time felt most in Central Asia. Local rulers increasingly came to see the Kremlin as the ultimate guarantor of their security against the perceived Islamist threat.[86] For Russia, the Islamist threat was real enough (the first Chechen war was then at its peak), but the strategic advance into Central Asia also was part of the reaction against the West led by Primakov.

The Putin years witnessed a concerted return to Central Asia on the part of Russian diplomacy. Of course, much of the increased focus on the region is an outgrowth of the September 11 attacks and the deployment of U.S. troops to Uzbekistan and Kyrgyzstan thereafter. Yet Moscow's gaze was already turning to Central Asia at the very beginning of Putin's term in office. Putin's first foreign trip as prime minister was to Tajikistan, in November 1999, when he sought to promote the electoral fortunes of the secularist, pro-Russian incumbent then named Emomali Rakhmonov (the Tajik leader subsequently de-Russified his surname, and officially became Emomali Rakhmon). The following month Putin traveled to Uzbekistan, signing a series of bilateral deals aimed at bringing Tashkent more directly into the Russian orbit, though in practice the Uzbeks continued to hedge their bets, joining the independence-minded GU(U)AM forum in April 1999.[87]

Until the September 11 attacks, Moscow's interest in the region was largely driven by a desire to prevent any further loss of Russian prestige and influence. The invasion of Kyrgyzstan by Islamist militants from the Islamic Movement of Uzbekistan (IMU) in August 1999 provided Putin with an opportunity to step up Russian engagement in the region. The militants' threat to regional stability, coupled with the Kyrgyz government's clear inability to repulse them on its own suggested that only outside intervention could defend the secular status quo.[88] In response to the IMU's cross-border invasion, Putin immediately began seeking a rapprochement with Uzbekistan, the country most seriously threatened by the IMU and in many ways the key to regional stability. Though Tashkent refused for the time being to back out of GU(U)AM or to join Russian-sponsored multilateral groups like the Collective Security Treaty, it agreed to limited participation in training exercises with Russia and signed a series of bilateral security cooperation agreements with Moscow.[89]

Russia's leaders shifted the focus of their engagement in Central Asia following the September 11 attacks, which drew the attention of Washington directly to events in the region. Instead of seeking to keep the U.S. out of Central Asia, the Putin administration took advantage of the attacks to formulate a new approach, according to which Russia would be the indispensable ally in the U.S.-led war on terror and would use its newfound role as a springboard to attain Great Power status. It is notable that the U.S. deployments in Central Asia were approved directly by Putin in the face of serious opposition from his generals. Burdened by a seemingly endless war in Chechnya, Putin readily concluded, in the words of Gleb Pavlovsky, that "it is better to have Americans in Uzbekistan than to have the Taliban in Tatarstan."[90] Russian leaders recognized that, given the scale of the carnage unleashed on 9/11 and their own vulnerability to Islamic terrorism (Russia has over twenty million Muslim citizens and abuts some of the least stable of Islam's "bloody borders"), gaining the cooperation of the United States in the ongoing struggle against fundamentalism was enough of a strategic imperative to trump worries about the effects of American power inside the boundaries of the former USSR.[91]

At the same time, cooperation with the Americans seemed to offer the best opportunity for Russia to regain its role as one of the leading pillars of the international order, since it was essentially offering to play a key role in a campaign that (if successful) would have major implications for the future shape of the world. Besides, leaders in Uzbekistan, Tajikistan, and Kyrgyzstan made clear in the weeks immediately following the attacks that they wanted U.S. troops deployed in the region to protect their own governments against Taliban-inspired Islamists like the IMU.[92] Putin was thus in some sense reacting to events beyond his control—categorically refusing to allow U.S. troops into Central Asia risked sacrificing whatever influence Moscow retained in the region, and under the circumstances it appeared better to make a virtue of necessity.

Putin's gamble turned out to be only partially justified. On the one hand, the initial intervention drove the Taliban from power and inflicted a crushing blow on the strongest of the Central Asian Islamist groups, the IMU, which had contributed to regional instability through cross-border raids, kidnappings, and bomb attacks (including one that narrowly missed killing Uzbek president Karimov in 1999).[93] Then again, the U.S. invasion of Iraq, which Russia strenuously opposed, drew attention and resources away from the Afghan campaign, while the overall deterioration in U.S.-Russian relations since 2002 has complicated the Kremlin's plans for using an alliance with the U.S. as a springboard for achieving greater international influence. The result has been an increasing drive by the Kremlin to secure its own dominant role in the region, sidelining the U.S. (as well as China) in the process.

Shortly after agreeing to the establishment of semipermanent U.S. military installations at Manas, Kyrgyzstan, and Karshi-Khanabad, Uzbekistan, Russia moved to set up its own facilities in the region. The Russian air base at Kant in Kyrgyzstan, which opened in early 2003, was the first new long-term deployment of Russian troops outside the borders of the Russian Federation since the end of the Cold War. It was designed to counter the expansion of American influence in Central Asia that occurred in the wake of the Afghan invasion, and to take advantage of the Central Asians' disappointment that the U.S. presence in the region had not brought them more benefit.[94]

Since 2003, Moscow has moved to upgrade and expand the facilities at Kant in order to establish a permanent presence in Kyrgyzstan, on the basis of the Tashkent Collective Security Treaty. In 2006, the Russian government began improving facilities at the Kant base and moving in additional personnel. Moscow signed an agreement with Bishkek by which Russia receives free use of the base in exchange for providing the Kyrgyz military with helicopters and other kinds of basic military equipment. President Putin praised the Russian forces at Kant as "a mobile and operational element in the collective development of the CSTO in Central Asia" that Moscow looked forward to further enhancing in the future.[95]

Following the Tulip Revolution that overthrew longtime strongman Askar Akaev, the new Kyrgyz government stepped up pressure on the United States to downsize and eventually eliminate its base at Manas. These demands were in line with a collective call issued by the Shanghai Cooperation Organization in 2005 to set a date for the eventual liquidation of the entire U.S. military presence in Central Asia (the U.S. was forced to leave the Karshi-Khanabad base in Uzbekistan after Washington called for an international inquiry into the massacre of demonstrators by Uzbek security forces in Andijon in May 2005).[96] Bishkek ultimately succeeded in forcing Washington to increase its annual rent payments for the Manas facility to $200 million, while Russia continues to enjoy rent-free access to Kant. Even though the U.S. had initially supported the Tulip Revolution as an opportunity to move Kyrgyzstan back on the path to democratic development, the new government of President Kurmanbek Bakiev made a clear calculation that the country's interests ultimately lie more with Moscow than with Washington.[97] Bakiev accommodated Russia's demands to maintain the Kant facility, despite previous opposition to the Russian base when he was an opposition leader.[98]

The contrasting fates of the Russian and American air bases in Kyrgyzstan reflect the degree to which international relations in Central Asia (and in the CIS more generally) became more contested in the course of President Putin's second term. For Moscow, the strategy of bandwagoning with the United States against the Taliban gradually gave way to a more aggressive approach of attempting to restore Central Asia's traditional role as a buffer and to sharply limit the influence of outside powers in the region. Given the fall of the Taliban and the overall worsening of relations between Moscow and Washington, it is hardly surprising that U.S.-Russian dynamics in Central Asia have changed since 2001.

When he came to power in 2000, Putin emphasized on several occasions that the principal threat to Russian security came from the south, that is, from Islamic radicalism in the Caucasus and Central Asia.[99] As that threat diminished following the Taliban's fall from power and the winding down of hostilities in Chechnya, Moscow's fundamental threat calculus shifted.

The pro-Taliban IMU was decimated by U.S. bombing attacks in Afghanistan in 2001–2002, suffering hundreds of casualties and the death of its leader, Juma Namangani. Meanwhile, the peace treaty between government and (partially Islamist) opposition forces in Tajikistan signed in 1997 has, contrary to the expectations of many, held firm. The spate of bombings inside Russia conducted by Chechen and allied Islamist forces, which was responsible for much of Moscow's interest in stamping out Islamist groups throughout the CIS, has also abated. Russia's killing of Chechen rebel leaders Aslan Maskhadov, Ibn al-Khattab, and Shamil Basaev, coupled with the success of the pro-Moscow strongman Ramzan Kadyrov in restoring order to Chechnya, has made the Islamist threat to Russia less immediate—though Dagestan, Ingushetia, and other Muslim regions in the North Caucasus continue to simmer.[100]

Consequently, Moscow was able to pursue a broader strategic agenda toward its Muslim neighbors once the link between instability in Central Asia and instability in Russia itself was severed. With the Islamist threat from the south seemingly under control for the time being and U.S. aid no longer critical to achieving Russian aims, Putin began focusing on the longer-term project of re-establishing Russian hegemony in Eurasia, which requires limiting the role played by outside powers such as the United States and China. To be sure, a residual U.S. presence in the region actually benefits Russia, since it takes the burden of conducting and coordinating counterterrorism operations out of the hands of Russia's military, which remains in a state of transition. For that reason, then-U.S. ambassador to Russia Alexander Vershbow argued in 2004 in favor of continuing U.S.-Russian cooperation in Central Asia to help "establish a strong barrier on the road of the spread of religious extremism, terrorism, and instability."[101] The U.S. presence also works to limit Chinese penetration of Central Asia.[102] Since China is a regional power whose interest in Central Asia is likely to be permanent, Moscow can afford to see the (relatively) fleeting presence of U.S. troops as less threatening.

Instead of seeking common ground with Washington, though, Russia has moved to integrate the states of Central Asia into a security (and economic) bloc under its own direction, under what was for a time referred to as the "Ivanov Doctrine" in honor of Russia's former defense minister Sergei Ivanov, who was responsible for overseeing the creation of Russia's 2003 Military Doctrine. The Military Doctrine listed the presence of "foreign troops (without UN Security Council sanction) to the territory [sic] of contiguous states friendly with the Russian Federation" as one of the major threats to Russian security.[103] When the document was issued, the only foreign troops present in neighboring countries were those of the U.S. in Kyrgyzstan and Uzbekistan. To counter this perceived threat, Russia took the lead in promoting the unification of the post-Soviet republics—particularly in Central

Asia—into an integrated security space under Russian leadership, while also seeking to strengthen bilateral ties with the most important countries of the region (Uzbekistan and Kazakhstan) in a kind of zero-sum competition with the United States. Thus in August 2005, the states of the CIS signed a memorandum of understanding promising to enhance their cooperation in the struggle against terrorism and extremism. Notably, the memorandum underlined the dominant role of the United Nations and international law in combating terrorism, a clear signal of the signatories' displeasure with Washington's unilateral approach to a problem that affected all of them.[104]

One major element in Russia's strategy of security integration has been the creation and strengthening of multilateral institutions in which Russia plays a leading role. The SCO is in some ways the most visible such organization, but its lack of institutionalization (the SCO does not control any troops apart from the national forces of its members) and the presence of China limit its usefulness as a lever of Russian control in Central Asia. While the SCO's main role so far has been to manage the inevitable conflicts and disagreements that have emerged between Moscow and Beijing, it is the Collective Security Treaty Organization (CSTO) that has emerged as the primary vehicle for the re-establishment of Moscow's strategic influence in Central Asia.

The CSTO, which some Russian strategists have seen as a kind of Eurasian NATO, joins Russia with the Central Asian states (apart from officially neutral Turkmenistan), Armenia, and Belarus. It is one of several Russian-designed multilateral organizations in the region that took on new substance in the Putin years, along with the CIS Customs Union and Eurasian Economic Community (EurAsEC).[105] As its name implies, the CSTO is based on the principle of collective security, with its members committed to coming to one another's aid in the event of an outside attack. It maintains a series of joint institutions, including a general staff, though its cohesiveness remains open to doubt.

The origins of the CSTO lie in the 1992 Tashkent Treaty on Collective Security, which aimed at giving the newly independent states of the CIS some kind of overarching security framework to replace the joint structures of the Soviet Union. However, throughout the 1990s, the Tashkent Treaty was little more than a pious declaration of intent, as the various states of the CIS each pursued their own interests with little coordination. Shortly after his ascension to power in 2000, President Putin proposed revitalizing the various institutions underpinning the CIS. The immediate result was an agreement on the creation of a joint CIS Counterterrorism Center based in Kyrgyzstan, followed in 2001 by a joint Rapid Deployment Force.[106] When the CSTO itself was formed the following year, the Rapid Deployment Force became the nucleus of the organization's combined military capability. With the deterioration of the security situation in Afghanistan beginning in

2007, Moscow began laying the groundwork for the deployment of CSTO forces to curb the spread of drugs and Islamic radicalism into Central Asia. The CSTO summit in September 2008 agreed on the formation of a ten-thousand-man joint security force that could be deployed to Afghanistan, while Lavrov called for coordination between the CSTO and NATO forces to combat the spread of instability from Afghanistan to Central Asia.[107]

In his press conference announcing the formation of the CSTO in May 2002, Putin explained that the need for such an organization grew out of the post-Soviet region's failure to adapt to new realities:

> After the fall of the Soviet Union . . . an entirely new situation emerged. Inattention to the new situation in the world had in the final analysis terrible consequences; like those of last September 11. All this means that we must build new security structures in the world, new mechanisms for cooperation.[108]

While leaving open the possibility for the new organization to cooperate with similar blocs elsewhere in the world (specifically NATO and the SCO), the Russian president made clear that the CSTO was first and foremost a regional organization and part of his broader agenda for rebuilding the ties binding Russia to its former dependencies in Central Asia. Given the vast power disparity between Russia and the other members of the CSTO (a problem that takes a different form in the SCO as a result of China's immense influence), the organization has largely served as a vehicle for expanding Russian influence over its neighbors, particularly in Central Asia. Thus, despite its focus on the CIS, the CSTO has not hesitated to follow Russia's lead in staking out positions critical of the Western powers when those powers appear to be undermining Moscow's international position. For instance, the organization's members adopted a collective declaration in mid-2007 criticizing NATO and the United States for planning to establish antiballistic missile defense systems in Eastern Europe, even though Russia is the only CSTO member with a missile force that could be affected by the proposed deployment.[109] Moreover, the CSTO depends on Russia for its hardware, and the Kremlin has agreed to sell military equipment to its CSTO partners at the same price paid by the Russian military. Unconstrained by Chinese concerns, the CSTO also took a more overtly pro-Russian stance on the 2008 Georgian war than did the Shanghai Cooperation Organization—though it, too, stopped short of extending recognition to South Ossetia and Abkhazia.[110]

On the level of bilateral relations, Russia similarly moved to shore up its standing with the states of Central Asia as a way of increasing its own influence and limiting that of the U.S. (as well as China). This increased emphasis during the Putin years on bilateral relations resulted both from the increasingly competitive dynamic of international politics in Central

Asia and from Moscow's growing tendency to see influence over its post-Soviet neighbors as a prerequisite for its ambition of enhancing its global standing. While Putin's Russia devoted more attention to Central Asia as a whole, the orientation of Kazakhstan and Uzbekistan in the global balance is a particularly important indicator of Russia's evolving global role and key to the success of the so-called Ivanov Doctrine.[111] Kazakhstan's importance derives in particular from its location and ownership of substantial gas and oil reserves. Uzbekistan, on the other hand, has fewer resources but a larger population, a (comparatively) powerful military, and a more serious problem with terrorism and Islamist extremism. Both Astana and Tashkent have balanced carefully between Russia and the United States (as well as China to a lesser extent), though recently Uzbekistan has found itself both pushed and pulled increasingly into Moscow's orbit.

Situated on the Caspian coast, Kazakhstan is the largest oil producer in the former Soviet Union apart from Russia itself, with output reaching 1.4 million barrels per day.[112] Given its location, it is also critical as a transport route for energy bound for other countries in both Europe and Asia. During the Putin years, Moscow relentlessly pursued economic integration with Kazakhstan while also seeking Kazakh support for its broader international objectives. Kazakhstan was among the first littoral countries to agree with Russia on a pact establishing national sectors of the Caspian Sea (in 1998). Astana and Moscow also signed a friendship and cooperation treaty in 2002, opening the way for greatly expanded Russian investment in the country, giving Kazakhstan access to Russia's Baltic pipeline system to Europe, and encouraging the participation of Russian energy companies in developing Kazakhstan's resources (Lukoil alone has invested over $3 billion in Kazakhstan since the agreement).[113] Kazakhstan has also been an enthusiastic supporter of Russian attempts to create a single economic space in Central Asia and other forms of economic integration being pushed by Moscow.[114]

In the security sphere, Moscow and Astana agreed on a long-term lease for the Baikonur Cosmodrome (from which almost all Russian space launches are conducted) and on training Russian soldiers at Kazakh facilities. Putin's January 2004 visit to Astana paved the way for Kazakhstan to adopt an increasingly pro-Russian leaning in its foreign policy, with the two countries agreeing on a joint plan for security cooperation a month later that called for greatly enhanced collaboration against terrorism and external threats.[115] In April 2006, Putin and Kazakh president Nursultan Nazarbaev spoke in favor of deepening integration between the two countries. While praising the level of integration already achieved, according to the Russian president, "We need instruments for resolving problems that arise in order to move forward. . . . We will continue to work toward strengthening all the integration processes in the post-Soviet space."[116]

Russia's interest in seeking greater influence in Kazakhstan has had its analogue in U.S. attempts to recruit Astana as a major ally in the war on terrorism. U.S. Secretary of State Condoleezza Rice has praised Kazakhstan for its commitment to fighting Islamic terrorism and its role as Washington's key partner in Central Asia.[117] Kazakhstan participated in the U.S.-led campaign in Afghanistan, providing several of its facilities for refueling of planes involved in anti-Taliban operations, while Nazarbaev allowed the U.S. military to train and supply their Kazakh counterparts.[118]

Yet the government of President Nazarbaev has become increasingly authoritarian since the start of the war on terror and has refused to place itself firmly in the U.S. camp in opposition to Russia and China. Instead, Astana has pursued a careful balancing act. On the one hand, Nazarbaev agreed after much prodding to build a link from Kazakhstan's enormous Kashagan oil field to the Baku-Tbilisi-Ceyhan pipeline in June 2006. Kazakhstan agreed to link its oil production with BTC only after signing a separate agreement committing to ship more than twice as much oil (sixty-seven million tons per year, versus twenty-five million tons through BTC) through the Caspian Pipeline Consortium (CPC), which is privately owned but crosses Russian territory. Effectively connecting Kazakhstan to BTC will require building a new pipeline beneath the Caspian Sea at enormous cost.[119]

Yet for geographical as well as demographic reasons, Astana continues to see Russia, rather than the United States, as the principal guarantor of its security.[120] Despite its cooperation with the U.S. in the context of Operation Enduring Freedom in Afghanistan and its active participation in NATO's Partnership for Peace program, Astana remains a member of the Russian-dominated CSTO, whose members are prohibited from joining any competing security organization (i.e., NATO). The Kazakh economy is also heavily dependent on Russia, thanks to the fact that Soviet industries and supply chains were constructed around the assumption that inter-republican borders were essentially meaningless (as they were while the USSR existed). Since the collapse of the Soviet Union, Kazakhstan's economy has benefited substantially from cross-border remittances and the migration of workers to Russian cities.[121]

Another, less discussed component of Russia's enduring influence in Astana is the presence of a large Russian diaspora in the northern third of Kazakhstan and in major cities. Not only are the ethnic Russians heavily concentrated in scientific and technical sectors of the economy that Astana would be loath to harm, but the potential for ethnically based politics and even irredentism (which nationalist groups in Russia have at times pressed) is never far from the surface. Indeed, Nazarbaev's decision to move the capital from Almaty in the southeastern corner of Kazakhstan to the newly built city of Astana in the north has often been interpreted as a carrot to the large Russian population of the northern region.[122] For all these reasons, and despite concerted diplomatic and economic inducements offered by Washington, Kazakhstan remains balanced precariously between outside powers seeking to influence its foreign policy and gain access to its energy riches.

The struggle for influence between Russia and the U.S. has been even more intense in Uzbekistan, the most populous and militarily potent of the Central Asian states. In contrast to Kazakhstan, Uzbekistan's government has vacillated over time between Moscow and Washington, and the battle for Tashkent has in many ways served as a kind of proxy for the broader evolution of Russian foreign policy in Central Asia. For much of the 1990s, Uzbekistan confronted a simmering Islamist insurgency (which eventually coalesced into the IMU) and pursued a fairly independent line in foreign policy, rapidly ridding itself of Russian advisers and resisting Moscow's overtures for a closer relationship, while seeking a dominant role for itself within Central Asia, often at Russian expense.[123] Tashkent withdrew from the CST and joined GU(U)AM in 1999, in part because the former refused to take a firm line against the emerging Islamist threat.

Putin made a concerted effort to heal the breach between Moscow and Tashkent, particularly following the IMU's 1999 incursion into Kyrgyzstan and attempts on the life of Uzbek president Karimov. The attacks allowed Putin to link Russia's own campaign in Chechnya with Uzbekistan's battle against the IMU as part of a larger struggle against radical Islam. More fundamentally, the growth of the IMU threat convinced Tashkent that Russia had a central role to play in defending the status quo in Central Asia. However, the two sides continued to disagree, most notably over what to do about the impending takeover of Afghanistan by the Taliban.[124] Despite the warming climate in relations with Moscow, Uzbekistan did not rejoin the CST and remained wary of falling too far under Russia's influence.

In the aftermath of the September 11 attacks, Tashkent moved rapidly to accommodate the U.S. and participate in the campaign against the Taliban. Following a phone call by President Bush on September 19, 2001, Karimov acceded to the U.S. request to base coalition troops in Uzbekistan (the U.S. considered Uzbekistan a more palatable rear zone than its old ally Pakistan because of the strength of anti-American and pro-Taliban feeling in Pakistan).[125]

Karimov promised the U.S. use of the old Soviet Karshi-Khanabad air base in exchange for a security guarantee from Washington and a tacit promise to look the other way at Uzbekistan's abysmal human rights record. On October 5, 2001, Karimov agreed to allow the U.S. to base both troops and aircraft at the base (but not to use it for launching attacks into Afghanistan). Karshi-Khanabad soon became a major staging point for U.S. aircraft ferrying supplies into the Afghan theater.[126] Washington meanwhile gave Tashkent a series of wide-ranging security guarantees, solemnized during a visit by Secretary of State Colin Powell to Uzbekistan in early December.[127] The relationship was upgraded to a strategic partnership in March 2002.[128] The presence of U.S. troops strengthened Karimov's hand against the Russians. Shortly after the agreement on U.S. access to Karshi-Khanabad, Uzbekistan pulled out of an SCO summit meeting, a move interpreted at the time as a snub to Moscow and a signal that Tashkent viewed itself as part of the U.S.-dominated security sphere emerging around Afghanistan.[129]

Even during the high point of U.S.-Russian cooperation in Central Asia during 2001–2002, the government of Uzbekistan consciously sought to balance between the two major powers in order to maximize its own flexibility and independence, essentially acting as if Washington and Moscow remained rivals for influence in Central Asia. Karimov sought to modernize the Uzbek military with arms purchased from the U.S. and other NATO countries and rejected Russian calls to set a deadline for the coalition troops' departure from Karshi-Khanabad. Yet at the same time, Karimov pursued a series of energy deals with Moscow, including a major cooperation agreement between Gazprom and Uzbekneftegaz signed in 2002 and deals with both Lukoil and Gazprom in 2004 that assigned the Russian firms a major role in developing new oil and gas deposits in Uzbekistan.[130] Tashkent and Moscow even signed a strategic partnership agreement in June 2004, while Uzbekistan remained committed to supporting U.S. operations in Afghanistan.[131]

Russia then moved rapidly to consolidate its position as the dominant influence in Uzbekistan following Karimov's brutal crackdown on demonstrators in the city of Andijon in May 2005 (which the Uzbek government blamed on Islamist radicals attempting to overthrow the government). Following the massacre, Washington rapidly, if tepidly, criticized the Karimov government's excesses, claiming to "condemn the indiscriminate use of force against unarmed civilians and deeply regret any loss of life."[132] Along with the EU, Washington called for a formal investigation into the Andijon events. In response, Karimov declared that the Western powers had no business interfering in Uzbekistan's internal affairs and communicated through the UN that he would not allow an outside investigation.[133] Karimov fulminated, "Is Uzbekistan an independent, sovereign state? . . . Why should we have to give you answers as though we're the accused?"[134]

At the end of July, Karimov moved more concretely, demanding that the U.S. vacate the Karshi-Khanabad base in six months' time. The eviction notice, delivered to the U.S. embassy with insulting formality, did not give a reason for Tashkent's change of heart, but was clearly in response to the continuing fallout over the Andijon crisis.[135] The implicit bargain—access to Karshi-Khanabad in exchange for diplomatic support and silence about Uzbekistan's human rights record—had quickly unraveled. Karimov believed the U.S. had broken a promise. If he could not rely on Washington to defend his regime in a crisis, Karimov rapidly came to the conclusion that his alliance with the U.S. had lost its value.

Unable to lean on the U.S. in his struggle against Islamic extremists (Karimov blamed the Andijon uprising on fanatical Islamists who had led a prison break with the assistance of sympathizers in the town), the Uzbek leader maneuvered his country back into a partnership with Russia. Just days after the U.S. call for an investigation, Karimov announced Uzbekistan's departure from GUUAM, which thus reverted to its pre-1999 appellation of GUAM. More broadly, Karimov began reconsidering his alliance with the United States in a way that opened the door for an increased Russian presence in Central Asia.

Moscow had quickly concluded that the post-Andijon tension between Tashkent and Washington could be used for its own purposes. Even before Karimov's decision to evict U.S. forces from Karshi-Khanabad, a summit of the SCO heads of state adopted a declaration calling on Washington to set a date for the departure of its forces from the territory of SCO member states. Putin welcomed the declaration, claiming "Russia is completely satisfied with the conclusions, the decisions that were taken, [which are] in our general interest."[136] Moscow also invited Tashkent to join the plethora of Russian-sponsored organizations throughout Eurasia. During a visit to Tashkent in October 2005, Russian foreign minister Lavrov discussed Uzbekistan's possible membership in the Eurasian Economic Association, receiving a favorable response from the Uzbek authorities.[137] Uzbekistan formally joined EurAsEc in January 2006.[138]

Uzbekistan also signed an alliance agreement with Russia in November 2005 during Karimov's visit to Moscow, committing both sides to upholding the supremacy of the UN as arbiter of international security and containing an unconditional mutual defense clause, essentially committing Russia to defend Uzbekistan against outside aggression. According to the Russian president, the 2005 agreement "brings our countries to a qualitatively new [level] and the maximum degree of cooperation."[139] Karimov praised the re-assertion of Russian power in the region, claiming in his joint press conference with Putin that "the strengthening of Russia's position in Central Asia is a firm guarantee of peace and stability in our region, and answers the deep interests of our two countries as well as the international community as a whole."[140] Finally, in June 2006, Karimov attended a summit of CSTO heads of state, where Putin announced to journalists that Uzbekistan had formally rejoined the organization from which it had withdrawn in 1999 when it joined GU(U)AM. The announcement of Tashkent's membership in the CSTO ended Uzbekistan's attempt to use its value to the U.S. in the war on terror as a means of shielding itself from Russia.[141]

Although Uzbekistan is in many ways the most important and influential of the Central Asian states, Russian policy there has been extremely cautious. When Putin agreed to the presence of U.S. troops in Central Asia following the September 11 attacks, he was in many ways making the best of a bad situation, since Karimov and other regional leaders had made clear they would offer Washington basing rights regardless of Russian concerns. However, until the fallout over Andijon, Russia's growing interest in Central Asia in general and Uzbekistan in particular was usually filtered through the prism of Moscow's relationship to the United States and its broader global ambitions. Despite mounting tensions with the U.S. throughout the war on terror, Russia remained content to leave Uzbekistan alone as the linchpin of the U.S. security alliance in Central Asia until 2005. Even then, it was the SCO (at Chinese behest), along with Uzbekistan itself, that were instrumental in forcing U.S. troops out of Karshi-Khanabad and ultimately reversing Tashkent's alliance posture. Moscow was more than willing to take advantage of circumstances to strengthen its own hand in the region but generally awaited developments rather than initiating them itself. In this way, Russia's growing influence in Central Asia was as much the result of strategic opportunism as of any overt desire to challenge U.S. hegemony. Once again, the major objective of Russian foreign policy has been to enhance its own global role, in partnership with the U.S. if possible, in opposition to it if necessary.

The second major factor driving Russia's intervention in the politics of Central Asia besides security is energy. Russia's emergence as a key supplier of both oil and gas owes much to its presence in Central Asia. Moscow has moved aggressively to lock up production and transit infrastructure in countries like Kazakhstan and Turkmenistan, both as a means of asserting its own influence in these countries and to limit other states' ability to cut Moscow out of deals involving Central Asian hydrocarbons. Central Asia is a major producer of both oil and gas, and growing interest on the part of European (and American) energy companies has also placed the region at the forefront of pipeline diplomacy.

The struggle to control pipelines has been a key piece of Moscow's attempts to exert influence over all the Caspian littoral states of the CIS. With the Western powers dreaming of access to the Caspian's energy riches, Brussels and Washington have aggressively promoted new pipeline deals bypassing Russia, while Moscow has responded with its own attempts to bottle up Central Asia's energy in Russian-controlled pipelines. Azerbaijan, with the BTC and BTE pipelines, had largely escaped Russian domination by the late 1990s. Kazakhstan managed to balance between the competing demands of Russia, the West, and China by signing multiple deals.[142] Turkmenistan, which is one of the world's largest producers of natural gas, is the post-Soviet state most in play among the various Great Powers at the beginning of Medvedev's presidency. Gazprom has long eyed Turkmenistan hungrily as a solution to mounting demand and stagnant supply inside Russia. For the time being, Russia essentially possesses a monopoly over the Turkmen pipeline network, controlling Turkmenistan's ability to ship its gas to the outside world, with both economic (higher prices) and geopolitical consequences, not only for Turkmenistan but also for Ukraine and the countries of the EU who are the ultimate customers for Turkmen gas shipped across Russia.[143]

The death of Turkmenistan's eccentric and autocratic leader Saparmurat Niyazov in December 2006 made the country the object of an intense geopolitical and geo-economic struggle between Russia and the other major powers. Washington and Brussels have sought to gain Turkmen cooperation in the Nabucco project. With mounting interest from Western energy firms as well as from China, which is building its own pipeline to Turkmenistan, Moscow was forced to agree in early 2008 to start paying Ashgabat (as well as the other Central Asian gas-producing countries) "European prices" for their gas, rather than the deeply discounted rate it had been getting up to that point. Turkmenistan meanwhile used the possibility of a deal with outside powers as a form of leverage in negotiations with the Russians, holding discussions with other powers (including the Europeans and Americans, Iranians, and Indians) to explore the possibility of breaking the effective Russian monopoly on Ashgabat's gas exports.[144]

In a more general sense, Russia's involvement in Central Asia, as along many of its foreign policy vectors, has emphasized using economic means to achieve geopolitical ends. In November 2005, Putin praised the signing of the Russo-Uzbek alliance primarily for clearing the way for greater trade and economic cooperation between Moscow and Tashkent.[145] Russian diplomats often emphasize the importance of ties with the other Central Asian countries in similar terms, with economic integration taking precedence (at least rhetorically) over security cooperation.[146]

Of course, such economic ties often have security consequences, especially when it comes to the energy sector. In the major energy-producing countries, Russian participation in the energy sector has overlapped with the Kremlin's broader foreign policy goals, as Russian businessmen with Kremlin connections have sought to establish cartel arrangements solidifying Russia's influence over the politics and economies of the Central Asian states and coordinating their move into Central Asia.[147] This process also coincides with the Kremlin's more direct attempts to promote political and economic integration in the region by way of multilateral organizations like EurAsEC and the Central Asian Cooperation Organization (CACO).[148] Even in the states that are not major energy players in their own right—Kyrgyzstan, Tajikistan, and (to some degree) Uzbekistan—the Kremlin has moved to establish Russia as the major supplier and pipeline operator with an eye to promoting economic integration on its own terms.

Russian domination of the energy sector has significantly constrained the Central Asian states' foreign policy autonomy (in contrast to Georgia and Azerbaijan, which rely on the non-Russian BTC and BTE pipelines). Not surprisingly, leaders of several Central Asian republics have sought to regain some of that autonomy by bringing in outside powers to break the Russian stranglehold on their economies—though others do not perceive their dependence on Russia as necessarily problematic. Kazakhstan has been the most successful practitioner of balancing, allowing Western firms to develop its major oil fields, even while much of its gas transportation network remains controlled by the Kremlin. For Georgia (as well as Azerbaijan), the war of August 2008 was a stark reminder that Moscow has not entirely reconciled itself to a loss of influence in the region, despite the existence of pipelines outside its control.[149] The Central Asian leaders perceived the war as altering the region's balance of power, diminishing their enthusiasm for Western-sponsored pipeline projects such as Nabucco. At a minimum, the war seriously complicated efforts to expand the West's energy corridor through the Caucasus by highlighting the region's political (and economic) risks.

With the Western powers unable to offer sufficiently attractive proposals, many Central Asian leaders have looked to China as a potential hedge against overweening Russian influence. With its neighboring location and nearly insatiable appetite for foreign energy, China has emerged as the most important alternative pole of attraction for the Central Asian states. Beijing has tended to see Central Asia's energy infrastructure as a strategic asset for whose acquisition it is willing to pay a premium. The most notable such example is the Chinese National Petroleum Company's August 2005 decision to purchase a controlling stake in Petrokazakhstan, the largest oil company in Kazakhstan, for well above market price.[150] Uzbekistan also signed a deal with Beijing in mid-2007 to construct a new gas pipeline to China, while Turkmenistan is also building a pipeline to the Middle Kingdom.[151]

With the West largely frozen out and a significant Chinese role still in the future, Russia remains the most important player in Central Asian energy politics. Russia's ability to dominate the energy transport routes out of Central Asia is in part a result of strategic opportunism. The United States in particular was slow to recognize the significance of Central Asia as both a battleground in the ideological struggle between Islamism and secularism and a potential alternative to the Middle East (and Russia itself) as a source of energy. Until the late 1990s, the U.S. government viewed Central Asia as a neutral zone, where no outside power exercised a predominant influence as local elites pursued economic development and political stabilization on their own terms.[152] U.S. diplomacy was critical to sustaining support for the construction of BTC, which proved to be an enormously complex and expensive undertaking, but Washington was less successful in tying producers on the east side of the Caspian into the energy corridor it sought to build around Russia and Iran. Unlike Georgia or Azerbaijan, the Central Asian states did not have unresolved territorial disputes that Moscow sought to manipulate; of the Central Asian republics, only Uzbekistan participated in GU(U)AM, and then only temporarily. Worried, too, about the spread of Islamic radicalism, Central Asia's leaders had reason to patch up their disputes with the Russians.

U.S. attention to the economic importance of Central Asia wavered in the aftermath of the invasion of Iraq in 2003. With mounting concerns about Gazprom's ability to produce enough gas to meet its existing contracts, Russia is again moving aggressively into Central Asia, promoting its own pipelines (most notably the Pre-Caspian pipeline from Kazakhstan, designed to undermine the competing Trans-Caspian line backed by Western energy firms) and seeking to deny outsiders direct access to Central Asia's gas. With less attention now being paid to the threat of Islamic extremism in Central Asia, it is energy that remains the most important prize in the geopolitical competition among Russia, China, and the West.

CONCLUSION

While the effects of Russia's more assertive foreign policy have been felt most strongly inside the CIS, the post-Soviet republics have, for the most part, mattered to Moscow primarily insofar as they have become a contested zone between Russia and other major power blocs—the United States and Europe on the one hand, and China on the other. Russia possesses unique advantages in the CIS relative to other parts of the world where it has attempted to exert influence since the end of the Soviet Union. The history of Russian-Soviet control has created a series of cultural, economic, and political linkages that make reliance on Moscow a relatively familiar strategy for the Soviet-trained elites of most CIS countries. Then again, nearly two decades of independence have trained the populations of the post-Soviet states in the habits of independence, including the benefits of maneuvering between competing suitors. With the paradoxical and partial exception of Belarus, none of the Soviet successor states has exhibited a strong inclination to return to provincial status under Moscow—whatever fantasies Russia's Eurasianist fringe may indulge in.

In response to the perception that its periphery was slipping out of its control in a way that posed real threats to its security, the Kremlin responded with an active, assertive, and initially defensive strategy designed to stop the bleeding while it was busy putting its own house in order. The invasion of Georgia was a clear indication that, at last, Russia's leaders were ready to use the full range of tools available to them to restore Russian influence over its former empire. Moscow has made use of tools like the CSTO and the frozen conflict zones to ensure that the non-Baltic states of the former Soviet Union retain a significant degree of dependence on Russia for their military and economic security. Like Putin, Medvedev has been keen to demonstrate Russia's interest in the states of the former Soviet Union, making his first foreign stop as president in Kazakhstan and presiding over the unleashing of Russian military power in Georgia.

Zbigniew Brzezinski's grand chessboard metaphor is nowhere more apt than in the CIS. To be sure, while the Kremlin claims to be playing the same game as its rivals, with influence over the foreign policy orientations of the CIS states the prize, the West has repeatedly been caught off guard through its inability to understand the rules. Western leaders may say that the spread of Western ideals and institutions to the CIS is a natural step in the progression of liberalism and democracy, but Moscow still sees geopolitics around every corner. Not that the West itself has been immune to the lures of geopolitics: the BTC pipeline was a geopolitical tour de force. The problem is that, having played the game (quite successfully) by Russian rules in the past, the West has a credibility problem in Moscow when it announces that the rules have changed now that Russia is itself equipped to play the old game more successfully.

The spread of liberalism and democracy in the CIS has the potential to benefit millions of people, but until such political transformations can be divorced from the competing geopolitical ambitions of the Great Powers, they also pose the danger of deepening instability as well as the progressive deterioration of relations between Russia and the Western powers. That is, if democratization is to spread throughout the CIS, it will have to be an organic, homegrown process, and even then, Moscow will insist that democratic governments respect its interests. Following the war in Georgia, the Western powers look set to adopt a more cautious approach to promoting political change in the region.

The Ukrainian experience proved that democratization can occur without dramatically upsetting the balance of power in the affected region. The standoff between Yushchenko and Yanukovych reflected a real divide in Ukrainian society (and one that appears to exist in most of the non-Russian parts of the CIS) between those who would prefer to remain in the Russian orbit and those favoring closer ties with outside powers as a means of limiting Russian influence, and also demonstrated the value of a democratic system in which the losers can hold onto the hope of coming to power at some point in the future. Only if democratization comes to be valued for its own sake, as an organic result of developments within the affected society and not as a means of installing pro-American or pro-Western regimes, can prospects for a cooperative relationship between Russia and the Western powers in the CIS be realized.

Russia, to be sure, has not sought to completely exclude outside powers from a role in the affairs of the CIS. China is a leader in the SCO, while even NATO has a substantial presence in the CIS through its Partnership for Peace program. Confrontation with outside powers is not a development that stands to benefit Russia, and for that reason it has never been an aim of Russian foreign policy in the region per se. What continues to matter for the Kremlin is the protection of Russian strategic and financial interests. In particular, the expansion of NATO into the former Soviet Union is seen as a profoundly threatening development by many in the Russian political and security establishment. By invading Georgia, Moscow demonstrated it would take vigorous steps to check its loss of influence and that for all their rhetoric, the Western powers' options in the region remain much more limited than Russia's.

NOTES

1. This ambiguity is above all reflected in the politically fraught "Near Abroad [*blizhnoe zarubezh'e*]," used to distinguish the CIS states from the rest of the world (the "Far Abroad"). Though no longer normally employed in official statements, "Near Abroad" can still be found in the Russian academic and popular press.

2. Roy Allison, "The Military and Political Security Landscape in Russia and the South," in *Russia, the Caucasus and Central Asia: The 21st Century Security Environment*, ed. Rajan Menon, Yuri E. Fedorov, and Ghia Nodia (Armonk, NY: M. E. Sharpe, 1999), 42–55; Dmitri Trenin, "Southern Watch: Russia's Policy in Central Asia," *Journal of International Affairs*, Spr 2003, 56(2): 120–22.

3. A country-by-country breakdown of proven reserves of oil and natural gas is available at British Petroleum, "Statistical Review of World Energy, 2007," http://www.bp.com/productlanding.do?categoryId = 6848&contentId = 7033471.

4. The so-called Russia-Belarus Union State has never had much substance. By late 2007, there was some speculation that the union would be upgraded and given a strong executive, presumably so that Putin could take over as chairman and continue to wield power after the end of his term as Russian president. See Fred Weir, "Putin Eyes Full Merger with Belarus," *Christian Science Monitor*, 10 Dec 2007. Under such a scenario, Russia would essentially absorb Belarus.

5. See Pavel K. Baev, "Assessing Russia's Cards: Three Petty Games in Central Asia," *Cambridge Review of International Affairs*, Jul 2004, 17(2): 269–83; Fiona Hill, "Russia's Newly Found Soft Power," *The Globalist*, 26 Aug 2004, http://www.theglobalist.com/StoryId.aspx?StoryId = 4139.

6. Ariel Cohen, "Putin's Foreign Policy and U.S.-Russian Relations," Heritage Foundation Backgrounder #1406, 18 Jan 2001, http://www.heritage.org/Research/RussiaandEurasia/BG1406.cfm. The locations of Russian troop deployments and a full order of battle are available at the Russian Armed Forces website, http://www.geocities.com/pentagon/9059/RussianArmedForces.html. Russian troops withdrew from Georgia (excepting South Ossetia and Abkhazia) by the end of 2007,

before temporarily returning to Georgia proper in the course of the August 2008 war.

7. Sherman W. Garnett, "Europe's Crossroads: Russia and the West in the New Borderlands," in *The New Russian Foreign Policy*, ed. Michael Mandelbaum (New York: Council on Foreign Relations, 1998), 70.

8. According to the 2001 census, 67.5 percent of the inhabitants of Ukraine listed Ukrainian as their native language, versus 29.6 percent who listed Russian. Such statistics require context, however, since most Ukrainians understand Russian, and a large number (including President Yushchenko) speak Russian or a mixed dialect known as *surzhyk* in everyday life. See "Chislennost' i sostav naseleniya Ukrainy po itogam Vseukrainskoi perepisi naseleniya 2001 goda," http://ukrcensus .gov.ua/rus/results/general/language.

9. GUAM (an acronym of its members' names: Georgia, Ukraine, Azerbaijan, Moldova) was formed in 1994 and aimed at (in the words of the organization's charter) "promoting democratic values, ensuring rule of law and respect of human rights; ensuring sustainable development; strengthening international and regional security and stability. . . ." See "Charter of Organization for Democracy and Economic Development GUAM [sic]," 23 May 2006, http://www.guam.org.ua/ 267.0.0.1.0.0.phtml. GU(U)AM has often been seen as a counterweight against Russian influence, even though all of its members are also members of the Commonwealth of Independent States. From 1999 to 2004, the organization was known as GUUAM, reflecting Uzbekistan's decision to join, then leave the group.

10. On the formation and significance of GU(U)AM for Ukraine, see John A. Armstrong, "Ukraine: Evolving Foreign Policy in a New State," *World Affairs*, Sum 2004, 167(1): 34–38. Also see Armstrong, "Independent Ukraine in the World Arena," *Ukrainian Quarterly*, Spr–Sum 1998, 54(1–2): 5–15.

11. See especially Taras Kuzio, "Neither East nor West: Ukraine's Security Policy under Kuchma," *Problems of Post-Communism*, Sep–Oct 2005, 52(5): 59–68.

12. Michael Wines, "Report of Arms Sale by Ukraine to Iraq Causes Consternation," *New York Times*, 7 Nov 2002; Tatyana Ivzhenko, "Kuchme grozit arest," *Nezavisimaya Gazeta*, 18 Nov 2005.

13. Russian Ministry of Foreign Affairs, "Stenogramma vystuplenii Ministrov inostrannykh del Rossii S. V. Lavrova i Ukrainy K. I. Grishchenko po itogam sovmestnogo zasedaniya Kollegii Ministerstv inostrannykh del Rossii i Ukrainy," 28 May 2004.

14. Taras Kuzio, "Russian Policy toward Ukraine during Elections," *Demokratizatsiya*, Aut 2005, 13(4): 492.

15. Adrian Karatnycky, "Ukraine's Orange Revolution," *Foreign Affairs*, Mar–Apr 2005, 84(2): 38–42.

16. For a detailed examination of the Kremlin's participation in the dirty tricks campaign against Yushchenko, see Kuzio, "Russian Policy toward Ukraine during Elections," 493–99. Pavlovsky admitted in a 2007 interview that he had come to Ukraine in 2004 under an agreement between Putin and Kuchma. See "Russian Spin Doctor Views Moscow's Relations with Ukraine, Georgia," *Ukrainska Pravda*, JRL #241, 21 Nov 2007.

17. See Karatnycky, "Ukraine's Orange Revolution," 35–37.

18. Robert Coalson, "Analysis: Kremlin Wary of New Ukrainian President," *RFE/RL Feature*, 24 Jan 2005; Askold Krushelnycky, "Ukraine: Russian President Stops Short of Openly Endorsing Yanukovych During Visit," *RFE/RL Newsline*, 27 Oct 2004.

19. V. Putin, "Vstupitel'noe slovo i otvety na voprosy v khode sovmestnoi press-konferentsii po itogam sammita Rossii-ES," 25 Nov 2004, http://www.kremlin.ru/appears/2004/11/25/2239_type63377type63380_80195.shtml.

20. Colin Powell, State Department Briefing, 24 Nov 2004, http://www.state.gov/secretary/former/powell/remarks/38738.htm. Notably, though, President Bush was more circumspect, refraining from criticism of Russia's role in particular.

21. Tatyana Ivzhenko, "'Oni khotyat delat' iz nashikh lyudei idiotov,'" *Nezavisimaya Gazeta*, 24 Dec 2004.

22. Richard L. Armitage, interview with Oleksandr Tkachenko, Novy Kanal TV, 8 Dec 2004.

23. Matt Kelley, "U.S. Money Has Helped Opposition in Ukraine," *San Diego Union-Tribune*, 11 Dec 2004. According to Kelley, the U.S. government alone spent $65 million on promoting democracy in Ukraine.

24. Dmitri Trenin, "Vneshnee vmeshatel'stvo v sobytiya na Ukraine i rossiisko-zapadnye otnosheniya," Carnegie Moscow Center Briefing 7(2), Feb 2005.

25. Andrew Kuchins, "A Turning Point in US-Russian Relations?" Carnegie Endowment for International Peace (originally published in *Vedomosti*, 20 Nov 2006, 1), http://www.carnegiendowment.org/publications/index.cfm?fa=view&id=18872&prog=zru.

26. Anders Åslund, "Ukraine's Voters Do Not Need Moscow's Advice," *Financial Times*, 11 Nov 2004.

27. "Pavlovsky: U nas ne voznikaet problem s Tymoshenko," RIA-Novosti, 3 Feb 2005, http://www.rian.ru/politics/cis/20050203/17111699.html.

28. "Rossiya namerena kardinal'no izmenit' svoyu politiku na postsovetskom prostranstve," *Izvestiya*, 23 Aug 2005.

29. Alexander Rahr, "Rossiya reabilitiruetsya za Ukrainu," *Izvestiya*, 15 Sep 2005.

30. Ivanna Gorina, "Shutki v storonu," *Rossiiskaya Gazeta*, 13 Nov 2006.

31. Jan S. Adams, "Russia's Gas Diplomacy," *Problems of Post-Communism*, May–Jun 2002, 49(3): 18–19.

32. On Kyiv's charge that Moscow was violating existing agreements, see Mykhailo Krasnyanskiy, "Who Is Blackmailing Whom?" *Ukrayinska Pravda*, 12 Dec 2005, http://pravda.com.ua/en/news/2005/12/12/4919.htm. Moscow also signed a new deal in December 2005 to buy more gas from Turkmenistan, the major supplier in Central Asia, thus reducing the amount of non-Russian gas available to the Ukrainians.

33. A detailed overview of the events leading up to the January 2006 gas cutoff is provided in Nikolai Sokov, "Alternative Interpretations of the Russian-Ukrainian Gas Crisis," Center for Strategic and International Studies, PONARS Policy Memo No. 404, Jan 2006. The cutoff affected not only gas produced inside Russia but also gas originating in Turkmenistan and Uzbekistan that flowed to Ukraine through Russian pipelines.

34. Quoted in Igor Torbakov, "Kremlin Uses Energy to Teach Ex-Soviet Neigh-

bors a Lesson in Geopolitical Loyalty," *Jamestown Foundation Eurasia Daily Monitor*, 2 Dec 2005.

35. Russian Ministry of Foreign Affairs, "Zayavlenie MID Rossii o situatsii v rossiisko-ukrainskikh otnosheniyakh v gazovoi sfere," 1 Jan 2006.

36. Additionally, the agreement specified that Russian gas would be sold to Ukraine through the joint company RosUkrEnergo, which would pay $230 per thousand cubic meters, then mix the Russian gas with cheaper gas from Central Asia before selling it to Naftohaz Ukrainy at $95. The deal also resolved a related Russo-Ukrainian dispute over tariffs paid by Gazprom for the use of Ukraine's pipeline network for moving its gas to Europe. See "Russia: Moscow, Kyiv Announce End of Gas Dispute," *RFE/RL Newsline*, 4 Jan 2006.

37. Tatyana Ivzhenko, "Kiev ugrozhaet Putinu," *Nezavisimaya Gazeta*, 23 Dec 2004.

38. See, for example, Ariel Cohen, "Russia's Gas Attack on Ukraine: An Uneasy Truce," Heritage Foundation Web Memo #954, 4 Jan 2006, http://www.heritage.org/Research/RussiaandEurasia/wm954.cfm; Torbakov, "Kremlin Uses Energy."

39. Judy Dempsey, "Russia Tells Ukraine Gas Price Could Triple," *International Herald Tribune*, 1 Aug 2005.

40. "Dvoinoi standarty 'gazovoi voiny,'" *Izvestiya*, 3 Jan 2006.

41. Russian Ministry of Foreign Affairs, "Intervyu Posla Rossii na Ukraine V. S. Chernomyrdina zhurnalu 'Profil','" 19 Sep 2007.

42. Ivanna Gorina, "Finskii proval," *Rossiiskaya Gazeta*, 30 Oct 2006.

43. Oleg Gavrish and Natalya Grib, "Tsena Oprosa," *Kommersant*, 20 Oct 2006.

44. Yanukovych termed this linkage a completely natural result of the close economic integration between Russia and Ukraine. See Aleksandr Martynenko, interview with Viktor Yanukovych, *Rossiiskaya Gazeta*, 20 Oct 2006.

45. Tony Halpin, "Ukraine Gas Deal Marred by Fears of Dwindling Autonomy," *Times*, 25 Oct 2006. On the Black Sea Fleet, see G. B. Karasin, interview in *Vremya Novostei*, 12 Oct 2007; Russian Ministry of Foreign Affairs, "Otvet ofitsial'nogo predstavitelya MID Rossii M. L. Kamynina na vopros agenstva 'Interfaks' po povodu situatsii vokrug ob"ektov Chernomorskogo flota," 9 Mar 2007.

46. Dmitri K. Simes, "Losing Russia," *Foreign Affairs*, Nov–Dec 2007, 86(6): 47.

47. Charles King, "A Rose among Thorns," *Foreign Affairs*, Mar–Apr 2004, 83(2).

48. M. Mayorov, "South Ossetia: Conflict Zone," *International Affairs: A Russian Journal of World Politics, Diplomacy, and International Relations*, 2002, 48(2): 112, 117. The peacekeepers, dispatched at the end of Georgia's early 1990s civil war, comprised Georgian, South Ossetian, North Ossetian, and Russian detachments. Tbilisi long resented their presence and charged that they were not impartial, especially since three-quarters of the soldiers (i.e., all but the Georgians) were de facto controlled by Moscow. See Vladimir Socor, "JCC, 'Peacekeeping' Formats in South Ossetia Shown to Be Unstable," *Jamestown Foundation Eurasia Daily Monitor*, 26 Oct 2005.

49. See Andrei Terekhov, "Demokraticheskaya missiya Kondolizy," *Nezavisimaya Gazeta*, 19 Apr 2005.

50. "Shevardnadze Accuses Soros of Financing Coup d'Etat in Georgia," *Pravda.ru* (English), 1 Dec 2003, http://newsfromrussia.com/world/2003/12/01/51582.html.

51. See Pavel Zarifullin, "Pri chem zdes' Saakashvili?" *Russkii Kur'er*, 6 Nov 2006.

52. NATO agreed to offer Georgia an "intensified dialogue" with the aim of eventual membership in September 2006.

53. Sergey B. Ivanov, "International Security in the Context of the Russia-NATO Relationship," speech to Fortieth Munich Conference on Security Policy, 7 Feb 2004, http://www.securityconference.de/konferenzen/rede.php?menu_2005 = & menuekonferenzen = &sprache = en&id = 126&.

54. Mikheil Saakashvili, "The Way Forward: Georgia's Democratic Vision for the Future," *Harvard International Review*, Spr 2006, 71–72.

55. Alexander Y. Skakov, "Russia's Role in the South Caucasus," *Helsinki Monitor*, 2005, (2): 121.

56. Ahto Lobajakas, "CIS: Referendums Seen as Kremlin's Master Plan," *RFE/RL Feature*, 20 Sep 2006. The South Ossetian and Abkhaz conflicts have also influenced the debate in the U.S. government about backing Georgia's candidacy for membership in these organizations. See "Background Briefing by Senior Administration Officials on the NATO Summit," 29 Nov 2006, http://www.whitehouse.gov/news/releases/2006/11/20061129-4.html.

57. Stephen Erlanger, "Yeltsin Voices Russia's Anger at Ethnic Wars Roiling the Old Soviet Empire," *New York Times*, 22 Jun 1992. The International Crisis Group estimates 180,000–200,000 ethnic Georgians fled Abkhazia in the course of the 1991–1992 conflict. Almost none of them has returned.

58. On the dispute over Russian peacekeepers, see Aleksandr Gol'ts, "Voennoe mirotvorchestvo Rossii," *Pro et Contra*, Sep–Dec 2006: 65–74; Christine Ben Bruusgaard, "Budushchee rossiiskikh mirotvortsev," Moscow Carnegie Center Briefing, Jun 2007, 9(2). The South Ossetian peacekeepers were dispatched in 1992 with the assent of both Tbilisi and Tskhinvali, although the Georgian side began calling for their withdrawal in 2000. See Mayorov, "South Ossetia," 117.

59. Putin suggested holding referenda on the fate of Abkhazia and South Ossetia in a joint press conference with Saakashvili following their negotiations in St. Petersburg in June 2006. "Press-konferentsiya po okonchanii vstrechi s Prezidentom Gruzii Mikhailom Saakashvili," http://www.kremlin.ru/text/appears/2006/06/107067.shtml.

60. On the Russian response to Kosovo's independence, see Sergei Lavrov, "Stenogramma press-konferentsii Ministra inostrannykh del Rossii S. V. Lavrova, Zheneva, 12 fevralya, 2008 goda," 12 Feb 2008.

61. See Andrei Ryabov, "Gruzino-abkhazskii tupik," *Pro et Contra*, Sep–Dec 2006: 35–36.

62. See Theresa Freese, "Abkhazia: At War with Itself," *Transitions Online*, 6 Dec 2004.

63. Arkady Dubnov, "Razmorozhennaya druzhba," *Vremya Novostei*, 12 Feb 2004.

64. "Press-konferentsiya po okonchanii vstrechi s Prezidentom Gruzii Mikhailom Saakashvili."

65. Ariel Cohen, "Saakashvili Visits Washington amid Heightening Geopolitical Tension in the Caucasus," *EurasiaNet Insight*, 24 Feb 2004, http://www.eurasianet.org/departments/insight/articles/eav022404.shtml.

66. Oleg Zorin and Gennady Sysoev, "Moskva podstraivaetsya pod Mikhaila Saakashvili," *Kommersant*, 19 Jan 2004.

67. Seth Mydans, "Georgia's President Risks Showing Warlord Who's Boss," *New York Times*, 18 Mar 2004.

68. "Georgia's Leader Declares Victory After Rebel Flees," *New York Times*, 6 May 2004.

69. When Chechen fighters sought refuge in Kodori in mid-2001, Moscow accused the Georgian government of aiding the separatists. Russian troops, along with pro-Russian Abkhaz militiamen, drove the Chechens out militarily while Tbilisi protested the Russian incursion as a violation of its sovereignty. After the Chechens left, Shevardnadze's government deployed Georgian forces to the area over the opposition of Moscow (and the Abkhaz leadership in Sukhumi). The UN eventually negotiated a withdrawal agreement in the spring of 2002, though Russian forces made an abortive attempt to return later that year, nearly starting a firefight with the Georgians. See Keti Bochorishvili, "Georgia: Fear and Poverty in the Kodori Gorge," Institute for War & Peace Reporting, 31 May 2002, http://iwpr.net/?p=crs&s=f&o=160838&apc_state=henicrs2002.

70. Ryabov, "Gruzino-abkhazskii tupik," 33–34.

71. Jean-Christophe Peuch, "Caught between Russia and Georgia, South Ossetia Rift Widens," *RFE/RL Feature*, 14 Nov 2007.

72. The Georgian Foreign Ministry linked the arrest of the Russian officers with the participation of both South Ossetian and Abkhazian leaders in a Russian-sponsored economic forum in Sochi. See Vladimir Solov'ev, "Zapad na vorot," *Kommersant*, 2 Oct 2006.

73. See Yury Simonyan et al., "Tbilisi proshel tochku vozvrata," *Nezavisimaya Gazeta*, 29 Sep 2006.

74. "Georgia: Hundreds Left Stranded after Deportations from Russia," *RFE/RL Feature*, 17 Oct 2006.

75. Sergei Ivanov, interview with Vesti Nedeli TV, 8 Oct 2006, JRL #230.

76. "Putin Fury at Georgia 'Terrorism,'" BBC News, 2 Oct 2006, http://news.bbc.co.uk/2/hi/europe/5397102.stm. The sociopathic Beria was an ethnic Mingrelian from Abkhazia (which was then part of the Georgian SSR). Putin's remark thus carried the implication that in political terms Saakashvili was Beria's descendant.

77. "Vnutrenyaya diplomatiya," *Kommersant*, 6 Oct 2006.

78. Claire Bigg, "Is Moscow Behind Georgian Unrest?" *RFE/RL Feature*, 14 Nov 2007; Sergei Lavrov, interview with *Rossiiskaya Gazeta*, 28 Sep 2007.

79. Sergei Lavrov, "Zayavlenie Ministra inostrannykh del S. V. Lavrova na press-konferentsii dlya rossiiskikh i zarubezhnykh SMI v svyazi s situatsiei v Yuzhnoi Ossetii," 8 Aug 2008, http://www.mid.ru/brp_4.nsf/2fee282eb6df40e643256999005e6e8c/82bf30d2efb07313c325749f005cede0?OpenDocument.

80. Dmitry Medvedev, "Zayavlenie v svyazi s situatsiei v Yuzhnoi Ossetii," 8 Aug 2008, http://www.kremlin.ru/appears/2008/08/08/1522_type63374type63378type82634 ...205027.shtml.

81. By and large, the looting and attacks on civilians appear to have been the work of the irregular South Ossetian militias rather than the Russian military, which in places worked to stop the depredations (and in others did nothing). Sabrina Tavernise, "Signs of Ethnic Attacks in Georgia Conflict," *New York Times*, 14 Aug 2008.

82. Andrew E. Kramer, "Peace Plan Offers Russia a Rationale to Advance," *New York Times*, 13 Aug 2008. The cease-fire agreement negotiated by Sarkozy was ambiguous on the question of troop withdrawals. While calling on both Tbilisi and Moscow to withdraw their forces to prewar positions, it permitted Russia to station peacekeepers in designated regions abutting South Ossetia and Abkhazia, where they were allowed to take unspecified "additional security measures." Moscow refused Sarkozy's attempts to modify this provision of the cease-fire. It eventually withdrew forces from Georgia proper but kept them in the "independent" enclaves of South Ossetia and Abkhazia.

83. Adeeb Khalid, *Islam After Communism: Religion and Politics in Central Asia* (Berkeley, CA: University of California Press, 2007), 153–58.

84. Jeronim Perovic, "From Disengagement to Active Economic Competition: Russia's Return to the South Caucasus and Central Asia," *Demokratizatsiya*, Win 2005, 13(1): 62.

85. See Kathleen Mihalisko, "Yeltsin's CIS Decree: An Instrument for Regaining Russia's Superpower Status," *Jamestown Foundation Prism*, 6 Oct 1995, 1(21), http://jamestown.org/publications_details.php?volume_id = 1&issue_id = 84&article_id = 984.

86. Dina Malysheva, "Konflikty u yuzhnykh rubezhei Rossii," *Pro et Contra*, 2000, 5(3): 7–32; Roy Allison, "Strategic Reassertion in Russia's Central Asia Policy," *International Affairs*, 2004, 80(2): 285–86.

87. On the significance of these visits, see Lena Jonson, *Vladimir Putin and Central Asia: The Shaping of Russian Foreign Policy* (London: I. B. Tauris, 2004), 65.

88. For an overview of the IMU's 1999 invasion of Kyrgyzstan and firsthand reporting of the event, see Aleksandr Kim, "Batkenskaya voina 1999: Kak eto bylo na samom dele," *TsentrAziya.ru*, 30 Aug 2002, http://www.centrasia.ru/newsA.php4?Month = 8&Day = 30&Year = 2002. See also Igor Rotar, "The Islamic Movement of Uzbekistan: A Resurgent IMU?" *Jamestown Foundation Terrorism Monitor*, 18 Dec 2003, 1(8).

89. Jonson, *Vladimir Putin and Central Asia*, 70–71.

90. "Kremlin Adviser Explains Putin's Decision to Ally with West," RFE/RL Report, 10 Oct 2001.

91. Leonid F. Ryabikhin, "Rossiya i Zapad: Soderzhanie i perspektivy vzaimootnoshenii," in *Rossiya i Zapad posle 11 sentyabrya*, materials from roundtable sponsored by Russian Academy of Sciences European Institute (Moscow: RAN-Institut Evropy, 2002), 68–69.

92. Alan Kasaev and Armen Khanbabyan, "Den' velikogo peredela," *Nezavisimaya Gazeta*, 20 Sep 2001. See also Jonson, *Vladimir Putin and Central Asia*, 85–86.

93. For a brief history of the IMU, see Mark Burgess, "In the Spotlight: Islamic Movement of Uzbekistan (IMU)," CDI Terrorism Project, 25 May 2002, http://www.cdi.org/terrorism/imu.cfm.

94. "Russia to Establish Air Base in Kyrgyzstan, Deals Blow to U.S. Strategic Interests in Central Asia," *EurasiaNet Eurasia Monitor*, 3 Dec 2002, http://www.eurasianet.org/departments/insight/articles/eav120302.shtml.

95. V. Putin, "Zayavlenie dlya pressy po itogam rossiisko-kirgizskikh peregovorakh," 24 Apr 2006, http://www.kremlin.ru/appears/2006/04/24/1828_type63377type63380_104861.shtml.

96. Russia's initial assent to the American presence in both Kyrgyzstan and Uzbekistan was predicated on the understanding that the deployment of U.S. troops in the region would be temporary.

97. Aleksandr Zhelenin, "Sud'bu voennoi bazy reshit referendum," *Nezavisimaya Gazeta*, 5 Jun 2007; Aleksandr Knyazev, "Vashington v Kirgizii ne dostig zhelaemogo rezul'tata," *Nezavisimaya Gazeta*, 15 May 2007.

98. See Charles Carlson, "Kyrgyzstan: President Defends Russian Presence in Central Asia," *RFE/RL Newsline*, 24 Sep 2003; Pavel Felgenhauer, "Moscow Hopes Crisis Will Drive Bakiyev Back into Russian Camp," *Jamestown Foundation Daily Monitor*, 8 Nov 2006.

99. Trenin, "Southern Watch," 121–22. See also Putin's autobiography. Vladimir Putin, *Ot pervogo litsa: Razgovory s Vladimirom Putinim* (Moscow: Vagrius, 2000), 135–37.

100. Khattab, the Saudi-born leader of the Chechens' Arab sympathizers, was poisoned by the Russian security services in March 2002. Maskhadov, the relatively moderate president of the Republic of Ichkeria (Chechnya), was killed in murky circumstances in March 2005. Basaev, by far the most notorious of the Chechen field commanders and the man responsible for the most spectacular acts of terrorism in the Chechen conflict (including the 1995 Budyennovsk hospital seizure, the 1999 invasion of Dagestan, the 2002 Dubrovka theater siege, and the 2004 Beslan school seizure), died in an explosion in July 2006. The FSB claims its agents detonated a truck full of explosives driving next to Basaev's car, while Chechen rebel sources claim the truck explosion was an accident. See Sergei Mashkin, "Shamilya Basaeva ubila firmennaya bomba," *Kommersant*, 13 Jul 2006.

101. Quoted in Flemming Splidsboel-Hansen, "A Grand Strategy for Central Asia," *Problems of Post-Communism*, Mar–Apr 2005, 52(2): 49.

102. See Richard Weitz, "Averting a New Great Game in Central Asia," *Washington Quarterly*, Sum 2006, 29(3): 158–60.

103. Ilan Berman, "The New Battleground: Central Asia and the Caucasus," *Washington Quarterly*, Win 2004, 28(1): 64. The Russian Military Doctrine is available in English at http://www.fas.org/nuke/guide/russia/doctrine/991009-draft-doctrine.htm.

104. See Russian Ministry of Foreign Affairs, "Kontseptsiya sotrudnichestva gosudarstv-uchastnikov Sodruzhestva Nezavisimykh Gosudarstv v bor'be s terrorizmom i inymi nasil'stvennymi proyavleniyami ekstremizma," 26 Aug 2005.

105. "Korotko: Evraziiskii NATO," *Nezavisimaya Gazeta*, 17 May 2002.

106. Richard Weitz, "The CIS Is Dead: Long Live the CSTO," *Central-Asia Caucasus Monitor*, 8 Feb 2006, http://www.cacianalyst.org/?q=node/3725.

107. Nurshat Ababakirov, "The CSTO Plans to Increase Its Military Potential," *Central Asia-Caucasus Institute Analyst*, 17 Sep 2008; "NATO-CSTO cooperation advisable—Lavrov," Interfax, 10 Dec 2008, http://www.interfax-news.com/3/453633/news.aspx.

108. V. Putin, "Zayavlenie dlya pressy i otvety na voprosy zhurnalistov po okonchanii zasadaniya Soveta kollektivnoi bezopasnosti," 14 May 2002, http://www.kremlin.ru/appears/2002/05/14/0000_type63374type63377type63380 ...28902.shtml.

109. CSTO, "Zayavlenie Parlamentskoi Assemblei Organizatsii Dogovora o Kollektivnoi Bezopasnosti ob Izmenenii Konfiguratsii Voennogo Prisutstviya NATO v Evrope," http://www.dkb.gov.ru/start/indexb.htm.

110. "CSTO Condemns Georgia's Actions in S. Ossetia, Backs Russia," RIA-Novosti, 5 Sep 2008, http://en.rian.ru/russia/20080905/116583797.html.

111. Berman, "The New Battleground," 65.

112. U.S. Department of Energy, "Kazakhstan Country Analysis Brief 2007," http://www.eia.doe.gov/emeu/cabs/Kazakhstan/Background.html. See also Jeffrey Mankoff, "Energy Security in Eurasia," Council on Foreign Relations Special Report, Oct 2008.

113. Perovic, "From Disengagement," 69–70. Lukoil and Gazprom are collaborating in a joint venture with Kazakhstan's energy monopoly Kazmunaigaz to develop a major field along the Russo-Kazakh border, while Lukoil is the largest foreign investor in Kazakhstan.

114. Russian Ministry of Foreign Affairs, "Interv'yu ofitsial'nogo predstavitelya MID Rossii A. V. Yakovenko agenstvu 'Interfaks' po rossiisko-kazakhstanskim otnosheniyam," 20 Apr 2004.

115. Berman, "The New Battleground," 65; "Kazakh, Russian Security Council Chiefs Sign Annual Cooperation Plan," RFE/RL Newsline 11 Feb 2004.

116. Russian Ministry of Foreign Affairs, "Press-konferentsiya Prezidenta Rossii V. V. Putina i Prezidenta Kazakhstana N. A. Nazarbaeva po itogam rossiisko-kazakhstanskikh peregovorov," 4 Apr 2006.

117. Condoleezza Rice, "Remarks at Eurasian National University," 13 Oct 2005, http://www.state.gov/secretary/rm/2005/54913.htm.

118. Doulatbek Khidirbekughli, "U.S. Geostrategy in Central Asia: A Kazakh Perspective," Comparative Strategy, 2003 (22): 160–61.

119. Sergei Kulikov, "Kazakhstanskaya neft' poplyvet v obkhod," Nezavisimaya Gazeta, 9 Aug 2007.

120. See Stephen Blank, "U.S. Interests in Central Asia and Their Challenges," Demokratizatsiya, Sum 2007, 15(3): 320.

121. Weitz, "Averting a New Great Game," 157.

122. See Charles E. Ziegler, "The Russian Diaspora in Central Asia: Russian Compatriots and Moscow's Foreign Policy," Demokratizatsiya, Win 2006, 14(1): 111–12.

123. In the 1990s, Tashkent intervened repeatedly in the affairs of its neighbors, ignoring Russian interests in the process. In the Tajik civil war, for instance, it supported a faction (the Khojandis) opposed by the Russian government. See Mukhammed-Babur Malikov, "Uzbekistan: A View from the Opposition," Problems of Post-Communism, Mar–Apr 1995, 42(2).

124. Aleksei Mironov, "Plany Moskvy nikogo ne udivili v Tashkente," Nezavisimaya Gazeta, 25 May 2000.

125. Vladimir Mukhin, "Pentagon v Tashkente," Nezavisimaya Gazeta, 28 Sep 2001.

126. "Khanabad, Uzbekistan: Karshi-Khanabad (K2) Airbase Camp Stronghold Freedom," http://www.globalsecurity.org/military/facility/khanabad.htm; "Uzbekistan Places One Airbase at U.S. Disposal," RFE/RL Newsline, 9 Oct 2001.

127. "Joint Statement between the Government of the United States of America

and the Government of the Republic of Uzbekistan," 12 Oct 2001, http://www
.state.gov/r/pa/prs/ps/2001/5354.htm.

128. "Declaration on the Strategic Partnership and Cooperation Framework between the United States of America and the Republic of Uzbekistan," 12 Mar 2002, http://www.state.gov/p/eur/rls/or/2002/11711.htm.

129. Bruce Pannier, "U.S. Alliance Leaves Tashkent Feeling Confident (Part 1)," *RFE/RL Feature*, 12 Oct 2001, http://www.rferl.org/features/2001/10/1210200 1114721.asp.

130. Perovic, "From Disengagement to Active Economic Competition," 70.

131. Russian Ministry of Foreign Affairs, "Dogovor o strategicheskom partnerstve mezhdu Rossiiskoi Federatsiei i Respublikoi Uzbekistan," 16 Jun 2004.

132. Andrew Tully, "Uzbekistan: U.S. Criticizes Both Sides in Unrest," *RFE/RL Feature*, 17 May 2005. The words were spoken by U.S. State Department spokesman Richard Boucher.

133. "Karimov Nixes International Probe into Andijon Crackdown," EurasiaNet, 20 May 2005, http://www.eurasianet.org/departments/insight/articles/pp051805 .shtml.

134. Daniel Kimmage, "Analysis: The Discrete Charm of 'Non-Interference' in Uzbekistan," *RFE/RL Feature*, 18 May 2006, http://www.rferl.org/featuresarticle/ 2006/05/90b78341-c3d8-4a5b-8de4-c54b1b4a0 cac.html.

135. Aleksei Bausin, "Tashkent dal Vashingtonu na vyvod voisk 180 dnei," *Izvestiya*, 1 Aug 2005.

136. Ekaterina Grigorieva, "ShOS vystupilo protiv chuzhikh voennykh baz," *Izvestiya*, 6 Jul 2005.

137. Russian Ministry of Foreign Affairs, "Stenogramma otvetov Ministra inostrannykh del Rossii S. V. Lavrova po itogam vizita v Uzbekistan," 21 Oct 2005.

138. Gulnoza Saidazimova, "Uzbek Membership in Russia-Led Group Comes amid Isolation from West," *RFE/RL Report*, 30 Jan 2006.

139. Russian Ministry of Foreign Affairs, "Zayavlenie dlya pressy Prezidenta Rossii V. V. Putina i Prezidenta Uzbekistana Islama Karimova po itogam rossiisko-uzbekskikh peregovorov," 15 Nov 2005. See also Russian Ministry of Foreign Affairs, "Dogovor o soyuznicheskikh otnosheniyakh mezhdu Rossiiskoi Federatsiei i Respublikoi Uzbekistan," 14 Nov 2005.

140. Russian Ministry of Foreign Affairs, "Zayavlenie dlya pressy Prezidenta Rossii V. V. Putina i Prezidenta Uzbekistana Islama Karimova po itogam rossiisko-uzbekskikh peregovorov," 15 Nov 2005.

141. Vladimir Socor, "Uzbekistan Accedes to Collective Security Treaty Organization," *Jamestown Foundation Eurasia Daily Monitor*, 27 Jun 2006, http://www.james town.org/edm/article.php?article_id=2371223.

142. Adam N. Stulberg, *Well-Oiled Diplomacy: Strategic Manipulation and Russia's Energy Statecraft in Eurasia* (Albany, NY: State University of New York Press, 2007).

143. Daniel Kimmage, "Turkmenistan: The Achilles Heel of European Energy Security," *RFE/RL Feature*, 30 Jun 2006, http://www.rferl.org/featuresarticle/ 2006/06/d07bcab3-c72d-4eaa-a1eb-456b146c0 859.html.

144. "Indiya voznamerilas' 'peresest" na turkmenskuyu gazovuyu trubu," *Izvestiya*, 10 Nov 2007; "Turkmenistan Threatens Gas Cutoff to Russia After Talks Fail," *RFE/ RL Newsline*, 29 Jun 2006.

145. Russian Ministry of Foreign Affairs, "Zayavlenie dlya pressy Prezidenta Rossii V. V. Putina i Prezidenta Uzbekistana I. Karimova po itogam rossiisko-uzbekskikh peregovorov," 15 Nov 2005.

146. Russian Ministry of Foreign Affairs, "Intervyu ofitsial'nogo predstavitelya MID Rossii A. V. Yakovenko agenstvu 'Interfaks' po rossiisko-kazakhstanskim otno-sheniyam," 20 Apr 2004.

147. "'LUKOIL' i 'Gazprom' budut rabotat' v Kazakhstane, Uzbekistane, i Ukraine ruka ob ruku," *Izvestiya*, 16 Nov 2004.

148. Perovic, "From Disengagement to Active Economic Competition," 71–72.

149. Indeed, much discussion of Russian war aims centered on the fate of the BTC/BTE pipelines. Some Western analysts asserted either that Russian forces had deliberately attacked the pipelines or that gaining direct control of them (by ousting Saakashvili in place of a pro-Russian leader in Tbilisi and intimidating Baku into falling in line) was part of Moscow's long-range plan.

150. See Keith Bradsher and Christopher Pala, "China Ups the Ante in Its Bid for Oil," *New York Times*, 22 Aug 2005.

151. "Kitai zaruchilsya 'gazovoi podderzhkoi' Uzbekistana," *Izvestiya*, 2 May 2007.

152. See Eugene Rumer, "SShA i Tsentral'naya Aziya posle 11 sentyabrya," *Kosmo-polis*, Spr 2003, (3). This view of Central Asia was associated in particular with Bill Clinton's deputy secretary of state, Strobe Talbott, an expert in Russian and post-Soviet affairs.

Conclusion

Dealing With Russia's Foreign Policy Reawakening

The August 2008 war in Georgia is a good place to end a story about post-Soviet Russia's foreign policy reawakening. The war encapsulated several features of the grand strategic vision underlying Russian foreign policy in the post-Soviet era. The conflict highlighted Russia's resurgence as a major power, at least in its own region, capable of employing overwhelming force to protect its perceived interests even in the face of international condemnation, and cemented Russia's identity as a state outside the confines of the collective known as the West. While the source of the war lay in Georgia's attempts to uncouple its history from that of Russia, its impact resonated far beyond the Caucasus in part because of Russia's evolving position in the Great Power concert that represents the primary plane for Russian foreign policy maneuvering. The war was therefore as much about sending a message to outside powers like the United States and the European Union about the reality of Russia's resurgence as it was about punishing the way-ward Georgians.

The attainment of Russia's Great Power ambitions requires the rest of the world to give Moscow the deference it feels is due to one of the leading world powers. Failure to do so has long been a leading cause of Russian resentment and revisionism toward the post–Cold War order. Indeed, the Georgian war cannot be understood without reference to the whole series of perceived slights Moscow endured at the West's hands since the end of the Cold War, with the struggle over Kosovo's independence having the most immediate bearing on the Russia-Georgia conflict. In understanding Russia's foreign policy behavior, the substance—or validity—of these objections is in a sense less important than the very fact of their existence.

Of course, Moscow has objected to a range of policy choices undertaken by outside powers (especially in the West) since the breakup of the Soviet Union. August 2008, however, was the first time the Russian Federation used force outside its own borders in an attempt to block developments it opposed, in this case, the assertion of Georgian control over South Ossetia, and more broadly Georgia's aspiration to join NATO. It did so in large part because the balance of power between Russia and the states that supported Saakashvili has changed fundamentally since the beginning of the twenty-first century.

Between Moscow's disdain for Saakashvili, interest in keeping the frozen conflicts frozen, and opposition to NATO expansion, in a sense its war with Georgia was overdetermined. The real question then is not why Georgia, but why August 2008? Some factors, of course, were contingent, including the timing of Saakashvili's attempt to retake the rebellious province. Still, the extent of Russian military preparations and the steady campaign to raise tensions in both South Ossetia and Abkhazia in the weeks leading up to the conflict attest to a high degree of preparation on the Russian side. Moscow may not have known when Saakashvili would try to seize the breakaway provinces, but it seemed intent on provoking him to do so—a trap about which the U.S. and other Georgian allies repeatedly cautioned him.[1] If the timing of Saakashvili's ill-conceived move into South Ossetia was contingent, however, the broader forces at work were not. By August 2008, many Russians had come to believe that the country's post-Soviet recovery had succeeded, that the economic upheavals of the 1990s and the decay of Russian military power had been reversed during the period of consolidation under Putin.

Russian elites never stopped believing that the Near Abroad was for Moscow a zone of special interest and responsibility, a point Medvedev merely made explicit in the aftermath of the 2008 war.[2] Russia's temporary cession of initiative to outside powers in the region was always more a result of Russian weakness than any sort of more fundamental transformation in the nature of the Russian state or the way its leadership identified its interests.

As a powerful state lacking natural frontiers, Russia has throughout its entire history viewed having some measure of control over the states along its borders as a condition necessary for its security. The forceful assertion of Russian interests in Georgia was thus also a familiar response by a post-imperial state to the loss of colonial outposts. It is worth remembering that Russia never existed as a self-contained national state. Lacking both natural frontiers and ethnic cohesion, its borders have expanded and contracted with the power of the state. Since Ivan IV (the Terrible) conquered the Muslim khanates of Kazan and Astrakhan in the mid-sixteenth century, Russia was an empire, and its imperial legacy continues to inform Russia's foreign policy debate. Russian rulers never stopped trying to expand the frontiers of that empire until the end of the Soviet Union (even if much of the USSR's empire was informal and based on the rule of indigenous Communist parties whose ultimate loyalty was to the Kremlin).

Sometimes, the drive to expand outstripped the economic, political, and military capabilities of the state, with catastrophic results. Like the Russian Empire in 1917, the Soviet Union in the mid-1980s found that its imperial commitments exceeded its capacity to pay for them. Facing rising opposition to Communist rule in Eastern Europe and military defeat in Afghanistan, Mikhail Gorbachev made the bitter but necessary decision to embark on a period of retrenchment. Gorbachev ordered Soviet troops out of Afghanistan and told his counterparts in East Germany, Poland, and elsewhere that the Red Army would no longer prop them up. Without their Soviet minders, these Communist outposts crumbled with astonishing rapidity. The process of disintegration soon spread to the Soviet Union itself, and Soviet troops found themselves called on to put down demonstrations in Tbilisi, Vilnius, and elsewhere on the USSR's fringes. But the empire, as then constituted, could not be saved.

Still, even without the other fourteen Soviet republics, the Russian Federation was itself a massive patchwork that reflected the centuries-long process of expansion responsible for its creation. To a Russian in Moscow, the distinction between North Ossetia, which remained part of the Russian Federation, and South Ossetia, which was part of the now independent state of Georgia, could seem somewhat arbitrary. Indeed, the entire CIS, whose economy was intimately tied to that of Russia and whose populations shared a common Soviet (and largely Russophone) culture, remained bonded to Moscow by a common past, and in those states with a significant Russian population, by ties of ethnicity. Two decades after the Soviet collapse, those bonds have only partially loosened.

Establishing a new paradigm for relations between the Russian Federation and the other republics of the former USSR has been in many ways the most challenging aspect of Russia's strategic evolution since 1991. Slowly and painfully, Russia is shedding the burden of its imperial past. The colored revolutions, especially those in Ukraine and Georgia, marked a crisis of legitimacy for Russian influence in the former Soviet Union, even as that influence was coming under pressure from the stepped-up American and Chinese presence, as well as the consolidation of non-Russian (or even anti-Russian) national identities in many of the post-Soviet successor states. Moscow's decision to move to market prices for gas sales to the CIS states, a step precipitated by the fiasco of its attempts to head off the Orange Revolution, was a critical step in the emergence of a postimperial framework for relations between Russia and its onetime dependencies.

The war in Georgia in 2008 showed both the successes and the failures of this evolution. On the one hand, important constituencies in the Russian security establishment argued—successfully—for intervention, believing that Georgia remained a less than fully sovereign country by virtue of its past as a Russian/Soviet dependency. It was also easy to believe that Putin, who famously remarked that the collapse of the USSR was "the greatest geopolitical catastrophe of the [twentieth] century," was interested in reversing the verdict of Russia's imperial collapse.[3]

Yet despite Russia's overwhelming military triumph and the clear inability of outside powers to influence the course of events, Moscow did not follow an explicitly imperial strategy during and after the war. It refused calls to annex South Ossetia and Abkhazia, which were left in a kind of legal and political limbo. Nor did Russian forces advance on Tbilisi, much less seek to incorporate Georgia into the Russian state. Russian bête noire Saakashvili remained in office (though Moscow sought to undermine his authority, which was waning anyway as a result of the suffering brought on by his own rashness). For all these reasons, Georgia in 2008 was not Kazan in 1552, or even Czechoslovakia in 1968. If anything, Russia's actions in the Caucasus looked much more like the kind of interventions long undertaken by the U.S. in Latin America or France in La Francophonie, that is, the actions of a Great Power claiming an exclusive sphere of influence in an area where it has strong historical links.

To be sure, the world is much changed in the four decades since Soviet tanks put an end to the Prague Spring, and even in the two decades since the fall of the Berlin Wall. Imperialism as such is no longer a viable modus operandi for states, even along their borders. During the Georgian conflict, not only the United States and Europe, but even China cautioned Moscow about the danger it was courting if it pushed too far. For Russia, a country with an almost insatiable desire to be taken seriously as a pillar of the international order, throwing away whatever respectability it had accumulated through the careful husbanding of resources and cautious diplomacy merely to teach the Georgians a lesson would be a step of breathtaking rashness. Foreign diplomats, including U.S. Secretary of State Rice, cautioned Moscow that the very goals it had sought for a decade plus to attain were at risk thanks to its unilateral, disproportionate, and misleading actions against Georgia.[4] Russia's convoluted response to such outside pressure was an indication that strong divisions continue to exist in Moscow about whether to prioritize relations with the outside world or to focus on Russia's special role inside the former Soviet Union.

In other words, the debate between Eurasianists and others remains very much a part of the Russian political scene, notwithstanding former president Putin's success at imposing a veneer of uniformity at the top. This debate is at once about the proper vector for Russian foreign policy, but at the same time, it reflects differing understandings of how to attain that which the bulk of the Russian elite desires, namely for Russia to be acknowledged and respected as a serious international actor. For the Eurasianists, who appear to have played a key role in fomenting and propagating the conflict in Georgia (South Ossetian "president" Eduard Kokoity is a member of Dugin's International Eurasianist Movement, and Dugin himself championed both the war and Russia's decision to recognize the breakaway enclaves), the war was a vindication of their belief that the West will take Russia seriously only when Russia stands up for itself. Indeed, Dugin favors an intensification of Russian pressure on Georgia and across the South Caucasus, which he sees as the front line in an American attempt to encircle and destroy Russia as a Great Power.[5]

The Eurasianists and their supporters in government were at best indifferent about how the West responded to the invasion. They did not see integration with Western-dominated institutions like the WTO as holding any particular value to Russia anyway. Most of them would just as soon proceed with the construction of a statist, corporatist, and autarkic economic system based on the state-controlled energy sector as well as a series of newly created state conglomerates (many controlled by *siloviki*) in fields including weapons production, nanotechnology, high-tech exports, atomic energy, infrastructure construction, development banking, and residential utilities.[6] An attempt to alter the geopolitical status quo, like attempting to fast-track Georgia and Ukraine for membership in NATO, would give the extremists a perfect excuse to intensify the conflict over the fate of other parts of the CIS. Given the West's anemic response to the invasion of Georgia, the Eurasianists are confident further instability would only play into their hands. Ukraine in particular could fragment if forced to decide once and for all whether to throw in its lot with Russia or with NATO, and Dugin's followers would be happy to encourage the process of fragmentation if the West gives them an opportunity to do so.[7]

For the opponents of Eurasianism, the critical imperative in war's aftermath was to contain the fallout on Russia's broader international relationships. Putin and Medvedev did not appear to see the war as a fundamental reversal of Russia's strategy of seeking good relations with the West to the extent that doing so is in line with the broader objective of promoting Russia's claim to Great Power status. Arguments against the war, or at least arguments in favor of its sharp limitation, focused on the need for Russia to maintain its position as a respected member of the international community. For instance, the centrist military analyst Andrei Piontkovsky suggested parallels between Russia's invasion of Georgia and the way 1930s Germany used limited military adventures against its neighbors to prove its geopolitical resurgence. As Piontkovsky pointed out, Germany found itself lured by easy success, believing that the outside world would never, under any circumstances, stand up to aggression.[8]

While Russian troops appeared initially to be staying in Georgian territory in violation of the cease-fire agreement negotiated by French president Sarkozy, their gradual withdrawal coupled with attempts on the part of Putin and Medvedev to turn down the heat in their exchanges with the Western powers showed the limited appetite for Dugin's schemes at the top levels of power. The war in Georgia notwithstanding, Putin and Medvedev made clear that they wanted to continue cooperating with the United States in Afghanistan, where they perceived the resurgence of the Taliban as a direct threat to their own interests; that they wanted to continue making progress on the arms control agenda; and that they wanted to continue pursuing economic integration despite the suspension of some commitments made as part of WTO ascension talks.[9] Dugin's talk of an almost apocalyptic confrontation between Russia and the United States is not realistic, as most Kremlin officials seem to understand.[10]

If the conflict in Georgia was partially about vindicating Russians' belief in their special responsibility for the area of the former Soviet Union, it was also about changing the contours of Russia's relationship with the West. For nearly two decades, the fundamental challenge confronting Russian diplomacy lay in figuring out how to manage relations with a West that was at the end of the Cold War the world's dominant political, military, economic, and ideological bloc. Much of what the West stood for—prosperity, stability, and security—was appealing to Russians fresh off the tumultuous experience of the Soviet 1980s. Yet neither Kozyrev nor anyone else in the Russia of the early 1990s could snap his fingers and make Russia a Western country. Indeed, the trade-offs that would have been necessary for Russia to truly join the West were more than the country's political class was willing to make—in contrast to post-Communist states like Poland and Hungary, with their ties to the Catholic/Protestant world and their recent experiences of Russian domination.

With the option of following the Eastern Europeans into the arms of the West foreclosed for both domestic and foreign policy reasons, the Russian elite spent much of the next decade trying to articulate another model for its interactions with this collection of wealthy and powerful states whose motivations often remained obscure. From the Russian vantage point, the language of human rights, employed by NATO to justify its military intervention in Serbia in 1999, appeared a useful tool to justify what seemed to be of a piece with the Alliance's long-standing desire to contain Russian power.

The 9/11 attacks provided Moscow with an opening to suggest that the Chechen conflict was part of a larger struggle between radical Islamism and a secular, pluralistic worldview shared by Russia and the Western powers. The attacks allowed Russia, with Putin in the lead, to argue that the fundamental distinction in world politics was no longer between the West and the non-West, but between those who abetted terrorists and those who did not, a framework that fit neatly with George W. Bush's famous statement that "either you are with us, or you are with the terrorists." Moscow was essentially aiming to, in Medvedev's words, "once and for all put an end to the division in the world that was created by the Cold War."[11]

By adopting Bush's global war on terror as an organizing principle for relations with the West, Putin attempted to refashion the relationship from one based on integration to one based on the idea of partnership. Such a partnership would rest on an acknowledgment by the U.S. that Russia was, in essence, an equal. It would not be hectored about its pummeling of Chechnya, any more than it would hector Washington about the latter's tactics in Afghanistan. It would grant Washington its cooperation—including access to facilities in Central Asia—but it would do so as a matter of choice and with the right to terminate its cooperation when it no longer served Russian interests. Looking back on Primakov's promotion of multipolarity as a description of the structure of international relations, it would assert its position as a pole.

Nonetheless, the Russian leadership was smart enough to realize that even in a multipolar world, all poles are not created equal. Only the U.S. had the capacity to be a truly global power, capable of projecting significant force far from its borders, as in Afghanistan, Iraq, and elsewhere. Russia, however well it had recovered from the ravages of the 1990s, was not in that league. Unlike the Soviet Union, it would not seek to project its power and influence globally. It would, in fact, stand down from some of its more far-flung commitments, such as the military outposts it had inherited at Cam Ranh Bay, Vietnam, and Lourdes, Cuba. It would, though, proclaim its special interest in the former Soviet Union and demand that the United States, the European Union, and even China respect its primacy in that region. And since the partnership on offer was a classic bit of realpolitik, Moscow would not allow its new partners to intervene with their liberal democratic moralizing in the Russian sphere of influence. Unlike the Kozyrev era, this offer of partnership was not based on the idea of Russia seeking integration in the existing security architecture, but on an agreement negotiated between states with a limited range of common interests.

To the extent that Putin's Russia had a grand strategy, its hallmarks were state-driven economic development, the employment of Russia's newfound wealth to rebuild the foundations of national power (military, political, and economic), and a concerted effort to minimize conflicts with the other Great Powers to allow Russia time to recover from the upheavals of the 1990s. Russia, of course, had followed a similar pattern after past catastrophes like the Crimean War or the Russo-Japanese War. Putin was well aware of that history and of the role played by men like Gorchakov and Stolypin in restoring Russia to what they considered its rightful place as one of the world's major powers. The conscious emulation of these prerevolutionary statesmen, along with the creation of a hypertrophied state apparatus alongside a (reasonably) vibrant private economy led many analysts to see in "Putin's project" a form of tsarist restoration.

Yet neither the tsarist nor the Soviet experience offers modern Russia a viable foreign policy model. The Russian Empire was a perpetually revisionist power. The tsars continually pushed Russia's frontiers outward, impervious to considerations of ethnicity. From the sixteenth to the nineteenth centuries, Russia's frontier continually expanded, taking in everyone from Poles in the West to Mongols and Evenks in the East. The emergence of modern nationalism in the second half of the nineteenth century was a development for which Imperial Russia, like the German, Austrian, and Turkish empires, was ill prepared. Nationalism emerged, of course, not only among the minority peoples of the Russian Empire, but among its largest ethnic contingent, the Russians themselves. This development of nationalism as a political force among Russians and others spelled the end for the empire's traditional strategy of expansion and amalgamation on the basis of dynastic loyalty.

The importance of ethnic Russian national sentiment has often been overlooked. Russian nationalism was long subsumed by the multinational Soviet Union, which downgraded the national claims of ethnic Russians in the interest of reconciling the country's non-Russian population to Soviet rule. The Soviet Union could function as an empire precisely because it claimed to be non-Russian. Despite its occasionally violent manifestations, the re-emergence of Russian ethnic nationalism as a potent force in modern Russian politics and society also reflects the transition away from an imperial identity in favor of belief in a self-contained national state.[12] In a postimperial world, in short, Putin (and Medvedev) cannot, like Gorchakov or Stolypin, restore Russian power simply to embark on a new quest for expansion.

Nor like the leaders of the Soviet Union can they seek to build an ideologically cohesive bloc of states to challenge the supremacy of the liberal Atlanticist West—though Dugin and his followers might hope otherwise. No doctrine has emerged to replace Marxism-Leninism as a potentially universalist alternative to capitalist globalization. Eurasianism has few adherents outside the former Soviet Union; within the former USSR, more states worry about a potential Russian threat to their independence than about alleged Western designs to contain Russia. Likewise, Russian nationalism by its nature has a rather limited constituency and is liable to generate more hostility than influence among states with significant Russian minorities such as Ukraine, Kazakhstan, Latvia, and Estonia.

Globally, the most powerful challenge to liberalism and capitalism is posed by radical Islam. Though Russia has on the order of twenty million Muslim inhabitants, a country that consciously appropriates symbols of

Orthodox Christianity (such as the three-barred cross impaling an Islamic crescent found atop many Russian churches) and that is more than 80 percent Orthodox cannot aspire to a leading role in an international Islamist movement merely to spite the West. And despite Samuel Huntington's worries about Orthodoxy forming the nucleus of a non-Western civilizational identity, the Orthodox world is far too fragmented (the Orthodox Greeks, Bulgarians, Romanians, and eventually, Serbs and Montenegrins are members of the EU, and the first three are also in NATO) and too heterogeneous to form the nucleus of an anti-Western bloc.[13]

One other possible way Russia could seek to create a counterhegemonic bloc of states is on the basis of authoritarianism itself. Some scholars have noted that as democracy becomes an increasingly important factor uniting its practitioners, nondemocratic states find they have a common interest in preventing the spread of democracy.[14] Indeed, Russia and, especially, China have found themselves on the same side of a number of critical international issues, in part for this reason. Moscow and Beijing share an aversion to the notions of humanitarian intervention and democracy promotion. Both prefer to work through the UN Security Council, which gives them the power to veto initiatives they see as threatening. Both moved to block the U.S.-led invasion of Iraq as well as intervention in Sudan's Darfur region out of a desire to preserve the veneer of absolute sovereignty protecting even the most odious regimes from interference in their internal affairs. Through organizations like the SCO, Russia and China have formed a group that to some appears the nucleus of a new authoritarian international.

Yet authoritarianism as such is hardly an idea capable of forming a broad international consensus. China, for instance, may have a political system that denies the public much in the way of meaningful participation in government. Yet, in contrast to Russia, China has clearly and unambiguously thrown in its lot with a world of economic globalization and is seeking to expand public participation in government even as Russia seeks to restrict it. In some ways, China's view of the international order has more in common with that of the Western powers than with that of Russia.[15] Political upheaval, of the sort Russia unleashed with its invasion of Georgia, is inimical to the Chinese belief in order and stability as the essential factors enabling it to achieve a peaceful rise. Beijing was appalled by the hypocrisy of Russia's Georgian adventure; as the Chinese recognized, to matter as a principle in international relations, state sovereignty and inviolability have to apply equally as much to Georgia as they do to Serbia or Iraq. With its own separatist dramas in Tibet and Taiwan, China had no interest in legitimating Russia's territorial revisionism.

Authoritarianism, in other words, is not a coherent worldview like Marxism-Leninism (and even when Marxism-Leninism still mattered, the Sino-

Soviet split demonstrated how national rivalries could crop up independent of ideological affinity). Despite its authoritarian tendencies, China has more to gain from partnering with the West in a globalized world than from seeking to overturn a global order that has made it one of the fastest-growing, most dynamic countries in the world in just over a generation. Only an extraordinary string of mistakes by the West could unite Russia and China in a counterhegemonic bloc based on a shared commitment to authoritarianism.

The last remaining possible partners for a Russia that seeks to challenge the prevailing global order as the Soviet Union once did are those states that have by their own behavior isolated themselves from the international mainstream. Iran under its theocratic regime is one option (and one in which Dugin places particular hopes). Still, Iran is unstable, its "mullahocracy" deeply unpopular. In a generation, Iran may look much different from its present incarnation. Other rogue states, such as North Korea, are in even worse shape. Hugo Chávez's Venezuela has been happy to tweak the Americans at every opportunity but still sells them oil. In any case, Venezuela is at best a third-rate power. Most importantly, a partnership with global outcasts on the basis of opposition to American, or liberal Atlanticist, hegemony would be a strange way for Russia to pursue its long-standing aim of becoming a powerful and respected member of the global community.

In short, Russia has few choices apart from seeking some kind of modus vivendi with the existing world order in which the United States is gradually losing its unquestioned dominance but is nonetheless the leading power and, in partnership with Europe, China, Japan, and others operates an increasingly globalized economy. Autarkic fantasies may of course appeal to some Russians, but certainly those who like their bank accounts in Switzerland or Cyprus and their villas in London understand what they stand to lose were Russia to retreat from the Atlanticist world that so many of Dugin's acolytes condemn. Russia is not, and may never be, part of the West as such, but its only choice is between isolation and increasing irrelevance on the one hand, and seeking to participate, Chinese-style, in a system it did not design but from which it can nonetheless benefit on the other. In his more multilateralist moments, Putin has made clear his preference for a Russia that follows this path to prosperity and respect. Medvedev, the lawyer, has been even more pronounced in his calls for Russia to pursue economic integration even as it seeks its own path in cultural, geopolitical, and institutional terms.[16]

Since appearing onstage as Yeltsin's designated successor in 1999, Putin—now in partnership with Medvedev—has pursued some variant of this strategy, seeking to return Russia to the ranks of the world's Great Powers and ensuring its voice is heard on a wide range of issues (above all, those connected with the fate of the former Soviet Union). Neither Putin nor Medvedev has shown an inclination to follow Dugin into a real confrontation with the United States or the West. Their goal has been, and remains, partnership, but only on terms acceptable to Russia—which is to say on terms that Russia itself has a hand in defining.

Two interconnected dangers threaten this vision: the rise of rejectionist sentiment among important elements of the Russian elite, and a misplaced desire to punish and isolate Russia on the part of the West. In geopolitical terms, the war in Georgia was dangerous precisely because it strengthened both of these tendencies. Taking advantage of the power transition in Moscow, Eurasianist hard-liners seem to have sensed an opportunity to go after Saakashvili, striking a blow at his patrons in the West at the same time. After some initial vacillation, the untested Dmitry Medvedev fell into line, such that even Dugin was driven to praise the new president's tough response.[17] That even Russia's president, a man invested with enormous constitutional powers on paper, could not overawe or outmaneuver those who would embark Russia on such a perilous adventure does not speak well for the balance of forces in the Kremlin's hall of mirrors. Once the consequences of the war for Russia's international standing and economic stability had become clear, however, Medvedev actively sought to reassure the West (and Western investors) of Russia's commitment to stability, order, and progress.

Yet the Western impulse to assign blame and punishment for the Georgia crisis solely to Russia risks only emboldening such atavistic forces inside Russia itself. To be fair, the Bush administration was relatively careful to point out Saakashvili's own poor judgment and excessive use of force against South Ossetia as factors contributing to the conflict and was very limited in its attempts to punish the Russians. The most substantive step, cancellation of an accord on civilian nuclear cooperation, will affect the U.S. as much as Russia. Still, insofar as the war came in the midst of an election season in the United States, it facilitated a substantial amount of posturing by political candidates eager to demonstrate their toughness— American missteps in the war on terror and in Iraq having not entirely succeeded in convincing the U.S. political class that toughness and statesmanship are not always the same. Prominent among the proposed U.S. responses were suggestions to expel Russia from the G8, abolish the NATO-Russia Council, or fast-track NATO membership for Ukraine and Georgia.[18] Notably, Democrat Barack Obama, who was elected to succeed George W. Bush as president of the United States in November 2008, had adopted a much more nuanced view of the fighting in Georgia than his Republican challenger John McCain. Even though most Russians were skeptical that Obama could rapidly bring about an improvement in ties between Washington and Moscow, they appreciated that his election offered an opportunity to break with many of the failed policies of the past.

Western, especially U.S., policy in the aftermath of the Georgian crisis needs to focus on shaping the terms of the debate under way within the Russian elite about how to make use of Russia's newfound strength, which was put on display so dramatically during the fighting in Georgia. Seeking to isolate Russia, as McCain and many other U.S. politicians and academics called for, would indeed send a clear message to Moscow—namely, that the West is unwilling to live with and accommodate itself to a powerful Russia. Doing so would push Russia further toward the isolation and autarky favored by the likes of Dugin.

One important reason why that path remains attractive has to do with the fact that the Russian elite (and much of the broader public as well) has derived personal benefit from the country's post-Soviet evolution. As long as oil and gas prices were rising alongside the Russian standard of living, it was easy for many Russians to channel their energies into material consumption. The aftermath of the Georgia war proved just how fragile Russian prosperity was; the stock market lost close to half its total value in barely a month, and trading had to be halted repeatedly in the autumn of 2008 to avoid greater damage. Amid what appeared to be the beginning of a global recession, oil prices dropped from over $140 a barrel to below $50. Russia, which failed to diversify its economy during the flush times, faced the prospect of a deep recession.[19] With memories of the 1998 default still raw for many, the prospect of renewed economic instability at least raised questions about the durability of Russia's Putin-era consolidation.

Given Russia's still-stratified socioeconomic makeup, it was the surviving oligarchs who caught the initial brunt of the downturn. With many oligarchs forced to turn to the state for financial assistance, the officials behind Kremlin, Inc. had an opportunity to scoop up strategic assets at bargain prices. Sechin in particular was responsible for coordinating the seizure of industrial assets from the oligarchs as the price of bailing them out.[20] In the short run, at least, the economic crisis looked set to strengthen the consolidation of state control over key industrial sectors, with implications for Russia's willingness to accept the rules of economic globalization. Of course, Russia was not alone in using the crisis to extend state ownership, but in a world where money is tighter than it had been for the decade leading up to 2008, Moscow ultimately may find itself forced to step back from extensive state control in order to keep its economy competitive. Such would be the case especially if energy prices remain low (especially if oil trades at under $70 per barrel) for an extended period.

In the long run, Russia may well have little choice but to participate constructively in a globalized world; the question is what happens in the interim (it has been said that Germany miraculously evolved from a militaristic empire into a liberal democracy in the span of only half a century—except that the half century in question was marred by the two world wars Germany started). Like Germany after World War I, a Russia that is deliberately excluded and isolated will turn inward on itself, becoming more authoritarian and more aggressive. The Western powers' ability to shape Russian political development is limited, particularly in terms of domestic politics. In terms of foreign policy though, the West has a much greater capacity to shape Russian behavior, for good or ill.

NATO expansion is perhaps the most salient example from the past two decades of how, with the best of intentions, Western leaders succeeded in marginalizing Russia and succoring the most atavistic, anti-Western elements of the Russian elite. The much stronger Russia of the early twenty-first century will need to be handled with much greater care than the West paid to the decrepit Russia of the 1990s. The United States and Europe need to show Russia that it can have what it most craves—respect, recognition, and responsibility for upholding order around the world—without having to resort to force or threats of force to make itself heard. A Russia that feels itself backed into a corner and in need of lashing out isolates itself (as during the war in Georgia) but also creates suffering and instability for others. In part, that means being open to rethinking the question of how Russia should fit into the institutional web comprising Europe.

Ever since Peter the Great ordered his boyars to cut their beards and trade their caftans for suits, Russia has struggled to define its identity as a state (and a civilization) between Europe and Asia. Momentous as the end of the Cold War was, it was hardly sufficient to achieve that which Peter and his successors never fully accomplished and make Russia into a truly Western country. The ambition to do so on the part of men like Kozyrev, not to mention many Western leaders at the time, seems hopelessly quixotic from the vantage point of the early twenty-first century. Policy makers in Moscow, Washington, Brussels, and elsewhere need to acknowledge that Russia's integration with the West, if it ever happens, is a project requiring a generation or more to reach fruition. In the interim, policy makers will, to paraphrase former U.S. defense secretary Donald Rumsfeld, have to work with the Russia that they have rather than the Russia they would like to have.

Without abandoning its unique identity or Great Power aspirations, Russia can play a constructive role in the world. China is (largely) already doing so. As its economy starts taking off, India is beginning to as well. The Great Powers of the twenty-first century will not be the Great Powers of the twentieth century, though Russia, like the United States, may be fortunate enough to play a leading role in both. It will do so on its own terms, which for now means a rejection of norms-based institutions in favor of bilateral relationships and Great Power bargaining, and a focus on power maximization attained, for now, largely through channeling energy rents to the state.

Dealing with this Russia will require the West to reach out to Moscow, seeking to make it a partner in promoting mutual security wherever possible. It also requires the West to be firm about its own values and identity. The West's success has been as much a result of its commitment to democracy, the rule of law, and political liberalism as anything else. Western leaders should not compromise on these fundamental values, including in their dealings with Russia. Europe, for instance, should look skeptically at Gazprom's dealings on the continent not because Gazprom is Russian, but because it is a nontransparent monopolist. There is no need for Europe to discriminate against Gazprom or other Russian companies as long as the Europeans are clear and consistent about enforcing their own laws, whether the target is Gazprom or Microsoft.

In security terms, the West has largely failed to reach a workable compromise with Russia. With the failure of integration as a strategy, the fallback option has far too often been confrontation on the model of the Cold War. Western talk about punishing Russia, whether over the decision to cut gas supplies to Ukraine or over the invasion of Georgia, bears an unfortunate whiff of Cold War thinking, where every Russian action has to breed an equal and opposite Western reaction. Russia poses a significant challenge for Western diplomacy, but so, too, do other large states like China, India, South Africa, Brazil, Mexico, Pakistan, and many more. Russia is hardly unique in this regard, apart from its nuclear arsenal. Yet habits of thinking about Russia dating from the Cold War have made it much harder for the West to elucidate a new framework for dealing with Russia that does not involve either isolating and containing Russia or seeking its complete merger with the ideological and institutional apparatus of the West.

Successfully managing relations between the West and Russia will require moving beyond the rather simplistic framework that sees Russia as either an ally or an enemy. That framework overlooks the central thrust of the dominant worldview existing in Russia itself, namely, that Russia is one Great Power among many that must look out for itself in a world dominated by the principle of self-help. This outlook makes it well-nigh impossible for Russia to be a full member in a West that is moving haltingly into the posthistorical world envisioned by Francis Fukuyama almost two decades ago. But neither does it doom Russia and the West to constant confrontation, as during the Cold War.

Since the end of the Cold War, the U.S. and Europe have struggled to settle on a narrative to describe what is happening in a Russia that is no longer a rival but is neither an ally, and to form a coherent policy for dealing with it. For all its ambiguity, the notion of a strategic partnership between Russia and the Western powers may offer the best hope for maximizing cooperation and minimizing the scope and consequences of the inevitable disagreements. For understandable reasons, Russia wishes to remain outside of the West's institutional framework. Yet problems ranging from nuclear security to counterterrorism to energy security cannot be solved without active Russian participation. Securing Moscow's cooperation will, however, require the U.S. and EU to take Russian concerns seriously and to occasionally make difficult concessions.

Having too often tried to insulate themselves from Russia's maddening complexities, the U.S. and Europe need to reach out to Moscow, seeking a model of integration that simultaneously respects Russia's stature and does not require the Western powers to sacrifice their own values. While the concept being sold seems flawed, the Bush administration's attempts to overcome Russia's suspicions about its European missile defense program offer some lessons about building bridges to Moscow. First, whether or not the system was designed to check Russian capabilities, important constituencies in Moscow (especially the military) believed it was. Russian post–Cold War solipsism means that any major hard power initiative will be seen as somehow directed against Russia. That said, the Bush administration's willingness to address Russian concerns patiently yet firmly almost succeeded in finding a mutually acceptable compromise (agreement was ultimately derailed by the conflict in Georgia). Despite its fears about its deterrent capacity being eclipsed, Russia proposed a series of plausible alternatives, including offering to build a joint antimissile system involving Russian radar facilities.

As also with the issue of Iran's nuclear program, where the Russians offered to maintain custody of fuel for the Iranian reactors throughout its use for power production, the fact that Russia's interests (as the Kremlin chooses to define them) differ from the interests of the Western powers does not mean that compromise is impossible. The Russian leadership has proposed creative solutions to a number of problems where it has not been given sufficient recognition or follow-up by a West that too often sees Russia intent on playing the role of spoiler. Treating Russia as a real strategic partner would mean acknowledging the likelihood that differences will continue to exist while encouraging Moscow to make a positive contribution to resolving them.

Sometimes, of course, agreement about an issue will remain out of reach no matter what. Further NATO expansion may prove to be such an issue. The process of NATO expansion, now long under way, need not stop simply out of deference to Russian wishes. The countries of the former Soviet Union, like their neighbors in Eastern Europe, are fully sovereign members of the international community. As such, they should have the right to determine their own orientation to Europe's dominant security organization. Geographical considerations as well as NATO's ability and willingness to provide new members with the credible security guarantee that lies at the heart of the Atlantic Alliance will matter, too. While the prospect of membership should not be automatically foreclosed for additional post-Soviet states, neither should NATO rush into admitting new members that are not ready to undertake the burdens of collective security that membership implies or whose own publics are not strongly behind ascension. For instance, Ukraine, which like Georgia was promised future membership by the 2008 Bucharest summit, needs to develop a domestic consensus that joining NATO is in the national interest before the Alliance makes an offer to Kyiv. President Yushchenko's promise that Ukraine will hold a referendum on membership is an encouraging sign, though it is one that his successors—whether pro- or anti-NATO—may not feel bound to follow.

Equally important, NATO and its current members must do all they can to make the process of expansion less explosive in relations with Moscow. Doing so means being more explicit about the nature of the challenges NATO is designed to confront in the twenty-first century, and also beginning to take seriously Russian proposals for some kind of broader security pact. In the early 1990s, the hope was that Russia itself would eventually make its way into NATO. In the early twenty-first century, that prospect looks exceedingly remote: Russia's authoritarian political system disqualifies it, and few Europeans or Americans would seriously contemplate extending NATO's Article 5 collective security guarantee all the way to the Russo-Chinese frontier (a prospect to which Beijing would no doubt object strenuously). For a time, Moscow hoped to use the OSCE as an alternative, only to sour on the idea when the OSCE began openly criticizing the conduct of Russian elections.

That experience shows the importance of separating domestic politics from international security, where the Western powers have direct interests at stake. Medvedev's proposal for some kind of pan-European security arrangement, which was made before the outbreak of hostilities in Georgia, is an alternative that deserves a serious hearing. To be sure, Washington and Brussels have to be careful that any Russian approach, especially to Europe, does not come at the expense of transatlantic ties or the effective functioning of NATO. For these reasons, the new security organization proposed by Medvedev in July 2008 has little chance of being accepted in the form presented.[21]

Still, the basic idea of building a security system that embraces Russia more comprehensively than existing institutions such as the NATO-Russia Council is one to which the U.S. and Europe should pay more attention. NATO, with its proven collective security track record, should be central to this program of engaging Russia on security issues such as arms limitation, nuclear proliferation, terrorism, counternarcotics, and other transnational issues.[22] A more active effort on the part of NATO to engage and address

Russia would also help build trust between Moscow and the Atlantic Alliance, especially if NATO chooses to increase its emphasis on such nontraditional security threats. The West in general, and NATO in particular, suffer from a credibility problem in Russia, and it will take a more concerted campaign to convince Moscow that NATO does not harbor aggressive designs against it and that indeed it can benefit Russia through a kind of enhanced partnership. And as former U.S. ambassador to Ukraine Steven Pifer notes, a process of engagement leading to better NATO-Russian relations would be among the most effective ways of ameliorating Russian hostility to the idea of bringing Ukraine and Georgia into NATO.[23]

Another area where Russia needs to be engaged is on the issue of energy security.[24] For the foreseeable future, Europe will continue to depend on Russia and Gazprom for the efficient operation of its economy. In the long run, Europe needs to develop alternatives, including non-Russian hydrocarbon sources (from the Middle East, North Africa, and Central Asia) and postcarbon sources of power such as wind and, perhaps, nuclear power. For the time being, though, Europe needs to find ways of making Russia a reliable partner in the energy market. Europe should thus develop incentives to encourage greater Russian oil and gas production to insure against forecasted shortfalls.

Pipelines like Nord Stream and South Stream are mainly problematic from the standpoint of particular countries, such as Poland, that would be bypassed. The solution is not to block the pipelines' construction or keep Russia out of European energy markets, but to ensure that Moscow does not gain untoward leverage against Poland, Ukraine, and other Eastern European gadflies. Energy market integration (potentially including states on the EU's borders like Ukraine) is the most effective answer, albeit difficult to achieve in practice. Strong leadership from Brussels, as well as from the United States, will be needed to overcome the resistance of European energy firms as well as individual countries that benefit from the status quo. At the same time, Russian participation in European markets needs to be predicated on observance of EU rules on competition and transparency. Gazprom need not be singled out, but it should be made to follow the same rules as everyone else, especially regarding disclosure and the unbundling of its refining and transportation assets.

The war in Georgia (in which Medvedev's role remains unclear) was at once the culmination of changes under way in Russia for over a decade and a sharp break with the recent past insofar as it represented Moscow's first bid to use force to overturn the verdict of 1991. For the West, the war should serve as a wake-up call about the risks of alienating and ignoring Russia. Europe in particular cannot be secure as long as it seeks security in opposition to Russia. The Russia created by Putin and inherited by Medvedev may be an increasingly difficult partner for Europe and the

United States, but it must be a partner nonetheless. Russia's identity and self-perception as one of a handful of Great Powers in a multipolar world is too well entrenched. So are the political and economic foundations of Russian power despite the downturn of late 2008–2009.

Hoping for a return to the Russia of the 1990s, the Russia of Yeltsin and Kozyrev, is fruitless. Instead, the West must get used to dealing with a new, more powerful, and more confident Russia that has not entirely freed itself of the baggage accumulated during its imperial and Soviet past, regardless of the economic crisis overtaking the country at the start of 2009. The West should do what it can to encourage Russia's transformation into a responsible stakeholder in the international system, even while standing up for its own interests and values. Above all, the West must understand that the Russians themselves will determine what kind of country they will have in the twenty-first century and how that country will interact with the rest of the world.

NOTES

1. For a discussion of these provocations and the Georgian reaction, see Daniel Fried, "U.S.-Russia Relations in the Aftermath of the Georgia Crisis," testimony to U.S. House Committee on Foreign Affairs, 9 Sep 2008.

2. Dmitry Medvedev, "Interv'yu Dmitriya Medvedeva telekanalam 'Rossiya,' Pervomu, NTV," 31 Aug 2008, http://www.kremlin.ru/appears/2008/08/31/1917_ type63374type63379_205991.shtml.

3. Putin's remark was made during his 2005 annual address to parliament. Putin, "Poslanie Federal'nomu Sobraniyu Rossiiskoi Federatsii," 25 Apr 2005, http://www.kremlin.ru/appears/2005/04/25/1223_type63372type63374type826 34_87049.shtml.

4. Condoleezza Rice, "Secretary Rice Addresses U.S.-Russia Relations at the German Marshall Fund," 18 Sep 2008, http://www.state.gov/secretary/rm/2008/09/ 109954.htm.

5. Marlène Laruelle, "Neo-Eurasianist Alexander Dugin on the Russia-Georgia Conflict," *Central Asia-Caucasus Analyst*, 3 Sep 2008.

6. Clifford Gaddy, "How Not to Punish Moscow," *Newsweek*, 23 Aug 2008; Dmitry Butrin, "Tsarevye dary," *Kommersant Vlast'*, 24 Dec 2007; Ilya Amladov and Polina Ivanova, "'Oboronprom' poshel v nastuplenie," *Kommersant*, 27 Dec 2007.

7. Aleksandr Dugin, "Russian Nationalist Advocates Alliance against the U.S.," interview with *Los Angeles Times*, 4 Sep 2008.

8. Megan K. Stack, "Russia Sees Georgia Outcome as Proof of Its Dominance," *Los Angeles Times*, 25 Aug 2008.

9. "Russia Still Seeks WTO Membership, Broader Ties with EU," RIA-Novosti, 2 Sep 2008, http://en.rian.ru/russia/20080920/116989116.html.

10. "What the Russian Papers Say," RIA-Novosti, 19 Sep 2008, http://en.rian.ru/ analysis/20080919/116976285-print.html.

11. Dmitry Medvedev, "Vystuplenie na Konferentsii po mirovoi politike," 8 Oct 2008, http://www.kremlin.ru/text/appears/2008/10/207422.shtml.

12. Eduard Solovyev, "Russian Geopolitics in the Context of Globalization," in *Russia and Globalization: Identity, Security, and Society in an Era of Change*, ed. Douglas W. Blum (Washington, DC: Woodrow Wilson Center, 2008), 303.

13. In his well-known book on the clash of civilizations, Huntington does see Orthodoxy as one of the civilizational blocs that will emerge in the twenty-first century as the world increasingly fragments along cultural lines. See Samuel Huntington, *The Clash of Civilizations and the Remaking of World Order* (New York: Touchstone, 1996), 72–80, 163–67.

14. See especially Robert Kagan, *The Return of History and the End of Dreams* (Washington, DC: Carnegie Endowment for International Peace, 2008).

15. See Anne-Marie Slaughter's statement to *The Economist*'s online debate over the consequences of the Georgian war, http://www.russiablog.org/2008/09/the_economist_hosts_oxfordstyl.php.

16. See especially Dmitry Medvedev, "Vystuplenie na V Krasnoyarskom ekonomicheskom forume 'Rossiya 2008–2020. Upravlenie rostom,'" 15 Feb 2008, http://www.medvedev2008.ru/performance_2008_02_15.htm.

17. Dugin, "Russian Nationalist."

18. For several months after the end of active hostilities, the U.S. blocked meetings of the NATO-Russia Council, a move denounced by Moscow as unhelpful. "U.S. Blocks NATO's Activities—Russian Envoy," *Russia Today*, 23 Sep 2008.

19. Clifford J. Levy, "Stock Slump Imperils Putin's Effort to Pump Up Russian Wealth, and His Legacy," *New York Times*, 12 Oct 2008.

20. Clifford J. Levy, "In Hard Times, Russia Tries to Reclaim Industries," *New York Times*, 8 Dec 2008.

21. Judy Dempsey, "Russian Proposal Calls for Broader Security Pact," *New York Times*, 28 Jul 2008.

22. Steven Pifer, "What Does Russia Want? How Do We Respond?" Lecture at Texas A&M University, 11 Sep 2008, http://www.brookings.edu/speeches/2008/0911_russia_pifer.aspx.

23. Ibid.

24. See Jeffrey Mankoff, "Energy Security in Eurasia," Council on Foreign Relations Special Report, Jan 2009.

Bibliography

Ababakirov, Nurshat. "The CSTO Plans to Increase Its Military Potential." *Central Asia-Caucasus Institute Analyst,* 17 Sep 2008.

Adams, Jan S. "Russia's Gas Diplomacy." *Problems of Post-Communism* 49(3) (May–Jun 2002).

Allison, Roy. "The Military and Political Security Landscape in Russia and the South." In *Russia, the Caucasus and Central Asia: The 21st Century Security Environment,* edited by Rajan Menon, Yuri E. Fedorov, and Ghia Nodia. Armonk, NY: M. E. Sharpe, 1999.

———. "Strategic Reassertion in Russia's Central Asia Policy." *International Affairs* 80(2) (2004).

Ambrosio, Thomas. *Challenging America's Global Pre-eminence: Russia's Quest for Multipolarity.* Aldershot: Ashgate, 2005.

———. "The Geopolitics of Demographic Decay: HIV/AIDS and Russia's Great-Power Status." *Post-Soviet Affairs* 22(1) (Jan–Mar 2006).

American Enterprise Institute. "Russian Oil and U.S. Energy Security." 6 Mar 2003, http://www.aei.org/events/filter.all,eventID.254/transcript.asp.

Arbatov, Aleksei G. *Rossiiskaya natsional'naya ideya i vneshnyaya politika (mify i real-nosti).* Moscow: Moskovskii obshchestvennyi nauchni fond, 1998.

———. "Russia's Foreign Policy Alternatives." *International Security* 18(2) (Aut 1993): 5–43.

———. "Russian National Interests." In *Damage Limitation or Crisis? Russia and the Outside World,* edited by Robert D. Blackwill and Sergei A. Karaganov. Washington, DC: Brassey's, 1994.

Arbatova, Nadezhda. "L'échéance de 2007 et l'état des relations politiques entre la Russie et l'UE." Institut Français des Relations Internationales (IFRI), Russie.Nei.-Visions (20).

———. "'Problema-2007': Chto dal'she?" *Rossiya v global'noi politike* (1) (Jan–Feb 2006).

Arkhangel'sky, Yu., and P. Yermolaev. "Politicheskaya elita i strategicheskie priori-tety RF: Mezhdu 'metologicheskim idealizmom' i 'naivnym realizmom.'" *Miro-vaya ekonomika i mezhdunarodnye otnosheniya* (11) (Nov 2006).

Armitage, Richard L. Interview on Novy Kanal TV with Oleksandr Tkachenko, 8 Dec 2004.

Armstrong., John A. "Independent Ukraine in the World Arena." *Ukrainian Quarterly* 54(1–2) (Spr–Sum 1998): 5–15.

———. "Ukraine: Evolving Foreign Policy in a New State." *World Affairs* 167(1) (Sum 2004).

Aron, Leon. "The Foreign Policy Doctrine of Postcommunist Russia and Its Domestic Context." In *The New Russian Foreign Policy*, edited by Michael Mandelbaum. New York: Council on Foreign Relations, 1998.

———. "Putin-3." *AEI Russia Outlook*. 16 Jan 2008, http://www.aei.org/publica tions/filter.all,pubID.27367/pub_detail.asp.

Åslund, Anders. *How Capitalism Was Built*. New York: Cambridge University Press, 2007.

———. "Putin's Lurch toward Tsarism and Neoimperialism: Why the United States Should Care." *Demokratizatsiya* (16) (Win 2008): 17–25.

———. *Russia's Capitalist Revolution: Why Market Reform Succeeded and Democracy Failed*. Washington, DC: Peterson Institute for International Economics, 2007.

———. "Russia's Economic Transformation under Putin." *Eurasian Geography & Economics* 45(6) (Sep 2004): 397–420.

———. "Russia's Energy Policy: A Framing Comment." *Eurasian Geography & Economics* 47(3) (May–Jun 2006): 321–8.

———. "Russia's WTO Ascension." Testimony at the Hearing on EU Economic and Trade Relations with Russia, European Parliament Committee on International Trade. 21 Nov 2006, http://www.iie.com/publications/papers/paper.cfm?Re searchID = 686.

Avdonin, Vladimir. "Rossiiskaya transformatsiya i partnerstvo s Evropoi." *Kosmopolis* 4(6) (Win 2003–2004).

Azfal, Amina. "Russian Security Policy." *Strategic Studies* 25(1) (Spr 2005).

Baburin, S. N. *Territoriya gosudarstva: Pravovye i geopoliticheskie problemy*. Moscow: Izd-vo MGU, 1997.

Baev, Pavel K. "Assessing Russia's Cards: Three Petty Games in Central Asia." *Cambridge Review of International Affairs* 17(2) (Jul 2004): 269–83.

———. "The Evolution of Putin's Regime: Inner Circles and Outer Walls." *Problems of Post-Communism* 51(6) (Nov–Dec 2004): 3–13.

———. "Putin's Court: How the Military Fits In." Center for Strategic and International Studies PONARS Policy Memo #153, Nov 2000.

———. "The Trajectory of the Russian Military: Downsizing, Degeneration, and Defeat." In *The Russian Military*, edited by Steven E. Miller and Dmitri V. Trenin. Cambridge, MA: American Academy of Arts and Sciences, 2004.

Baluevsky, Yuri. "Strategic Stability in a Globalized World." *Russia in Global Affairs* (4) (Oct–Dec 2003).

———. "Struktura i osnovnye soderzhanie novoi Voennoi doktriny Rossii." 20 Jan 2007, http://www.mil.ru/847/852/1153/1342/20922/index.shtml.

Baran, Zeyno. "EU Energy Security: Time to End Russian Leverage." *Washington Quarterly* 30(4) (Aut 2007).

Bastian, Katrin, and Roland Götz. "Deutsch-russische Beziehungen im europäischen

Kontext: Zwischen Interessenallianz und strategischer Partnerschaft." Stiftungs Wissenschaft und Politik Berlin (SWP-Berlin) Diskussionspapiere, May 2005.

Bastian, Katrin, and Rolf Schuette. "The Specific Character of EU-Russia Relations." In *Russia versus the United States and Europe*, edited by Hannes Adomeit and Anders Åslund. Berlin: SWP Berlin, 2005.

Bazhanov, Yevgeny. *Sovremennyi mir*. Moscow: Izvestiya, 2004.

Beehner, Lionel. "Energy's Impact on EU-Russian Relations." Council on Foreign Relations Backgrounder. Jan 2006, http://www.cfr.org/publication/9535/energys _impact_on_eurussian_relations.html.

———. "The Rise of the Shanghai Cooperation Organization." Council on Foreign Relations Backgrounder. 12 Jul 2006, http://www.cfr.org/publication/10883/.

———. "Severing of U.S.-Uzbek Ties over Counterterrorism." *Council on Foreign Relations Backgrounder*, 30 Sep 2005, http://www.cfr.org/publication/8940/ severing_of_usuzbek_ties_over_counterterrorism.html.

Berman, Ilan. "The New Battleground: Central Asia and the Caucasus." *Washington Quarterly* 28(1) (Win 2004).

Bilenkin, Vladimir. "The Ideology of Russia's Rulers in 1995: Westernizers and Eurasians." *Monthly Review* (Oct 1995).

Blagov, Sergei. "Balancing China in the Russian Far East," *JRL* #2007-77, 2 Apr 2007.

———. "Russia Hails Border Agreement with China Despite Criticism." *Jamestown Foundation Weekly Monitor*, 25 May 2005, http://www.jamestown.org/publica tions_details.php?volume_id = 407&issue_id = 3345&article_id = 2369795.

———. "Russia's Pacific Pipeline Seen as Double Edged Sword." *Jamestown Foundation Eurasia Daily Monitor*. 12 Jan 2005, http://www.jamestown.org/edm/ article.php?article_id = 2369078.

Blank, Stephen J. "China Makes Policy Shift, Aiming to Widen Access to Central Asian Energy." EurasiaNet.org. 13 Mar 2006, http://www.eurasianet.org/depart ments/business/articles/eav031306.shtml.

———. "The Dynamics of Russian Weapons Sales to China." U.S. Army War College Strategic Studies Institute. 1997, http://www.fas.org/nuke/guide/china/doctrine/ ruswep.pdf.

———. "The Eurasian Energy Triangle: China, Russia, and the Central Asian States." *Brown Journal of World Affairs* 12(2) (Win–Spr 2006).

———. "U.S. Interests in Central Asia and Their Challenges." *Demokratizatsiya* 15(3) (Sum 2007).

Bochkarev, Danila. *Russian Energy Policy during President Putin's Tenure: Trends and Strategies*. London: GMB, 2006.

Bochorishvili, Keti. "Georgia: Fear and Poverty in the Kodori Gorge." Institute for War & Peace Reporting. 31 May 2002, http://iwpr.net/?p = crs&s = f&o = 160838& apc_state = henicrs2002.

Bogaturov, Alexei. "International Relations in Central-Eastern Asia: Geopolitical Challenges and Prospects for Political Cooperation." Brookings Institution Center for Northeast Asian Policy Studies (CNAPS), Jun 2004.

Bordatchev, Timofeï. "L'UE en crise: Des opportunités à saisir pour la Russie?" IFRI Russie.Nei.Visions (7) (Oct 2005).

Borer, Douglas A., and Jason J. Morrissette. "Russian Authoritarian Pluralism: A Local and Global Trend?" *Cambridge Review of International Affairs* 19(4) (Dec 2006): 571–88.

Bremmer, Ian. "Who's in Charge in the Kremlin?" *World Policy Journal* (Win 2005–2006).

Bremmer, Ian, and Samuel Charap. "The *Siloviki* in Putin's Russia: Who They Are and What They Want." *Washington Quarterly* 30(1) (Win 2006–2007): 83–92.

British Petroleum. "Statistical Review of World Energy, 2007," http://www.bp.com/productlanding.do?categoryId=6848&contentId=7033471.

Brooke, James. "Russia Rattles Asia with Attack on Shell's Sakhalin-2." Bloomberg News, 19 Oct 2006, JRL #2006-235.

Brookings Institution. "The Russian Federation." Energy Security Series Report, Oct 2006.

Brown, Archie. "Vladimir Putin's Leadership in Comparative Perspective." In *Russian Politics under Putin*, edited by Cameron Ross. Manchester: Manchester University Press, 2004.

Bruusgaard, Christine Ben. "Budushchee rossiiskikh mirotvortsev." Moscow Carnegie Center Briefing 9(2) (Jun 2007).

Brzezinski, Zbigniew. *Game Plan: A Geostrategic Framework for the Conduct of the U.S.-Soviet Contest.* Boston: Atlantic Monthly Press, 1986.

———. *The Grand Chessboard: American Primacy and Its Geostrategic Imperatives.* New York: Basic Books, 1997.

———. "Putin's Choice." *Washington Quarterly* 31(2) (Spr 2008): 95–116.

Bugajski, Janusz. "Russia's New Europe." *The National Interest* (74) (Win 2002–2003): 84–91.

Bukkvoll, Tor. "Putin's Strategic Partnership with the West: The Domestic Politics of Russian Foreign Policy." *Comparative Strategy* (23): 222–42.

Burgess, Mark. "In the Spotlight: Islamic Movement of Uzbekistan (IMU)." CDI Terrorism Project. 25 May 2002, http://www.cdi.org/terrorism/imu.cfm.

Burns, R. Nicholas. "The NATO-Russia Council: A Vital Partnership in the War on Terror." Speech, 4 Nov 2004, http://www.state.gov/p/eur/rls/rm/38244.htm.

Burns, William J. "Coffee Break at the State Department: U.S. Ambassador to Russia." JRL #2007-8, 12 Jan 2007.

———. "Georgia and Russia." Testimony to U.S. Senate Foreign Relations Committee, 17 Sep 2008.

Bush, George W., and Vladimir Putin. "Joint Statement by U.S. President George Bush and Russian Federation President V. V. Putin Announcing the Global Initiative to Combat Nuclear Terrorism." *Joint Communiqué of 2006 G8 Summit*, http://en.g8russia.ru/docs/5.html.

———. "President Bush and Russian President Putin Discuss Progress." Press conference, 21 Oct 2001, http://www.whitehouse.gov/news/releases/2001/10/2001 1021-3.html.

———. "Remarks by the President and Russian President Putin in Press Availability Camp David." 27 Sep 2003, http://moscow.usembassy.gov/bilateral/transcript .php?record_id=18.

"Bushehr-Iran Nuclear Reactor." GlobalSecurity.org. Report, http://www.globalsec urity.org/wmd/world/iran/bushehr.htm.

Buszynski, Leszek. "Oil and Territory in Putin's Relations with China and Japan." *Pacific Review* 19(3) (Sep 2006).

Carothers, Thomas. "The Backlash against Democracy Promotion." *Foreign Affairs* 85(2) (Mar–Apr 2006): 55–68.

Central Election Commission of the Russian Federation, "Svedenie o provodyash-chikhsya vyborakh i referendumakh," http://www.vybory.izbirkom.ru/region/region/izbirkom?action = show&root = 1&t v d = 100100021960186&vr n = 1001 00021960181&region = 0&global = 1&sub_region = 0&prver = 0&pronetvd = null &vibid = 100100021960186&type = 242.

Center for Analysis of Strategies and Technologies. "Identified Contracts for Russian Arms Deliveries Signed in 2003." Moscow Defense Brief #2.

Center for Defense Information. "Here There Be Dragons: The Shanghai Coopera-tion Organization." China Report, 26 Sep 2006.

Chang, Felix K. "Russia Resurgent: An Initial Look at Russian Military Performance in Georgia." Foreign Policy Research Institute (FPRI) analysis paper, 13 Aug 2008.

Chang, Gordon G. "How China and Russia Threaten the World." *Commentary* (Dec 2006).

Checkel, Jeffrey. "Structure, Institutions, and Process: Russia's Changing Foreign Policy." In *The Making of Foreign Policy in Russia and the New States of Eurasia*, edited by Adeed Dawisha and Karen Dawisha. Armonk, NY: M. E. Sharpe, 1995.

Chen, Yun. "Kitai i Rossiya v sovremennom mire." *Svobodnaya Mysl'* (3) (2006).

Cheney, Richard. "Vice President's Remarks at the 2006 Vilnius Conference." 4 May 2006, http://www.whitehouse.gov/news/releases/2006/05/20060504-1.html.

"China, Russia: An End to an Island Dispute." Stratfor, 17 Jul 2008, http://www.stratfor.com/analysis/china_russia_end_island_dispute.

"China, Russia Sign Good-Neighborly Friendship, Cooperation Treaty." *People's Daily.* 17 Jul 2001, http://english.people.com.cn/english/200107/16/eng2001 0716_75105.html.

Chizhov, V. A. "Rossiya-EC: Strategiya partnerstvo." *Mezhdunarodnaya zhizn'* (9) (Sep 2004).

Cohen, Ariel. "Bringing Russia into an Anti-Saddam Coalition." Heritage Founda-tion Executive Memorandum #812. 29 Apr 2002, http://www.heritage.org/Research/RussiaandEurasia/EM812.cfm.

———. "The North European Gas Pipeline Threatens Europe's Energy Security." Heritage Foundation Backgrounder #1980 (26 Oct 2006): 2.

———. "Putin's Foreign Policy and U.S.-Russian Relations." Heritage Foundation Backgrounder #1406. 18 Jan 2001, http://www.heritage.org/Research/Russiaand Eurasia/BG1406.cfm.

———. "The Russia-China Friendship and Cooperation Treaty: A Strategic Shift in Eurasia?" Heritage Foundation Backgrounder #1459 (18 Jul 2001), http://www.heritage.org/Research/RussiaandEurasia/BG1459.cfm.

———. "Russia's Gas Attack on Ukraine: An Uneasy Truce." Heritage Foundation Web Memo #954. 4 Jan 2006, http://www.heritage.org/Research/Russiaand Eurasia/wm954.cfm.

———. "Saakashvili Visits Washington amid Heightening Geopolitical Tension in the Caucasus." *EurasiaNet Insight.* 24 Feb 2004, http://www.eurasianet.org/departments/insight/articles/eav022404.shtml.

———. "Washington Ponders Ways to Counter the Rise of the Shanghai Cooperation Organization." *Eurasia Insight.* 15 Jun 2006, http://www.eurasianet.org/
departments/insight/articles/eav061506_pr.shtml.

Collective Security Treaty Organization. "Zayavlenie Parlamentskoi Assamblei
Organizatsii Dogovora o Kollektivnoi Bezopasnosti ob Izmenenii Konfiguratsii
Voennogo Prisutstviya NATO v Evrope," http://www.dkb.gov.ru/start/indexb
.htm.

Collins, James. Foreword to *Putin's Russia: Past Imperfect, Future Uncertain,* edited by
Dale R. Herspring. Lanham, MD: Rowman & Littlefield, 2005.

Colton, Timothy J. *Yeltsin: A Life.* New York: Basic, 2008.

Colton, Timothy J., and Michael McFaul. "America's Real Russian Allies." *Foreign
Affairs* 80(6) (Nov–Dec 2001): 46–58.

"A Confusing Turn in Russia: Does Khodorkovsky's Arrest Signal a Retreat from Economic Reform?" Brookings Institution panel discussion, 25 Nov 2003, http://
www.brookings.edu/comm/events/20031125.pdf.

Council on Foreign Relations. "Russia's Wrong Direction: What the U.S. Can and
Should Do." Independent Task Force Report No. 57, Mar 2006.

"Crisis in Georgia: Frozen Conflicts and U.S.-Russian Relations." Carnegie Endowment for International Peace meeting summary. 11 Oct 2006, *JRL* #2006-237.

Daalder, Ivo, and James Goldgeier. "Global NATO." *Foreign Affairs* 85(5) (Sep–Oct
2006): 105–13.

Daly, John. "'Shanghai Five' Expands to Combat Islamic Radicals." *Jane's Terrorism &
Security Monitor,* 19 June 2001.

Dawisha, Adeed. Introduction to *The Making of Foreign Policy in Russia and the New
States of Eurasia,* edited by Adeed Dawisha and Karen Dawisha. Armonk, NY: M. E.
Sharpe, 1995.

Degoev, Vladimir. "Fenomen Putina kak faktor mirovoi politiki." *Svobodnaya mysl'*
(6) (2006): 17–26.

Delyagin, Mikhail. "Energeticheskaya politika Rossii." *Svobodnaya mysl'* (9–10)
(2006): 5–14.

Dibb, Paul. "The Bear Is Back." *The American Interest* 2(2) (Nov–Dec 2006).

Dobretsov, Nikolai, et al. "The 'Altai' Trunk Gas Pipeline and Prospects of Russia's
Outlet to the Fuel-and-Energy Market of the Asia-Pacific Region and the Development of Transit Regions." *Far Eastern Affairs* 35(2) (2007).

Dogan, Mattei, and John Higley. "Elites, Crises, and Regimes in Comparative Analysis." In *Elites, Crises, and the Origins of Regimes,* edited by Mattei Dogan and John
Higley. Lanham, MD: Rowman & Littlefield, 1998.

Doherty, Caitlin B. "Inside Track: The SCO and the Future of Central Asia." *The
National Interest* (7 Sep 2007).

Donaldson, Robert H., and Joseph L. Nogee. *The Foreign Policy of Russia: Changing
Systems, Enduring Interests,* 2nd ed. Armonk, NY: M. E. Sharpe, 2002.

Doyle, Michael W. "Politics and Grand Strategy." In *The Domestic Bases of Grand
Strategy,* edited by Richard Rosencrance and Arthur A. Stein, 22–47. Ithaca, NY:
Cornell University Press, 1993.

Dugin, Aleksandr. "Kondopoga: A Warning Bell." *Russia in Global Affairs* 4(4)
(2006): 8–13.

Dugin, Aleksandr G. *Osnovy geopolitiki: Geopoliticheskoe budushchee Rossii*. Moscow: Arktogeya, 1997.

Dunlop, John B. "Aleksandr Dugin's *Foundations of Geopolitics*." *Demokratizatsiya* 12(4) (Win 2004).

Eberstadt, Nicolas. "The Russian Federation at the Dawn of the Twenty-first Century: Trapped in a Demographic Straightjacket." *National Bureau of Asian Research (NBR) Analysis* 15(2) (Sep 2004).

European Commission. "The Policy: What Is the European Neighborhood Policy?" http://ec.europa.eu/world/enp/policy_en.htm.

European Council. "Conclusions and Plan of Action of the Extraordinary European Council Meeting on 21 September 2001," http://www.eurunion.org/partner/ EUUSTerror/ExtrEurCounc.pdf.

———. "A Secure Europe in a Better World." 12 Dec 2003, http://www.consiliu m.europa.eu/uedocs/cms_data/docs/2004/4/29/European%20Sec urity%20Strat egy.pdf.

European Union. "Declaration by the Presidency on Behalf of the European Union on the Deterioration of the Situation in South Ossetia (Georgia)." 11 Aug 2008, http://europa.eu/rapid/pressReleasesAction.do?reference = PESC/08/99&format = HTML&aged = 0&language = EN&guiLanguage = en.

European Union External Relations Directorate-General. "Russia: Country Strategy Paper, 2007–2013." 7 Mar 2007, http://ec.europa.eu/external_relations/russia/ csp/index.htm.

"European Union: Quick Deal Undermines Unbundling Plan." *Oxford Analytica* (9 Jun 2008).

"Fact Sheet: U.S.-Russia Strategic Framework Declaration." 6 Apr 2008, http://www .whitehouse.gov/news/releases/2008/04/20080406-5.html.

Falin, Valentin. "Der Kalte Krieg ist nicht zu Ende." *Russland.ru*, http://russland.ru/ kapitulation1/morenews.php?iditem = 39.

Fedorov, Yury E. "'Boffins' and 'Buffoons': Different Strains of Thought in Russia's Strategic Thinking." Chatham House Russia and Eurasia Program Briefing Paper, Mar 2006.

———. "Vneshnyaya politika Rossii: 1991–2000. Chast' I." *Pro et Contra* 6(1–2) (2001).

Feigenbaum, Evan A. "The Shanghai Cooperation Organization and the Future of Central Asia." Speech at the Nixon Center. 6 Sep 2007, http://www.state.gov/p/ sca/rls/rm/2007/91858.htm.

Felgenhauer, Pavel. "Moscow Hopes Crisis Will Drive Bakiyev Back into Russian Camp." *Jamestown Foundation Daily Monitor*, 8 Nov 2006.

Fischer, Sabine. "Die EU und Russland: Konflikte und Potentiale einer schwierigen Partnerschaft." SWP-Berlin Diskussionspapiere, Dec 2006.

Forsberg, Tuomas. "Russia's Relationship with NATO: A Qualitative Change or Old Wine in New Bottles?" *Journal of Communist Studies and Transition Politics* 21(3) (Sep 2005).

Freedman, Lawrence. "The New Great Power Politics." In *Russia and the West: The 21st Century Security Environment*, edited by Alexei Arbatov et al. Armonk, NY: M. E. Sharpe, 1999.

Freedman, Robert O. "Putin, Iran, and the Nuclear Weapons Issue." *Problems of Post-Communism* 53(2) (Mar–Apr 2006): 39–48.

Freese, Theresa. "Abkhazia: At War with Itself." *Transitions Online*, 6 Dec 2004.

Fried, Daniel. "The Future of NATO: How Valuable an Asset?" Testimony to House of Representatives Committee on Foreign Affairs. 22 Jun 2007, http://foreignaf fairs.house.gov/110/fri062207.htm.

———. "Remarks before the U.S. Senate Foreign Relations Committee." 21 Jun 2007.

———. "U.S.-Russia Relations in the Aftermath of the Georgia Crisis." Testimony to U.S. House Committee on Foreign Affairs, 9 Sep 2008.

Friedman, George. "The Medvedev Doctrine and American Strategy." *Stratfor Geopolitical Intelligence Report*, 2 Sep 2008, http://www.stratfor.com/weekly/medve dev_doctrine_and_american_strategy.

Fukuyama, Francis. "The End of History?" *The National Interest* (16) (Sum 1989).

———. *The End of History and the Last Man.* New York: Free Press, 1992.

———. "The Kings and I." *The American Interest* 3(1) (Sep–Oct 2007).

Fukuyama, Francis, and Michael McFaul. "Should Democracy Be Promoted or Demoted?" *Washington Quarterly* 31(1) (Win 2007–2008): 23–45.

Gaddy, Clifford G. "As Russia Looks East: Can It Manage Resources, Space, and People?" *Gaiko Forum*, Jan 2007.

———. "How Not to Punish Moscow." *Newsweek*, 23 Aug 2008.

Gaddy, Clifford, and Fiona Hill. "Putin's Agenda, America's Choice: Russia's Search for Strategic Stability." Brookings Institution Policy Brief #89, May 2002.

———. *The Siberian Curse: How Communist Planners Left Russia Out in the Cold.* Washington, DC: Brookings Institution, 2003.

Gaddy, Clifford G., and Barry W. Ickes. *Russia's Virtual Economy.* Washington, DC: Brookings, 2002.

Gaddy, Clifford G., and Andrew C. Kuchins. "Putin's Plan." *Washington Quarterly* 31(2) (Spr 2008): 117–29.

Gaidar, Yegor. "The Collapse of the Soviet Union: Lessons for Contemporary Russia." Address to the American Enterprise Institute, 13 Nov 2006, http://www.aei .org/events/filter.all,eventID.1420/transcript.asp.

———. *Gibel' imperii: Uroki dlya sovremennoi Rossii.* Moscow: ROSSPEN, 2006.

———. "The Soviet Collapse." AEI Online, On the Issues, 19 Apr 2007, http:// www.aei.org/publications/pubID.25991,filter.all/pub_detail.asp.

Gamaleeva, Mariya. "Formirovanie obraza Rossii kak aspekt publichnoi vneshnei politiki." *Mezhdunarodnik.ru.* 2 Aug 2006, http://www.mezhdunarodnik.ru/mag azin/4812.html.

Garnett, Sherman W. "Challenges of the Sino-Russian Strategic Partnership." *Washington Quarterly* 24(4) (Aut 2001).

———. "Europe's Crossroads: Russia and the West in the New Borderlands." In *The New Russian Foreign Policy*, edited by Michael Mandelbaum. New York: Council on Foreign Relations, 1998.

———. "Limited Partnership." In *Rapprochement or Rivalry? Russia-China Relations in a Changing Asia*, edited by Sherman W. Garnett, 7–15. Washington, DC: Carnegie Endowment, 2000.

Gat, Azar. "The Return of Authoritarian Great Powers." *Foreign Affairs* 86(4) (Jul–Aug 2007).

Giegerich, Bastian, and William Wallace. "Not Such a Soft Power: The External Deployment of European Forces." *Survival* 46(2) (Sum 2004): 163–82.

Gladkyy, Oleksandr. "American Foreign Policy and U.S. Relations with Russia and China after 11 September." *World Affairs* 166(1) (Sum 2003): 3–24.

"Glava Genshtaba Baluevsky otpravlen v otstavku." *Polit.ru*, 3 Jun 2008, http://www.polit.ru/news/2008/06/03/otstav.html.

Goble, Paul. "Putin Restricts Russian Foreign Ministry's Role in CIS Countries." Window on Eurasia (blog). 14 May 2008, http://windowoneurasia.blogspot.com/2008/05/window-on-eurasia-putin-restricts.html.

Goldgeier, James M. "NATO Expansion: Anatomy of a Decision." *Washington Quarterly* 21(1) (Win 1998): 85–102.

———. "The United States and Russia: Keeping Expectations Realistic." *Policy Review* (Oct–Nov 2001): 47–65.

Goldgeier, James M., and Michael McFaul. *Power and Purpose: U.S. Policy toward Russia after the Cold War.* Washington, DC: Brookings, 2003.

———. "What to Do about Russia." *Policy Review* (133) (Oct–Nov 2005).

Goldman, Marshall. *Petrostate: Putin, Power and the New Russia.* Oxford: Oxford University Press, 2008.

Goldstein, Lyle, and Vitaly Kozyrev. "China, Japan, and the Scramble for Siberia." *Washington Quarterly* 48(1) (Spr 2006).

Gol'ts, Aleksandr. "Voennoe mirotvorchestvo Rossii." *Pro et Contra* (Sep–Dec 2006): 65–74.

Goodby, James E., Vladimir I. Ivanov, and Nobuo Shimotomai, eds. *'Northern Territories' and Beyond: Russian, Japanese, and American Perspectives.* Westport, CT: Praeger, 1995.

Gorodetsky, Gabriel, ed. *Russia between East and West: Russian Foreign Policy on the Threshold of the Twenty-First Century.* London: Frank Cass, 2003.

Gorvett, Jon. "End of the Line for Baku-Ceyhan?" *Middle East* (312) (May 2001).

Götz, Roland. "Europa und das Erdgas des kaspischen Raums." SWP-Berlin Diskussionspapiere, Aug 2007.

Government of Ukraine. "Chislennost' i sostav naseleniya Ukrainy po itogam Vseukrainskoi perepisi naseleniya 2001 goda," http://ukrcensus.gov.ua/rus/results/general/language.

Graham, Thomas. "Remarks at Russia: Today, Tomorrow—and in 2008." Conference, American Enterprise Institute. 14 Oct 2005, http://www.aei.org/events/eventID.1119,filter.all/event_detail.asp.

Grant, Charles. "A More Political NATO, a More European Russia." In *Europe after September 11,* edited by Charles Grant. London: Centre for European Reform, 2001.

GUAM. "Charter of Organization for Democracy and Economic Development GUAM [sic]." 23 May 2006, http://www.guam.org.ua/267.0.0.1.0.0.phtml.

Haass, Richard. "The Age of Nonpolarity: What Will Follow U.S. Dominance?" *Foreign Affairs* 87(3) (May–Jun 2008).

Hanson, Philip, and Elizabeth Teague. "Big Business and the State in Russia." *Europe-Asia Studies* 57(5) (Jul 2005): 657–80.

Hart, Gary, and Gordon Humphrey. "Creating a Cold Peace by Expanding NATO." Cato Institute brief. 20 Mar 1998, http://www.cato.org/pub_display.php?pub_id=5929.

Herspring, Dale R. "Putin and Military Reform." In *Putin's Russia: Past Imperfect, Future Uncertain*, edited by Dale Herspring. Lanham, MD: Rowman & Littlefield, 2005.

Herspring, Dale R., and Peter Rutland. "Russian Foreign Policy." In *Putin's Russia: Past Imperfect, Future Uncertain*, edited by Dale R. Herspring. Lanham, MD: Rowman & Littlefield, 2005.

Hill, Fiona. "Beyond Co-Dependency: European Reliance on Russian Energy." Brookings Institution U.S.-Europe Analysis Series, Jul 2005.

——. "Russia's Newly Found Soft Power." *The Globalist* (26 Aug 2004), http://www.theglobalist.com/StoryId.aspx?StoryId=4139.

Hill, Fiona, and Omer Taspinar. "Turkey and Russia: Axis of the Excluded?" *Survival* 48(1) (Mar 2006): 81–92.

de Hoop Schaeffer, Jap. "Opening Statement by the Secretary General [to] Informal Meeting of the NATO-Russia Council and the Level of Foreign Ministers." 26 Apr 2007, http://www.nato-russia-council.info/htm/EN/documents26apr07.shtml.

Hopf, Ted. *Social Construction of International Politics: Identities & Foreign Policies, Moscow 1955 and 1999*. Ithaca, NY: Cornell University Press, 2002.

Huashen, Jao. "Kitai, Tsentral'naya Aziya i Shankhaiskaya Organizatsiya Sotrudnichestva." Carnegie Moscow Center Working Paper No. 5, 2005.

Hunter, Robert E. "Solving Russia: Final Piece in NATO's Puzzle." *Washington Quarterly* 23(1) (Win 2000): 118–23.

Huntington, Samuel. *The Clash of Civilizations and the Remaking of World Order*. New York: Touchstone, 1996.

——. "The West and the World." *Foreign Affairs* 75(6) (Nov–Dec 1997).

Inozemtsev, Vladislav, and Sergei Karaganov. "Imperialism of the Fittest." *The National Interest* (80) (Sum 2005): 74–80.

Isakova, Irina. *Russian Governance in the Twenty-First Century: Geo-strategy, Geopolitics and Governance*. London: Frank Cass, 2005.

Ivanov, Igor. "A New Foreign-Policy Year for Russia and the World." *International Affairs: A Russian Journal of World Politics, Diplomacy and International Relations*, 49(6) (2003): 33–38.

——. *The New Russian Diplomacy*. Washington, DC: Nixon Center/Brookings Institution, 2002.

——. "The New Russian Identity: Innovation and Continuity in Russian Foreign Policy." *Washington Quarterly* 24(3) (Sum 2001).

——. "Otvety Ministra inostrannykh del Rossiiskoi Federatsii I. S. Ivanova na voprosy zhurnala 'Kosmopolis.'" *Kosmopolis* (1) (Aut 2002).

Ivanov, Sergei B. "International Security in the Context of the Russia-NATO Relationship." Speech to Fortieth Munich Conference on Security Policy. 7 Feb 2004, http://www.securityconference.de/konferenzen/rede.php?menu_2005=&menu ekonferenzen=&sprache=en &id=126&.

——. Interview with Vesti Nedeli TV, 8 Oct 2006. *JRL* #2006-230.

——. "Speech at the 42nd Munich Conference on Security Policy." 5 Feb

2006, http://www.securityconference.de/konferenzen/rede.php?id=171&sprache=en&.

Jingjie, Li. "From Good Neighbors to Strategic Partners." In *Rapprochement or Rivalry? Russia-China Relations in a Changing Asia*, edited by Sherman W. Garnett. Washington, DC: Carnegie Endowment, 2000.

Jonson, Lena. *Vladimir Putin and Central Asia: The Shaping of Russian Foreign Policy.* London: I. B. Tauris, 2004.

Kagan, Frederick W. "The Russian Threat to International Order: Challenge and Response." Testimony to U.S. House Committee on Foreign Affairs, 9 Sep 2008.

Kagan, Robert. *The Return of History and the End of Dreams.* Washington, DC: Knopf, 2008.

Kahlid, Adeeb. *Islam after Communism: Religion and Politics in Central Asia.* Berkeley: University of California Press, 2007.

Karaganov, Sergei A. "Russia and the International Order." *Military Technology* (Jan 2006): 221–26.

———. "Russia and the West after Iraq," translated for Project Syndicate. Jun 2003, http://www.project-syndicate.org/commentary/karaganov8.

———. "Russia Pulled East and West," translated by Project Syndicate. Feb 1997, http://www.project-syndicate.org/commentary/kar5.

———. "Russia's Elites." In *Damage Limitation or Crisis? Russia and the Outside World*, edited by Robert D. Blackwill and Sergei A. Karaganov. Washington, DC: Brassey's, 1994.

Karatnycky, Adrian. "Ukraine's Orange Revolution." *Foreign Affairs* 84(2) (Mar–Apr 2005).

"Karimov Nixes International Probe into Andijon Crackdown." *EurasiaNet*, 20 May 2005, http://www.eurasianet.org/departments/insight/articles/pp051805.shtml.

Kassianova, Alla. "Russian Weapons Sales to Iran: Why They Are Unlikely to Stop." Center for Strategic and International Studies PONARS Policy Memo No. 427, Dec 2006, http://www.csis.org/media/csis/pubs/pm_0427.pdf.

Katz, Mark N. "Primakov Redux? Putin's Pursuit of 'Multipolarism' in Asia." *Demokratizatsiya* 14(1) (Win 2006).

Kay, Sean. "What Is a Strategic Partnership?" *Problems of Post-Communism* 47(3) (May–Jun 2000): 15–24.

"Kazakhstan Considers to Divert [sic] Oil Export Route from BTC to Russia." *Hürriyet.* 10 Sep 2008, http://www.hurriyet.com.tr/english/finance/9714319.asp?scr=1.

Kelin, A. V. "Spokoino negativnoe otnoshenie k rasshireniyu NATO." *Mezhdunarodnaya zhizn'* (31 Dec 2003).

"Khanabad, Uzbekistan: Karshi-Khanabad (K2) Airbase Camp Stronghold Freedom," http://www.globalsecurity.org/military/facility/khanabad.htm.

Khidirbekughli, Doulatbek. "U.S. Geostrategy in Central Asia: A Kazakh Perspective." *Comparative Strategy* (22) (2003).

Kim, Aleksandr. "Batkenskaya voina 1999: Kak eto bylo na samom dele." *TsentrAziya.ru.* 30 Aug 2002, http://www.centrasia.ru/newsA.php4?Month=8&Day=30&Year=2002.

King, Charles. "A Rose among Thorns." *Foreign Affairs* 83(2) (Mar–Apr 2004).

Kiselev, Evgeni. "The Future of Russian Politics: What the West Perceives and Misperceives." Lecture to Carnegie Endowment for International Peace. 14 Nov 2006, http://www.carnegieendowment.org/events/index.cfm?fa = eventDetail&id = 934 &&prog = zru.

Klepatskii, L. N. "The New Russia and the New World Order." In *Russia between East and West: Russian Foreign Policy on the Threshold of the Twenty-First Century*, edited by Gabriel Gorodetsky. London: Frank Cass, 2003.

Klussmann, Uwe, Christian Neef, and Matthias Schepp. "Russland: Annähern und verflechten." *Der Spiegel*, 2 Oct 2006.

Knight, Gavin. "The Alarming Spread of Fascism in Putin's Russia." *New Statesman*, 24 Jul 2007.

Kochladze, Manana. "The BTC Pipeline: Botched, Tardy, and Chilling." *Transitions Online*, 7 Feb 2005.

Konuzin, A. V. "Sil'naya OON—osnova zdorovykh mezhdunarodnykh otnoshenii." *Mezhdunarodnaya zhizn'* (11) (2006).

Kozyrev, Andrei. "The Lagging Partnership." *Foreign Affairs* 73(3) (May–Jun 1994): 59–71.

———. "Partnership or Cold Peace?" *Foreign Policy* (99) (Sum 1995).

———. *Preobrazhenie*. Moscow: Mezhdunarodnye otnosheniya, 1995.

———. "Riski svoi i chuzhie." *Moskovskie novosti*, 1 Aug 2000.

Kramarenko, Aleksandr M. "Ideologiya vneshnei politiki sovremennoi Rossii." *Mezhdunarodnaya zhizn'* (2008) (8–9).

Krasnyanskiy, Mykhailo. "Who Is Blackmailing Whom?" *Ukrayinska Pravda*. 12 Dec 2005, http://pravda.com.ua/en/news/2005/12/12/4919.htm.

Kryshtanovskaya, Olga, and Stephen White. "Inside the Putin Court: A Research Note." *Europe-Asia Studies* 57(7) (Nov 2005): 1065–75.

———. "Putin's Militocracy." *Post-Soviet Affairs* 19(4) (2003): 289–306.

Kubicek, Paul. "Russian Energy Policy in the Caspian Basin." *World Affairs* 166(4) (Spr 2004).

Kuchins, Andrew. "État terrible." *The National Interest* (91) (Sep–Oct 2007).

———. "A Turning Point in US-Russian Relations?" Carnegie Endowment for International Peace (originally published in *Vedomosti*, 20 Nov 2006), http://www .carnegiendowment.org/publications/index.cfm?fa = view&id = 18872&prog = zru.

Kuchkanov, Vladimir. "Demokraticheski orientirovannye perevoroty v SNG i geopoliticheskie perspektivy Rossii v regione." *Mezhdunarodnik.ru* (28 Sep 2005), http://www.mezhdunarodnik.ru/magazin/1439.html.

Kuzio, Taras. "Neither East nor West: Ukraine's Security Policy under Kuchma." *Problems of Post-Communism* 52(5) (Sep–Oct 2005): 59–68.

———. "Russian Policy toward Ukraine during Elections." *Demokratizatsiya* 13(4) (Aut 2005).

Kvint, Vladimir. "The Internationalization of Russian Business." Lecture at Kennan Institute, 16 Oct 2006, JRL #2006-237.

Lake, David A., and Robert Powell. "International Relations: A Strategic Choice Approach." In *Strategic Choice and International Relations*, edited by David A. Lake and Robert Powell, 3–38. Princeton, NJ: Princeton University Press, 1999.

Lanskoy, Miriam, Jessica Stern, and Monica Duffy Toft. "Russia's Struggle with Chechnya: Implications for the War on International Terrorism." Kennedy School of Government/Belfer Center Report, Caspian Studies Program, November 26, 2002.

Laruelle, Marlène. *Aleksandr Dugin: A Russian Version of the European Radical Right?* Washington, DC: Woodrow Wilson Center, 2006.

———. "Neo-Eurasianist Alexander Dugin on the Russia-Georgia Conflict." *Central Asia-Caucasus Analyst*, 3 Sep 2008.

Lasswell, Harold, et al. *The Comparative Study of Elites*. Stanford, CA: Stanford University Press, 1952.

Lavrov, Sergei V. "Rossiya i SShA: Mezhdu proshlym i budushchim." *Mezhdunarodnik.ru* (26 Sep, 2006), http://www.mezhdunarodnik.ru/magazin/5308.html.

———. "Rossiya-Kitai: Partnerstvo otkryvayushchee budushchee." 12 Oct 2004, http://www.mid.ru.

———. "Russia and India: Mutually Beneficial Cooperation and Strategic Partnership." *International Affairs: A Russian Journal of World Politics, Diplomacy, and International Relations* 53(3) (2007): 24–29.

———. "Speech at MGIMO University, Moscow, 3 Sep 2007." *JRL* #2007-188, 4 Sep 2007.

———. "Stenogramma otvetov Ministra Inostrannykh del Rossii S. V. Lavrova po itogam vizita v Uzbekistan." 21 Oct 2005.

———. "Stenogramma press-konferentsii Ministra inostrannykh del Rossii S. V. Lavrova, Zheneva, 12 fevralya 2008 goda." 12 Feb 2008, http://www.mid.ru.

———. "Stenogramma vystupleniya Ministra inostrannykh del Rossii S. V. Lavrova na 'Myurdalevskikh chteniyakh,' Zheneva, 12 fevralya 2008 goda." 12 Feb 2008, http://www.mid.ru.

———. "Vystuplenie Ministra Inostrannykh Del Rossii S. V. Lavrova na zasedanii MID ShOS, Bishkek, 7 iyulya 2007." 7 Jul 2007, http://www.mid.ru.

———. "Vystuplenie Ministra Inostrannykh Del S. V. Lavrova na Postministerskoi Konferentsii Rossiya-ASEAN, Manila, 1 avgusta 2007." 1 Aug 2007, http://www.mid.ru.

———. "Zayavlenie Ministra inostrannykh del S. V. Lavrova na press-konferentsii dlya rossiiskikh i zarubezhnykh SMI v svyazi s situatsiei v Yuzhnoi Ossetii." 8 Aug 2008, http://www.mid.ru.

Lavrov, Sergei, and K. I. Grishchenko. "Stenogramma vystuplenii Ministrov inostrannykh del Rossii S. V. Lavrova i Ukrainy K. I. Grishchenko po itogam sovmestnogo zasedaniya Kollegii Ministerstv inostrannykh del Rossii i Ukrainy." 28 May 2004, http://www.mid.ru.

Legvold, Robert. "All the Way: Crafting a U.S.-Russian Alliance." *The National Interest* (Win 2002–2003): 21–31.

LeVine, Steve. *The Oil and the Glory: The Pursuit of Empire and Fortune on the Caspian Sea*. New York: Random House, 2007.

———. *Putin's Labyrinth: Spies, Murder, and the Dark Heart of the New Russia*. New York: Random House, 2008.

Light, Margot, John Löwenhardt, and Stephen White. "Russia and the Dual Expansion of Europe." In *Russia between East and West: Russian Foreign Policy on the*

Threshold of the Twenty-First Century, edited by Gabriel Gorodetsky. London: Frank Cass, 2003.

Likhachev, V. "Russia and the European Union." *International Affairs: A Russian Journal of World Politics, Diplomacy, and International Relations* 52(2) (2006).

Lo, Bobo. "The Long Sunset of Strategic Partnership: Russia's Evolving China Policy." *International Affairs* 80(2) (2004).

———. "The Securitization of Russian Foreign Policy under Putin." In *Russia between East and West: Russian Foreign Policy on the Threshold of the Twenty-First Century*, edited by Gabriel Gorodetsky. London: Frank Cass, 2003.

———. *Vladimir Putin and the Evolution of Russian Foreign Policy*. London: Royal Institute of International Affairs, 2003.

Lotspeich, Richard. "Perspectives on the Economic Relations between China and Russia." *Journal of Contemporary Asia* 36(1) (2006).

Lucas, Edward. *The New Cold War: Putin's Russia and the Threat to the West*. New York: Palgrave Macmillan, 2008.

Lukin, Alexander. "Russia's Image of China and Russian-Chinese Relations." Brookings Institution CNAPS Working Paper. May 2001, http://www.brookings.edu/fp/cnaps/papers/lukinwp_01.pdf.

Lukin, V. P., and A. I. Utkin. *Rossiya i Zapad: Obshchnost' ili otchuzhdenie?* Moscow: Yabloko, 1995.

Lukin, Vladimir. "New Century, Greater Concerns." *International Affairs: A Russian Journal of World Politics, Diplomacy and International Relations* 48(2) (2002).

———. "Our Security Predicament." *Foreign Policy* (88) (Aut 1992): 57–58.

———. "Rossiiskii most cherez Atlantiku." *Rossiya v global'noi politike*. Nov–Dec 2002 (1).

Lynch, Dov. "Russia's Strategic Partnership with Europe." *Washington Quarterly* 27(2) (Spr 2004).

Lyne, Roderic, Strobe Talbott, and Koji Watanabe. "Engaging with Russia: The Next Phase." Report to the Trilateral Commission, Triangle Papers 59, 2006.

MacFarlane, S. Neil. "The 'R' in BRICs: Is Russia an Emerging Power?" *International Affairs* 82(1) (2006): 41–57.

Mackinder, H. J. *Democratic Ideals and Reality*. London: Constable, 1919.

———. "The Geographical Pivot of History." *Geographical Journal* 23(4) (Apr 1904): 421–37.

Mahbubani, Kishore. "The Case against the West." *Foreign Affairs* 87(3) (May–Jun 2008).

Makarenko, B. "Rossiiskii politicheskii stroi: Opyt neoinstitutsional'nogo analiza," *Mirovaya ekonomika i mezhdunarodnye otnosheniya* (2) (Feb 2007): 32–42.

Malashenko, Vladimir. "The Russian-Eurasian Idea (Pax Rossica)." *Russian Analytica* (6) (Sep 2005): 5–14.

Malcolm, Neil, et. al. *Internal Factors in Russian Foreign Policy*. Oxford: Clarendon, 1996.

Malikov, Mukhammed-Babur. "Uzbekistan: A View from the Opposition." *Problems of Post-Communism* 42(2) (Mar–Apr 1995).

Malysheva, Dina. "Konflikty u yuzhnykh rubezhei Rossii." *Pro et Contra* 5(3) (2000): 7–32.

Mandelbaum, Michael. "Introduction: Russian Foreign Policy in Historical Perspective." In *The New Russian Foreign Policy*, edited by Michael Mandelbaum. New York: Council on Foreign Relations, 1998.

Mankoff, Jeffrey. "Energy Security in Eurasia." Council on Foreign Relations Special Report, Oct 2008.

———. "Russia and the West: Taking the Longer View." *Washington Quarterly* 30(2) (Spr 2007).

———. "Russian Foreign Policy in the Putin Era." Yale University International Security Studies Working Paper. Jan 2007, http://www.yale.edu/macmillan/iac/mankoff.pdf.

Mantyskii, A., and V. Khodzhaev. "New Vistas of Russia-India Cooperation." *International Affairs: A Russian Journal of World Politics, Diplomacy, and International Relations* 51(1) (2005): 49–55.

Marat, Erica. "Fissures in the Force: Multilateral Security Integration Can Only Go So Far." *Jane's Intelligence Review* (12 May 2007).

Margelov, Mikhail. "Russia and the U.S.: Priorities Real and Artificial." *International Affairs: A Russian Journal of World Politics, Diplomacy, and International Relations* 52(1) (2006).

Mayorov, M. "South Ossetia: Conflict Zone." *International Affairs: A Russian Journal of World Politics, Diplomacy, and International Relations* 48(2) (2002).

McClintick, David. "How Harvard Lost Russia." *Institutional Investor.* Feb 2006, http://www.dailyii.com/article.asp?ArticleID = 1020662.

McFaul, Michael. "Democracy Promotion as a World Value." *Washington Quarterly* 28(1) (Win 2005):147–63.

———. "Getting Russia Right." *Foreign Policy* (117) (Win1999–2000): 58–74.

———. "Realistic Engagement: A New Approach to American-Russian Relations." *Current History* 100(648) (Oct 2001): 313–22.

———. "Russia and the West: A Dangerous Drift." *Current History* 104(684) (Oct 2005): 307–12.

———. "U.S.-Russia Relations in the Aftermath of the Georgia Crisis." Testimony to U.S. House Committee on Foreign Affairs, 9 Sep 2008.

McFaul, Michael, and Kathryn Stoner-Weiss. "The Myth of the Authoritarian Model." *Foreign Affairs* 87(1) (Jan–Feb 2008): 68–84.

McFaul, Michael, and Alexandra Vacroux. "Russian Resilience as a Great Power: A Response to Ambrosio." *Post-Soviet Affairs* 22(1) (Jan–Mar 2006): 24–33.

Medvedev, Dmitry. "Interv'yu Dmitriya Medvedeva telekanalam 'Rossiya,' Pervomu, NTV." 31 Aug 2008, http://www.kremlin.ru/text/appears/2008/08/205991.shtml.

———. "Nachalo vstrechi s prezidentom Gruzii Mikhailom Saakashvili." 6 Jun 2008, http://www.kremlin.ru/appears/2008/06/06/1618_type63377_202182.shtml.

———. "Press-konferentsia po okonchanii vstrechi s Prezidentom Frantsii Nikolya Sarkozy," 8 Sep 2008, http://www.kremlin.ru/text/appears/2008/09/206269.shtml.

———. "Stenograficheskii otchet o vstreche s uchastnikami mezhdunarodnogo kluba 'Valdai.'" 12 Sep 2008, http://www.kremlin.ru/text/appears/2008/09/206408.shtml.

———. "Vystuplenie na Konferentsii po mirovoi politike." 8 Oct 2008, http://www.kremlin.ru/text/appears/2008/10/207422.shtml.

———. "Vystuplenie na soveshchanii s poslami i postoyannymi predstavitelyami Rossiiskoi Federatsii pri mezhdunarodnykh organizatsiyakh." 15 Jul 2008, http://www.kremlin.ru/appears/2008/07/15/1635_type63374type63376type82634_204113.shtml.

———. "Vystuplenie na V Krasnoyarskom ekonomicheskom forume 'Rossiya 2008–2020' upravlenie rostom." 15 Feb 2008, http://www.medvedev2008.ru/performance_2008_02_15.htm.

———. "Vystuplenie na Voennom parade v chest' 63-i godovshchiny Pobedy v Velikoi Otechestvennoi Voine." 5 Sep 2008, http://www.kremlin.ru/appears/2008/05/09/1111_type82634type122346_200412.shtml.

———. "Vystuplenie na vstreche s predstavitelyami politicheskikh, parlamentskikh i obshchstvennykh krugov Germanii." 5 Jun 2008, http://www.kremlin.ru/appears/2008/06/05/1923_type63374type63376type63377 ... 202133.shtml.

———. "Vystuplenie na zasedanii Soveta glav gosudarstv—chlenov Shankhaiskoi organizatsii sotrudnichestva." 28 Aug 2008, http://www.kremlin.ru/text/appears/2008/08/205835.shtml.

———. "Zayavlenie posle podpisaniya dogovorov o druzhbe, sotrudnichestve i vzaimnoi pomoshchi s respublikami Abkhaziya i Yuzhnaya Ossetiya." 17 Sep 2008, http://www.kremlin.ru/text/appears/2008/09/206560.shtml.

———. "Zayavlenie v svyazi s situatsiei v Yuzhnoi Ossetii." 8 Aug 2008, http://www.kremlin.ru/appears/2008/08/08/1522_type63374type63378type82634_205027.shtml.

Medvedev, Dmitry, and Hu Jintao. "Zayavleniya dlya pressy po itogam rossiisko-kitaiskikh peregovorov." 23 May 2008, http://www.kremlin.ru/appears/2008/05/23/1933_type63377type63380_201233.shtml.

Mendelson, Sarah E., and Theodore P. Gerber. "Failing the Stalin Test." *Foreign Affairs* 85(1) (Jan–Feb 2006).

Menon, Rajan. "The Sick Man of Asia: Russia's Endangered Far East." *The National Interest* (Aut 2003).

Menon, Rajan, and Alexander J. Motyl. "Why Russia Is Really Weak." *Newsweek*, Sep 2006.

Merkushev, Vitaly. "Relations between Russia and the EU: The View from across the Atlantic." *Perspectives on European Politics and Society* 6(2) (2005).

Merry, E. Wayne. "Moscow's Retreat and Beijing's Rise as Regional Great Power. *Problems of Post-Communism* 50(3) (May–Jun 2003): 17–31.

Mihalisko, Kathleen. "Yeltsin's CIS Decree: An Instrument for Regaining Russia's Superpower Status." *Jamestown Foundation Prism* 1(21) (6 Oct 1995), http://jamestown.org/publications_details.php?volume_id = 1&issue_id = 84&article_id = 984.

Milov, Vladimir. "Can Russia Become an Energy Superpower?" *Social Sciences* 38(1) (2007).

———. "The Future of Russian Energy Policy." Address to the Brookings Institution, 30 Nov 2006, http://www.brookings.edu/comm/events/20061130.htm.

———. Presentation to "Whither Russia's Oil?" Conference, American Enterprise

Institute. 19 May 2006, http://www.aei.org/events/eventID.1314,filter.all/ event_detail.asp.

Mir vokrug Rossii: 2017. Kontury nedalekogo budushchego. SVOP/State Higher School of Economics/RIO-Tsentr, 2007.

Monaghan, Andrew. "'Calmly Critical': Evolving Russian Views of US Hegemony." *Journal of Strategic Studies* 29(6) (Dec 2006): 987–1013.

Morse, Edward L., and James Richard. "The Battle for Energy." *Foreign Affairs* 81(2) (Mar–Apr 2002).

"Moscow Says Japan-Russia Diplomacy 'in a State of Catastrophe.'" AFP News, *JRL* #2006-255, 13 Nov 2006.

Murphy, Paul J. *Wolves of Islam: Russia and the Faces of Chechen Terror.* Washington, DC: Brassey's, 2004.

Nation, R. Craig. "Beyond the Cold War: Change and Continuity in U.S.-Russian Relations." In *The United States and Russia into the 21st Century,* by R. Craig Nation and Michael McFaul, 9–13. Carlisle Barracks, PA: Strategic Studies Institute, U.S. Army War College, 1997.

"NATO-CSTO cooperation advisable—Lavrov." Interfax. 10 Dec 2008, http:// www.interfax-news.com/3/453633/news.aspx.

"NATO-Russia Relations: A New Quality." Declaration by Heads of State and Government of NATO Member States and the Russian Federation. 28 May 2002, http://www.nato-russia- council.info/htm/EN/documents28may02_1.shtml.

Neef, Christian. "Russian Bear Roars: Why Is Moscow Risking a New Cold War?" *Der Spiegel,* 25 Jun 2008, http://www.spiegel.de/international/world/0,1518, 562073,00.html.

Negroponte, John D. "Annual Threat Assessment." Testimony to Senate Select Committee on Intelligence, 11 Jan 2007. *JRL* #2007-8, 12 Jan 2007.

Niazi, Sadique. "Pushback to Unilateralism: The China-India-Russia Alliance." *Foreign Policy in Focus, JRL* #2008-3, 3 Jan 2008.

Nichols, Thomas M. "Russia's Turn West." *World Policy Journal* 19(4) (Win 2002–2003).

Nikitin, Alexander. "Russian Perceptions of the CFSP/ESDP." European Institute for Security Studies Analysis. May 2006, www.iss-eu.org/new/analysis/analy145.pdf.

North Atlantic Treaty Organization. "Founding Act on Mutual Relations, Cooperation and Security between NATO and the Russian Federation." 27 May 1997, http://www.nato.int/docu/basictxt/fndact-a.htm.

———. "Joint Statement on the Occasion of the Visit of the Secretary General of NATO, Lord Robertson, in Moscow on 16 February 2000," http://www.nato.int/ docu/review/2000/0001-0c.htm.

———. "The Partnership for Peace," http://www.nato.int/issues/pfp.

———. "Riga Summit Declaration." 29 Nov 2006, http://www.nato.int/docu/pr/ 2006/p06-150e.htm#eapc_pfp.

Olcott, Martha. "Vladimir Putin i neftyanaya politika Rossii." Carnegie Moscow Center Working Paper (1) (2005).

"Opposition to NATO Expansion." Open letter to Bill Clinton. 26 Jun 1997, http:// www.armscontrol.org/act/1997_06-07/natolet.asp.

Oznobishchev, Sergei. "Rossiya-NATO: Realisticheskoe partnerstvo ili virtual'noe protivostoyanie?" *Mirovaya ekonomika i mezhdunarodnye otnosheniya* (1) (Jan 2006).

———. "Russia and the United States: Is 'Cold Peace' Possible?" *International Affairs: A Russian Journal of World Politics, Diplomacy, and International Relations* 50(4) (2004).

Pascual, Carlos. "The Geopolitics of Energy: From Security to Survival." Brookings Institution, Jan 2008, http://www.brookings.edu/papers/2008/01_energy_pascual.aspx.

Perovic, Jeronim. "From Disengagement to Active Economic Competition: Russia's Return to the South Caucasus and Central Asia." *Demokratizatsiya* 13(1) (Win 2005).

Peskov, Dmitry. "On Iran and Energy, According to Russia." Interview with *The National Interest* online, 28 Dec 2006. JRL #2007-4, 5 Jan 2007.

Pifer, Steven. "What Does Russia Want? How Do We Respond?" Lecture at Texas A& M University. 11 Sep 2008, http://www.brookings.edu/speeches/2008/0911_russia_pifer.aspx.

Pinto, Brian, Evsey Gurevich, and Sergei Ulatov. "Lessons from the Russian Crisis of 1998 and Recovery." *Managing Volatility and Crises: A Practitioner's Guide*, http://www1.worldbank.org/economicpolicy/documents/mv/pgchapter10.pdf.

Pipes, Richard. "Flight from Freedom: What Russians Think and Want." *Foreign Affairs* 83(3) (May–Jun 2004).

"PM Outlines Goals for Next Three Years." RosBusinessConsulting, JRL #2008-7, 8 Jan 2008.

Polikanov, Dmitrij. "U-Turns in Russia-NATO Relations." *Perspectives* (17) (2001).

Polikanov, Dmitry, and Graham Timmins. "Russian Foreign Policy under Putin." In *Russian Politics under Putin*, edited by Cameron Ross. Manchester: Manchester University Press, 2004.

Powell, Colin. State Department Briefing. 24 Nov 2004, http://www.state.gov/secretary/former/powell/remarks/38738.htm.

Pravda, Alex. "Putin's Foreign Policy after 11 September." In *Russia between East and West: Russian Foreign Policy on the Threshold of the Twenty-First Century*, ed. Gabriel Gorodetsky. London: Frank Cass, 2003.

"President Hu Vows to Push Forward Sino-Russian Strategic Partnership." Xinhua Online. 20 Nov 2006, http://english.gov.cn/2006-11/19/content_446644.htm.

"Primakov on Russian Relations with the West." *OMRI Daily Digest*, 30 May 1996.

Primakov, Yevgeny. "Intervention." Speech to North Atlantic Cooperation Council ministerial session. 11 Dec 1996, http://www.nato.int/docu/speech/1996/s9612115.htm.

———. "Is the Russia-U.S. Rapprochement Here to Stay?" *International Affairs: A Russian Journal of World Politics, Diplomacy and International Relations* 48(6) (2002).

———. "Opening Statement by H. E. Mr. E. Primakov, Minister of Foreign Affairs of Russia." May 1997, http://www.shaps.hawaii.edu/security/arf/primakov-arf-9707.html.

———. *Russian Crossroads: Toward the New Millennium.* Translated by Felix Rosenthal. New Haven, CT: Yale University Press, 2004.

———. "Russia's Foreign Policy in 2005 Was Successful in Every Area." *International*

Affairs: A Russian Journal of World Politics, Diplomacy, and International Relations 52(2) (2006): 13–22.

———. "Turning Back over the Atlantic." *International Affairs: A Russian Journal of World Politics, Diplomacy and International Relations* 48(6) (2002): 65–74.

Prizel, Ilya. *National Identity and Foreign Policy: Nationalism and Leadership in Poland, Russia, and Ukraine.* Cambridge: Cambridge University Press, 1998.

Pursianinen, Christer. *Russian Foreign Policy and International Relations Theory.* Aldershot: Ashgate, 2000.

Pushkov, A. "Quo Vadis? Posle vstrechi Putin-Bush." *Mezhdunarodnaya zhizn'* (Jun 2002).

Putin, Vladimir. "50 Years of the [sic] European Integration and Russia." Translated in *JRL* #2007-72, 25 Mar 2007.

———. "Full Text: Vladimir Putin Interview." Remarks to Valdai Discussion Club. 9 Sep 2006, http://en.valday2006.rian.ru/materials/20060910/52329444.html.

———. "Interview with Wenmin Jiabao." 13 Oct 2004, http://www.kremlin.ru/text/appears/2004/10/77852.shtml.

———. "Intervyu zhurnalistam pechatnykh sredstv massovoi informatsii iz stranchlenov 'gruppy vos'mi.'" 4 Jun 2007, http://www.kremlin.ru/text/appears/2007/06/132615.shtml.

———. *Ot pervogo litsa: Razgovory s Vladimirom Putinim.* Moscow: Vagrius, 2000.

———. "Otvety na voprosy rossiiskikh i inostrannykh zhurnalistov po okonchanii sammita Shankhaiskoi organizatsii sotrudnichestva." 16 Jun 2005, http://www.mid.ru/ns- rasia.nsf/1083b7937ae580ae432569e7004199c2/432569d80021985fc325718f0028c259?Op enDocument.

———. "Poslanie Federal'nomu Sobraniyu Rossiiskoi Federatsii." 8 Jul 2000, http://www.kremlin.ru/appears/2000/07/08/0000_type63372type63374type82634_28782.shtml.

———. "Poslanie Federal'nomu Sobraniyu Rossiiskoi Federatsii." 3 Apr 2001, http://www.kremlin.ru/appears/2001/04/03/0000_type63372type63374type82634_28514.shtml.

———. "Poslanie Federal'nomu Sobraniyu Rossiiskoi Federatsii." 18 Apr 2002, http://www.kremlin.ru/appears/2002/04/18/0000_type63372type63374type82634_28876.shtml.

———. "Poslanie Federal'nomu Sobraniyu Rossiiskoi Federatsii." 16 May 2003, http://www.kremlin.ru/appears/2003/05/16/1259_type63372type63374_44623.shtml.

———. "Poslanie Federal'nomu Sobraniyu Rossiiskoi Federatsii." 26 May 2004, http://www.kremlin.ru/appears/2004/05/26/0003_type63372type63374type82634...71501.shtml.

———. "Poslanie Federal'nomu Sobraniyu Rossiiskoi Federatsii." 25 Apr 2005, http://www.kremlin.ru/appears/2005/04/25/1223_type63372type63374type82634...87049.shtml.

———. "Poslanie Federal'nomu Sobraniyu Rossiiskoi Federatsii." 10 May 2006, http://www.kremlin.ru/text/appears/2006/05/105546.shtml.

———. "Poslanie Federal'nomu Sobraniyu Rossiiskoi Federatsii." 26 Apr 2007, http://www.kremlin.ru/appears/2007/04/26/1156_type63372type63374type82634...125339.shtml.

———. "Press-konferentsiya po okonchanii vstrechi s Prezidentom Gruzii Mikhailom Saakashvili," http://www.kremlin.ru/text/appears/2006/06/107067.shtml.

———. "Vstupitel'noe slovo i otvety na voprosy v khode sovmestnoi press-konfer entsii po itogam sammita Rossii-ES." 25 Nov 2004, http://www.kremlin.ru/appears/2004/11/25/2239_type63377type63380_80195.shtml.

———. "Vstupiel'noe slovo na zasedanii Soveta bezopasnosti." 3 Dec 2003, http://www.kremlin.ru/appears/2003/12/03/1821_type63374type63378_56602.shtml.

———. "Vstupitel'noe slovo na zasedanii Soveta Bezopasnosti." 20 Dec 2006, http://president.kremlin.ru/appears/2006/12/20/1548_type63374type63378ty pe82634_115648.shtml.

———. "Vstupitel'noe slovo na zasedanii Soveta Bezopasnosti, posvyashchennom meram po realizatsii Poslaniya Federal'nomu Sobraniyu." 20 Jun 2006, http://www.kremlin.ru/text/appears/2006/06/107450.shtml.

———. "Vystuplenie i diskussiya na Myunkhenskoi konferentsii po voprosam politiki bezopasnosti." 10 Feb 2007, http://www.kremlin.ru/appears/2007/02/10/1737_type63374type63376type63377t yp e63381type82634_118 097.shtml.

———. "Vystuplenie na Balkanskom sammite po energeticheskoi bezopasnosti." 24 Jun 2007, http://www.kremlin.ru/appears/2007/06/24/1200_type63374 type63377_135699.shtml.

———. "Vystuplenie na soveshchanii rukovodyashchego sostava sotrudnikov diplomaticheskoi sluzhby Rossii." 26 Jan 2001, http://www.kremlin.ru/appears/2001/01/26/0000_type63374type63377type63378_28464.shtml.

———. "Vystuplenie Prezidenta Rossii V. Putina na Bishkekskom sammite." 16 Aug 2007, http://www.sectsco.org/html/01671.html.

———. "Zayavlenie dlya pressy i otvety na voprosy na sovmestnoi press-konferentsii s Predsedatel'em Kitaiskoi Narodnoi Respubliki Jiang Zeminem." 16 Jul 2001, http://www.kremlin.ru/appears/2001/07/16/0003_type63377type63380_28588.shtml.

———. "Zayavlenie dlya pressy i otvety na voprosy zhurnalistov po okonchanii zasedaniya Soveta kollektivnoi bezopasnosti." 14 May 2002, http://www.kremlin.ru/appears/2002/05/14/0000_type63374type63377type63380_28902.shtml.

———. "Zayavlenie dlya pressy po itogam rossiisko-kirgizskikh peregovorakh." 24 Apr 2006, http://www.kremlin.ru/appears/2006/04/24/1828_type63377type 63380_104861. shtml.

———. "Zayavlenie Prezidenta Rossii." Statement to the press, 24 Sep 2001, http://www.kremlin.ru/appears/2001/09/24/0002_type63374type63377_28639.shtml.

Putin, Vladimir, and Hu Jintao. "Zayavleniya dlya pressy Prezidenta Rossii V. V. Putina i Predsedatelya Kitaiskoi Narodnoi Respubliki Khu Tsintao i otvety na voprosy zhurnalistov po okonchanii kitaisko-rossiiskikh peregovorov." 27 May 2003, http://www.ln.mid.ru/brp_4.nsf/sps/76C04FB86CB13A8F43256D3400 32EEFB.

Ra'anan, Uri, and Kate Martin, eds. *Russia: A Return to Imperialism?* New York: St. Martin's, 1995.

Ramo, Joshua Cooper. *The Beijing Consensus.* London: The Foreign Policy Centre, 2004.

Rangsimaporn, Paradorn. "Russian Elite Perceptions of the Russo-Chinese 'Strategic Partnership' (1996–2001)." *Slovo* 18(2) (Aut 2006): 129–45.

————. "Russia's Debate on Military-Technological Cooperation with China: From Yeltsin to Putin." *Asian Survey* 46(3) (May–Jun 2006).

"Report of the Russian Working Group." In *U.S.-Russian Relations at the Turn of the Century*. Washington, DC: Carnegie Endowment for International Peace/Moscow: Council on Foreign and Defense Policy, 2000.

Rice, Condoleezza. "Campaign 2000: Promoting the National Interest." *Foreign Affairs* 79(1) (Jan–Feb 2000).

————. "Remarks at Eurasian National University." 13 Oct 2005, http://www.state.gov/secretary/rm/2005/54913.htm.

————. "Secretary Rice Addresses U.S.-Russia Relations at the German Marshall Fund." 18 Sep 2008, http://www.state.gov/secretary/rm/2008/09/109954.htm.

Richter, James. "Russian Foreign Policy and the Politics of National Identity." In *The Sources of Russian Foreign Policy after the Cold War*, edited by Celeste A. Wallander. Boulder, CO: Westview, 1996.

Rogowski, Ronald. "Institutions as Constraints on Strategic Choice." In *Strategic Choice and International Relations*, edited by David A. Lake and Robert Powell. Princeton, NJ: Princeton University Press, 1999.

Romanova, T. A. "Rossiya i ES: Dialog na raznykh yazykakh." *Rossiya v global'noi politike* (6) (Nov–Dec 2006).

Rose, Richard. *New Russia Barometer III: The Results*. Glasgow: Strathclyde University Press, 1994.

Rosenberger, Chandler. "Moscow's Multipolar Mission." *ISCIP Perspective* 8(2) (Nov–Dec 1997), http://www.bu.edu/iscip/vol8/Rosenberger.html.

Rosencrance, Richard, and Arthur A. Stein. "Beyond Realism: The Study of Grand Strategy." In *The Domestic Bases of Grand Strategy*, edited by Richard Rosencrance and Arthur A. Stein, 3–21. Ithaca, NY: Cornell University Press, 1993.

Rosencrance, Richard, and Arthur A. Stein, eds. *The Domestic Bases of Grand Strategy*. Ithaca, NY: Cornell University Press, 1993.

"Rossiya i mir." Levada Center Poll, http://www.levada.ru/press/2007081001.html.

"Rossiya i SShA." Levada Center poll, http://www.levada.ru/russia.html.

Rotar, Igor. "The Islamic Movement of Uzbekistan: A Resurgent IMU?" *Jamestown Foundation Terrorism Monitor* 1(8) (18 Dec 2003).

Roy, Denny. "China's Reaction to American Predominance." *Survival* 45(3) (Aut 2003).

Rumer, Eugene. "SShA i Tsentral'naya Aziya posle 11 sentyabrya." *Kosmopolis* (3) (Spr 2003).

Rumsfeld, Donald. "Prepared Statement to Senate Foreign Relations Committee." 17 Jul 2002, http://www.defenselink.mil/speeches/speech.aspx?speechid=269.

"Russia: START II Overview." Nuclear Threat Initiative NIS Nuclear and Missile Database, 4 Dec 2002, http://www.nti.org/db/nisprofs/russia/treaties/s2descr.htm.

"Russia Thinks Globally." *Russia Profile* Experts Panel, 27 Jun 2008.

"Russia to Establish Air Base in Kyrgyzstan, Deals Blow to U.S. Strategic Interests in Central Asia." *EurasiaNet Eurasia Monitor*. 3 Dec 2002, http://www.eurasianet.org/departments/insight/articles/eav120302.shtml.

"Russia Warns EU over Ex-Soviet Sphere of Influence." *JRL* #2007-30, 7 Feb 2007.

"Russian-Chinese Joint Declaration on a Multipolar World and the Establishment of a New International Order." 23 Apr 1997, http://www.fas.org/news/russia/1997/a52—153en.htm.

Russian Federation. "Plan deistvii po realizatsii polozhenii o Dogovore o dobrososedstve, druzhbe i sotrudnichestve mezhdu Rossiiskoi Federatsiei i Kitaiskoi Narodnoi Respublikoi (2005-2008g.)." 14 Oct 2004, http://www.kremlin.ru/interdocs/2004/10/14/0000_type72067_78193.shtml?typ e = 72067.

Russian Federation and European Union. "Agreement on Partnership and Cooperation." 1 Dec 1997, http://eur-lex.europa.eu/LexUriServ/LexUriServ.do?uri = CELEX:21997A1128(01):E N:HTML.

Russian Federation and People's Republic of China. "Sovmestnaya deklaratsiya Rossiiskoi Federatsii i Kitaiskoi Narodnoi Respubliki." 27 May 2003, http://www.kremlin.ru/interdocs/2003/05/27/1649_type72067_46160.shtml?type = 72067.

Russian Federation Academy of Sciences. *Rossiya i Zapad posle 11 sentyabrya.* Moscow: RAN-Institut Evropy, 2002.

Russian Federation Security Council. "Kontseptsiya natsional'noi bezopasnosti Rossiiskoi Federatsii." 2000, http://www.scrf.gov.ru/documents/decree/2000_24_1.shtml.

Russian Ministry of Defense. "Military Doctrine of the Russian Federation." http://www.fas.org/nuke/guide/russia/doctrine/991009-draft-doctrine.htm.

Russian Ministry of Foreign Affairs. "Dogovor o soyuznicheskikh otnosheniyakh mezhdu Rossiiskoi Federatsiei i Respublikoi Uzbekistan." 14 Nov 2005.

———. "Dogovor o strategicheskom partnerstve mezhdu Rossiiskoi Federatsiei i Respublikoi Uzbekistan." 16 Jun 2004, http://www.mid.ru.

———. "Ekonomicheskaya diplomatiya Rossii v 2003 godu." http://www.mid.ru.

———. "Intervyu ofitsial'nogo predstavitelya MID Rossii A. V. Yakovenko agenstvu 'Interfaks' po rossiisko-kazakhstanskim otnosheniyam." 20 Apr 2004, http://www.mid.ru.

———. "Intervyu Posla Rossii na Ukraine V. S. Chernomyrdina zhurnalu 'Profil'.'" 19 Sep 2007, http://www.mid.ru.

———. "Interv'yu zamestitelya Ministra inostrannykh del Rossii A. P. Losyukova agenstvu 'Interfaks' po rossiisko-kitaiskim otnosheniyam." 16 Jul 2001, http://www.mid.ru.

———. "Kontseptsiya sotrudnichestva gosudarstv-uchastnikov Sodruzhestva Nezavisimykh Gosudarstv v bor'be s terrorizmom i inymi nasil'stvennymi proyavleniyami ekstremizma." 26 Aug 2005, http://www.mid.ru.

———. "Kontseptsiya vneshnei politiki Rossiiskoi Federatsii." 2000, http://www.mid.ru.

———. "Kontseptsiya vneshnei politiki Rossiiskoi Federatsii." 2008, http://www.mid.ru.

———. "Medium-term Strategy for Development of Relations between the Russian Federation and the EU" (translation). 22 Oct 1999, http://presidency.finland.fi/netcomm/News/showarticle1610.html.

———. "Obzor vneshnei politiki Rossiiskoi Federatsii." 27 Mar 2007, http://www.mid.ru/brp_4.nsf/sps.

————. "O peregovorakh Prezidenta Rossii V. V. Putina s Predsedatelem KNR Khu Tsintao." 21 Mar 2006, http://www.mid.ru/ns-rasia.nsf/1083b7937ae580ae 432569e7004199c2/432569d80021985fc3257139002ba25d?OpenDocument.

————. "Otvet ofitsial'nogo predstavitelya MID Rossii M. L. Kamynina na vopros agenstva 'Interfaks' po povodu situatsii vokrug ob"ektov Chernomorskogo flota." 9 Mar 2007, http://www.mid.ru.

————. "Press-konferentsiya Prezidenta Rossii V. V. Putina i Prezidenta Kazakhstana N. A. Nazarbaeva po itogam rossiisko-kazakhstanskikh peregovorov." 4 Apr 2006, http://www.mid.ru.

————. "Zayavlenie dlya pressy Prezidenta Rossii V. V. Putina i Prezidenta Uzbekistana Islama Karimova po itogam rossiisko-uzbekskikh peregovorov." 15 Nov 2005, http://www.mid.ru.

————. "Zayavlenie MID Rossii o situatsii v rossiisko-ukrainskikh otnosheniyakh v gazovoi sfere." 1 Jan 2006, http://www.mid.ru.

"The Russian Model: Do Russia and China Provide an Alternative to Liberal Democracy?" *Russia Profile*. 5 Oct 2007, http://www.russiaprofile.org/page.php?page id = Experts%27 + Panel&articleid = a1191582534.

"Russian Spin Doctor Views Moscow's Relations with Ukraine, Georgia." *Ukrainska Pravda*, JRL #2007-241, 21 Nov 2007.

"Russians Consider NATO as Hostile." *JRL* #2007-186, 31 Aug 2007.

"Russia's Dangerous, but Mostly for Russians." *The Economist* (2 Dec 2006).

"Russia's Place in the World after September 11." *International Affairs: A Russian Journal of World Politics, Diplomacy, and International Relations* 48(2) (2002): 78–91.

Russo, Alan. "Mir v Yugoslavii: Komu eto vygodno?" Carnegie Moscow Center Briefing 1(6) (Jun 1999), http://www.carnegie.ru/ru/print/48347-print.htm.

Ryabikhin, Leonid F. "Rossiya i Zapad: Soderzhanie i perspektivy vzaimootnoshenii." In *Rossiya i Zapad posle 11 sentyabrya* (materials from roundtable sponsored by Russian Academy of Sciences European Institute), 68–69. Moscow: RAN-Institut Evropy, 2002.

Ryabov, Andrei. "Gruzino-abkhazskii tupik." *Pro et Contra* (Sep–Dec 2006).

————. "Moskva prinimaet vyzov 'tsvetnykh revolyutsii.'" *Pro et Contra* 9(1) (Jul–Aug 2005).

Saakashvili, Mikheil. "The Way Forward: Georgia's Democratic Vision for the Future." *Harvard International Review* (Spr 2006).

Safonov, A. E. "Neobkhodima global'naya sistema protivodeistviya terrorizmu." *Mezhdunarodnaya zhizn'* (1) (Jan 2003).

————. "Terrorizm apokalipsisa." *Mezhdunarodnaya zhizn'* (5) (2006).

Schmidt, Matthew. "Is Putin Pursuing a Policy of Eurasianism?" *Demokratizatsiya* 13(1) (Win 2005).

Sempa, Francis P. *Geopolitics: From the Cold War to the 21st Century*. New Brunswick, NJ: Transaction, 2002.

Sestanovich, Stephen. Testimony to U.S. Senate Committee on Foreign Relations. 29 Jun 2006, http://www.cfr.org/publications/11019/testimony_to_committee_on_foreign_relations_us_senate.html?breadcrumb = default.

Shanghai Cooperation Organization. "Deklaratsiya o sozdanii Shankhaiskoi organizatsii sotrudnichestva." 15 Jun 2001, http://www.sectsco.org/html/00651.html.

———. "Dushanbe Declaration of Heads of SCO Member States." 28 Aug 2008, http://www.sectsco.org/news_detail.asp?id = 2360&LanguageID = 2.

———. "Joint Communique of the Council of Governmental Heads (Prime Ministers) of Shanghai Cooperation Organization Member States." 23 Sep 2004, http://www.shaps.hawaii.edu/fp/russia/2004/20040923_sco_jc.html.

———. "Predsedatel' KNR: ShOS ne yavlyaetsya antiamerikanskoi organizatsiei." IBK.ru News. 21 Apr 2006, http://www.ibk.ru/news/predsedatel_knr_shos_ne_ yavlyaetsya_antiamerikanskoi_organizatsiei-16946/.

Sherr, James. "Russia's Current Trajectory." *Russia in the International System*, Conference Report of the U.S. National Intelligence Council, 1 Jun 2001, http://www.dni.gov/nic/confreports_russiainter.html.

"Shevardnadze Accuses Soros of Financing Coup d'Etat in Georgia." *Pravda.ru* (English). 1 Dec 2003, http://newsfromrussia.com/world/2003/12/01/51582.html.

Shevtsova, Lilia. *Putin's Russia*. Translated by Antonina W. Bouis. Washington, DC: Carnegie, 2003.

Shlapentokh, Vladimir. "The Dying Russian Democracy as a Victim of Corrupt Bureaucrats." *JRL* #2007-126, 18 May 2007.

———. "Looking for Other Options: Russia's National Identity Cannot Be Based on Western Models." *Russia Profile*, 30 Oct 2006.

———. "Serdiukov as a Unique Defense Minister in Russian History: A Sign of Putin's Absolute Power." Comment on *JRL* #2007-76, 1 Apr 2007.

———. "Two Simplified Pictures of Putin's Russia, Both Wrong." *World Policy Journal* (Spr 2005): 61–72.

Shlyndov, Alexander. "Military Technical Collaboration between Russia and China: Its Current Status, Problems, and Outlook." *Far Eastern Affairs* 33(1) (2005).

Simes, Dmitri K. "Losing Russia." *Foreign Affairs* 86(6) (Nov–Dec 2007).

———. "The Results of 1997: No Dramatic Upheavals." *International Affairs* 44(1) (1998).

———. "A View from Russia: Grading the President." *Foreign Policy* (137) (Jul–Aug 2003).

Simonia, Nodari A. "Priorities of Russian Foreign Policy and the Way It Works." In *The Making of Foreign Policy in Russia and the New States of Eurasia*, edited by Adeed Dawisha and Karen Dawisha, 38–39. Armonk, NY: M. E. Sharpe, 1995.

Skak, Mette. "The Logic of Foreign and Security Policy Change in Russia." In *Russia as a Great Power: Dimensions of Security under Putin*, edited by Jakob Hedenskog. London: Routledge, 2005.

———. "The Mismatch of Russia and the EU as Actors in a Globalized World." Presentation to the "Russia and the European Union after Enlargement: New Prospects and Problems" Conference, *JRL* #9265, 11 Oct 2005.

Skakov, Alexander Y. "Russia's Role in the South Caucasus." *Helsinki Monitor* (2) (2005).

Snyder, Jack. "Democratization, War, and Nationalism in the Post-Communist States." In *The Sources of Russian Foreign Policy after the Cold War*, edited by Celeste A. Wallander. Boulder, CO: Westview, 1996.

Snyder, Timothy. *The Reconstruction of Nations: Poland, Ukraine, Lithuania, Belarus, 1569–1999*. New Haven, CT: Yale University Press, 2003.

Socor, Vladimir. "EU-Russia Summit Targets New Partnership Agreement." *Jamestown Foundation Eurasia Daily Monitor*, 2 Jul 2008.

———. "JCC, 'Peacekeeping' Formats in South Ossetia Shown to Be Unstable." *Jamestown Foundation Eurasia Daily Monitor*, 26 Oct 2005.

———. "Moscow Confronts the West over CFE Treaty at OSCE." *Jamestown Foundation Eurasia Daily Monitor*, 25 May 2007.

———. "Uzbekistan Accedes to Collective Security Treaty Organization." *Jamestown Foundation Eurasia Daily Monitor*. 27 Jun 2006, http://www.jamestown.org/edm/article.php?article_id=2371223.

Sokov, Nikolai. "Alternative Interpretations of the Russian-Ukrainian Gas Crisis." Center for Strategic and International Studies. PONARS Policy Memo #404, Jan 2006.

Solov'ev, E. G. "The Foreign Policy Priorities of Liberal Russia." *Russian Politics and Law* 44(3) (May–Jun 2006).

———. *Natsional'nye interesy i osnovnye politicheskie sily sovremennoi Rossii*. Moscow: Nauka, 2004.

Solovyev, Eduard. "Russian Geopolitics in the Context of Globalization." In *Russia and Globalization: Identity, Security, and Society in an Era of Change*, edited by Douglas W. Blum. Washington, DC: Woodrow Wilson Center, 2008.

Sovet Vneshnei i Oboronoi Politiki. "Novye vyzovy bezopasnosti i Rossiya." 11 Jul 2002, http://www.svop.ru/live/materials.asp?m_id=6729&r_id=6758.

———. "Oboronnaya politika Rossii." 14 Oct 2003, http://www.svop.ru/live/materials.asp?m_id=7271&r_id=7272.

Splidsboel-Hansen, Flemming. "A Grand Strategy for Central Asia." *Problems of Post-Communism* 52(2) (Mar–Apr 2005).

———. "Past and Future Meet: Aleksandr Gorchakov and Russian Foreign Policy." *Europe-Asia Studies* 54(3) (2002): 377–96.

Stent, Angela E. "America and Russia: Paradoxes of Partnership." In *Russia's Engagement with the West: Transformation and Integration in the Twenty-First Century*, edited by Alexander J. Motyl, Blair A. Ruble, and Lilia Shevtsova. Armonk, NY: M. E. Sharpe, 2005.

———. "Berlin's Russia Challenge." *The National Interest* (Mar–Apr 2007).

Stent, Angela, and Lilia Shevtsova. "America, Russia, and Europe: A Realignment?" *Survival* 44(4) (Win 2002–2003): 121–34.

Stern, Jonathan P. *The Future of Russian Gas and Gazprom*. Oxford: Oxford University Press, 2005.

Stratfor. "Annual Forecast 2008: Beyond the Jihadist War—Former Soviet Union." Stratfor Analytical Report, Jan 2008, http://www.stratfor.com/analysis/annual_forecast_2008_beyond_jihadist_war_former_soviet_union.

Straus, Ira. "NATO: The Only West Russia Has?" *Demokratizatsiya* 11(2) (Spr 2003).

Stulberg, Adam N. *Well-Oiled Diplomacy: Strategic Manipulation and Russia's Energy Statecraft in Eurasia*. Albany, NY: State University of New York Press, 2007.

Surkov, Vladislav. "Natsional'naya budushchego (polnaya versiya)." http://surkov.info/publ/4-1-0-37.

———. "News Conference of Presidential Aide Vladislav Surkov, Deputy Head of the Presidential Administration." 4 Jul 2006, http://en.g8russia.ru/news/2006 0704/1168817.html.

———. "Stenogramma: Suverenitet—eto politicheskii sinonim konkurentosposob-nosti (chast' 1)." http://surkov.info/publ/4-1-0-13.

Talbott, Strobe. *The Russia Hand: A Memoir of Presidential Diplomacy*. New York: Random House, 2002.

Taylor, Brian D. "Power Surge? Russia's Power Ministries from Yeltsin to Putin and Beyond." Center for Strategic and International Studies PONARS Policy Memo No. 414, Dec 2006.

Torbakov, Igor. "Kremlin Uses Energy to Teach Ex-Soviet Neighbors a Lesson in Geopolitical Loyalty." *Jamestown Foundation Eurasia Daily Monitor*, 2 Dec 2005.

Trenin, Dmitri. "After the Empire: Russia's Emerging International Identity." In *Russia between East and West: Russian Foreign Policy on the Threshold of the Twenty-First Century*, edited by Gabriel Gorodetsky. London and Portland, OR: Frank Cass, 2003.

———. *The End of Eurasia: Russia on the Border between Geopolitics and Globalization*. Washington, DC: Carnegie Endowment, 2002.

———. "Pirouettes and Priorities." *The National Interest* (74) (Win 2003–2004).

———. "Russia: Back to the Future?" Statement to U.S. Senate Committee on Foreign Relations, 29 Jun 2006.

———. "Russia Leaves the West." *Foreign Affairs* 85(4) (Jul–Aug 2006): 87–96.

———. Russia Redefines Itself and Its Relations with the West." *Washington Quarterly* 30(2) (Spr 2007): 95–105.

———. *Russia's China Problem*. Washington, DC: Carnegie Endowment for International Peace, 1999.

———. "Russia's Foreign and Security Policy under Putin." Carnegie Moscow Center. 24 Jun 2005, http://www.carnegie.ru/en/pubs/media/72804.htm.

———. "Russia's Security Integration with America and Europe." In *Russia's Engagement with the West: Transformation and Integration in the Twenty-First Century*, edited by Alexander J. Motyl, Blair A. Ruble, and Lilia Shevtsova. Armonk, NY: M. E. Sharpe, 2005.

———. "ShOS i vybor za mir." *Ezhednevnyi zhurnal* (29 Aug 2007).

———. "Southern Watch: Russia's Policy in Central Asia." *Journal of International Affairs* 56(2) (Spr 2003).

———. "Vneshnee vmeshatel'stvo v sobytiya na Ukraine i rossiisko-zapadnye otnosheniya." Carnegie Moscow Center Briefing 7(2) (Feb 2005).

Trenin, Dmitri, and Bobo Lo. *The Landscape of Russian Foreign Policy Decision Making*. Moscow: Carnegie Moscow Center, 2005.

Trenin, Dmitri, and Vitaly Tsygichko. "Kitai dlya Rossii: Tovarishch ili gospodin?" *Indeks bezopasnosti* 82(2).

Tsereteli, Mamuka. "The Blue Stream Pipeline and Geopolitics of Natural Gas in Eurasia." *Central Asia-Caucasus Analyst*, 30 Nov 2005.

Tsygankov, Andrei P. "Projecting Confidence, Not Fear: Russia's Post-Imperial Assertiveness." *Orbis*, Aut 2006: 677–90.

———. *Russia's Foreign Policy: Change and Continuity in National Identity*. Lanham, MD: Rowman & Littlefield, 2006.

Twigg, Judyth. "Differential Demographics: Russia's Muslim and Slavic Populations." Center for Strategic and International Studies PONARS Policy Memo No. 338, Dec 2005.

"Ugroza po sosedstvu: Pered rossiiskim Dal'nem Vostokom vstaet real'naya ugroza 'polzuchei' kitaiskoi ekspansii." *Vzglyad*. 4 Aug 2005, http://www.vzglyad.ru/politics/2005/8/42962.html.

Umland, Andreas. "'Neoevraziistvo,' vopros o russkom fashizme i rossiiskii politicheskii diskurs." *Zerkalo nedeli* 48(627) (16–22 Dec 2006), http://www.zn.ua/1000/1600/55389.

———. "The Rise of Integral Anti-Americanism in the Russian Mass Media and Intellectual Life." History News Network, 26 Jun 2006, http://hnn.us/articles/26108.html.

United Nations Security Council. "Security Council Imposes Sanctions on Iran for Failure to Halt Uranium Enrichment, Unanimously Adopting Resolution 737 (2006)." 23 Dec 2006, http://www.un.org/News/Press/docs/2006/sc8928.doc.htm.

United States Commission on Security and Cooperation in Europe. "The Shanghai Cooperation Organization: Is It Undermining U.S. Interests in Central Asia?" Hearing, 26 Sep 2006.

United States Department of Energy. "Kazakhstan Country Analysis Brief 2007," http://www.eia.doe.gov/emeu/cabs/Kazakhstan/Background.html.

———. "Russia Country Analysis Brief." Apr 2007, http://www.eia.doe.gov/emeu/cabs/Russia/Background.html.

United States Department of State. "Declaration on the Strategic Partnership and Cooperation Framework between the United States of America and the Republic of Uzbekistan." 12 Mar 2002, http://www.state.gov/p/eur/rls/or/2002/11711.htm.

———. "Joint Statement between the Government of the United States of American and the Government of the Republic of Uzbekistan." 12 Oct 2001, http://www.state.gov/r/pa/prs/ps/2001/5354.htm.

United States Government. "Background Briefing by Senior Administration Officials on the NATO Summit." 29 Nov 2006, http://www.whitehouse.gov/news/releases/2006/11/20061129-4.html.

United States National Intelligence Council. "Russia in the International System." Conference Report. 1 Jun 2001, http://www.dni.gov/nicconfreports_russia inter.html.

United States Open Source Center. "Analysis: Russian Draft Military Concept Views U.S. as Main Threat." JRL #2008-141, 1 Aug 2008.

———. "Russia: Foreign Policy Thinkers Undaunted by Rising China." *JRL* #2007-191, 7 Sep 2007.

United States Senate Committee on Foreign Relations. "U.S. Policy toward Russia." Congressional hearing, 21 Jun 2005.

Valdez, Jonathan. "The Near Abroad, the West, and National Identity in Russian Foreign Policy." In *The Making of Foreign Policy in Russia and the New States of Eurasia*, edited by Adeed Dawisha and Karen Dawisha. Armonk, NY: M. E. Sharpe, 1995.

"Vladislav Surkov's Secret Speech: How Russia Should Fight International Conspiracies." *MosNews*, 12 Jul 2005, http://www.mosnews.com/interview/2005/07/12/surkov.shtml.

"Vliyanie konflikta v Gruzii na otnoshenie rossiyan k Gruzii, SShA, i Ukraine." Levada Center poll, 21 Aug 2008, http://www.levada.ru/press/2008082103.html.

Vnukov, Konstantin V. Interview. 12 Mar 2007, http://www.mid.ru/ns- rasia.nsf/1083b7937ae580ae432569e7004199c2/432569d80021985fc325729c003ay79 71?OpenDocument.

———. "Russkii s kitaitsem brat'ya navek?" *Mezhdunarodnaya zhizn'* (1–2) (2006).

———. "The Year of Russia in China and Year of China in Russia: Two Halves of a Single Whole." *Far Eastern Affairs* 34(1) (2007): 33–37.

"Voennaya operatsiya SShA v Irake." Levada Center poll, http://www.levada.ru/irak.html.

Vogel, Heinrich. "Prospects for Coordination of Western Policies." In *Russia versus the United States and Europe—or 'Strategic Triangle': Developments in Russian Domestic and Foreign Policy, Western Responses, and Prospects for Policy Coordination*, edited by Hannes Adomeit and Anders Åslund. Berlin: SWP Berlin, 2005.

Voronin, A. I. "Russia-NATO Strategic Partnership: Problems, Prospects." *Military Thought* 14(4) (2005).

Vorontsov, Alexander. "Current Russia-North Korea Relations: Challenges and Achievements." Brookings Institution, CNAPS Working Paper, Feb 2007.

VTsIOM. "Rossiyane khotyat druzhit' s Kitaem, no na rasstoyanii." 16 Apr 2007, http://wciom.ru/arkhiv/tematicheskii-arkhiv/item/single/4397.html.

Wallander, Celeste A. "The Challenge of Russia for U.S. Policy." Testimony to U.S. Senate Committee on Foreign Relations, 21 Jun 2005.

Waltz, Kenneth N. *Theory of International Politics*. Reading, MA: Addison-Wesley, 1979.

Weitz, Richard. "Averting a New Great Game in Central Asia." *Washington Quarterly* 29(3) (Sum 2006).

———. "The CIS Is Dead: Long Live the CSTO." *Central-Asia Caucasus Monitor* (8 Feb 2006), http://www.cacianalyst.org/?q = node/3725.

Wen, Hsiu-Ling, and Chien-Hsun Chen. "The Prospects for Regional Economic Integration between China and the Five Central Asian Countries." *Europe-Asia Studies* 56(7) (Nov 2004).

Wendt, Alexander. *Social Theory of International Politics*. New York: Cambridge University Press, 1999.

White, Stephen, and Olga Kryshtanovskaya. "Russia: Elite Continuity and Change." In *Elites, Crises, and the Origins of Regimes*, edited by M. Dogan and J. Higley. Lanham, MD: Rowman & Littlefield, 1998.

Wilson, Jeanne L. "Strategic Partners: Russian-Chinese Relations and the July 2001 Friendship Treaty." *Problems of Post-Communism* 49(3) (May–Jun 2002): 3–13.

Winner, Andrew C. "The Proliferation Security Initiative: The New Face of Interdiction." *Washington Quarterly* 28(2) (Spr 2005): 129–43.

Wolf, Amy F., and Stuart D. Goldman. "Arms Control after START-II: Next Steps on the U.S.-Russian Agenda." Congressional Research Service Report for Congress, 22 Jun 2001.

World Policy Institute and Harriman Institute. "The New Post-Transitional Russian Identity: How Western Is Russian Westernization?" Project Report, Jan 2006.

Xiang, Lanxin. "China's Eurasian Experiment." *Survival* 46(2) (Sum 2004).

Yakovenko, A. V. "Stat'ya ofitsial'nogo predstavitelya MID Rossii A. V. Yakovenko po voprosam rossiisko-kitaiskikh otnoshenii." 29 Jun 2005, http://www.mid.ru/ ns-rasia.nsf/1083b7937ae580ae432569e7004199c2/432569d80021985fc3257 02f001ca314?OpenDocument.

Yasmann, Victor. "Red Religion: An Ideology of Neo-Messianic Russian Fundamentalism." *Demokratizatsiya* 1(2) (Spr 1993).

Yavlinsky, Grigory. "Domestic and Foreign Policy Challenges in Russia." Speech to Carnegie Endowment for International Peace. 31 Jan 2002, *JRL* #2002-6059, 6 Feb 2002.

Zamyatin, Dmitry. "Nado zabyt' Evraziyu!" Agenstvo Politicheskoi Novosti, 1 Jun 2007, http://www.apn.ru/publications/article17194.htm.

Zarifullin, Pavel. "Pri chem zdes' Saakashvili?" *Russkii Kur'er*, 6 Nov 2006.

Ziegler, Charles E. "The Russian Diaspora in Central Asia: Russian Compatriots and Moscow's Foreign Policy." *Demokratizatsiya* 14(1) (Win 2006).

Zimmerman, William. *The Russian People and Foreign Policy: Russian Elite and Mass Perspectives, 1993–2000.* Princeton, NJ: Princeton University Press, 2002.

Zyuganov, G. A. "Kak vernut'sya Rossii doverie i uvazhenie mezhdunarodnogo soobshchestva." *Pravda*, 6 Sep 2006.

Index

Abashidze, Aslan, 261
Abkhazia, 1, 27, 82, 99, 123, 134, 206, 245, 255–58, 260–61, 294, 296; Russian peacekeepers in, 259, 262; Russian recognition of, 160, 264, 271; war in (1992–1993), 258, 261
Adygea (Russia), 255, 258
Afghanistan, 100, 111–12, 154, 174, 270–71, 273; civil war in (1978–), 111–13, 204; ethnic groups in, 112–13; NATO involvement in, 173; Northern Alliance, 112, 113; and SCO, 216, 221; Soviet-Afghan war (1979–1989), 108, 112, 265, 295; Taliban, 111–12, 113, 217, 221, 243, 266–68, 274, 298; U.S. invasion of, 4, 18, 24, 31, 114–15, 267, 274–75; U.S.-Russian cooperation in, 105, 116–18, 120, 123, 134, 174, 207, 247, 250, 268, 298–99
Africa, 103; North, 148, 309; South, 306
Akaev, Askar, 245, 268
Albania, Republic of, 184n2
Albright, Madeleine, 79, 108
Alexander II (Emperor), 39
al Qaeda. *See* Qaeda, al
Americas: Latin, 67, 296; North, 175, 213. *See also* Canada; United States of America (U.S.)
Amur River, 203

Anti-Ballistic Missile (ABM) Treaty, 19, 101, 106, 109–10, 117, 131, 134, 205, 207
anti-Semitism, 66
Armenia, Republic of, 66, 174, 244, 255; Russian troops stationed in, 245
Armitage, Richard, 112
arms control, 100, 105, 109, 116, 118, 206, 298, 308; Anti-Ballistic Missile Treaty, 19, 101, 106, 109–10, 117, 131, 134, 205, 207; Cooperative Threat Reduction (Nunn-Lugar) program, 114; mutually assured destruction, 110; SORT Treaty, 109, 137n37, 196; START I Treaty, 106, 118, 196; START II Treaty, 106, 109, 134, 230n8
Asia, 26, 68, 80, 152, 175–76, 178, 197, 225–27, 305; East, 228; Southeast 213
"Asian Tigers," 225
Asia-Pacific Economic Cooperation organization (APEC), 79, 225
Association of Southeast Asian Nations (ASEAN), 201–2, 225; Regional Forum, 225
Astrakhan khanate, 294
Atlanticism/Atlanticists, 62, 71–74, 82, 300, 302
Austro-Hungarian Monarchy, 300

About the Author

Jeffrey Mankoff, a specialist in Eurasian/Russian affairs, is associate director of International Security Studies (ISS) at Yale University and adjunct fellow for Russia studies at the Council on Foreign Relations (CFR). Previously, he was a John M. Olin National Security fellow at the Olin Institute for Strategic Studies, Harvard University, a Henry Chauncey Fellow in Grand Strategy at Yale University, and a fellow at Moscow State University.

Dr. Mankoff has written on a range of topics connected to post-Soviet politics and foreign policy. He is the author of the forthcoming CFR Council Special Report entitled "Eurasian Energy Security" and has written for a wide range of journals and newspapers. His areas of functional expertise include Great Power relations, foreign policy decision making, ethnic conflict, and energy security.

In addition to research, he teaches classes at Yale on modern diplomatic and military history. He received his PhD in diplomatic history from Yale in 2006. He also holds an MA in political science from Yale and a BA in international studies and Russian from the University of Oklahoma.